D1577316

SOURCE AND MEANING IN
SPENSER'S ALLEGORY

Source and Meaning in Spenser's Allegory

A STUDY OF
The Faerie Queene

JOHN ERSKINE HANKINS

OXFORD
AT THE CLARENDON PRESS
1971

Oxford University Press, Ely House, London W. 1

GLASGOW NEW YORK TORONTO MELBOURNE WELLINGTON
CAPE TOWN IBADAN NAIROBI DAR ES SALAAM LUSAKA ADDIS ABABA
DELHI BOMBAY CALCUTTA MADRAS KARACHI LAHORE DACCA
KUALA LUMPUR SINGAPORE HONG KONG TOKYO

PRINTED IN GREAT BRITAIN
AT THE UNIVERSITY PRESS, OXFORD
BY VIVIAN RIDLER
PRINTER TO THE UNIVERSITY

Preface

THE 1960s will be remembered as a great period of Spenser scholarship, for then were published a record number of books about *The Faerie Queene*. Not since the 1930s, when the *Variorum Spenser* was begun and when C. S. Lewis published *The Allegory of Love*, has there been so significant a period for students of Spenser. In 1960 appeared Pauline Parker's *Allegory of The Faerie Queene*, in 1961 A. C. Hamilton's *Structure of Allegory in* The Faerie Queene, in 1962 Graham Hough's *Preface to* The Faerie Queene, in 1963 William Nelson's *Poetry of Edmund Spenser*, in 1964 Alastair Fowler's *Spenser and the Numbers of Time* and Thomas P. Roche's *The Kindly Flame*, in 1965 Robert Kellogg and Oliver Steele's introduction to selected portions of *The Faerie Queene*, in 1966 Donald Cheney's *Spenser's Image of Nature* and Kathleen Williams's *Spenser's World of Glass*, in 1967 Paul J. Alpers's *Poetry of* The Faerie Queene, Arnold Williams's *Flower on a Lowly Stalk* (on courtesy), and C. S. Lewis's *Spenser's Images of Life* (posthumously edited by Alastair Fowler), in 1968 T. K. Dunseath's *Spenser's Allegory of Justice*, and in 1969 Jane Aptekar's *Icons of Justice*. All of these books contribute importantly to our understanding of *The Faerie Queene*.

To this goodly collection of volumes, I wish to add my own. My research for this book began shortly after the first volume of the *Variorum* appeared in 1932, and it has proceeded slowly ever since. The section of Chapter V called 'Spenser and the Revelation of St. John' was printed by *PMLA* in 1945. The section of Chapter II called 'External and Internal Allegory' is based on a paper read before the Stanford meeting of the Modern Language Association of America in 1949. I have sought to base my work on primary sources as far as possible and to quote other scholars only when their work is immediately relevant to the topic under discussion at the moment. This practice may have resulted in some errors of omission with, I hope, the compensating virtue of clarity. While a review of earlier scholarship is not a part of my plan, I do wish to acknowledge my indebtedness to the various works which have helped to build up my conception of *The Faerie*

Queene. Among authors not yet mentioned, I have found most helpful the work of B. E. C. Davis, Isabel E. Rathborne, and Josephine Waters Bennett. I also appreciate some hours of 'good talk' about Spenser with Douglas Bush, John Pope, Brents Stirling, Theodore Silverstein, and Merritt Y. Hughes. To simplify the critical apparatus of this book, I assume the reader's knowledge of the *Variorum Spenser* and refer to it whenever practicable. I use the abbreviation *PL* for J. P. Migne's *Patrologia Latina.* For items read in the Short-Title-Catalogue Microfilms, I am indebted to the University of Washington and the University of Kansas. I am also deeply indebted to the libraries of Harvard University, Yale University, the University of Connecticut, Bowdoin College, Colby College, and the University of Maine for the use of their facilities. For checking my translations from the Latin, I am indebted to David Tatem of the University of Maine. For reading my manuscript and making useful suggestions, I thank Frederick Pottle of Yale, Sears Jayne of Brown University, Richard Sprague and Jacob Bennett of the University of Maine, and my wife, Nellie Pottle Hankins.

J. E. H.

Orono, Maine

Contents

I

The Basis of the Allegory

THE student of Spenser's *Faerie Queene* soon recognizes a variety of approaches to his subject. The poem may be taken as a chivalric romance of knightly adventures, or as an extended allegory, or as both. In this study I propose to investigate the meaning of the allegory on several different levels. Chapters I–IV contain materials applicable to the poem as a whole, while Chapters V–XI interpret particular segments of it. From these separate and disparate interpretations of the material, the reader may construct or amplify his own interpretation of the poem.

Edmund Spenser liked to have an authority for his ideas and a traditional basis for his allegorical figures. For instance, he might never have personified Furor if Virgil had not already done so.[1] In his *Letter to Raleigh*, he names some of his principal sources and models: Homer, Virgil, Ariosto, Tasso, 'Aristotle and the rest'. Since he names Aristotle in connection with the moral virtues, he is pretty clearly referring to the *Nicomachean Ethics*; yet his divergences from that volume are so marked as to suggest that 'the rest' have considerably modified his borrowings from Aristotle. Scholars have laboured in vain to find the book or books which account for Spenser's selection of virtues. The most assiduous investigator, Viola Blackburn Hulbert, concludes that there was for a time a tradition of twelve moral virtues among Aristotelian commentators (Aristotle gives only eleven), but these twelve do not agree at all with the partial list revealed by Spenser: holiness, temperance, chastity, friendship, justice, courtesy, and constancy.[2]

It has been my good fortune to discover what I believe to be the major source for Spenser's use of the virtues. An examination of this work not only reveals his authority for many allegorical

---

[1] *Aeneid*, i. 294–6. Furor in chains is pictured in Vicenzo Cartari's *Imagini de gli Dei delli Antichi* (edn. of Padua, 1626), p. 326.

[2] For her discussion see *Var.* i. 353–7.

personifications but also frequently suggests what those personifications may mean and how the action is to be interpreted in terms of moral allegory.

FRANCESCO PICCOLOMINI AND THE MORAL VIRTUES

The book in question is the *Vniuersa Philosophia de Moribus* (1583) of Francesco Piccolomini. The author is mentioned by Padelford in a list of Aristotelian commentators,[1] but apparently the work has never been examined carefully with relation to Spenser. It appeared three years later than Gabriel Harvey's letter of 1580, which contains our first reference to *The Faerie Queene*.[2] It was printed in Venice, and the author's preface is dated July 1583. The date 1583 also appears on the title-page.

At some time during the period 1582–4 Spenser was present at a gathering of English gentlemen in Lodowick Bryskett's Irish cottage, as reported in Bryskett's *Discourse of Ciuill Life* (1606). At that time Spenser announced that he was writing a poem to illustrate the moral virtues but did not then have it in a presentable state. It may well be that the moral virtues were not a part of the earlier poem mentioned by Harvey, which was described as emulous of Ariosto and did not seem to Harvey very successful. Francesco Piccolomini's book may have come into Spenser's hands just at the time when he was changing the emphasis of his poem and making a fresh start upon it; for the internal evidence seems to show a considerable debt to Piccolomini.

A cousin of Francesco Piccolomini (1520–1604) was Alessandro Piccolomini (1508–78), whom Bryskett mentions by name. Both men were born and died at Sienna; both attended the University of Padua. Alessandro became an archbishop; Francesco became a professor of philosophy, first in the University of Sienna, afterwards in the University of Padua. Both men wrote treatises of moral philosophy based on the *Nicomachean Ethics* of Aristotle.

J. J. Jusserand refers to one treatise of Alessandro Piccolomini, Viola Hulbert to another.[3] These are *Della institutione di tutta la vita dell' huomo nato nobile, e in città libera* (1552), and *Della Institutione*

---

[1] *Var.* iii. 321.

[2] Spenser, *Poetical Works*, Cambridge edn., ed. R. E. N. Dodge (1908), p. 773. Passages from Spenser's poems are quoted from this edition. Dodge normalizes the letters *u* and *v* in accordance with modern usage.

[3] See p. 1 n. 2 above, and *Var.* i. 327–30.

Morale (edns. in Venice, 1560, 1575, 1594). These two works are not the same, though both are based on Aristotle's *Ethics*. The first has ten books, following closely the outline of Aristotle's work. The second is freer in form; it contains twelve books and does not follow exactly the order of Aristotle's discussion. In the first work the author says that Aristotle named eleven moral virtues, which he gives as follows: justice, fortitude, mansuetude, magnificence, magnanimity, temperance, liberality, honesty, desire of honour, affability, urbanity.

He prefixes to these virtues a remark on the desirability of wisdom. In the *Della Institutione Morale*, however, his virtue of honesty is changed to verity and his remark on wisdom becomes a discussion of prudence: 'Beyond the eleven moral virtues already given, there remains the final one, called Prudence, which, although spoken of as moral in a certain way, is nevertheless an intellectual virtue.'[1] As a complement to all the other moral virtues and as perfecting human actions, it is moral. As a power of the soul, in which it resides, it is intellectual.

It is clear that Bryskett, in so far as he borrowed from Alessandro, used the second work, for Bryskett's list of virtues includes fortitude, temperance, justice, prudence, liberality, magnificence, magnanimity, mansuetude, desire of honour, verity, affability, urbanity.[2]

In his *Vniuersa Philosophia de Moribus* Francesco discusses the moral virtues at length in Book iv. The three heads and fountains of virtues are temperance, controlling the concupiscent appetite; fortitude, controlling the irascible appetite; and justice, controlling one's attitudes towards other people (iv. 34; p. 211c). He decides that Aristotle has named eleven moral virtues, but that this number seems either diminished or augmented; i.e. ten or twelve would have seemed more suitable. Accordingly he speculates as to what unnamed virtues may be comprehended within the virtues which are named. He expresses regret that Aristotle made no mention of holiness, piety, faith, hope, charity, modesty, sobriety, honesty, fasting or abstinence (*jejunium*), obedience, reverence, benignity, concord, friendship, grace, penitence, shamefastness (*pudicitia*), chastity, humility, pity, and the like, which shine most brightly in the crown of virtues and are commended by theologians (iv. 33;

---

[1] *Della Institutione Morale* (edn. of Venice, 1560), bk. viii, ch. 10, p. 365.
[2] Bryskett, *A Discourse of Ciuill Life* (London, 1606), p. 214.

p. 210c). He gives the list of Aristotelian virtues in outline form, just as we have already given them, except that he uses the word *amicitia* for Aristotle's *philia*, explaining that it includes affability, humanity, familiarity, and facility. He explains that mansuetude includes mercy and lenity, and that verity is the same as candour (iv. 29; pp. 202D, 204A). He considers justice the queen of all the virtues and notes the division into universal justice, suitable for rulers in their dealings with their states, and particular justice, which concerns private citizens in their relations with each other (iv. 30; p. 205D). He omits prudence, because it is an intellectual virtue, not a moral one (iv. 34; p. 211C).

Francesco is much concerned about Aristotle's omission of holiness (*sanctitas*). He declares that Plato in the *Protagoras* names five major virtues: sapience, temperance, fortitude, justice, holiness. Justice is right conduct towards men, holiness right conduct towards God (iv. 33; p. 211A). Holiness may be called heroic justice and is a part of justice. Nevertheless, Plato had listed it separately. Since Aristotle himself says that magnificence includes liberality and that magnanimity includes the moderate desire of honour and yet has chosen to list them as four distinct virtues, by a similar reasoning holiness may be listed separately, though included in justice (iv. 34; p. 211C). Since piety, religion, and holiness are necessarily bound in one knot, holiness may also be called religious justice. Aristotle fails to mention it because it concerns man's relationship to God instead of to other people. Also, Aristotle, living before the Christian era, saw only as under a cloud and from a distance things pertaining to the knowledge of God (iv. 35; p. 212D). In Book vi he states that Suessanus and others identify holiness with Aristotle's 'heroic virtue', a conclusion with which he disagrees (vi. 9; p. 338A). In recapitulation, Francesco remarks again that justice, the enemy of all vices, includes within its bounds piety, religion, and holiness, which restore us to God, convey us to God, and unite us most happily with God (iv. 52; p. 233B).

Francesco's treatment of holiness as a virtue seems to have established something of a tradition. His arguments were repeated in Antonio Riccoboni's commentary upon the *Nicomachean Ethics* (1593).[1] About 1620 Franco Burgersdyck, a professor of philo-

---

[1] The commentary is bound with Riccoboni's translation of the *Nicomachean Ethics*. Later editions appeared in 1596 (Frankfurt) and 1610 (Hanover). On the

sophy at the University of Leyden, wrote a little book entitled *Idea Philosophiae Moralis*, in which he named the eleven Aristotelian virtues and placed piety at the head of them, making twelve in all. He observed that piety was not derived from Aristotle but from Pythagorean and Platonic writings. He stated that piety towards God corresponds to probity or right conduct towards men;[1] it was on this ground that Francesco included them both in justice. Later in the century Johann Crell defined holiness or piety as a Christian virtue which is the *complexus* of all the moral virtues joined together.[2]

As we read Francesco's words, we can see clearly how Spenser derived his treatment of holiness. Other virtues concern man's conduct towards men, but holiness concerns his attitude towards God and his pilgrimage towards final unity with God. Exactly this subject is presented allegorically in Book 1 of *The Faerie Queene*. Since justice is the noblest virtue, and holiness the noblest form of justice, it should logically be the first virtue presented, even though this would require a change in Spenser's original plan. He could assume that holiness was implied by Aristotle's justice, since that author had in two other instances listed as separate virtues what were really different degrees of the same virtue.

Francesco's work also serves to explain Spenser's treatment of magnificence. Spenser's *Letter to Raleigh* states that Prince Arthur represents magnificence, 'for that (according to Aristotle and the rest) it is the perfection of all the rest, and conteineth in it them all'. This is puzzling, inasmuch as Aristotle names two superior moral virtues and indicates that of the two magnanimity is superior to magnificence. Most critics have assumed that Spenser, through forgetfulness or deliberate choice, intended magnanimity to be the equivalent of magnificence. Such a confusion of the two virtues sometimes occurred, as in La Primaudaye's *French Academie*, pt. i, ch. 27: 'Of Magnanimitie and Generositie'. In the text magnanimity is defined as 'Generositie or noblenes of hart, as that which vndoubtedly is comprehended vnder the first part of *Fortitude*, which Cicero calleth Magnificence, or a doing of great

title-page of the commentary Riccoboni states that his work is based on that of Francesco Piccolomini, 'the greatest philosopher of our times'.

[1] Leyden, 1622 (2nd edn.), ch. 13, p. 128.

[2] Crell, *Ethica Christiana*, II. ii, p. 93, appended to his *Ethica Aristotelica ad Sacrarum Literarum normam emendata* (Venice, n.d.).

and excellent things'.[1] Here the two major virtues are confused with each other and seem indistinguishable in the mind of the author.[2] La Primaudaye's words may serve as authority for the one occasion when Spenser does let Arthur represent magnanimity (below, p. 183). But he had the two virtues clearly distinguished in his mind, and Francesco Piccolomini's account of them enables us to see why Arthur represents the twin meanings of magnificence and heavenly grace, and how these two are associated with each other.

Francesco, in his attempt to revise Aristotle's list to include only the major virtues, finally reduces them to six: justice, temperance, fortitude, magnanimity, magnificence (including liberality), and mansuetude (iv. 50). These can be yet further reduced, since it is possible to consider magnanimity a part of fortitude (iv. 52; p. 233B). But in his description of the virtues he lists magnanimity separately. This description, which occurs in chapter 50 (pp. 230–1), may be summarized as follows:

It is difficult to determine, he says, which is the most excellent virtue, since each of the six has its special claim. Justice, the queen of virtues, is necessary in large states and in small social units, such as the home. Even thieves have a semblance of justice towards each other, else they could not act together as a group. 'Take away Justice from men's breasts, and at once you shall see them more beastly than the beasts and their cities wilder (*sylvestriores*) than the forests' (p. 230B).

Temperance may claim eminence because of the difficulty of its task: to subdue and control the concupiscent desires of the body. Seneca says, 'He rules a great power who rules himself, and he who conquers desire is stronger than he who overcomes an enemy'. Solomon says, 'He who conquers his soul is stronger than he who conquers cities' (p. 230C).

Yet fortitude does not yield place, since it controls the irascible faculty, which is more eminent than the concupiscible faculty and is nearer to reason. In fortitude the quality of heroism most greatly shines and by it heroes are elevated above the human condition; e.g. Hercules (pp. 230–1).

[1] Edn. of London, 1586, p. 289. Italics not mine. (In all quotations italics are mine unless otherwise specified.)

[2] Michael F. Moloney in 1953 questioned the identification of magnificence with magnanimity, pointing out Aquinas's statement that magnificence was connected with holiness (*Journal of English and Germanic Philology*, lii. 58–62).

Magnanimity cannot be held inferior to any, because nothing is more outstanding than the great soul and nothing should be considered more eminent. Through the other virtues we arrange human affairs rightly; through magnanimity we despise them and, spurred on by it, are lifted towards God. By its agency we contemn as vile the goods of fortune and throw at our feet what the race of men generally admire and covet. Seneca in Epistle 108 says that the great soul is he who surrenders himself to God. Its opposite, the pusillanimous soul, complains, judges the world order to be evil, and wishes to change the gods rather than to change himself. Francesco (p. 231B) then quotes Aristotle's definition of the magnanimous man in *Nicomachean Ethics*, iv. iii. 1, 10, 16.

The account of magnificence merits a complete translation:

But Liberality, adorned by the amplitude of its Magnificence, yields not to it [magnanimity], but rather strives to show itself more illustrious. For if Charity is the prince of theological virtues, Liberality, which among moral virtues is most like unto it, seems by the best right to stand ahead of the others; especially since by no action do we approach nearer to God and become more like him than when we liberally and magnificently bring help to others. This is the virtue by which we bind all others to us in a certain royal knot, which succours the needy, nourishes virtues, and directs the goods of fortune into a suitable channel. Its action is most like the actions of God and of Nature. For God by his immense liberality alone created the world; his handmaid Nature, when she labours for men and bestows her gifts upon things, most amply preserves Liberality. This virtue seems to be preferable to Justice, because Justice distributes equitably the goods of others, but Liberality distributes its own, which is far more difficult. And especially Magnificence, which is the height of Liberality, seems preferable to the others, because the other virtues were born to accompany all ranks and conditions of men; alone this one seeks the highest state and condition of men, since it may unite only with those splendidly born and most richly supplied with the goods of fortune. Indeed Liberality is that which takes treasures from the hands of fortune and stores them most securely; for by its reward we have the power to say: whatever I have given, that I have. (p. 231C)

Liberality and magnificence have an affinity and likeness to charity, the chief of the theological virtues (iv. 52; p. 233A).

In a later chapter on the nature of grace, Francesco writes:

The office of Liberality and Magnificence is especially worthy the name of Grace . . . of this kind, the effusion of Graces first and truly agrees with God alone, because he only lacks nothing, depends on no one, hopes for nothing for himself from anyone; therefore is he truly a living fountain of Graces, from which first flows Grace freely given. (viii. 36; p. 435C)

Mansuetude, or gentleness, deserves eminence because it is best accommodated to the nature of man. It frees us from wrath and keeps man within the bounds of reason. It binds together societies of men, which wrath disturbs and dissipates. It allows men to dwell in peace and tranquillity, than which nothing is sweeter or more pleasing to them (p. 231D).

It will be observed that in this description magnanimity and magnificence have become essentially religious virtues. Magnificence is the virtue most characteristic of God himself. The outpouring of his grace to man, shown in the first creation of the world and in Nature's care for man's bodily needs, is the most princely example of magnificence possible. It is a virtue which can be possessed only by the greatest and most splendid of men and characterizes their attitudes toward those less powerful and fortunate. Hence it is the virtue best fitted to Prince Arthur and to the gift of heavenly grace (below, p. 15).[1]

Francesco does not say that magnificence contains all other virtues (as Spenser does) but he does say that it is most like charity among the theological virtues. And charity, he says, is fervent love, the mother, root, nerve, form, and spirit of all other virtues (iv. 36; p. 214B). He might have added, as the most magnificent gift of all, God's sacrifice of his Son for the redemption of Man.

Francesco's book also furnishes authority for the inclusion of chastity as a major virtue. He names as virtues which constitute a part of temperance: fasting, abstinence, virginity, chastity, honesty, modesty, sobriety (iv. 34; p. 212A). These were later consolidated by Burgersdyck to chastity and frugality, by Crell to chastity and sobriety. Chastity is stressed by Francesco on the last page of his book in these words:

We are rightly affected towards ourselves through Temperance, towards others through Justice, and towards God through Piety;

---

[1] Josephine Waters Bennett has noted an occasional theological significance attached to the word *magnificence* (*The Evolution of* The Faerie Queene [Chicago, 1942], pp. 59–60). In an unpublished Yale dissertation Martha Alden Craig finds a similar suggestion in the Magnificat: 'My soul doth *magnify* the Lord' ('Language and Concept in *The Faerie Queene*' [1959], p. 85).

hence we shall live *chastely*, justly, and piously. Of this best institution, *Chastity* or Temperance is the beginning, Justice the middle, and Piety the end; thence in so salutary an end may we rest most cheerfully with the Glory of God. (x. 34; p. 596c)

Here chastity is used as a near equivalent of temperance, as earlier it had been declared a part of temperance. One form of chastity, virginity, is characterized by Francesco as heroic temperance (vi. 3; p. 331B). The same logic that allowed holiness (heroic justice) to be listed as a separate major virtue would allow chastity (heroic temperance) to be listed separately also. It must be noted that Book III of *The Faerie Queene* stresses both Belphoebe (virginity) and Britomart (chastity) as essentially the same virtue, the latter representing the chastity that culminates in marriage.

Another striking borrowing from Francesco Piccolomini occurs in Spenser's use of Mutabilitie to illustrate the Legend of Constancie. At first glance such a usage seems a contradiction in terms, but we can see how it came about. The 'ever-whirling Wheele of Change' (*FQ* VII. vi. 1) is reminiscent of Fortune's wheel and suggests an indebtedness of Mutabilitie to the goddess Fortuna. Natalis Comes, Spenser's favourite mythographer, states a tradition that Fortune once rebelled against Jove and almost pushed him from his throne.[1] The resemblance to Mutabilitie's conduct is marked, for she seeks to unseat the moon and boldly declares her pre-eminence over all the gods, including Jove. Francesco writes of Fortune: 'There is another opinion of certain people who judge that Fortune is a certain goddess and divine power . . . Others say that Fortune is a sort of intelligent force, presiding over the mortal sphere in much the same way as the powers that move the heavens preside over the heavenly spheres' (viii. 40; p. 441A, C).

In this assertion of Fortune's power in the 'mortal sphere', the world of change below the moon, and of her comparative equality with the movers of the heavenly bodies, we find the ground for Mutabilitie's recognized authority over the sublunar realm and her determination to extend it over the moon and the planets.

A second passage relates Fortune to mutability and to constancy. In one sense she is inconstant because she is always

---

[1] These suggestions were made by R. B. Levinson and H. G. Lotspeich, respectively (*Var.* vi. 400, 410).

changing, but in another sense she is constant to the principle of
her nature, which is change: 'Secondly, she is firm and *constant* by
reason of the conservation of her condition and of her *mutability*;
for she is *immutably mutable*' (viii. 48; p. 452C). Francesco expands
this paradox at length with supporting quotations from Aristotle,
Ovid, Boethius, and Alciatus. In this curious statement of the constancy of mutability lies the suggestion for Spenser's association
of the two.

Another image in Spenser which is drawn primarily from the
work of Francesco is the golden chain which binds all the virtues
together:

> O goodly golden chayne: wherewith yfere
> The vertues linked are in lovely wize.   (I. ix. I)

Again Guyon (temperance), Britomart (chastity), and Prince
Arthur (heavenly grace) are bound together by 'that golden
chaine of concord' (III. i. 12). In his image of Concord as the
goddess who reconciles Love and Hate, Spenser describes the
'inviolable bands', ordained by God and maintained by Concord,
which control the world of matter and keep the elements from
conflict with each other (IV. x. 35).

Francesco gives several theories of the relations between the
world of ideas and the world of phenomena:

> Another most likely manner is that of Plato, judging that the Divine
> Mind includes not so much the ideas of individuals as the ideas of
> species, to which the reasons of the [World-] Soul, the seeds of Nature,
> the participations and shadows of matter may respond: by which *golden
> chain* [*aurea catena*] he declares the steps of the universe to be bound, and
> all things to descend from the first to the lowest and to be recalled
> from the lowest to the first.   (ii. 26; p. 119C)

This golden chain appears to be the same as Spenser's 'inviolable
bands' and 'golden chaine of concord'.

Francesco also declares that the moral virtues are bound together in an indissoluble knot by certain bonds (*vincula*); one
virtue reinforces another after the manner of the three Graces,
who never appear singly but always embrace each other (iv. 39;
p. 217B). His *vincula* are identified by Spenser with his *aurea catena*,
the golden chain of concord which harmonizes both the virtues
and the universe itself.

In the House of Alma appear two other Aristotelian virtues (or half-virtues). Guyon speaks to Shamefastness, or Shame-facedness, who is too bashful to speak but is described by Alma as the fountain of modesty (II. ix. 40–3). A few moments before, Prince Arthur spoke to another lady, Prays-desire, 'that by well doing sought to honour to aspyre', and who describes herself as 'sad in mind Through great desire of glory and of fame' (36–9). These two are grouped together by Aristotle when he says that citizen soldiers, though untrained, are prompted to courageous action by a sense of shame and by the desire of something noble, honour, and by a fear of public disgrace if they show cowardice (*Nic. Eth.* III. viii. 3). In two other passages (II. vii. 14; IV. ix. 1–8), he explains that modesty is the mean between shamefastness and lack of shame, or impudence. Francesco quotes all these passages in a chapter on shamefastness (*verecundia*), concluding that it is 'a half virtue, a seed of virtue, a way to virtue, born from a desire of honesty or honour and a fear of infamy, which are the beginnings of virtue and the spurs to it' (iv. 32; p. 209c). The uniting of these two qualities, the sense of shame and the desire of honour, by Aristotle has caused Spenser to associate them in the House of Alma as Shamefastness and Prays-desire.[1]

Spenser's most notable innovation is his adoption of courtesy as a moral virtue, for it is not so listed by Aristotle or his commentators. Instead, it appears in various lists of the chivalric virtues, those appropriate to a medieval knight.[2] Spenser may have drawn a hint from Alessandro Piccolomini through Pierre Larivey's French translation of *Della institutione di tutta la vita dell'huomo nato nobile, e in città libera*, for Larivey renders 'urbanità o piacevolezza' as 'courtoisie ou gayeté'.[3] Courtesy is thus equated with urbanity, which is an Aristotelian virtue. But courtesy also

---

[1] J. K. Neill (*Var.* ii. 294) noted the two passages on shamefastness and modesty in *Nic. Eth.* II. vii. 14 and IV. ix. 1–8, but he overlooked the one in III. viii. 3, which associates shamefastness with the desire of honour as stimuli to noble action. For the iconographical significance of the two ladies see Paul J. Alpers, *The Poetry of The Faerie Queene* (1967), pp. 205–8.

[2] Huon de Mery, *Le Tournoiement d'Antechrist*; Watriquet de Couvin, *Li Mireoirs as Dames*; Brunetto Latini, *Il Tesoretto* (see W. A. Neilson, *The Origins and Sources of the Courts of Love* [1899], pp. 49, 72, 111); Vegetius, *The Art of Chivalry* (see B. E. C. Davis, *Edmund Spenser* [1933], p. 110); Stephen Hawes, *The Pastime of Pleasure*, line 3425 (EETS, o.s., no. 173 [1928], p. 131).

[3] *Var.* i. 329.

includes affability, which seems equivalent to Spenser's 'civility'.
Alessandro Piccolomini says of this virtue:

> Inasmuch as one should not converse in just the same manner with
> friends, with strangers, with nobles, with common men, with princes,
> with private citizens, with lords, with gentlewomen, and the same
> I say of all other kinds of persons with whom meetings occur in
> varying circumstances; where always, instead, one ought in every case
> so to consider the quality of the place, of the time, of the persons,
> of the natures of such persons, and finally of every other diversity,
> that one speaks no word which is not well chosen and suitable for each
> situation.[1]

Spenser writes of:

> friendly offices that bynde,
> And all the compliments of curtesie:
> They teach us, how to each degree and kynde
> We should our selves demeane, to low, to hie,
> To friends, to foes; which skill men call civility.
>
> (VI. X. 23)

Francesco Piccolomini joins the conversational virtues of affability and urbanity under the title of *iucunditas*, or agreeableness:

> And of these which pertain to Agreeableness, one is concerned with
> Jests, the other with associations and common affairs of the rest of life.
> For the prudent man in every action and word, and with every condi-
> tion of men, should preserve decorum and show himself such as the
> place, person, and occasion demand. Therefore also in salty remarks and
> jests he is held to observe due measure, and for the sake of recreation
> he should sometimes give place to jests that he may make himself more
> pleasing to others, may lead a more cheerful life, may refresh his mind
> and return to serious things with more alacrity. (iv. 29; p. 205B)

Francesco further defines affability and urbanity as means between
opposite extremes. He describes an excess of affability as bland,
obsequious, studious of pleasing, and its possessor as a 'yes-man'
(*assentator*). One deficient in affability is quarrelsome, morose,
difficult, and contentious (p. 203C). An excess of urbanity leads to
scurrility and ridiculousness. One deficient in urbanity is 'Insulsus,
Agrestis, Rusticus' (p. 205A). The first of these terms means 'un-
salted', dull, flat, or insipid. The other two both mean rustic or
'countrified'. This fact is sufficient to mark urbanity as a primary

---

[1] *Della Institutione Morale* (edn. of Venice, 1560), vi. 12; p. 278.

ingredient of Spenser's courtesy, since Spenser himself opposes courtesy to rusticity in his account of Belphoebe:

> Well may I weene, faire ladies, all this while
> Ye wonder how this noble damozell
> So great perfections did in her compile,
> Sith that in savage forests she did dwell,
> So farre from court and royall citadell,
> The great schoolmaistresse of all *courtesy*:
> Seemeth that such wilde woodes should far expell
> All civile usage and gentility,
> And gentle sprite deforme with rude *rusticity*. (III. vi. 1)

The same contrast is used for Calidore among the shepherds:

> Thus did the *gentle* knight himselfe abeare
> Amongst that *rusticke* rout in all his deeds. (VI. ix. 45)

And it is made evident in Calidore and Coridon. Coridon is not deficient in affability; i.e. he is not naturally morose or quarrelsome. But he is *rustic* and is lacking in the wit that distinguishes Calidore; hence he is deficient in urbanity.

Francesco also associates urbanity with dexterity (p. 205B), a hint that Spenser may have followed in portraying Calidore's athletic ability (VI. ix. 44). These various elements all seem to have a part in the author's ideal of courtesy.

While Bryskett follows Alessandro Piccolomini in listing prudence as a moral virtue, Francesco Piccolomini calls it an intellectual virtue which is a companion of the various moral virtues (v. 35; p. 296A). It is reason applied to the action of the moral virtues (v. 31; p. 291A). Only prudence supplies the arms by which man overcomes vices and perturbations (v. 35; p. 296B). It is more common in old people than in young people (v. 31; p. 291C).

Spenser has supplied as companions of his major figures several embodiments of prudence: Una's Dwarf in Book I, the Palmer in Book II, Britomart's Nurse Glauce in Book III, and the Hermit in Book VI. The Dwarf exemplifies caution, which Francesco lists as an 'affection' of prudence (v. 30; p. 290D). The Palmer, Glauce, and the Hermit represent the wisdom of advanced age. When the Palmer brings Guyon's sword to the weaponless Arthur for use against Pyrochles (*FQ* II. viii. 40), he illustrates Francesco's statement that only prudence can supply man the arms to overcome vices and perturbations of the soul.

We can see from this example how Spenser borrows from Francesco not only the virtues and vices which his characters represent, but also some of the actions which they perform. Further instances of such borrowing will be pointed out later in this book. It is precisely here that interpreters of Spenser's allegory have been most at fault, in failing to realize fully that he presents virtues and vices *in action* within the individual soul.

Francesco Piccolomini has supplied additional hints for the representation of other virtues in *The Faerie Queene*. For example, Scudamour thinks Britomart an example of 'huge heroicke magnanimity' (III. xi. 19). This reflects Francesco's statement that, while all magnanimity is the moderate desire of honour raised to a heroic pitch, there is a further division into ordinary magnanimity and heroic magnanimity (vi. 5; p. 333C). Britomart is thus used to represent two virtues, chastity and magnanimity. Spenser's use of her and Belphoebe as companion examples of heroic virtue probably stems from Francesco's statement that virginity is heroic temperance and the neglect of worldly advantage is heroic magnanimity (vi. 3; p. 331B). Again, Francesco gives these two as instances of heroic moderation (vi. 7; p. 336C). His repeated association of virginity with magnanimity may have caused Spenser to associate magnanimity with chastity as pre-marital virginity in the person of Britomart and with the heroic vow of perpetual virginity in the person of Belphoebe (cf. Francesco, iv. 6; p. 174A). He recognizes chastity and virginity as different degrees of the same virtue (below, p. 148).

Timias is similarly used to represent two virtues. The first of these is the moderate desire of honour, since Timias's name means 'honour' in Greek. As the excess of this virtue, Francesco gives *philotimia* (love of honour); as its deficiency, he gives *aphilotimia* (no love of honour). The first term is used (in *FQ* II. vii. 49) for Philotime, who represents ambition. Timias represents moderation in the pursuit of honour, and this virtue becomes almost an equivalent of modesty in Francesco's view (iv. 29; p. 202B). Later, Burgersdyck definitely substituted modesty for desire of honour, stating that it has the same relationship to magnanimity that liberality has to magnificence.[1]

---

[1] *Idea Philosophiae Moralis*, ch. 17 (edn. of Oxford, 1654, p. 163).

Just as Spenser identifies Arthur with heavenly grace and Una with truth (verity) in i. viii. 1, so he identifies Timias with grace in ii. xi. 30, where Timias saves Arthur's life by driving off the two hags Impotence and Impatience while Arthur is fighting Maleger:

> So greatest and most glorious thing on ground
> May often need the help of weaker hand . . .
> Proofe be thou, Prince the prowest man alyve . . .
> That had not Grace thee blest, thou shouldest not survive.

This is not a reference to heavenly grace, which is represented by Arthur himself, but to the poise and equanimity which we associate with a *graceful* person and which we may call natural grace. These qualities subdue minor annoyances, making it easier for heavenly grace to fight the major battles of the soul. The qualities of natural grace are discussed at length in Chapter IX.

Spenser has used Guyon to represent both temperance and fortitude as two forms of self-control. This becomes evident when we read in Francesco Piccolomini's book that temperance controls the lusts of the concupiscible faculty of the soul, but that fortitude controls the passions of the irascible faculty, including the passion of anger (iv. 34; p. 211B). Without using the word 'fortitude', Spenser assigns to Guyon its functions in describing the Palmer

> Who suffred not his wandring feet to slide;
> But when *strong passion* or *weak fleshlinesse,*
> Would from the right way seeke to draw him wide,
> He would, through *temperaunce* and *stedfastnesse,*
> Teach him the weak to strengthen, and the strong suppresse.
>
> (ii. iv. 2)

Here are named twin virtues, temperance and steadfastness, the latter being an equivalent of fortitude. The two virtues control weak fleshliness and strong passions, respectively. When Guyon fights Pyrochles, or wrath, he exercises fortitude, which pertains to the irascible faculty; but when he fights Cymochles, or sexual licence, he exercises temperance. Obviously the two virtues are closely related, as both involve the problem of self-control.

These examples are sufficient to show how pervasive was the influence of Francesco Piccolomini upon Spenser's treatment of the moral virtues. Francesco based his work upon that of Aristotle, but he was no slavish imitator and in fact produced his own system of ethics, with his own analysis of human conduct. Spenser used something of the same freedom and prepared his own list of virtues, yet remained close to his sources in 'Aristotle and the rest'. He was at once an innovator and a traditionalist.

II

The Method of the Allegory

WE sometimes use 'allegory' as an omnibus term to include every artistic or literary representation that has a meaning other than the apparent one. In the sixteenth century considerable debate was devoted to the allegory, the symbol, the emblem, and the device (*impresa*) as forms representing a figurative meaning.[1] Some of this debate is reflected in Spenser's usage.

SPENSER'S 'CONTINUED ALLEGORY AND DARKE CONCEIT'

These phrases, by which Spenser describes *The Faerie Queene* in his *Letter to Raleigh*, require some explanation. What does he mean by a continued allegory, and does this imply the existence of non-continued allegory? Most acknowledged allegories are narratives and are continued through a series of events. If all were like this, Spenser's qualifying term 'continued' would be unnecessary.

In Tasso's discussion of the heroic poem and the use of allegory therein, he gives several examples of allegory. One of these is Nebuchadnezzar's dream of the giant statue made of gold, silver, brass, and iron, but having feet of clay (Dan. 2 : 31–5). Another is the Cave of the Nymphs in Homer's *Odyssey*, Book xiii, as interpreted by Porphyry.[2] These might be called 'still life' allegories; for, while there is some action involved, there is no continuous narrative. The organization of material is descriptive, with various parts combining to make an allegorical whole. Spenser may have had such examples in mind and may have felt it necessary to specify that his work is a continued allegory; i.e. an allegory in narrative form.

Whether Spenser's description is correct for the entire poem may be questioned, for, as Paul J. Alpers points out, his allegory

---

[1] For extended discussion see Rosemary Freeman, *English Emblem Books* (1948), and Rosemond Tuve, *Allegorical Imagery* (1966).

[2] *Trattato del Poema Eroico*, bk. v, in *Works* (Venice, 1834), vol. i, pp. 115–16.

is sometimes intermittent.[1] Most passages can be interpreted as representations of the moral virtues in action, but not all of them can. Britomart confessing to Glauce her love for Artegall (III. ii. 38) is difficult to see as anything but a girl in love. Malbecco's grief at the seduction of his wife Hellenore (III. ix–x) seems to be the affliction of a real person, not of an abstraction, even though Spenser gives him an Ovidian transformation into Gelosy at the end of the episode. This phenomenon of intermittent allegory may be partially explained by Edwin Honig:

> In *The Faerie Queene* the world is presented morally, as an emanation of inner experience. There the virtues and the vices exist as personified motivations to action in the guise of fictional characters. Some vices, like Archimago and Duessa, are realized as persons, while those like Mammon or Despair need to wear only the obvious clothing of the psychic forces which Spenser intends them briefly to represent. But the well-drawn figures of Britomart (Chastity) and Arthur (Magnificence) surge across the borders of abstraction and become vivid, dramatically incarnated personalities.[2]

In other words, Spenser's characters become real people for him as well as for his readers, though he had planned them originally as figures like those in a morality play, representing abstract ideas. At such moments he pictures them as human beings in human situations; his interest in personality supplants his interest in allegorical portrayals.

Spenser's phrase 'darke conceit', used by Honig as the title of his book, raises additional questions. Since a conceit is a metaphorical identification of unlike things, it obviously resembles allegory, which is usually identified as an extended metaphor. The term 'darke' may be explained by Erasmus's comments upon the nature of proverbs: 'Metaphor is almost always present. . . . Allegory is not less prevalent, although this is in certain instances a species of metaphor. . . . Sometimes I have discovered even an enigma, which according to Quintilian is nothing other than *a darker allegory*, of which kind is "The half is greater than the whole".'[3] Thus the term 'darke' conveys no sinister or evil connotation but

---

[1] 'Narrative and Rhetoric in *The Faerie Queene*', *Studies in English Literature: The Renaissance*, ii (1962), 27–46, quoted in Tuve, *Allegorical Imagery*, p. 290. In his book *The Poetry of* The Faerie Queene (1967) Alpers minimizes too far the allegorical action of the poem.

[2] *Dark Conceit: The Making of Allegory* (Evanston, Ill., 1959), pp. 174–5.

[3] *Adagia* (Frankfurt, 1670), pp. 1–2.

simply refers to obscurity of meaning, like that in a riddle, or enigma.

Macrobius expresses a reason for presenting deep truths in riddling or allegorical form. The general run of men and women are not fitted for the comprehension of profound truths; only the wise have the right to lift the veil of truth. The fable or allegory veils the truth from unfit spectators and reveals it only to those who are equipped to understand it.[1]

Spenser uses the concept of veiled truth in his portrayal of Una, who never lifts her veil for Redcross until he has approached perfection in holiness (below, p. 121). In the Proem to Book II, Spenser applies the same concept to the poem as a whole:

> And thou, O fayrest Princesse under sky,
> In this fayre mirrhour maist behold thy face,
> And thine owne realmes in land of Faery,
> And in this antique ymage thy great auncestry.

> The which O pardon me thus to enfold
> In *covert vele*, and wrap in shadowes light,
> That feeble eyes your glory may behold,
> Which ells could not endure those beames bright,
> But would be dazled with exceeding light. (stanzas 4–5)

In the language of compliment, Spenser describes Queen Elizabeth as shining too brightly for the vision of ordinary mortals; hence the veil of allegory is necessary to protect the eyesight of the beholders. This veil of allegory is thus comparable to the veil which protected the Israelites from the brightness of Moses' face after he returned from Sinai and the presence of God (Exod. 34: 33–5).

Spenser's uses of allegory seem to follow Natalis Comes's three methods of interpreting Greek myths: the historical, the physical, and the ethical or moral. Some mythical figures can be interpreted in one way, some in two, and some in all three ways. Comes interprets Jupiter and Saturn in all three ways.

Historically, writes Comes, Jupiter and Saturn were kings of antiquity who became elevated to gods in popular belief, which sought to deify great men. Physically, Jupiter variously represents air, aether, the sun, fate, the sky, and the World-Soul. Saturn

---

[1] *In Somnium Scipionis*, I. ii. 17, quoted in C. S. Lewis, *Spenser's Images of Life* Cambridge, 1967), p. 43.

represents time. Ethically, Jupiter signifies that happiness and the abundance of all good things follow upon the wisdom and integrity of the prince. Saturn's expulsion from the throne by Jupiter means that no great work can be done without great dangers and perturbations of the soul.[1]

Comes explains Circe physically and ethically. Physically, she represents the process in nature of corruption and generation by which life is carried on, and this change is represented when Ulysses' companions are turned to beasts. But Ulysses is immune to this change, since he signifies man's immortal soul, which is not subject to the corruption of the flesh. Ethically, Circe is lust (*libido*) which impresses into man's soul vices like those of beasts. The soul that is prudent and divine can avoid capture by these vices, but only by divine aid can it finally overcome so great a multitude of pleasures and of dangers.[2]

Comes gives numerous other interpretations. His three methods of interpretation are adopted by Claudius Minos, or Claude Mignaut, in his edition of Alciatus's *Emblemata*, another favourite source-book of Spenser's work. Minos thinks of an 'allegorical' treatment as the turning of a historical or physical 'symbol' so as to give it a moral point.[3] In symbols, he states, 'whatever is hidden is yet propounded to be understood by informed ears'.[4] He is blamed for this statement by N. W., the anonymous friend of Samuel Daniel. N. W. insisted that Minos used the word 'symbol' too loosely and should seek for greater precision in his terms.[5]

Christoforo Landino, the Virgilian allegorist (below, p. 68), varies slightly the three methods of interpreting Greek fables: Mythicon, or fables for entertainment; Physicon, representing forces of nature; and Civile, imparting precepts for virtuous living.[6]

While moral allegory is the dominant form throughout most of *The Faerie Queene*, Spenser does have some instances of historical allegory and of physical allegory. These are given separate attention at the end of this book.

---

[1] *Mythologiae* (edn. of Padua, 1616), bk. x, pp. 532–3.
[2] Ibid., p. 543.
[3] Alciatus, *Emblemata*: 'Syntagma de Symbolis' (edn. of Lyons, 1614), pp. 10–11.
[4] Ibid., p. 2.
[5] Daniel, *The Worthy Tract of Paulus Iouius* (1585), Introd. (unpaged).
[6] *Disputationes Camaldulensis* (Strasbourg, 1508), bk. iii, sig. Hiiii.

EXTERNAL AND INTERNAL ALLEGORY

After noting the kinds of allegory used by Spenser, we must necessarily study the method by which they are presented. For the concrete presentation of abstract qualities, some type of visible embodiment must be used. In moral allegory Spenser's method is twofold. A character may be an *exemplum* or a type of a particular virtue or a particular vice. But he may also be the virtue or vice itself as it presents itself within the soul of the individual man; or he may be a faculty of the soul capable of being influenced by virtue or vice, or by affections and perturbations, the preliminary stages of vice (below, p. 64). In such a case he is never a person but is a quality or impulse within the individual soul. The interior of the soul is the battle-ground on which the action is fought.

This conception of allegory is not new. In the fourth century Prudentius used it in his *Psychomachia*, or *Battle of the Soul*. After his work the war of the virtues and vices gradually became the most popular subject of medieval allegory. W. A. Neilson has quoted a sermon by St. Bernard which combines the method with Aristotelian psychology. There is a city of Mansoul. In it are three castles, Rationabilitas, Irascibilitas, and Concupiscibilitas, presided over by Faith, Hope, and Charity, assisted by minor virtues. The ruler of the town is Free Will, who is attacked and overcome by Blasphemy, Luxury, and Pride, and is liberated only by the arrival of Grace and Fear with an army of virtues.[1] In some instances the virtues and vices are personified as knights. In Stephen Hawes's *Pastime of Pleasure*, for example, Grandamour rides forth from the Tower of Chivalry with Sir Truth, Sir Courtesy, Sir Fidelity, and others.[2] The method was a familiar one.

In reading these allegories, however, it is very difficult to keep in mind that these characters are not people but abstract qualities. The more skilful the author, the more they appear to be real people and seem to exemplify the qualities rather than to be the qualities themselves. Thus, we know that Una is truth, but we think of her as a lovely maiden in distress. The difficulty is heightened when the author's method is twofold, when some characters are actual persons and others are abstract qualities within the soul, or when the same character is now one and now the other. This

---

[1] *The Origin and Sources of the Courts of Love*, p. 19.
[2] *The Pastime of Pleasure*, line 3425 (EETS, o.s., no. 173, p. 131).

is the aspect of Spenser's method which is likely to thwart the modern reader. Yet in these days of psychological study, when the language of battle is once again used to explain the clashing impulses within the human mind, we are perhaps better fitted to understand *The Faerie Queene* than were the people of any other period since Spenser wrote it.

The increasing awareness of this aspect of *The Faerie Queene* by modern critics may be illustrated by a few quotations:

> The *vehicle* of the medieval mode normally operates to create a world of vision or fancy which is capable of representing the inner unseen world of the human mind.[1]

> In *The Faerie Queene* the function of the allegory and of the imagery is partly to externalize the psychomachia, the internal moral struggle between good and evil for possession of the soul, a subject popular since the fourth century.[2]

> The absolute conflict between heaven and hell, good and evil, is fought out relatively in every human soul, is fought out then, all through Spenser's poem, and marked by the symbolic opposites referred to. . . .[3] At the last resort, these good personages are only the attributes of Arthur himself. . . .[4] In actual fact, the whole action of all six books and all the land of faerie with its forests, castles, and sea-shores, exist in Arthur's soul, and there only.[5]

This last eloquent statement grasps the essence of the internal allegory but considerably overstates the case. In the internal world of the soul, Arthur represents heavenly grace, which is the most eminent example possible of magnificence because it is most characteristic of God. Magnificence, according to the *Letter to Raleigh*, 'is the perfection of all the rest and containeth in it them all'. It is the *complexus* of all the moral virtues raised to their most eminent degree and aids the less perfect individual virtues in their efforts to reach a similar degree of perfection, for no one virtue can reach perfection except in a bond of union with the other virtues (above, p. 10). Hence, magnificence can 'contain' the other

---

[1] Edward P. Sheridan, 'Modes of Allegory in *The Faerie Queene*', Yale Dissertation, 1949, p. 21. Italics not mine.

[2] Lyle Glazier, 'Spenser's Imagery: Imagery of Good and Evil in *The Faerie Queene*', Harvard Dissertation, 1950, p. 9.

[3] Pauline Parker, *The Allegory of* The Faerie Queene (Oxford, 1960), p. 48.

[4] Ibid., p. 87.   [5] Ibid., p. 169.

virtues without being identical with them. It would appear, however, from her statements that Mother Parker regards Arthur in
the external world as a hero comparable with Agamemnon–
Ulysses, Aeneas, Orlando, and Godfredo–Rinaldo. She seems to
consider him identical with 'a gentleman or noble person' who is
to be fashioned 'in virtuous and gentle discipline' as 'the general
end . . . of all the book' (*Letter to Raleigh*). Such an identification
does explain a seeming inconsistency in Spenser, who names
Arthur as his major hero in the *Letter* and then makes him appear
only infrequently. If the entire action is really taking place in
Arthur's soul, then obviously he is present at all times as the
scene of action, so to speak; his internal appearances need come
only at a time when is necessary for heavenly grace to effect a
rescue.

Certain difficulties arise in this interpretation. For one thing,
numerous scenes of the internal allegory, particularly in Books
III and IV, seem designed to take place within the soul of a woman.
Again, some of the action does not lend itself to internal allegory
but portrays people in their external relations with each other.
These elements suggest that possibly Spenser's 'gentleman or
noble person' is to be fashioned in virtuous and gentle discipline
by viewing the 'historical fiction' of Arthur rather than by being
Arthur himself. Spenser's words allow such an interpretation.
The gentleman could thus be instructed by the career of Arthur
as a citizen of the world, albeit the semi-legendary world of epic
heroes, and also by his example of perfection in the internal world
of the human soul. This soul is not limited to the gentleman or
to Arthur but may be the soul of any man or of any woman.

Spenser's twofold method is clearly foretold in Tasso's *Allegory
of the Poem*, which explains his epic *Gerusalemme Liberata*. This
allegory was printed with some editions as early as 1581 and with
most of those immediately thereafter.[1] In some instances relevant
comments were printed at the head of each canto, as though the
poetry beneath had been written expressly to illustrate the allegorical interpretation above. We know that Tasso fitted his allegory
to the poem after the poem had already been composed, but
Spenser could not be expected to know that. Actually, he has

---

[1] Tasso's *Allegoria*, or *Allegory of the Poem*, is translated into English and printed
at the end of Fairfax's translation of *Gerusalemme Liberata*, ed. H. Morley (Caris-
brooke Library, London, 1890).

applied the method described by Tasso much more extensively than Tasso himself did.[1]

Tasso divides the method of heroic poetry into imitation and allegory. The first is an image of human action, the second a figurative presentation of human life. Imitation presents costumes, actions, passions, opinions in an external manner. Allegory considers their intrinsic being, obscurely and mysteriously showing forth the nature of the thing. Dante and Ulysses, the lonely voyagers, represent the contemplative life, while Agamemnon and Achilles represent the civil or political life, since they are always shown among their fellows. Aeneas combines the two, the contemplative life in the first six books of the *Aeneid*, and the political life in the last six. Tasso says that he has formed his epic on the same plan and states that Godfredo represents the political man.

This passage almost certainly suggested Spenser's statement in his *Letter to Raleigh* that Agamemnon and Ulysses represent respectively a good governor and a virtuous man, that the two are combined in Aeneas and again in Ariosto's Orlando, and that Tasso has dissevered them again, showing the political virtues in Godfredo and the ethical virtues of a private man in Rinaldo. Spenser seems to have assumed this interpretation of Rinaldo, for Tasso does not interpret him in this particular way, though he does make clear that Rinaldo is in contrast with Godfredo. Of these several examples, Spenser apparently preferred to follow Virgil, since he planned to illustrate the private moral virtues by Prince Arthur and the political virtues by King Arthur, using the same hero in different periods of his career.

The important point to be noted here is that these characters are interpreted by what may be called external allegory. Perhaps we should prefer the term 'exemplification'. Godfredo is the political man, shown in his relations with his fellow soldiers. Tasso says that the death of Sveno and his companions shows the loss of friends suffered by the political man. Such circumstances are external and are examples of adverse fortune. Perhaps such a method was intended by Spenser for his complete portrait of

---

[1] I am here at variance with the opinion of Alpers, *The Poetry of* The Faerie Queene, p. 19 n. Alpers notices Tasso's reference to imitation and allegory, but not the further distinction between external and internal allegory, which Tasso illus trates without stating the double classification.

Arthur, who was to illustrate first the private moral virtues and later the political virtues.

After his introduction, Tasso comes to the other form of allegory, or internal interpretation. The entire Christian army represents one man, the ordinary troops being his body, the leaders representing the various faculties of his soul. Godfredo represents the intellect, or reason. The enchantress Armida represents the concupiscible faculty. Rinaldo represents the irascible faculty, which is much more than mere wrath. Its place in the faculties of the soul is like that of a warrior in the societies of men. It provides the emotional urge to unselfish action. When it obeys reason as its proper commander, it aids in subduing the savage lusts and desires that spring from the concupiscible faculty, and thus promotes true human happiness. But when it does not obey reason but follows its own bent, fighting not against but for concupiscence, then it is like a savage watchdog that kills not the thief but the watchman. Rinaldo, loving Armida, is the irascible faculty serving concupiscence, but when he returns to his proper commander and obeys Godfredo, or the rational faculty, then he easily cuts down the enchanted wood and forces a way into the city. The wood represents false images of good, the gardens of Armida empty and illusory pleasures, the city of Jerusalem the perfection of civil happiness which is the goal of every man. The victory of the army represents man's attainment of happiness, following the union of all the Christian warriors under Godfredo, which might be described as man's conquest of himself.

Tasso's account of the three faculties is probably drawn, directly or indirectly, from Aristotle's *Nicomachean Ethics*, VII. vi. Aristotle describes the irascible faculty and explains its impulses as more nearly rational and honourable than the desires and lusts of the concupiscible faculty. Francesco Piccolomini quotes Plato's saying in *Republic* iv that the duty of the irascible appetite is to fight for reason against desire (i. 13; p. 56c). One can easily see how this internal struggle of the soul became allied with the battle of the vices and the virtues. The primary source of the latter is Biblical. St. Peter speaks of 'fleshly lusts that war against the soul'. St. Paul, in a passage quoted by Spenser, refers to the 'whole armour of God' which is needed as a defence against the powers of darkness.[1] In this combination of Biblical and Aristotelian

[1] See 1 Pet. 2: 11; Eph. 6: 11–17; and the *Letter to Raleigh*.

material we find the clue to internal warfare in *The Faerie Queene*. The same combination accounts for another prominent element in Spenser, his use of beasts and monsters. Aristotle describes bestiality as the lowest stage of vice, when reason is completely absent and the two lower faculties have full control.[1] The Bible uses 'beast' constantly as a term for the devil acting through the lower impulses of man's nature. Francesco explains that the fables of Hercules slaying monsters are an allegory of man overcoming the vices within his soul (vi. 8; p. 337C, x. 34; p. 595A).

There are two ways in which we can force ourselves to follow the internal allegory. One is always to ask, Where is the field of action? The answer is always the same: Within the human soul. The second way is to try to reconstruct the external situation and actions of the individual whose internal conflict is allegorically presented. When holiness falls a victim to pride, or when temperance and chastity momentarily clash with each other, what is happening to the person whose internal thoughts are thus shown to us? There may be a variety of possible answers; the attempt to provide one will keep us cognizant of Spenser's method and will explain many puzzling inconsistencies in *The Faerie Queene*.

There is thus a twofold moral allegory in *The Faerie Queene*. In the first, Spenser follows essentially the method later used in Bunyan's *Pilgrim's Progress*. As Christian is a man progressing through various physical and mental perils to the heavenly land, so each of Spenser's major characters is a person progressing toward perfection in a particular virtue. Redcross is a holy man, Guyon a temperate man, Britomart a chaste woman, Artegall a just man, etc., each of whom undergoes perils in the quest for that perfection of virtue through which true glory is attained. Even when the perils are mental and are allegorically presented, the main characters remain real people. This method corresponds to Tasso's first form of allegory, or exemplification.

In the second method, only one person is concerned, the entire action taking place within his soul. Holiness, temperance, chastity, justice are not persons but are qualities of his soul which may be either strengthened or weakened by his conduct. Within the forest of his lower nature lurk the beasts, giants, and brutal men who rush out to destroy his nobler qualities when opportunity arises. These are lusts and affections of the concupiscible appetite.

[1] *Nic. Eth.* vii. v. 5–6.

But in his breast there lives a nobler nature, the irascible faculty which, though savage and untamed and fierce, recognizes reason with the rational virtues as its lawful guide and ruler.[1] Sometimes it is perverted to support the baser nature or may even suffer a 'split personality', part of it supporting and part opposing the governance of reason. If all else fails, heavenly grace (Arthur) comes to rescue the languishing virtue.

This 'inside-out method' of interpreting human conduct was especially congenial to medieval minds. They envisioned, with greater intensity than we can feel, the great world conflict as a struggle between opposing forces for possession of the soul of man. The field of conflict is within each soul; the crisis of each life comes when it makes a vital decision of the mind. Externally the climax of Christ's life came with the crucifixion, but internally it came in the Garden of Gethsemane, when he made his decision to face whatever God might send. The internal struggle is the more dramatic because it is more significant, its outcome determining man's future state through all eternity. The clashing impulses within the soul constitute the really vital struggle, to which external events and characters are relevant only in so far as they influence the tremendous internal decision.

A simple and illuminating example of the 'inside-out method' is found in a modern Russian play, Evreinov's *Theater of the Soul*.[2] The stage represents the interior of the human breast; its red curtains sway back and forth with the heartbeats. Here the Rational Entity and the Emotional Entity of the owner debate the relative merits of his wife and of a dancer with whom he is infatuated; images of the two women appear as they are envisioned by each of the two entities. The entities fight, and reason is slain by emotion, who then turns to the image of the dancer. She rebuffs him with the taunt that he has not enough money to be her gallant. In excitement he rushes to the telephone and shouts a command. There is a loud explosion and blood pours from the

[1] For an early discussion of the internal war among the three faculties of the soul see John Smith Harrison, *Platonism in English Poetry of the Sixteenth and Seventeenth Centuries* (Columbia University Press, 1903), pp. 13 ff. In 1935 Merritt Y. Hughes called the Palmer in Bk. II an externalization of conscience and suggested that other characters in Spenser had a similar dual role (*Journal of English Literary History*, ii. [1935], 151–64). The present study illustrates more fully the interplay of the internal struggle and the external action.

[2] Evreinov's play is available in English in T. H. Dickinson, *Chief Contemporary Dramatists*, 3rd series (Boston, 1930).

torn curtain; externally we know that the man has shot himself. As the Emotional Entity sinks down beside the Rational Entity, a third figure, the Eternal Entity, rouses himself from a corner where he has been sleeping. He rubs his eyes, picks up his suitcase, murmurs 'I have to change here', and walks out. The curtain falls.

In an obvious and somewhat crude fashion, this play illustrates the technique of internal allegory: the internal struggle of the mind is presented in objective form, and we must guess at the external action which accompanies it. This is essentially the technique described by Tasso and used by Spenser. The language of modern psychology may also assist our comprehension of it, for the id, the ego, and the super-ego have a rather close correspondence to the Aristotelian faculties of the soul: the concupiscible, the irascible, and the rational. From the concupiscible faculty come the appetites for food, drink, and sexual satisfaction which are necessary for the continuance of the race, and which must be controlled rather than destroyed. From the rational faculty comes the power of seeing general truths and making moral judgements; Thomas Aquinas interprets Aristotle to this effect.[1] The irascible faculty is the driving force or emotional impetus that leads to human action. It instinctively recognizes reason as its proper guide, but may be perverted to serve the concupiscible appetites or may itself get completely out of control, as in blind rage or anger. A man who surrenders wholly to the concupiscible appetites, unrestrained by the other faculties, is classed as bestial by Aristotle, since he lacks the rational faculty which distinguishes men from beasts.

In Shakespeare's *The Rape of Lucrece* external action and internal warfare are described together; Tarquin's deeds are accompanied by a play-by-play account of what goes on in his mind, here envisaged as a battle between reason and the affections or appetites. After his crime, his soul holds an internal dialogue with itself. The princess, or rational faculty, now spotted with crime, is visited by various Cares, who ask about her condition. She tells them that her subjects, the appetites, have risen in insurrection, burst through her fortress or 'consecrated wall', and brought her in subjection to a foreign power; i.e. to the devil. Her immortality

---

[1] Aquinas, *De Intellectu et Intelligibili*, Opusculum 49 in *Opuscula Omnia* (Paris, 1634), p. 378.

is in peril; she had sought to restrain the appetites but could not overcome their violent will. This theme is the same as that of the siege of Princess Alma's castle in Book II of *The Faerie Queene*, where the besiegers are the Affections, led by Maleger. Since Shakespeare has also given us the external action, the internal struggle is easily recognized as such; whereas Spenser has presented the internal struggle in objective form, expecting the reader to reconstruct the external action for himself. In Shakespeare the attack of the affections was successful. In Spenser the attack was unsuccessful; the affections were overcome through the aid of Prince Arthur, who is identified in Book I as heavenly grace. Most of Prince Arthur's other seemingly haphazard appearances are explained by this same conception. He arrives when the virtues appear to be on the point of destruction by the opposing vices or perturbations, and rescues the virtues. He is thus designed to illustrate the Christian dogma that man cannot stand in his own strength and can win the victory over sin only through the grace of God.

We must be careful not to confuse the virtues with the man who possesses them. When Guyon faints after emerging from the Cave of Mammon, he is on the point of being despoiled by Cymochles and Pyrochles in spite of the remonstrances of the Palmer. These three respectively suggest qualities of the concupiscible, irascible, and rational faculties of the soul. The person whose soul is represented does not faint. It is his virtue of temperance that fails, unable to endure longer after prolonged exposure to temptation. It is rescued by the timely arrival of heavenly grace, which preserves and revives it; i.e. the person is saved from intemperance through God's aid, when his normal powers of resistance have failed.

We should not identify Pyrochles as the irascible faculty itself. He is rather a 'perturbation' springing from the irascible faculty, furious and violent anger, just as in Book VI Sir Turpine represents inveterate and malicious anger, a rancorous temperament. Turpine is also overcome by Prince Arthur. Similarly, Cymochles is not the concupiscible faculty itself but a 'perturbation' springing from it, unrestrained appetite. He and his brother Pyrochles are thus the natural enemies of temperance in the human mind.

In Book I the counterpart of the brothers is Sansloy, or lawless violence. In his attempted seizure of Una he is opposed first by

Una's lion and afterwards by Sir Satyrane. Both the lion and Satyrane, by nature wild and violent, had recognized Una's goodness and had put themselves at her service. They reflect the irascible faculty of the soul, which instinctively recognizes the superiority of rational goodness and seeks to assist it in overcoming its opponents (below, pp. 124-5). The character of Satyrane has a good deal in common with Tasso's Rinaldo, who (by Tasso's own account) represents the irascible faculty. This good quality of the irascible faculty reappears in the Salvage Man of Book VI, who rescues Calepine from the unchivalrous Turpine. Here we have generous indignation, a virtue of the irascible faculty, subduing rancorous anger, a vice of the irascible faculty.

The concupiscible faculty is further represented in Spenser by the beasts, giants, and churls who represent various degrees of lust. These usually burst out of the forest to surprise their victims and the guardian virtues. The forest represents the flesh, an interpretation traceable to the Virgilian commentaries of Landino (below, p. 68). The beasts are vices which proceed from our fleshly nature and must be subdued by virtues proceeding from our spiritual nature. The fleshly nature should not be completely destroyed. For example, when Satyrane conquers the beast that feeds on women's flesh, he binds it with the Girdle of Chastity dropped by Florimell and can lead it wherever he will. This again refers to man's internal struggle, the irascible faculty subduing the concupiscible faculty (below, pp. 58, 147).

The most sustained instance of internal allegory in *The Faerie Queene* is presented in connection with Britomart. Since she represents chastity, the external situation is presumably a woman's struggle to remain chaste, the kind of situation shown in Richardson's *Pamela*. In the incident at Malecasta's castle, Britomart easily repulses Malecasta's knights, whose names, translated, are Ogling, Talking, Jesting, Kissing, Drinking, and Night Revelry. But after she goes to sleep, Malecasta, misapprehending her sex, seeks to slip into her bed. Remember that this is internal allegory; unchastity is on the verge of displacing chastity in the woman's thoughts—she is not asleep, but her chastity is. When Britomart suddenly awakes, seizes her sword, and causes a great uproar, chastity has suddenly revived. Externally, that is probably the moment when the lady slaps the gentleman's face. The six knights attempt to subdue Britomart, but Ogling, Jesting, Kissing, *et alii* cannot now prevail. Reinforced by holiness, the Redcross Knight, chastity puts them to flight. Virtue has triumphed. The six knights are obviously part of the external situation but are viewed from within the soul much as a televised image of the outside world is brought within a darkened room.

The incident involving Malecasta and Britomart takes place within the mind of a woman. Britomart is involved in another episode which takes place within the mind of a man. In IV. ix. 20–37 four knights are fighting over their claims to the false Florimell. In reality, they represent four different attitudes towards women. Druon is a misogynist who prefers to remain single and to have nothing to do with women. Claribell loves sincerely but too violently. Blandamour loves violently but for a short time only. Paridell disdains love but seduces women for his sensual gratification. Druon and Claribell fight Blandamour and Paridell; then they change partners, and Druon and Paridell combine against Blandamour and Claribell. When Britomart and Scudamour appear, the four attack them, Claribell and Blandamour attacking Britomart, while Druon and Paridell attack Scudamour. Alastair Fowler suggests the following scheme of qualities for the first four knights: Claribell—love, constancy; Blandamour—love, inconstancy; Paridell—disdain, inconstancy; Druon—disdain, constancy.[1] They change partners as the reason for fighting changes. Thus the first battle is between constancy and inconstancy, the second between love and disdain. In the third battle, violent love seeks to force the surrender of chastity, while those disdainful of love would force the knight of true love, Cupid's man, from his allegiance.

Fowler does not interpret this scene as internal allegory, though it can hardly be explained otherwise. Why should Druon, for example, fight about the false Florimell if he is an individual person? It seems completely unnecessary to fight in order to show that he does not want her; simply ignoring her would accomplish the purpose. But as an impulse within the soul of a man who meets a woman that attracts him, Druon is one of several alternatives: to forget her and preserve his 'single blessedness' (Druon), to fall uncontrollably and permanently in love (Claribell), to fall violently in love for a short time only (Blandamour), to seduce her without loving her (Paridell), to fall deeply in love but not

[1] Fowler, *Spenser and the Numbers of Time* (New York, 1964), pp. 31–2.

uncontrollably so (Scudamour), to seek her love only through honourable marriage (Britomart). These impulses may all exist together in a man's soul, either towards a particular woman or towards women generally, and may cause an emotional disturbance as he argues with himself now from one point of view, now from another. He can best compose his conflicting emotions through prayer and an appeal to heavenly grace, for it is Arthur who finally settles the confused quarrel of these six combatants.

As Arthur remains in Fairyland between the various rescues effected by him, so a modicum of heavenly grace resides in the soul of each man or woman who is not alienated from God. It is renewed periodically through the sacrament of communion and can be weakened or lost if man's will is turned away from God. It does not require a new visitation from heaven in every emergency. Spenser believed such visitations possible, as witness the angel who watches over Guyon after his emergence from the Cave of Mammon (II. viii. 1–8). But heavenly grace is a naturalized citizen, so to speak, and remains to strengthen a virtue against the assaults of its enemies after the angel has returned to heaven. It is God's viceroy residing in the world of the human soul, acting as a strategic reserve in the war against sin when human powers begin to fail.

Arthur's diamond shield, however, may represent the direct interposition of God in human affairs. It stems from the diamond shield in Tasso's *Gerusalemme Liberata*, vii. 82, and is identified in his *Allegory of the Poem* as 'the special safeguard of the Lord God'.[1] It is revealed three times in the poem, twice by accident (I. viii. 19, IV. viii. 42), once by design (V. viii. 37). It may signify that a man who stubbornly adheres to the error of his ways is sometimes frightened into repentance by a direct manifestation of God's power (below, p. 175).

More examples of internal allegory will be pointed out in later chapters of this book. Interestingly enough, here also Spenser shows a considerable debt to Francesco Piccolomini's *Vniuersa Philosophia de Moribus*. Though Francesco is not writing a chivalric allegory, he uses the language of battle in describing the action of virtues and vices. Even when he refers only to a difference in

---

[1] Alpers, like most other commentators, has overlooked the diamond shield of Tasso; he bases a lengthy discussion upon Atlante's shield in Ariosto (*The Poetry of The Faerie Queene*, pp. 174–9). See below, pp. 89, 109.

meanings of a word, the two meanings 'do battle' (*pugnant*). Most interesting of all is his statement that the virtues themselves, when in an imperfect state, may do battle with each other briefly until they recognize their true basis of concord, for the virtues are naturally harmonious (iv. 40; pp. 218–19). This provides the hint for the two clashes of Britomart and Artegall before they recognize each other, the clashes of Britomart with Guyon and Marinell, and the near-conflicts of Guyon with Redcross and of Arthur with Artegall. The battle of friends who fail to recognize each other in armour is a conventional situation in medieval romance, and Francesco's words give it an ethical rationale for use in the holy war. He also points out that opposing vices war against each other; e.g. avarice and prodigality do not exist together but either is more likely to change to the other than to the virtuous mean of liberality (ix. 48; p. 542c). Such conflicts occur between Archimago and Sansloy (I. iii. 38), Blandamour and Paridell (IV. ii. 15).

Again, Francesco names as the basic perturbations which disturb the soul love and hate, pursuit and flight. Love and hate are the beginnings, pursuit and flight are the middle stages, of a developing perturbation (i. 19; pp. 63–4, i. 21; p. 68D). But pursuit of the good and flight from the evil may assist in controlling perturbations (iv. 27; p. 198c). Here, though the flight of Florimell from various pursuers, good and bad, is doubtless imitated from Ariosto's Angelica, Francesco provides an ethical rationale which helps adapt it to Spenser's allegory. Una and Amoret likewise fly from evil forces upon occasion. The theme is reversed when perturbations or vices fly from the avenging virtues.

Other examples of internal warfare will emerge in the course of this book, for it is almost omnipresent in *The Faerie Queene*. The instances given will serve to illustrate the method and to help the reader to keep the internal perspective when interpreting this kind of allegory. It is not easy to do, for normally an author stands without and looks within the minds of his characters; but here he is 'standing on the inside, looking to the outside', and the reader must join him in the mysterious realm of the human soul.

III

The Allegorical Quest

WE can better understand *The Faerie Queene* if we can find some consistent pattern of the various adventures therein. The most obvious model for an Arthurian narrative is Malory's *Morte D'Arthur*, in which the knightly quests may be described as circular. They begin at Arthur's court, proceed through various mishaps and struggles to the accomplishment of the objective, then end at Arthur's court as each knight returns to report on the success of his mission. His reward is the increased honour accorded him by his fellow knights and by the world at large. Any other rewards, such as wealth, lands, or a wife, seem to be incidental to the acquirement of glory and honour, which is the main objective.

In his *Letter to Raleigh*, Spenser adopts this method with the knights of Gloriana's court and explains the quests of the first three books: (1) to release Una's parents from the dragon, granted to Redcross, later identified as St. George; (2) to seize and punish the enchantress Acrasia, granted to Guyon; (3) to rescue Amoret from the enchanter Busyrane, granted to Scudamour. These knights are to return to Gloriana's court at the end of a year to report on the success of their missions. To these may be added Artegall and Calidore as knights whose quests were assigned to them by Gloriana. The return to her court was to take place in Book XII, at which time Arthur also would presumably arrive, since Gloriana herself is the object of his quest.

The account of the first quest, that of Redcross, as given in the *Letter*, seems clearly to be drawn from Malory's account of Beaumains (actually Gareth),[1] but the poem itself departs from Malory to follow the adventures of St. George. In this and subsequent books of *The Faerie Queene*, the knight is to return to Cleopolis, the city of Glory. The tenth canto of Book I makes clear that this is earthly glory obtained during this life; the heavenly city

---

[1] *Morte D'Arthur*, bk. vii, chs. 1–21. Cf. *Var.* i. 391–5.

is a further stage, to be attained after the completion of the service due to Gloriana.[1] Thus, while heaven and union with God may be considered the ultimate objective, they are not the immediate objective of the quests in *The Faerie Queene*. Cleopolis is a city of Earth, or of that fairyland which allegorizes the Earth; it is not a part of heaven. In this Spenser's poem differs from Bunyan's *Pilgrim's Progress* and similar religious allegories, which end with the achievement of heaven after death.

THE PATTERN OF THE QUEST

In the various chivalric allegories which precede Spenser's work, there seems to be one of two final objectives possible to a quest, both achieved by way of the virtues. These are happiness and honour. Some quests culminate in one, some in the other. We may quote several examples of each.

The frontispiece of Thomas P. Roche's recent book *The Kindly Flame* reproduces the title-page of a Greek–Latin lexicon published at Basel in 1545.[2] The illustrated border, by Holbein, represents the pilgrimage of Man as the ascent of a mountain. Outside the garden gate at the bottom of the mountain, a cluster of naked babes wait until the venerable gatekeeper Genius admits them into life.[3] As each proceeds along the path, he passes figures labelled Fortune, Persuasion (evil), Opinions, Luxury, Avarice, Incontinence, Dolour, Sadness, Penitence, and False Discipline. At this point the path narrows and one must pass on hands and knees through a low stone gate and a very steep, narrow way beyond (cf. Matt. 7: 14), but Fortitude reaches a hand to aid the pilgrim. Afterwards he goes past Boldness, True Discipline, Truth, Persuasion (good), and the Virtues (not individualized). These stand outside the castle of True Happiness (*Arx Verae Felicitatis*), and the queen within is labelled Felicitas. Here the pilgrim's journey ends.

A second instance occurs in Tasso's *Allegoria* of *Gerusalemme Liberata*, discussed in the preceding chapter. The army, composed

---

[1] Isabel E. Rathborne, *The Meaning of Spenser's Fairyland* (New York, 1937), ch. 1.

[2] *Lexicon Graeco-Latinum . . . per Conradum Gesnerum Tigurinum* (Basel, 1545). In *The Kindly Flame: A Study of the Third and Fourth Books of Spenser's* Faerie Queene (Princeton, 1964).

[3] Cf. the similar image in the Garden of Adonis (below p. 269).

of various princes and other Christian soldiers, signifies the virile man, composed of soul and body; the soul not to be taken singly but distinguished into many and various powers. Jerusalem, strongly fortified in a rough, mountainous region, signifies civil happiness, which the army seeks and which comes to a Christian man. It is difficult to reach and must be approached by means of virtue.

Civil happiness, as understood by Tasso and Francesco Piccolomini, is man's happiness as a citizen (*civis*) among his fellow men and is the proper concern of the moral virtues, while the theological virtues of faith, hope, and charity are directed towards the happiness of heaven.[1]

A third instance is found in Jean Cartigny's *Voyage of the Wandering Knight*, translated into English by William Goodyear in 1581.[2] After a period in the Palace of Worldly Pleasure, the knight is saved from the mire of sin by God's Grace, goes through the School of Repentance, and ascends to the Palace of Virtue, which closely adjoins the Palace of True Felicitie. We know that this is an earthly palace, since he is granted a view of the City of Heaven from the Tower of Faith, which is part of the Palace of Virtue.

At this point we may note Lodowick Bryskett's statement of purpose in his *Discourse of Ciuill Life*: 'to discourse vpon the morall vertues, yet not omitting the intellectuall, to the end to frame a gentleman fit for ciuill conuersation, and to set him in the direct way that leadeth him to his ciuill felicitie'.

The *Discourse* itself, translated from Giraldi Cinthio, begins with these words:

The end of man in this life, is happinesse or felicitie: and an end it is called . . . because all vertuous actions are directed thereunto, and because for it chiefly man laboureth and trauelleth [travaileth] in this world . . . ciuill felicitie is nothing else then a perfect operation of the mind, proceeding of excellent vertue in a perfect life; and is atchieued by the temper of reason, ruling the disordinate affects stirred vp in vs by the vnreasonable parts of the mind, . . . and guiding vs by the meane of vertue to happy life.

---

[1] F. Piccolomini, *Vniuersa Philosophia de Moribus* (1583), iv. 36; pp. 213–14.

[2] For the extensive influence of this work on Book I, Canto x see Dorothy Atkinson, 'The Wandering Knight, the Redcross Knight, and "Miles Dei"', *Huntington Library Quarterly*, vii (1944), 109–34.

He continues by explaining how contemplative felicity differs from civil felicity (pp. 5, 40).

These examples may be called an 'Aristotelizing' of the virtuous quest, for they stem from Aristotle's attempt to define the *summum bonum* or highest good in the first pages of the *Nicomachean Ethics*. There he argues that virtue is not followed for its own sake but as a means to an end; therefore, virtue is pursued for the sake of something else. He recognizes three classes of men: the self-indulgent, who place their highest good in pleasures of the senses and are led into vice as a consequence; the citizens or *cives*, who consider honour to be their highest good and pursue virtues in order to achieve it; and the contemplative men, who find their highest good in the enjoyment of intellectual activity. Yet these three, pleasure, honour, and intelligence, are desired not only for themselves but also for the sake of happiness that they bring, while nobody desires happiness as a means of obtaining honour or pleasure or intelligence. Consequently, happiness represents the final end or *summum bonum* which mankind is seeking (*Nic. Eth.* I. v. 2–4, vii. 5).

Here we may see how both traditions of the virtuous quest stem from Aristotle. The progression may be either from virtue to happiness or from virtue to honour to happiness. Since honour is the particular road to happiness of *homo civilis*, the citizen among his fellow citizens, its choice as an objective at once eliminates the self-centred pleasure-lovers and the devotees of contemplation, and makes the quest appropriate to the moral virtues. Yet we should understand that the Palace of Honour is a place of happiness or else brings happiness to those who attain it. It must be actively sought. The *cives* seeking honour are men of action (I. v. 4), and the good of man is the active exercise of his soul's faculties in accordance with excellence or virtue (I. vii. 15, x. 9). If continually practised, such activity will produce happiness; opposite activities will produce the opposite of happiness (ibid.).

The Aristotelian origin of the quests for happiness by way of virtue and for honour by way of virtue seems to have been generally recognized. In Shakespeare's *Taming of the Shrew*, Lucentio comes to the University of Padua to study

> Virtue and that part of philosophy
> Will I apply that treats of happiness
> By virtue specially to be achieved.

His servant Tranio approves in general but adds:

> Only, good master, while we do admire
> This virtue and this moral discipline,
> Let's be no stoics nor no stocks, I pray,
> Or so devote to Aristotle's checks
> As Ovid be an outcast quite abjured. (1. i. 18–33)

Tranio opposes Aristotle's *Nicomachean Ethics* to Ovid's *Art of Love*. Lucentio's intent to study how happiness is achieved through virtue is a reference to Book 1 of the *Ethics*, as we have already discussed it.

In 1583 Richard Robinson published a short account of King Arthur's knights and their exploits 'tending vnto all honour and glory'. He adds: 'And it was no maruaile made amongst them if such personages (as exploited euery excellent deede of armes and matters of prowesse) were to be loued: Because *Honour and Glory are the Rewardes of Vertue*, as saith the *Philosopher*.'[1] The reference is to Aristotle and to those passages of the *Ethics* which we have already discussed.

The doctrine of the quest for honour as a life of strenuous action, opposed to a life of ease and pleasure, is clearly stated by Spenser in Belphoebe's dialogue with Braggadocchio upon their first meeting. The boaster pretends to follow the quest for honour but actually believes in the quest for pleasure. Belphoebe comments:

> 'Who so in pompe of prowd estate', quoth she,
> 'Does swim, and bathes him selfe in courtly blis,
> Does waste his dayes in darke obscuritee,
> And in oblivion ever buried is:
> Where ease abownds, yt's eath to doe amis:
> But who his limbs with labours, and his mynd
> Behaves with cares, cannot so easy mis.
> Abroad in armes, at home in studious kynd,
> *Who seekes with painfull toile, shal Honor soonest fynd.*
>
> 'In woods, in waves, in warres she wonts to dwell,
> And wilbe found with perill and with paine;
> Ne can the man, that moulds in ydle cell,
> Unto her *happy mansion* attaine:

---

[1] *The Auncient Order, Societie, and Unitie Laudable, of* Prince Arthure, *and his knightly Armory of the* Round Table. The quotation is from the introductory 'A Breefe Repetition of the Table Rounde'; italics not mine. Cf. Francesco Piccolomini, viii. 24; p. 418C.

Before her gate High God did sweate ordaine,
And wakefull watches ever to abide:
But easy is the way, and passage plaine
To Pleasures pallace; it may soon be spide,
And day and night her dores to all stand open wide.'

(II. iii. 40–1)

Here the palace of Honour is a 'happy mansion' and is thus equated with Cartigny's Palace of True Felicitie. It is likewise opposed to 'Pleasures pallace', or his Palace of Worldly Pleasure. No palace of Virtue is mentioned, but Spenser makes it clear that the active exercise of virtue is the way to the Palace of Honour. He mentions martial courage as the most praiseworthy example of virtue but adds the efforts of the 'studious kynde' (certainly including poets!) as another pathway to honour.

This primacy of martial courage may reflect the fact that this was originally the primary meaning of Latin *virtus* and to some extent of Italian *virtù*. The manner in which this significance was adapted to the holy war may be observed in an English emblem book, *The C Hystoryes of Troye*, translated from the French and printed by Robert Wyer (*c.* 1530). Emblem 11 is 'Valour' and is illustrated by a woodcut of Mars armed with spear and sword. The 'allegory' explains that Mars may be called the Son of God, who battled victoriously in this world, and the man of good spirit ought to follow his father Jesus Christ. And he should do battle against vices, as St. Ambrose says in his first book of *Offices*. The friend of God must be an enemy of the devil. As a man vainly wars in the field if his own city is full of spies, so may they not vanquish their evil outward, who do not make strong war against the sins of their souls. The most glorious victory is to vanquish oneself.[1]

The association of honour and virtue began quite early, and they are represented as companion figures on some Roman coins. About 212 B.C., Marcus Marcellus, the conqueror of Syracuse, built a temple to Virtus as an annexe to an already existing shrine to Honos, so that the two became one building. About 100 B.C. Marius built a second temple to Honos and Virtus, using his share of the booty gained in the Cimbrian War.[2] Jean Lemaire de

---

[1] For another reference see below, p. 161.
[2] A. O. Seyffert's *Classical Dictionary* (London, 1902), under *Honos*.

Belges, in his poem 'Le Temple d'honneur et de Vertus', states that the Romans had many such temples, now all fallen into decay. In his temple Honour and Virtue sit together upon a throne.[1] In Jean Froissart's 'Le Temple d'Onnour', the steps to Honour's throne are occupied by various virtues.[2]

Gavin Douglas's poem 'The Palice of Honour' has some interesting correspondences with Spenser. It has a 'cristall towr' and a 'cristall palice', reminding us of Spenser's Panthea, which is a 'towre of glass' (I. x. 58) or of 'christall' (II. x. 73). Honour is the king, attended by various Virtues. As the poet travels toward the tower, he passes the Court Rhetorical, beside the Springs of Helicon, presided over by Lady Cleo [*sic*], the eldest of the Nine Muses. This shows a resemblance to Cleopolis, Gloriana's capital city. In the Court Rhetorical dwell the poets of the past. Guided by a nymph assigned to him by Calliope, the poet approaches the palace and sees in a wondrous mirror the images of noble men and women from all past history. Within the palace are folk who had lived valiant and virtuous lives, fighting 'in just battell'. The guide explains that here honour is given only for virtue, not for wealth or noble birth, 'bot verteous honour never mair sall end' (p. 74). The poet ends with a short praise of virtue:

> For vertew is a thing sa precious,
> Quhair of the end is sa delicious,
> The warld can not consider quhat it is.
> It makis folk perfite and glorious,
> It makis sanctis of pepill vitious,
> It causes folk ay liue in lestand blis,
> It is the way to hie honour I wis,
> It dantis deith, and euerie vice throw micht;
> Without vertew, fie on all eirdlie wicht.
> Vertew is eik the perfite sicker way,
> And nocht ellis, till lestand honour ay.

Douglas does not assign Virtue a separate temple but makes the exercise of virtue the only road to honour.[3]

Concerning the temples of Honour and Virtue, Francesco

[1] For discussion see Rathborne, *Meaning of Spenser's Fairyland*, pp. 53–8.

[2] Froissart, *Poésies*, ed. Scheler (Brussels, 1871), vol. ii, pp. 162–93.

[3] Douglas, 'The Palice of Honour', pt. iii, in *Poetical Works* (Edinburgh, 1874), vol. i, p. 75. Miss Rathborne's discussion of the poem (pp. 48–52) omits some of the points here made, notably the reference to Cleo.

Piccolomini makes an interesting point not brought out in the sources already cited:

> Accordingly, Honour is co-joined in an indissoluble knot with Virtue. And therefore the Romans joined their temples of Honour and of Virtue in such a way that no one could enter into the temple of Honour unless he crossed through the temple of Virtue. (viii. 27; p. 421C)

The same point is made by Pierre de la Primaudaye:

> For this cause the ancient Romanes built two Temples ioyned together, the one being dedicated to Vertue and the other to Honor, but yet in such sort, that no man could enter into that of Honor, except he first passed through the other of Vertue.[1]

On the page preceding the quotation from Francesco, he distinguishes between terms which have substantially the same meaning: honour, glory, praise, fame, and encomium. Glory is more inclusive than honour, since it may be gained through strength of body and through works of art, whereas honour concerns only actions produced from the soul by virtue. Glory may be achieved through the inner satisfaction of successful accomplishment, but honour requires a measure of public recognition (viii. 26; p. 420B). But these are slight differences, and for practical purposes 'honour' and 'glory' are interchangeable terms. King Honour and Queen Gloriana represent ideals which are almost if not quite the same.

Francesco's comment on the temples of Honour and of Virtue furnishes the clue to what may be the basic pattern of *The Faerie Queene*. This pattern has already been partly perceived by Isabel E. Rathborne, who writes as follows:

> One of Spenser's favorite devices is the bringing of each subordinate hero shortly before his final adventure to an allegorical house in which he receives some important instruction as to the nature of the virtue he represents and the rewards of its successful practice. Thus St. George visits the House of Holiness, Guyon the Castle of Alma, Scudamour the Temple of Venus, and Artegall the Palace of Mercilla. . . . Calidore's open air vision of the Graces might be added to these.[2]

She thinks that Panthea would itself be the allegorical house in which Arthur is to receive a similar instruction. Perhaps so, but

---

[1] *The French Academie*, part one, ch. 23 (edn. of 1586, p. 247).
[2] Rathborne, *Meaning of Spenser's Fairyland*, pp. 128–9.

we do know that Panthea is the temple of Honour in the City of
Glory and is the objective towards which all the other knights are
striving. For them it is the end rather than the means to an end.
To fit themselves to enter it, each knight must pass through the
temple of Virtue, through a temple adapted to his particular
virtue, as Spenser represents it. In this temple he is strengthened
for the great test which is the climax of his quest, and these temples
may be called the places of perfecting the several virtues. The
knights may not return to the court of Gloriana in Cleopolis without passing through the temples of their several virtues and perfecting themselves therein. Spenser thus modifies the scheme of
Cartigny, who adjoins the Palace of Virtue to the Palace of True
Felicitie, by having a separate building for the perfecting of each
virtue but a single palace, Panthea, as the temple of Honour which
all are striving to reach. Physically, Spenser disjoins the palaces,
but he maintains the rule that the only way to the temple of
Honour is through the temple of Virtue.

Spenser had this image impressed upon him during his residence
at Cambridge. Some quarter of a mile from Pembroke, his college,
is Gonville and Caius College, which had been refounded and
largely rebuilt by Dr. John Caius, and which was still under
construction. In Spenser's time the main entrance, from Trinity
Street, was a low gateway marked *Humilitatis*. (Now it bears the
same inscription but is a stately gate which seems anything but
humble.) Behind this gate Dr. Caius constructed another, much
larger, one marked *Virtutis*; the reverse reads 'Io. Caius posuit
Sapientia 1567'.[1] This Gate of Virtue opens into a large court
surrounded on three sides by the student chambers. In the wall to
the left is a smaller gateway marked *Honoris*, above which is a
miniature temple, built in 1573. This gate opens into what is now
Senate House Lane, but in Spenser's time the Senate House was
not yet built. Instead, the gate opened on to the square in front
of the Old Schools, the most ancient of the University buildings,
used for administrative purposes. It is traditional that students of
Caius go out through the Gate of Honour when they go to the
final examination for their degrees in the neighbouring Senate
House, and Dr. Caius's whimsy may have intended something
of the sort. The student enters by the Gateway of Virtue; he

---

[1] Cf. Proverbs 4: 7–8: 'Wisdom . . . shall bring thee to *honour*, when thou dost
embrace her.'

remains in the college until he is prepared to enter the temple of Honour. This has the effect of making the college itself the temple of Virtue.

That Spenser was indeed influenced by this architectural allegory is shown by one salient feature, the Gate of Humility. This gate was already there and was retained when Dr. Caius refounded the college, perhaps in accordance with Proverbs 15 : 33, 'Before honour is humility'. It has no part in the Roman temples of Honour and Virtue; indeed, it would be contrary to the spirit of the Roman *Virtus*. But humility is a prelude to virtue at Gonville and Caius College, and so is it with Spenser. In Book 1 of *The Faerie Queene*, the place of perfecting holiness is the House of Coelia, which is the temple of Virtue for Redcross. When he and Una knock at the door,

> The porter opened unto them streight way.
> He was an aged syre, all hory gray,
> With lookes full lowly cast, and gate full slow,
> Wont on a staffe his feeble steps to stay,
> Hight Humiltà. They passe in, stouping low;
> For streight and narrow was the way which he did shew.
>
> (I. x. 5)

Thus one passes through the gate of Humility to enter the temple of Virtue. Here appear the 'strait gate and the narrow way' of Matthew 7 : 14, and such a meaning may well have been intended by the original builder of the Gonville entrance. Spenser's next lines show his characters passing into a courtyard rather than directly to the interior of the building:

> Each goodly thing is hardest to begin;
> But entred in, a spatious court they see,
> Both plaine and pleasaunt to be walked in. (I. x. 6)

This fits very well Caius Court, into which one emerges after passing through the Gate of Virtue.

As will be shown later, the place of perfecting chastity, visited by Britomart, is the Temple of Isis. She enters it 'with great humility' (v. vii. 3), thus repeating the theme of the Gonville gateway. The theme of humility does not appear at the entrances of the other temples of Virtue, perhaps because it is not especially appropriate for them.

In observing the pattern of Spenser's knightly quests, we may notice that each temple of Virtue is preceded by one or more houses of non-Virtue or anti-Virtue. These are not always evil in themselves but do provide severe tests of the knight in his or her particular virtue. Sometimes he wins by his own might, sometimes he is rescued by heavenly grace (Arthur). After the most severe of these he goes to his place of perfecting, or temple of Virtue, for strength and instruction. He then goes on to the most severe and fundamental test of all, in which victory completes the task of perfecting his virtue and fits him to return to Cleopolis, Panthea, and Gloriana's court.

We can make this clearer by giving in tabular form the quests of the major knights:

Name	Virtue	Place of Testing	Place of Perfecting	Final Test
Redcross	Holiness	House of Lucifera House of Orgoglio Cave of Despair	House of Coelia	Battle with Dragon
Guyon	Temperance	Phaedria's Isle Mammon's Cave	House of Alma	Overthrow of Acrasia
Britomart	Chastity	Castle Joyous House of Busyrane	Temple of Isis	Battle with Radigund
Artegall	Justice	House of Radigund	Mercilla's palace	Battle with Grantorto
Calidore	Courtesy	House of Briana House of Melibee	Mount Acidale (dance of Graces)	Subduing the Blatant Beast

These are the major quests, the pattern of which is fairly clear. Somewhat less evident are the quests of minor characters, but in them the same pattern is present:

Name	Virtue	Place of Testing	Place of Perfecting	Final Test
Calepine	Mildness	House of Turpine	Bower of Salvage Man	Rescue of Serena from Cannibals
Serena	Serenity	Forest—bitten by Blatant Beast	Hermit's cell	Ordeal of capture by Cannibals
Una	Truth	House of Archimago Forest—escapes Sansloy Cave of Despair—saves Redcross	House of Coelia	Defeats Duessa's attempt to win back Redcross
Florimell	Beauty	Witch's House House of Proteus	House of Marinell, as Bride	Defeats false Florimell
Marinell	Fertility	Rich Strand—wounded by Britomart	House of Liagore House of Proteus	Wins tournament
Amoret	'Womanhead'	House of Busyrane Cave of Lust House of Sclaunder	Temple of Venus	?
Scudamour	Physical Love	House of Busyrane House of Care	Temple of Venus	?

The pattern of Scudamour and Amoret is necessarily incomplete, since Spenser did not complete their story. Several critics accuse him of forgetting about them, but more probably he reserved the completion of their story for his seventh book, on constancy, since their loyalty to each other is repeatedly stressed. Interestingly enough, their place of perfecting or temple of Virtue follows the pattern of other quests by coming near the end of their narrative through the use of a 'flashback' technique, for in point of time it was the earliest episode involving them both.

This list is necessarily confined to 'continuing' characters, those whose adventures extend through several cantos or several books. *Exempla*, such as Medina and her sisters, Concord and her sons, are completed in brief space and do not involve a quest in the way that the continuing characters do. Yet several of the continuing characters do not fall easily into the pattern, though we might expect them to. These are Arthur, Timias, Belphoebe, and Satyrane. They undergo tests of strength and in some instances are rescued, but there seems to be no one place of perfecting and no one great test to prepare each of them for the visit to Cleopolis.

In the case of Arthur, Miss Rathborne thinks that Panthea itself was to be his place of perfecting, and that the final test would be the war 'twixt that great Faery Queene and Paynim King' (i. xi. 7). This is an ingenious suggestion.[1] In so far as Arthur represents magnificence, its perfection would seem to arrive when he becomes king. But in two earlier instances he shares the place of perfecting with the titular hero, after which the two ride forth on twin quests. Both Arthur and Guyon visit the House of Alma and learn of their ancestry, after which Arthur fights Maleger and Guyon captures Acrasia. Again, Arthur and Artegall visit together the palace of Mercilla and witness the trial of Duessa, after which Arthur rides to rescue Belge from Gerioneo and Artegall to rescue Eirena from Grantorto. Arthur is also tested when he spends the night with Amoret and Aemilia in the House of Sclaunder, both as to his sexual continence (iv. viii. 30) and as to his patience under Sclaunder's accusations (35). To this extent Arthur does fit into the pattern.

Timias and Belphoebe must be considered in relation to each other. Timias undergoes repeated injuries and cures. Injured by the 'fosters', he is healed in Belphoebe's bower (iii. v. 41).

---

[1] Rathborne, *Meaning of Spenser's Fairyland*, p. 129.

Deserted by Belphoebe, he pines away until restored to her favour by the agency of the little turtle-dove (iv. viii. 17). Bitten by the Blatant Beast, he joins Serena for a cure in the Hermit's cell (vi. vi. 15). One might consider his restoration to Belphoebe's favour as a form of perfecting his virtues of grace and honour. Similarly, one might see in Belphoebe's causeless jealousy a form of testing and in her restoration of Timias to her favour a form of perfecting her virtue of virginity, which for Spenser includes great 'bounty' and treasures of love. But no 'house' or 'temple' of any kind seems to be involved with Belphoebe, unless we consider Diana's forest haunt as parallel with Venus' garden and temple (iii. vi. 22), since Belphoebe was reared in one and Amoret in the other (iii. vi. 28).

Satyrane's failure to fit into the pattern of the virtues may be explained if we consider him the irascible faculty of the soul and not a particular virtue seeking perfection (above, p. 30).

The various quests listed here will be further analysed in later chapters. The recognition that there is a discernible pattern to Spenser's treatment of the virtues should go far toward clarifying the seeming obscurities of *The Faerie Queene*.

THE PLACE OF THE QUEST

There remains the question of where these quests take place. As internal allegory, they take place partially or fully within the human soul. But, if this is granted, they are still based upon the myth of Prince Arthur in Fairyland; and a myth must maintain some consistency within itself. What is the rationale of the allegory?

For the development of the myth, with its treatment of Fairyland as a land of heroes, the definitive work is still Miss Rathborne's *The Meaning of Spenser's Fairyland* (1937). In discussing Cleopolis as a city of earthly fame, she writes:

> This is the good fame of virtuous men, founders and preservers of just empires, expressed concretely in the honor and power they command during their lives on earth, and prolonged ideally in the memory of men by the enduring monuments of history and epic poetry.
>
> (p. 59)

May not this 'earth' be Spenser's Fairyland, a mythical land of fame where departed heroes, the ancestors of his royal and noble patrons, enjoy an extended, if not an immortal life, closely resembling their heroic lives on earth? In interpreting the symbolic meaning of Spenser's Fairyland, we have already seen cogent reasons for identifying it with the world of history, the land of earthly fame.   (pp. 142–3)

The world of *The Faerie Queene* is very largely the world of this history, and the life of Fairyland, kingdom of earthly glory, is still the life of that heroic age which succeeded the age of gold and still further partook of its splendors.   (pp. 148–9)

In explaining that Artegall is a Briton and no fairy, Merlin thus adopts phrasing which suggests the popular superstition which saw the fairies as members of a different race from men, instead of as members of the same race under different conditions. That the latter view of the basis for distinguishing fairies from Britons in the *Faerie Queene* represents Spenser's considered meaning is part of the hypothesis advanced in this book.   (p. 206)

The presence of these evil creatures [giants and monsters] in a heroes' paradise might seem to call for explanation . . . yet their presence . . . is not really inconsistent with the idea that Fairyland is a land of fame whose inhabitants partake of the nature of gods and demigods. There is good fame and ill fame.   (pp. 144–5)

All these points, which Miss Rathborne has deduced from obscure allusions in *The Faerie Queene* and an extensive study of its literary backgrounds, are clearly indicated by Francesco Piccolomini in the first two chapters of Book vi: 'De Virtute Heroica'. He starts by considering the possible derivations of the word 'hero' from several different Greek words, then begins a discussion of heroes and daemons. (The reader should remember that 'daemon' means a spirit, with no pejorative sense as in English 'demon'.)

Concerning this [derivation], doubtless we are unlikely to be made certain; nevertheless, I judge it very much in accordance with reason that the inventors of this name [*hero*] had indicated love and a burning desire of honour and of the divine condition; for that vehement love is a spirit elevating man and forming a hero. From whatever source the name is derived, the meaning is the same, and to this all agree: that the name *Hero* denotes a rank and condition above that of Man.

(p. 328c)

Francesco then discusses the nature of daemons as set forth in Iamblichus' *De Mysteriis Aegyptiorum*, section 2, and in Plato's

Epinomis, the latter of which suggests that heroes are merely aqueous spirits, while daemons are ethereal and aerial spirits, and that all of them are similar in being spirits of the elements. But Francesco would not include heroes in this classification:

> I judge that this opinion should not be accepted, since Plato [elsewhere] sets forth one generation and condition of Daemons, and another of Heroes; he affirms that Heroes are born from the love of gods towards human women or of men towards goddesses, as appears from his *Cratylus*, while in the *Timaeus* he sets forth another generation of Daemons.[1] Therefore, I should judge from the opinion of Plato that Heroes are not those who are Daemons by their nature and are distributed in ethereal, aerial, and aqueous forms, but are pilgrim Daemons; i.e. souls of illustrious men departed from life and dissolved from the crass body, and descended from the golden race of men.
>
> (pp. 328–9)

After quoting Socrates to the effect that the 'golden race' allegorically signifies good and praiseworthy men,[2] he continues:

> I judge that Plato called those Heroes who can also be called foreign and pilgrim Daemons, but not the aqueous Daemons, who are Daemons by their nature. These [Heroes] are placed by Iamblichus above human souls because they are the souls of those men who have exalted themselves above the human condition . . . He [Plato] clearly distinguishes Heroes from those who are Daemons by nature. Accordingly, we gather from the fictions of poets that a Hero is a Demigod, born from God and Man. From Plato's opinion, [the Hero] is the soul of an illustrious man departed from life and dissolved from the crass body, or else a [living] man elevated above the human condition by a burning love of Virtue. (p. 329A, B)

Here is clearly stated the existence of a land of heroes, both the myth itself and its allegorical significance. The distinction between daemons and heroes is just Spenser's distinction between fairies and men, and serves to explain that perplexing problem; Miss Rathborne is right in thinking them separate in kind. She is likewise right in thinking the heroes related to the Golden Age, for the greatest of them are those of the 'golden race'. Also, she is right in assuming that this land could contain both the

---

[1] Perhaps the reference is to *Timaeus*, 40, giving God's creation of the lesser deities. The reference is not clear.

[2] *Cratylus*, 397–8.

living and the dead, united in the sympathetic bond of heroic
virtue.

The second chapter of Book vi is equally stimulating, for in it
Francesco gives Britain as the fabulous locale of the land of
spirits, clarifies the nature of the land of heroes, and provides the
rationale by which the heroes may represent virtues and faculties
of the human soul. The chapter is called 'What according to
Aristotle's opinion is a Hero, and its opposite'.

> Various ones are mentioned by Poets, who are feigned to have taken
> their birth from the gods and are called Heroes and Demigods: as
> Pan, Hercules, Romulus, Aeneas, and others. Thus also Plutarch,
> giving Demetrius' opinion, speaks of islands, many around Britain,
> called by the Greeks Sporades [or Scattered Islands], which are said
> to be the islands of kindly spirits and Heroes.[1] But, since these are
> the inventions of Poets, the necessity is upon me to explain what
> truth (in Aristotle's view) is concealed under the cover of the fables.
> Heroes are illustrious men who through some extraordinary Virtue
> have attained to a condition shining above the human [condition],
> through which they either lead famous lives or are most notably
> praised by the mouths of men after their deaths. They are said to be
> elevated above the condition of man because, in so far as is permitted
> to man, they have raised themselves to the likeness of Gods. They are
> said to take their birth from the Gods; first, as it is observed that with-
> out a divine *afflatus* man cannot be elevated to the divine; and again,
> as only from an extreme delight in divine things, such as overflowing
> charity and a burning desire for the good and the honourable, can
> famous and generous actions proceed.   (p. 329C)

Francesco next proceeds to consider the presence of beastly
men and monsters in the land of heroes and to explain their
allegorical significance:

> To the race of Heroes is opposed that race of beastly men who,
> because of their conspicuous degradation and depravity, are feigned
> to be born of a man and a beast. Such are those men who, wrongly
> educated, become worse than beasts, as Aristotle says in *De Republica*,
> bk. i. And, as the nearest parents of the heroic man are nothing other
> than the mind turned towards the divine, and the feeling and appetitive
> power purged and conformed with the mind; so the parents of the

---

[1] In Eusebius' *Preparatio Evangelica*, v. 17, is a discussion of Demetrius' story in
Plutarch's *On the Ceasing of Oracles*. Violent thunderstorms take place when one of
the 'great souls' dies or becomes extinct. On one of the islands near Britain, Saturn
sleeps, guarded by Briareus and many daemons.

beastly man are sense and appetite, like a beast prone only to earthly things, which have claimed complete possession of reason and mind. We may fittingly say that Heroes and beastly men generate themselves, since by internal facuties as though by parents they are formed and produced. (pp. 329–30)

Not the physical bodies of men, but their qualities of heroism or beastliness, are the product of their internal faculties. Where the rational faculty controls the concupiscible (with the aid of the irascible) and itself aspires towards divine things, heroism will be produced; where the concupiscible faculty acts without any restraint from the other faculties, beastliness will be produced. These internal battles of the soul determine what kind of man one is to become.

Francesco continues:

For, since man is a little world, an epitome of the great world, a marriage of divine and mortal, by the image of Proteus he has strength to receive every form and to live every life . . . It is clear, therefore, what is meant by the name of *hero* and of *beastly man*, and who are their true parents, and what is the true allegory of the fable; from which it is evident that *hero* by common consent denotes only a certain excelling and eminent condition of man. (p. 330A, B)

As men can elevate themselves towards the gods through virtue, they can debase themselves to the level of beasts through vice. The extremes of both groups appear in Hero-land, which is at once the present world and the world of antiquity. And it is in or near Britain.

It seems quite probable that these two chapters provided Spenser with the rationale of his myth, in which Fairyland or Hero-land represents the internal world of moral struggle and the outer world of the virtuous quest. At least, they are an important element in the composite of sources upon which he drew.

THE CULMINATION OF THE QUEST

In Fairyland the successful ending of a quest is marked by a return to Gloriana, who had assigned the quest in the first place. In performing virtuous quests, the knights are serving their queen and strengthening her throne. This element of the poem may go back to Elizabeth's progress through the city of London on 14 January 1559, the day before her coronation. As she travelled from the Tower towards Westminster amid the tumultuous acclaim of the populace, she paused at five different points on the route where elaborate 'pageants' had been prepared for her reception. These are described in detail in a pamphlet printed by Richard Tottel nine days after the event. After recording the great enthusiasm of the people towards their new sovereign, and their awakening hope, the author describes the pageants. The second one is described thus:

This pageant standing in the nether ende of Cornehill was extended from thoneside of the strete to the other, and in the same pageant was deuised three gates all open, and ouer the middle parte thereof was erected one chaire a seate royall with clothe of estate to the same apperteyning wherein was placed a childe representing the Queenes highnesse with consideracion had for place conuenient for a table which conteined her name and title. And in a comelie wreathe artificially and wel deuised with perfite sight and vnderstanding to the people. In the front of the same pageant was written the name and title therof, which is *The seate of worthie gouernance*, which seate was made in such artificiall maner, as to the apperance of the lookers on, the foreparte semed to haue no staie, and therfore of force was stayed by liuely personages, which personages were in numbre foure, standing and staieing the forefront of the same seate royal, eche hauing his face to the Quene and people, wherof euery one had a table to expresse their effectes, which are vertues, namelie *Pure religion*, *Loue of subiectes*, *Wisedome* and *Iustice*, which did treade their contrarie vices vnder their feete, that is to witte, *Pure religion*, did treade vppon *Superstition*, and *Ignorance*, *Loue of subiectes*, did treade vpon *Rebellion* and *Insolencie*, *Wisedome* did treade vpon *follie* and *vaine glorie*, *Iustice* did treade vpon *Adulacion* and *Briberie*.[1]

Thus, in the popular consciousness, patriotic support of the throne involved the constant suppression of the vices by the virtues. Spenser found an audience already prepared for his moral allegory in *The Faerie Queene*. As a boy of seven residing in London, he may actually have seen this pageant on the eve of the coronation, and he could easily have read the description of it later. It serves to explain the reasoning by which the moral regulation of

[1] James M. Osborn, ed., *The Quenes Maiesties Passage through the Citie of London to Westminster the Day before her Coronacion* (Yale University Press, 1960), p. 38. Italics not mine.

one's own life could be deemed a political service to the Queen of England.

As Miss Rathborne has shown, the name Gloriana derives from Gloriande in several French metrical romances, in which she is a fairy lady-in-waiting and in one instance the fairy queen herself.[1] Spenser tells us in his *Letter to Raleigh* that Gloriana represents glory in his general intention and Queen Elizabeth in his particular intention. This seems to mean that Elizabeth is the human embodiment of the abstract quality of glory and also of those abstract virtues which serve to increase her glory. The projected union of Arthur and Gloriana need not refer to a marriage between Elizabeth and Leicester or Elizabeth and Essex, for the historical allegory is not always applicable. As internal allegory, the virtue of magnificence may be in Elizabeth's own mind, seeking deserving ways in which to promote her glory.

The association of glory with the Queen is well illustrated in a Latin poem describing her five-day visit to Cambridge University in August 1564. The poem, published in the next year, is Abraham Hartwell's *Regina Literata*.[2] The account of the Queen's entertainment is very interesting, but of especial significance is Hartwell's tribute to her glory. In a prose address to the reader, he writes: 'haec tamen quoquo modo extaret Regiae et virginalis imago gloriae, pariter ac communis boni diuturna memoria' ('but howsoever she may appear an image of Royal and virginal *glory*, and at the same time a lasting memorial of common goodness'). These words seem to involve the distinction which Spenser makes between Elizabeth as queen (Gloriana) and as a private person (Belphoebe), in the *Letter to Raleigh*.

Hartwell's climactic tribute to the Queen reads as follows:

> Virtutis merces eadem & labor, illa tropheum est,
>   Solaque dat nigrae vincere mortis iter.
> Nam nisi virtutis quaeratur gloria factis,
>   Omnis in extremos est abitura rogos.
> Non te Lethaeae carpent obliuia ripae,
>   Nec totam in cineres vertet auara dies . . .   (f. 43ʳ)
> Te fama excipiat vastum celebrata per orbem,
>   Gloriaque in Stygios non abitura lacus . . .   (f. 43ᵛ)

---

[1] *Meaning of Spenser's Fairyland*, pp. 211–12.

[2] A day-by-day account of this visit is found in John Nichols, *The Progresses and Public Processions of Queen Elizabeth* (London, 1823), vol. i, pp. 148–89.

Haec tua laus (Regina potens) tibi gloria summa
Quod casta colitur relligione Deus.   (f. 46ʳ)

(The same reward and labour of virtue—that is the trophy and alone
enables us to conquer the road of black death. For unless *glory* is sought
by deeds of virtue, all [glory] will disappear into [our] final graves. The
oblivion of Lethean shores shall not devour you, nor greedy Time
turn the whole into ashes . . . May your fame, celebrated through the
vast orb [of the world], prolong you nor let your *glory* disappear into
Stygian lakes . . . This your praise, powerful Queen, and your highest
glory: that God is worshipped with pure religion.)

The 'pure religion' of the final sentence is obviously intended
as a contrast with the enforced Romanism of Mary's reign.

As Gloriana's name suggests glory as the culmination of a
successful quest, so does the name of her capital city, Cleopolis.
Clio—or Cleo, in Gavin Douglas's spelling—was the leader of
the Nine Muses, but she was also an image of earthly glory. An
appendix to Natalis Comes's *Mythologiae* (1616) is a short work
by Geofredus Linocerius, *Mythologiae Musarum Libellus*. Chapter 2
is entitled 'De Clio: Quod omnes homines excitantur gloriae &
honoris stimulis' ('Of Clio: That all men are stirred by the stimuli
of glory and honour'). Clio is called 'the most ancient goddess of
glory'. The author states further:

So they [of old] represented her as the daughter of Jove: because
(as *kleio* simply means 'glory'), should we be permitted to leave behind
us for future generations the glory and name of deeds well done, we
should have no other source for that glory than Almighty God, who
from memory and contemplation creates for us a fame of well-doing
renowned in every age to come.

This same idea is expressed later in Milton's celebrated lines on
fame, which proceeds finally from the judgement of God:

As he pronounces lastly on each deed,
Of so much fame in Heaven expect thy meed.
                              ('Lycidas', ll. 83–4)

A similar identification of Clio is made in some editions of
Cartari's *Imagini de gli Dei delli Antichi*, under 'Apollo', where we
are told that the Nine Muses are patrons of knowledge: 'The first,

who is called Clio, signifies Glory, as through glory chiefly one may lead man to give his efforts to knowledge.'[1]

Glory is not an attribute of queens or noblemen only but may be won by those in all walks of life. 'Glory follows virtue as though its shadow', Thomas Cooper quotes Cicero as saying.[2] St. Paul states that God will give 'to them who, by patient continuance in well doing, seek for glory and honour and immortality, eternal life . . . glory, honour, and peace to every man that worketh good' (Romans 2: 7, 10). It is this shimmering vision of an ultimate glory from the virtuous performance of the daily task that provides the theme of *The Faerie Queene* and that gives true meaning to Christian faith.

[1] Cartari (edn. of Padua, 1626), p. 44. This sentence is missing from some early editions of Cartari. I have not examined them all.

[2] Cooper's *Thesaurus Linguae Romanicae & Britannicae* (London, 1578), under *Gloria*.

IV

The Allegorical Landscape

THOUGH the final destination of the virtuous quest is a city, Cleopolis, there is a surprising absence of cities throughout Spenser's Fairyland. Such centres of population as there are are castles or palaces or temples or cottages, but never a number of these close together. Each one seems to exist in isolation. The great country-houses with their spacious grounds, the fortified castles, stately temples, and remote cottages in the depths of the forest—these make up the world in which Spenser's characters move. Even such royal courts as the castle of Una's parents and the palace of Mercilla do not seem to be part of a larger urban community, though individually they may be quite populous. They stand in a boundless forest which is limited only by the surrounding sea but is broken here and there by glades and gardens, by roads, lakes, and streams.

CASTLES

We have already observed that some houses are places of perfecting one's virtue, while others are places of testing and may be called houses of anti-virtue. When the allegory is external, as we have defined it in Chapter II, the meaning of the houses is fairly clear; but if the allegory is internal, representing the *psychomachia*, then the houses must have a meaning pertaining to the internal struggle. For example, Redcross undergoes penance and absolution in Coelia's House of Holiness, which we naturally take to represent the Church. If Redcross is not a man, however, but an impulse towards holiness within the soul of a man, then the house becomes some inner fastness of the mind or dwelling-place of the soul, a refuge from the conflicting impulses that would destroy holiness. The external situation may be that of a man reading and meditating upon the Scriptures in an effort to regain his faith. He may read the words of St. Paul: 'Know ye not that ye are the temple of God, and that the spirit of God dwelleth in you? If any man defile the temple of God, him shall God destroy; for the temple of God is holy, which temple ye are' (1 Cor. 3: 16–17); 'Know ye not that your body is the temple of the Holy Ghost?' (1 Cor. 6: 19). Thus, his own body is a temple, or house of holiness, for in it dwells his soul, and in his soul dwells the spirit of God. Sins of the mind or of the body are a defilement of the temple, and the temple must be cleansed if the soul is to avoid destruction. The impulse towards holiness can be revived by the extirpation of pride, a sin of the mind which has caused him to accept false doctrine in preference to true faith. Internally, holiness had been almost destroyed by hypocrisy (Archimago), deceit (Duessa), and pride (Orgoglio) but had been saved by heavenly grace and truth (Arthur and Una), the latter of whom he had never seen clearly because of her veil. When the temple is cleansed, holiness is ready for his great battle with original sin or spiritual death, i.e. the dragon. Winning, he can at last look upon truth without her veil and is proof against further efforts of hypocrisy and deceit. His earlier fornication with Duessa was figurative only, signifying his yielding to deceit. Externally, the Christian had then accepted false doctrine but has now turned from false doctrine to the true faith and has reached a stage beyond repentance or conversion, a stage which in some communions is called sanctification, i.e. perfection in holiness.[1]

In Book II, Guyon's place of perfecting, where he accompanies Arthur, is the House of Alma, or House of the Soul. Here the house is again the human body, the meaning being so explicit that it cannot be missed. Guyon goes from Alma's castle to complete his conquest of Acrasia, whose Circean cup reduces men to beasts. Acrasia represents a voluptuous revelling in sexual excitement, or, as C. S. Lewis calls it, a diseased form of sexuality;[2] it is the 'human bondage' described by Somerset Maugham.[3] As such, it is a sin of the body, whereas pride had been a sin of the mind, conquered by Redcross. A. S. P. Woodhouse perceives the distinction and expresses it as one between nature and grace,[4] but his terminology is misleading. Heavenly grace (Arthur), residing in the soul, assists man to conquer all sin, corporal as well as in-

---

[1] *Encyclopedia of Religion and Ethics*, vol. xi, pp. 182–3.

[2] *The Allegory of Love* (Oxford, 1936), p. 332.

[3] See Maugham's novel *Of Human Bondage*.

[4] 'Nature and Grace in *The Faerie Queene*', *ELH* xvi (1949), 194–228; also in *RES*, N.S., vi (1955), 284–8, and *ELH* xxvii (1960), 1–15.

tellectual; and Arthur does not resign this function because Guyon fights sins of the body. Heavenly grace, holiness, and temperance are companion impulses within the soul of man, bound together by the golden chain which links all the virtues, and the entire soul of man will be redeemed even though his vision of the City of the Great King comes through holiness alone. It is like perceiving an object with the eyes and not with the senses of touch or taste; the whole mind reacts, whatever is the avenue of perpection.

In *Gerusalemme Liberata* Tasso uses the image of the castle in three ways. First, he speaks of souls possessing the castles of their bodies (xiv. 64). Again, he describes the heart as the castle where man's life and soul abide (xx. 120). And yet again, Godfredo's resolute resistance to Armida's seductive wiles is called a castle of goodness (v. 63). We have already noted St. Bernard's use of three castles to represent the three faculties of the soul: Rationabilitas, ruled by Faith; Irascibilitas, ruled by Hope; and Concupiscibilitas, ruled by Charity (above, p. 21). Physiologically, these castles would be the brain, the heart, and the liver, respectively.[1]

When the allegory is external, the Christian man must guard his soul against dangers from without, which lurk in the environment about him. For Redcross, these might be association with atheistic thinkers or exposure to perverted religious propaganda, as intellectual dangers. For Guyon, they might be the proximity of a brothel or acquaintance with a 'free love' society, as corporal temptation. Yet these external hazards are dangerous only in so far as they find a response within the man himself and become a part of his internal warfare by moving his fantasy, perplexing his judgement, and stirring his emotions. The first onset is a surprise attack; if successful, the invader sets up his own castle or strong point within the soul and can only be dislodged with great difficulty. If intellectual, the invaders are deceptive illusions of the man 'wise in his own conceit' (Prov. 26: 5, 12, 16, 28: 11; Rom. 11: 25, 12: 16); if corporal, they are perturbations or 'affections' proceeding from weakness of the flesh. They are indifferently called vices, but Aristotle says they are not vices until repeated acceptance has made them a matter of habit.[2] Before such

---

[1] Claudian, *The Fourth Consulship of Honorius*, ll. 235–54; Francesco Piccolomini i. 12; pp. 54–5. Cf. Shakespeare's *Twelfth Night*, i. i. 37.
[2] *Nic. Eth.* vii. viii. 3; Francesco, ii. 5; p. 94D.

acceptance, they are illusions and perturbations; afterwards, they are vices fortified within the soul and lessening the authority of reason.[1] The castles of Orgoglio (pride) and Busyrane (sexual perversion) may be taken as types of intellectual and corporal vices.

When the vices have established their fortresses within the soul, the rational faculty can no longer count the whole body as its castle but must withdraw into some inner keep or stronghold of the mind. Its defences are 'the pales and forts of reason' and the 'consecrated wall' which resists the onset of the affections.[2] To take the offensive, reason needs the aid of the irascible faculty, especially when the opposition stems from corporal temptations of the concupiscible faculty. Thus, Satyrane subdues and tames, but cannot kill, the beast that feeds on women's flesh, muzzling it with Florimell's Girdle of Chastity (III. vii. 36). This seems a clear instance of the irascible subduing the concupiscible within the human soul. But when the temptation is intellectual, the rational faculty is itself perplexed and confused. For example, Redcross is deceived by Archimago's illusions into believing Una unchaste and evil; but Satyrane, the lion, and the satyrs instinctively recognize her as good and do homage to her. Holiness, a virtue of the rational faculty, is deceived by illusions; the irascible faculty (lion, Satyrane) and the concupiscible faculty (satyrs) recognize her for what she is. Concupiscence can be kind when not aroused by desire; nevertheless, Una is nervous lest the satyrs should become aroused, and she welcomes her departure from them along with Satyrane.

The rival 'houses' of good and evil, of virtue and vice, which are the basic element of Spenser's narrative pattern, may go back ultimately to the House built upon the Rock and the House built upon the Sand (Matt. 7: 24–7). A more immediate parallel is with the rival palaces of Logistilla and Alcina in the *Orlando Furioso*. These two sisters are fairies, one good, the other evil. As fairies, they may have caught Spenser's attention as suitable prototypes for characters in *The Faerie Queene*. As a third sister, Ariosto introduces Morgan le Fay, apparently for authenticity, since she

---

[1] Francesco identifies perturbation and affection with each other and with Gk. *pathos* (i. 2; p. 41A). He sharply distinguishes these from vices, which have become ingrained through habitual indulgence. The whole of Book 1 is devoted to the study of perturbations.

[2] Shakespeare's *Hamlet*, I. iv. 28; *Lucrece*, l. 723.

takes almost no part in the action but is only named as an ally of Alcina. Alcina has a splendid palace of her own, but she is dissatisfied and conspires with Morgan against Logistilla, whose castle is on the same island but is difficult of access, unlike the easy road to Alcina's palace (cf. Matt. 7: 13–14). Porcacchi's annotation to Canto vi[1] explains that Logistilla represents the virtuous life, Alcina the lascivious life; the difficult road to Logistilla's palace illustrates the phrase 'Ardua ad virtutem via' ('Hard is the way to virtue').

Ruggiero, a captive of Alcina, is freed by Melissa, whom Porcacchi interprets in the 'Allegory' of Canto vii as 'the prevenient grace of divine Love, that makes us know our error and completely lift ourselves from vice'.[2] Melissa thus corresponds to Arthur, or heavenly grace, in Spenser's poem; and her aid was enlisted by Bradamante, Ruggiero's betrothed, just as Una persuaded Arthur to rescue Redcross. When Ruggiero's eyes are opened by the ring of reason, he sees Alcina as she really is: an old and hideous hag, pale, lean, wrinkled, toothless, bald (*OF* vii. 72–3), a close parallel to the exposure of Duessa after Orgoglio's death (*FQ* i. viii. 46–9). After escaping from Alcina, Ruggiero visits the palace of Logistilla, which he had earlier avoided. In the 'Allegory' of Canto vi, Porcacchi notes that in avoiding the difficult road to Logistilla's palace Ruggiero finds himself beset with a strange throng of monsters; these are the savage thoughts and vulgar desires that hinder the man who is not following virtue. The two ladies that direct him to Alcina signify lascivious love that at first seems simple and honest but gradually makes him a prey to vice. Such a gradual deterioration marked Redcross's relations with Duessa. Porcacchi states that the foundation of Logistilla's palace upon a rock (*OF* x. 57) signifies the virtuous man's intent to preserve 'the rock of his soul' (annotation to Canto vi). This contrasts with Lucifera's House of Pride, which is built on a sandy hill (*FQ* i. iv. 5), both palaces illustrating Christ's parable of the two houses.

Since Logistilla is described by Porcacchi as virtue and is not further particularized, her palace could correspond to any of

---

[1] *OF* (Venice, 1570).

[2] The moral interpretation of this episode by various sixteenth-century commentators, not including Porcacchi, is given by Kerby Neill, 'The Degradation of the Red Cross Knight', in Mueller and Allen, *That Soueraine Light* (Baltimore, 1952), pp. 100–2.

Spenser's houses of virtue, and Alcina–Logistilla could have influenced any of Spenser's antithetical pairs of maidens: Lucifera–Coelia, Duessa–Coelia, Acrasia–Alma, Malecasta–Britomart, Radigund–Britomart, and Duessa–Mercilla. The last of these seems most probable, because the richness and grandeur of Mercilla's palace most closely approach Ariosto's description of Logistilla's palace (*OF* x. 58). The easy road to Alcina's palace and the difficult road to Logistilla's palace signify the 'wide gate and broad way' and the 'strait gate and narrow way' of Matt. 7 : 13–14, which Spenser uses for the contrasting houses of Lucifera and Coelia (below, p. 115).

Other houses and castles that appear in *The Faerie Queene* will be discussed in their relevant chapters.

FORESTS

Before illusions and perturbations have developed into habitual vice,[1] their habitat is the forest surrounding the castle. The forest is often dark, in it one can easily lose one's way, and it may conceal hostile beasts or hostile men. In some sense it is always a place of mystery, full of unseen dangers and occasional pleasant surprises. Here, in a 'pleasant grove', one may chance upon the dance of the fairies, led by the Graces (VI. x. 12). Here one may see and pursue a fleeting vision of beauty that bursts from the dark trees, closely followed by ugliness (III. i. 15–17). Here one may encounter a wide assortment of giants, churls, and savage beasts, as well as adventurers who seek to overthrow them.

The forest as a place of illusions occurs at the very beginning of *The Faerie Queene* in the 'wandring wood', or Wood of Errour, in which Redcross and Una take refuge from a violent storm and afterwards lose their way. Here Redcross slays the dragon Errour, after which he and Una emerge from the wood, only to fall victim to the illusions created by Archimago with the aid of evil spirits. Archimago can make the true appear false and the false appear true.

This forest has several prototypes. Its catalogue of trees seems to be imitated from Ovid's forest on Mount Rhodope, the dwell-

---

[1] The term 'illusions' is not used by Francesco but describes accurately the part played by the mind or rational faculty in the development of perturbations by means of the fantasy (i. 6–7; pp. 44–6).

ing of Orpheus.[1] The technique of opening a poem with the incident of losing one's way in a forest is applied also in Dante's
Divine Comedy, which opens with the poet losing his way in a
'selva oscura', or dark forest, after straying from the direct path.
In both poems, the loss of the path appears to represent difficulties with religious belief.[2] Otherwise, the forests are different, for
Dante's is harsh and bitter, while Spenser's is pleasant.

This feature of Spenser's forest is probably indebted to the
magic wood of Oberon in *Huon of Bordeaux*. Huon chooses to pass
through this wood rather than take a longer way through the
desert, though he has been warned that the wood is 'full of ye
fayrey & straunge thynges'.[3] When he and his companions seek
to leave the wood, they are stopped by a violent storm conjured
up by Oberon, who finally makes friends with them. The association of the wood and the storm may have furnished this detail to
Spenser.

Ariosto and Tasso both have enchanted forests which deceive
through illusions. The second of Ariosto's supplementary cantos
to the *Orlando Furioso*[4] concerns Charlemagne's defeat of Tassi-
lone's army by superior swiftness. In the 'Allegory' Porcacchi
comments: 'Through the wood full of spirits that they caused to
be cut down at Prague—since these were held in veneration by
the pagans—is denoted the fact that diabolic illusions cannot in
any way do harm to a true Christian prince, a friend of God.'
In *Gerusalemme Liberata* Tasso presents a wood near Jerusalem
which the magician Ismeno fills with illusions of spirits and wild
beasts to frighten away the troops who seek timber for scaling-
ladders and siege-towers.[5] Ismeno's companion Armida, prototype of Acrasia, has seduced Rinaldo to desert the Christian army
for her garden of sexual bliss. The army makes no headway until

---

[1] Ovid, *Metamorphoses*, x. 86–105. Noted by Douglas Bush, *Mythology and the
Renaissance Tradition*, rev. edn., Norton, p. 102. See also *Var.* i. 179.

[2] See the discussion in Chapter V, below, p. 120.

[3] *Huon of Bordeaux*, tr. Berners, ch. 21, EETS, o.s., no. 40, p. 63.

[4] Ariosto wrote five cantos, apparently discarded, on the same matter as the
Orlando Furioso, which has forty-six cantos. These five are printed as an appendix
in the edition of Venice, 1570. As in the main poem, each canto begins with a poetic
one-stanza 'Argument' by Ludovico Dolce and a short prose 'Allegory' by Thomaso
Porcacchi, and is followed by prose annotations by Porcacchi.

[5] 'But most fascinating of all is the enchanted forest of the *Gerusalemme Liberata*,
where, as De Sanctis said, the forest is the poet himself' (John Arthos, *On the Poetry
of Spenser and the Form of Romances* [London, 1956], p. 78).

Rinaldo returns to his duty under Godfredo and disenchants the wood. Tasso explains in his 'Allegory' that Godfredo, Rinaldo, and Armida represent the rational, irascible, and concupiscible faculties of the soul. He adds:

> Ismen doth signify that temptation which seeketh to deceive with false belief the virtue, as a man may call it, opinative: Armida is that temptation which layeth siege to the power of our desires: so from that proceed the Errors of Opinion; from this, those of the Appetite. The enchantments of Ismen in the wood, deceiving with illusions, signify no other thing than the falsity of the reasons and persuasions which are engendered in the wood; that is, in the variety and multitude of opinions and discourses of men . . . The flowers, the fountains, the rivers, the musical instruments, the nymphs, are the deceitful enticements, which do here set down before us the pleasures and delights of the Sense, under the show of good. Let it suffice to have said thus much of the impediments which a man finds as well *within* as without himself: if the allegory of anything be untold, with these beginnings every man may find it out.[1]

As Armida is the prototype of Acrasia, even to the very words describing her dalliance, Ismeno seems to be a prototype of Archimago. He is an apostate Christian who now worships Mahomet but has not quite forsaken his early faith (*GL* ii. 2). So Archimago, falsely professing holiness in the guise of Redcross, is an ally of the Saracen Sansloy but has not quite become one of the Saracens (*FQ* I. iii. 39). Both magicians summon armies of sprites from hell.[2] Both create illusions to confound their opponents, making the false appear true. Their temptations are directed toward the intellect, encouraging false opinions. Both operate in or beside an enchanted wood. In Ismeno's wood, the Christian knight Tancred, having won through a wall of flame and defeated other illusions, is discomfited when addressed by a tree which he has gashed and which purports to contain a human soul (*GL* xiii. 32–43). This recalls another haunted spot in Spenser's forest, a spot shunned by superstitious shepherds, where Redcross finds Fradubio and Fraelissa changed to trees by the enchantments of Duessa (*FQ* I. ii. 28–43). As companion enchanters, Duessa and Archimago seem parallel to Armida and Ismeno. But Duessa is

---

[1] From the translation of Tasso's *Allegory of the Poem* appended to Fairfax's version of *Jerusalem Delivered*, ed. Henry Morley (1890), p. 439.

[2] *GL* xiii. 11; *FQ* I. i. 38.

more directly imitated from Ariosto's enchantress Alcina, and the Fradubio episode more closely parallels Alcina's enchantment of Astolfo who, in the form of a myrtle-tree, speaks to Ruggiero when agitated by the latter's horse (*OF* vi. 20–54).[1] Astolfo's account of Alcina's treachery resembles Fradubio's account of Duessa; and Ruggiero, like Redcross, nevertheless continues to become involved in the enchantress's power.

We may now turn to 'another part of the forest',[2] that outside the House of Alma. The Wood of Errour had seemed to confuse and perplex the intellect in Book I, but the dark wood of the next three books shelters the beasts and monsters which assault the soul through the physical senses, and the furious men who stir up the soul to excessive wrath. Spenser has carefully told us what they are:[3]

> Then gan the palmer thus: 'Most wretched man,
> That to *affections* does the bridle lend!
> In their beginning they are weak and wan,
> But soon through suff'rance growe to fearefull end.
> Whiles they are weake, betimes with them contend:
> For when they once to perfect strength do grow,
> Strong warres they make, and cruell battry bend
> Gainst fort of reason, it to overthrow:
> Wrath, gelosy, griefe, love this squyre have laide thus low.
>
> (II. iv. 34)

> What warre so cruel, or what siege so sore,
> As that which strong *affections* doe apply
> Against the forte of reason evermore,
> To bring the sowle into captivity? (II. xi. 1)

> Who ever doth to temperaunce apply
> His stedfast life, and all his actions frame,
> Trust me, shal find no greater enimy,
> Then stubborn *perturbation*, to the same. (II. v. 1)

Francesco Piccolomini discusses at some length the nature of affections and perturbations, which he uses as synonymous or

---

[1] For the speaking and bleeding tree, the ultimate sources are Virgil's Polydorus (*Aen.* iii. 24–46) and Dante's suicides (*Inferno*, xiii). The image appears in Renaissance painting (below, p. 83).

[2] A favourite stage direction of Shakespeare in *As You Like It* and *Two Gentlemen of Verona*, used by Lillian Hellman as the title of a play.

[3] In Bk. v these offenders represent lawless violence, and in Bk vi various kinds of discourtesy.

nearly synonymous terms.[1] They take their rise from pleasure and grief, which are sources of perturbations rather than perturbations themselves (i. 19; p. 63C). There are innumerable perturbations; they are like a Hydra with many heads (i. 10; p. 50A). The four main heads are illness, fear, merriment, and sexual desire (*libido*).[2] Perturbations or affections with vehement motions are called illnesses of the soul, to be cured by virtue, which has a calming influence. They are the spurs to vices; they fight against reason and stir up the soul to civil war (i. 23; p. 69D). Yet moderate perturbations may be good; e.g. pity and shamefastness (i. 26–7; pp. 74D, 75C). To some extent, perturbations and conduct depend upon the 'temperament' of the body as varied by age and illness (i. 28; pp. 76–7); but this is not entirely the case, for reason can fight and overcome an unfavourable bodily temperament, as it does in the case of the continent man. To deny this is to deny the existence of free will; the vicious man cannot give himself such an excuse (i. 29; pp. 77–8). Evil perturbations such as malevolence and envy are not vices unless they become habitual; but they are like vices, are occasions of vices, and are sinful (iv. 31; p. 208D).

Francesco has further significant words on vice, which is a sickness of the soul (iii. 17; pp. 160–1). Pleasure is the food of vice and causes bodily intemperance, which is the seedbed of all vices. We are joined to material and corporal substance; in us are planted the food of sin and the internal spur which incites us to vices; hence, we say that man is more prone to vice than to virtue (iii. 5; p. 149B, C). The Stoics disagree, believing that man is naturally virtuous, with no innate propensities to vice. Their opponents say that all men have propensities to vice by nature, since all are joined with privation, with the flesh, and with the senses, by which we are drawn to pleasure and are prone to vehement perturbations, which are the incitements to all evils (iii. 7; p. 151B). Francesco thinks there may be some measure of truth in each opinion, that neither is wholly correct (III. 9; pp. 152–3).

[1] For similar passages on the War of the Affections see chapters 5 and 6 of my book *Shakespeare's Derived Imagery* (1953; reprint by Octagon Books, 1967).

[2] Francesco, i. 7; p. 45D. Spenser names the four affections of wrath, jealousy, love, and grief; but these are the four that apply in the particular case of Phedon, not the four 'main heads' of perturbations. These are represented in Bk. II as follows: illness (Maleger), fear (Braggadocchio), merriment (Phaedria), sexual desire (Acrasia). Upton finds these four 'perturbations' in Cicero's *De Finibus*, iii. 10, but applies *aegritudo* or illness to Amavia (*Var.* ii. 233–4).

It thus becomes clear that vice is a habit produced by repeated surrender to affections or perturbations. They are different stages of the same things. The moral virtues are likewise habits of mind, and therefore the enemies of vice and the disciplinary officers of the affections.[1] Francesco remarks that 'every vice, as vice, is a recession from law, order, right, perfection, and whatever exists absolutely and truly' (ix. 48; p. 541B). Adopting an analogy with form and matter, he adds that virtue is form, while vice is deformity, depravity, defection, diminution, privation, and imperfection (p. 542C); that is, Vice represents a recession towards the formlessness of Chaos, or first matter. Vice is a living death; virtue is life (vi. 19; p. 351A).

This theme of Form versus Formlessness or Deformity is evident throughout Spenser's work. It colours his views on divine love, the creation of the world, the generation of life, Cosmos versus Chaos, order versus confusion, beauty versus ugliness, knowledge versus ignorance, light versus darkness, good versus evil, truth versus falsehood, love versus lust, virtue versus vice, and life versus death. The forest becomes a symbol of formlessness through an etymological accident. Latin *silva* or *sylva* was equated by Servius with Greek *hyle*.[2] *Hyle* signifies a forest but also refers to the primordial matter which is the basic substance of all created things. Chaos consists of this matter in its unformed state and is therefore an equivalent of *hyle*.

Hyle–forest–first matter became quite early a subject for allegory. Several scholars[3] have reviewed this theme as treated by Virgilian allegorists: Servius, Fulgentius, Bernard of Chartres, John of Salisbury, Ascensius (Badius), Landino. Virgil's several descriptions of forests, particularly the dark wood about Lake Avernus at the entrance to Hades, provided the material of allegory. Since this is the forest which sheltered the Golden Bough, the talisman which allowed the favoured ones to view the other world, it seems obvious that Virgil himself had some allegorical intent. The forest is a haunt of wild beasts, and on the road at the

---

[1] Cf. H. S. V. Jones, 'The *Faerie Queene* and the Medieval Aristotelian Tradition', *JEGP* xxv (1926), 283–98, for Aristotelian and Christian ethics.

[2] William Nelson, *The Poetry of Edmund Spenser* (New York, 1963), p. 159.

[3] Domenico Comparetti, *Virgil in the Middle Ages* (London, 1895); Elizabeth Nitchie, *Vergil and the English Poets*, (New York, 1919); Merritt Y. Hughes, *Virgil and Spenser* (Berkeley, Cal., 1929), and below, p. 68 n. 3; Nelson, *The Poetry of Edmund Spenser*.

forest's edge are figures of Grief, Care, Sickness, Age, Fear, Hunger, Penury, Death, Sleep, Travail, Guilty Pleasures of the Soul, War, the Furies, Discord. Next come the Tree of Dreams and the shades of various classical monsters: Centaurs, Scyllas, Briareus, the Hydra, the Gorgons, the Harpies, the three-bodied Geryon. Obviously, the allegorists would find a good deal of their material ready-made in Virgil's work.

To follow the commentaries more easily, we may observe the particular lines concerning the forest. In describing the difficulties of returning from Hades, the Sibyl says:

> Tenent media omnia silvae.   (*Aeneid*, vi. 131)

(Forests occupy all the middle space.)

Aeneas enters a forest outside the Sibyl's cave:

> Itur in antiquam silvam, stabula alta ferarum . . .   (179)
> Aspectans silvam immensam . . .   (186)

(They go into an ancient forest, deep lairs of wild beasts . . . beholding an immense forest . . .)

Having secured the Golden Bough, Aeneas reaches the cave by Lake Avernus:

> Spelunca alta fuit, vastoque immanis hiatu,
> Scrupea, tuta lacu nigro, nemorumque tenebris.   (237–8)

(There was a deep cave, with a monstrously vast mouth, strewn with sharp stones, protected by a black lake and the darkness of the woods.)

Virgil invokes the aid of the gods in describing the underworld, then resumes his account of Aeneas' journey:

> Di, quibus imperium est animarum, umbraeque silentes,
> et Chaos, et Phlegethon, loca nocte tacentia late,
> sit mihi fas audita loqui; sit numine vestro
> pandere res alta terra et caligine mersas.
> Ibant obscuri sola sub nocte per umbram,
> perque domos Ditis vacuas et inania regna:
> quale per incertam lunam sub luce maligna
> est iter in silvis . . .   (264–71)

(Gods, to whom is the command of souls, and silent shades, and Chaos, and Phlegethon, places broadly silent with night, allow me to speak as I have heard; let me by your will unfold things hidden by the deep earth and gloom! They went darkling under solitary night through the dusk, and through the vacant dwellings and empty king-doms of Dis, like going through a wood under the niggard light of an uncertain moon . . .)

In this passage Virgil invokes Chaos as part of the underworld, though he never pictures Aeneas as visiting Chaos. He is follow-ing the Homeric tradition of placing Chaos near Tartarus (*Iliad*, viii. 16)[1] and in the above passage he brings Chaos in close proximity to *silva* in the text, a fact which might cause their asso-ciation with each other. In addition, he describes the *silva* as being in 'domos . . . vacuas et inania regna'. It so happens that these two adjectives are used in the Vulgate version of Genesis 1 : 2 as the equivalent of 'without form and void' in the Authorized Version, describing the earth while it was still formless matter: Terra autem erat *inanis et vacua*, et *tenebrae* erant super faciem *abyssi*, et spiritus Dei ferebatur super *aquas*.' ('The earth, however, was void and empty, and darkness was above the face of the abyss, and the spirit of God was borne above the waters.') In hexameral litera-ture, the 'waters' are usually interpreted as formless matter before the separation of the elements, and 'abyss' is regularly used as an equivalent of Chaos.[2] Virgil uses *vacuas* and *inania* to describe the realms of Dis, his 'black lake' and 'deep cave' correspond to the dark waters of the abyss in Genesis, and these are located outside the gate of Hades in a vast forest or *silva*. Since *silva* or *hyle* signifies formless matter, and since Virgil's reference to Chaos comes while he is describing the *silva*, one may easily see in his passage a figur-ative description of Chaos, or first matter.

Sixteenth-century editions of Virgil's works are likely to have variorum notes of half a dozen commentators; each page has a small island of text surrounded by a sea of annotations in very fine print. The most respected and most often reprinted commentator was also the earliest, Servius (c. 400). He considers the forest as an allegory of human life. On line 131, as quoted above, he ex-plains why the Sibyl states that the return of souls from the under-world is not easy. It is because all are polluted and filthy; for through *silvae* Virgil signifies darkness and morasses, in which

[1] The Greek term used by Homer is *barathrum*, a gulf or abyss, distinct from Tartarus.

[2] As in the invocation of Bk. i of Milton's *Paradise Lost*. One Latin translation gives *fovebat* instead of *ferebatur*. Milton thus addresses the Holy Spirit, who 'dove-like, satst brooding o'er the vast abyss' (line 21), using the terms in the signification here stated.

savagery and lust are dominant. On this line and those immediately following, he gives another gloss assigned to line 136: 'We
know that Pythagoras of Samos divided human life as the forked
letter Y: the first age is uncertain, devoted neither to vices nor to
virtues, but with youth men begin to follow either the left fork,
vices, or the right fork, virtues. Therefore he says that the Golden
Bough is hidden in the midst of the forest because truly virtue and
integrity are hidden by the confusion and the many vices of this
life.' Servius refers back to this gloss in another gloss, to line
295: 'He [Virgil] follows that Pythagorean [teaching], saying that
those have held the way after the *error of the woods* (*errorem syluarum*), which leads either to vices or to virtues.'[1] The passage has
particular interest because it seems probable that the *errorem
syluarum* may have suggested to Spenser the dragon Errour of the
'wandring wood' (1. i. 13). This phrase would normally be rendered in Latin as *sylva erroris*, meaning 'wood of the wandering'
or 'wood of going astray', which seems to be Spenser's meaning,
for he is not suggesting that the wood uproots itself and wanders
to another spot.

In medieval times, John of Salisbury interpreted Aeneas as the
human soul inhabiting the body, since Greek *ennaios* signifies an
inhabitant. Bernard of Chartres saw in the first six books of the
Aeneid an allegory of 'all that the soul does or suffers during its
temporary abode in the body'.[2] But the most complete allegorist
of the *Aeneid* was Christoforo Landino (*c*. 1480), whose work has
been discussed by Hughes and Nelson.[3] His ideas were advanced
in a little book *Disputationes Camaldulensis* (1480) and in annotations to the *Aeneid*. Since he repeats himself extensively, one can
find his significant comments in several places. Recently, Graham
Hough has expressed doubt as to whether Spenser had read *Disputationes Camaldulensis*.[4] Even if he had not, he could still have
known Landino's interpretations of Virgil in any one of several
editions.[5]

We may summarize briefly Landino's Virgilian commentaries.
The Golden Bough is wisdom. The *antiqua silva* of line 179 is

---

[1] Virgil, *Opera*, with the commentaries of Servius (Venice, 1586, 1610).
[2] Comparetti, pp. 116–17.
[3] Hughes, 'Virgilian Allegory and *The Faerie Queene*', *PMLA* xliv (1929), 696–705; Nelson, *The Poetry of Edmund Spenser*, p. 159.
[4] *A Preface to* The Faerie Queene (1962), p. 122.
[5] Edns. of Venice, 1489, 1504, 1510, 1531; Nuremberg, 1492.

hyle or matter, from which all vices proceed and are unconquerable except by wisdom; the *stabula alta ferarum* signifies that vices change us from men into beasts. He defines Chaos (line 265) as first matter, called *hyle* or *silva*, from which all the elements were born. Chaos is a companion of Demogorgon.[1] Aeneas' entrance into hell is the entrance of the human soul into vices. The gloomy forest signifies matter and the body, from which all vices come to us. These same points are stated somewhat more extravagantly in the *Disputationes*, and two are added. Landino places God and *silva* at opposite ends of the great chain of being; and he says that, when Virgil shows Venus in human form, he always places her in a wood, since we all have to act while immersed in matter, or *silva*.[2]

In his commentary on Dante's *Divine Comedy*, Landino repeats these ideas with reference to the *selva oscura* in the second line of the poem. It is the same as *hyle* and *silva*, terms applied to corporeal matter. It represents the body and therefore represents vices. Dante, becoming lost in the wood, allegorically represents the soul's entrance into the body. Whoever loves the *selva* is in an earthly prison.[3]

This figurative equation of the forest and first matter with the human body and the sins of the flesh had become almost a commonplace by Spenser's time. In his edition of Petrarch's poems, Gesualdo glosses the several uses of *selva* in the third canzone, which begins 'A qualunque animale alberga in terra,' etc. On the *amorosa selva* (line 26), he explains that this is the myrtle wood of *Aeneid* vi, in which slain lovers wander. *Selva* may signify matter, from Greek *hyle* and Latin *silva*. Earth is the matter from which men are made, and the poet's journey into a dry forest or *secca selva* in line 37 may signify man's return to his original dust.[4]

Thomaso Porcacchi, in his 'Allegory' of *Orlando Furioso*, Canto i, explains the dark forest or *selva* as the darkness of corrupt appetites.[5] Tasso uses a fanciful variation of the theme in his

---

[1] Cf. *FQ* i. v. 22, iv. ii. 47, and below, p. 76.
[2] *Disputationes Camaldulensis* (Argentorati [Strasbourg], 1508), bk. iii, sig. Hvi.
[3] *Dante, con l'Espositioni di Christoforo Landino, e d'Alessandro Vellutello* (Venice, 1578), f. 1.
[4] *Il Petrarcha, con l'Espositione di M. Gio. Andrea Gesualdo* (Venice, 1574), f. 22ʳ. Cf. C. S. Lewis on Virgil's 'domos . . . vacuas et inania regna' as the prototype of the Waste House in Spenser's allegory (*Spenser's Images of Life*, p. 71).
[5] *Orlando Furioso* (Venice, 1570). See above, p. 61 n. 4.

Discorsi del Poema Eroico (1587, 1594). At the beginning of Book ii
he illustrates the difficulty of handling the materials of poetry by
a comparison to physical matter. Nothing is more uncertain, un-
stable, and inconstant than matter. 'La materia è simile ad una
selva oscura, tenebrosa e priva d'ogni luce.' ('Matter is like to an
obscure forest, dark and deprived of all light'). Some matter is
amenable to form, and some is not. Virgil and Homer described
scenes under the earth [and therefore dark], covering them with
a veil of allegory. He, Tasso, wishes to kindle a great light in the
darkness that obscures the great *selva* of poetic matter.[1]

We may note that, in the journey of Carlo and Ubaldo into the
underworld (*GL* xiv. 37), Tasso has borrowed the dark wood and
the uncertain moonlight of *Aeneid*, vi. 270:

> Debile e incerta luce ivi si scerne,
> Qual, tra boschi, di Cintia ancor non piena.

(A sickly and uncertain light shines there, like that in thick woods
when the moon is not yet full.)

And, with some variations, it reappears in Spenser's *Faerie Queene*
as Guyon enters Mammon's cave (*FQ* ii. vii. 20, 29).

An interesting variation of the forest-allegory is found in the
Distinctiones Dictionum Theologicalium of Alanus de Insulis, an
author whom Spenser has mentioned by name (vii. vii. 9). Under
silva he explains that this represents primordial matter, the Greek
hyle, which Plato called *silva* because, just as the forest provides
material for buildings, primordial matter provides the universal
material of bodies. But *silva* also represents the multitude of rude
and forest-dwelling (*silvestres*) men, because Christ can 'kindle'
a whole forest of such men with fire of the Holy Spirit. Again,
under *campus* Alanus quotes from Psalm 132: 6 (131: 6 in the
Vulgate) the words 'Invenimus eam in campis silvae' ('We found
her in the fields of the forest'). (The *eam* refers in this Psalm to the
tabernacle or temple which David has vowed to find as a suitable
house for the Lord.) Here, Alanus says, the *campis silvae* may refer
to the amplitude or latitude of vices, meaning 'We found her
wandering in vices'. But it can also refer to the Church among the
Gentiles; i.e. among rude and forest-dwelling men (*silvestribus
hominibus*).[2]

---

[1] Tasso, *Opere* (Milan, 1824), vol. iii, pp. 31–3.
[2] Alanus's work is available in *PL* ccx. This volume includes the *De Planetu*

It is difficult to render *silvestris* exactly in English. It means savage in a non-pejorative sense, as in Spenser's Salvage Man (VI. v. 1–6). It is intended to suggest the rough, crude, violent but not necessarily vicious, manners of primitive forest tribes. The passages here quoted may have a significance for Una among the satyrs or 'woodborne people' (1. vi. 16), since she represents the 'true Church' and seems to appeal to their better natures (below, p. 215).

An interesting footnote to Virgilian allegory concerns *Aeneid*, viii. 314:

> Haec nemora indigenae Fauni Nymphaeque tenebant.
>
> (Native-born Nymphs and Fauns held these woods.)

Gavin Douglas translates the line as follows:

> Thir woddis and thir schawis all, quod he,
> Sum tyme inhabit was and occupyit
> With *Nymphis* and *Faunis* apoun euery syde,
> Quhilk farefolkis [fairy folks] and then elfis clepin we.[1]

King Evander speaks these words to Aeneas as they sit within the grove which will later be occupied by the city of Rome. This has the effect of making Rome a fairy city of fame on enchanted ground, somewhat like the fairyland tradition attached to Glastonbury (below, p. 201).

Evander's speech to Aeneas follows closely upon his account of the cave of Cacus, which they can see from the spot where they sit, and of Cacus' death at the hands of Hercules, who had just arrived from a triumph over the monster Geryon (viii. 202). The battle with Cacus, a filthy, stinking, braying monster who breathed out clouds of smoke, seems to have furnished Spenser with some details for Gerioneo's unnamed monster who inhabits a cave beneath the temple altar (*FQ* v. xi. 21). Like Cacus, she is filthy and stinking (22–4), brays loudly (28), and breathes out clouds of smoke (32). Historically, she represents some aspect of the Roman Church, probably the Inquisition, and she much resembles the dragon Errour in I. i, who represents the false

---

Naturae and the *Anticlaudianus*, as well as the *Distinctiones*, which begin on p. 689 and are arranged alphabetically: *campus* (727), *silva* (944).

[1] Gavin Douglas's translation of the *Aeneid*, including the apocryphal Thirteenth Book by Maphaeus Vegius, was printed in London in 1553.

doctrine taught by the Roman Church. Spenser seems to have borrowed one detail in the battle with Errour from the battle with Cacus. Both Hercules and Redcross, impeded in using their weapons, choke their antagonists with a fierce hand-grip. Virgil calls Cacus a *semiferus* or half-beast (viii. 267), suggesting the bestial man. After Evander's account of the battle, the young people in the grove sing praises of Hercules, whose rites they are celebrating on that day. Their song enumerates his victories over various monsters: the two serpents which he strangled in his cradle, the Centaurs, the Cretan monsters, the Nemean lion, Cerberus, Typhoeus, the Hydra, and Cacus (viii. 288–304). We have already noted that Hercules' victories over these monsters represent man's conquest of the vices within his own soul (above, p. 26).

Spenser uses various beasts from the forest. Una's lion (I. iii. 5) is a benevolent beast, probably a quality of the irascible faculty in the soul (below, p. 124). The other beasts are hostile to man: the great dragon slain by Redcross (I. xi), the Witch's beast that feeds on women's flesh (III. vii), the monsters guarding Proteus' palace (IV. xi. 3), the Blatant Beast (V. xii; VI), the bear slain by Calepine (VI. iv. 22), the tiger slain by Calidore (V. x. 36), and the tiger who serves as Maleger's steed (II. xi). Most or all of these can be interpreted in terms of internal allegory. They are dangers within oneself; the forest which they inhabit can only be the self. We may identify the forest with the body or with the flesh, since from the weakness and imperfection of the flesh come most of the harms that annoy the soul. Thus, the body is simultaneously the castle of the soul and the forest of beasts surrounding the castle. In so far as the body obeys, protects, and nourishes the soul, it is a castle. In so far as its weakness clogs, annoys, and imperils the soul, it is a forest.[1] The beasts which inhabit the forest are themselves passions of the soul; the body provides the setting, but the warfare is within the soul.

It may well be that the beast from the forest is one of those archetypal symbols that recur naturally in man's consciousness and objectify some subconscious menace within himself.[2] De Quincey

---

[1] This dual capacity was recognized in an ancient heresy which taught that man's body above the waist was created by God, while the lower part containing the genital organs was created by the devil (St. Augustine, *De Haeresibus*, no. 85, quoted in my book *The Character of Hamlet* [1941], p. 122).

[2] Cf. Maud Bodkin, *Archetypal Patterns in Poetry* (Oxford, 1934).

mentions a recurrent childhood dream of meeting a lion and cowering before it, the inner threat being a paralysis of will that prevented any attempt at resistance or escape.[1] Blake's tiger conveys something of this visionary quality:

> Tiger, tiger, burning bright
> In the forests of the night.

The 'forests of the night' present the exact image of the *selva oscura*. In painting, this image appears repeatedly in the work of Henri Rousseau, where beasts look out from the forest with great, burning eyes. The most notable instance is Henry James's *Beast in the Jungle*, in which a man who is troubled from childhood with the fantasy that a beast will spring from the forest to destroy him, at last realizes that the forest or jungle is within himself and the beast an innate selfishness which detaches him from human kind.

The evil men and women in the forest are a step higher than the beasts but serve much the same purposes. Spenser's list of these includes Kirkrapine (I. iii), the Affections led by Maleger (II. xi), the three 'fosters' or foresters slain by Timias (III. v. 18–25), the giants Argante and Ollyphant (III. vii. 47–51), Lust (IV. vii. 5–32), the Witch's son (III. vii. 12), Malengin or Guile (V. ix. 4–19), the cannibals and the brigands (VI. viii. 35, x. 39). To these should be added the fisherman who attempts Florimell's virtue (III. viii. 25). These should perhaps be called perturbations, or perturbations blossoming into vices. The confirmed vices that have gained a measure of intellectual acceptance from the soul are likely to be represented as wizards or witches who cast strong spells or enchantments. They include Archimago, Duessa, Acrasia, the Witch who formed the false Florimell, Busyrane, Corflambo, Proteus, and Radigund.

Besides the various knightly virtues whose quests lead them through the dark forest, there are such native champions as Belphoebe, Satyrane, and the Salvage Man, all of whom delight to subdue the beasts of the forest. The forest is also traversed by evil knights who are not native to it and who are 'corrected' by the virtuous knights. In general, all the evil knights would undermine or destroy the just proceedings of reason, while the virtuous knights support the cause of order and rational justice.

---

[1] De Quincey's *The English Mail Coach*: 'A Vision of Sudden Death'.

CAVES

In Spenser's forests there are a number of caves. Some are the
dens of wild beasts: the cave of the dragon Errour and the cave
of Gerioneo's monster, which are associated in the religious allegory; the cave of the beast that feeds on women's flesh (III. vii.
22); and the cave of Malengin, or Guile (V. ix. 6). Caves inhabited
by evil men are the Cave of Despair (I. ix), the Cave of Mammon
(II. vii), the Cave of Lust (IV. vii), and the Cave of the Brigands
(VI. x, xi). These are caves of temptation. Added to these are the
dungeons in the palaces of Orgoglio and Proteus, where Redcross
and Florimell respectively are imprisoned, and the cave in the
Garden of Adonis where the destructive boar is shut up.

Since the deep cave or *spelunca alta* of Virgil is part of the forest
silva and shares its associations with the formlessness of primordial matter, the cave suggests the absence of light, the presence
of spiritual darkness, the 'abyss' of Chaos, and the descent to hell.
We may add to this Alanus de Insulis's explanation of the cave
(*antrum*, *caverna*) as 'the depraved heart of the wicked man', an
explanation which he also gives for 'abyss'.[1] Since the heart is
hollow, it suggests the image of a cave; e.g. Vachel Lindsay's 'the
red cave of my heart'.[2] Figuratively, then, it seems a suitable lair
or dwelling for wicked impulses when it has been turned away
from God and from the control of reason.

The 'abyss' of unformed matter in Genesis 1 : 2 is related to the
'bottomless pit', for this phrase is rendered as *abyssus* by the Vulgate in all instances. In Revelation 17 appears the vision of a
seven-headed beast, ridden by the Babylonian harlot, prototypes
of Duessa and her beast in *The Faerie Queene*, I. viii (below, p. 101).
In verse 8 we are told that this beast shall ascend from the 'abyss'
and shall go into 'interitus' or perishing;[3] in Revelation 19 : 20
this beast and the False Prophet are cast into a 'stagnum ignis
ardentis sulphure' ('a lake of fire burning with sulphur'). In
Revelation 20 : 2 the old dragon Satan—not the same as the

[1] *Distinctiones*, in PL ccx. 703, 735.
[2] Vachel Lindsay, 'The Chinese Nightingale'.
[3] In glossing Virgil's famous lines on the possible immortality of bees (*Georgica*,
iv. 225–7), Servius and Pomponius Sabinus distinguish between death as *interitus*
(a between-going), a transitional stage before another life, and death as *peritus*
(a through-going) or final extinction (Virgil, *Opera*, edns. of Antwerp, 1575, and
Basel, 1586).

seven-headed beast—is shut up in the 'abyss' by an angel for a thousand years (the millennium), at the end of which he shall escape and make great wars. After destroying his followers with fire from heaven, God shall throw him into the lake of fire where the beast and the False Prophet are. With him shall go Death, Hell, and the multitude of unbelievers.

Since the 'abyss' is different from the lake of fire, the pattern closely resembles Virgil's 'Chaos, et Phlegethon' (*Aeneid*, vi. 265), for Phlegethon is later identified as the Tartarean river of fire (551). Like Chaos and Tartarus, the 'abyss' and the *stagnum ignis* of Revelation represent companion realms in the world underground. Virgil's Phlegethon corresponds to the lake of fire; his Lake Avernus or *lacus niger* (vi. 238) is part of the *silva* and shares in the characteristics of Chaos.

The chaining of the 'old dragon' in the 'abyss' may have significance for Spenser's cave in the Garden of Adonis (iii. vi. 48). Adonis' bower is on a mountain in the midst of the garden, and within the mountain is imprisoned the boar that had wounded Adonis:

> There now he liveth in eternal blis,
> Joying his goddesse, and of her enjoyd:
> Ne feareth he henceforth that foe of his,
> Which with his cruell tuske him deadly cloyd:
> For that *wilde bore*, the which him once annoyd,
> She firmely hath emprisoned for ay,
> That her sweet love his malice mote avoyd,
> *In a strong rocky cave*, which is, they say,
> Hewen underneath that mount, that none him losen may.

In the same garden Spenser describes but does not localize Chaos, which supplies the needed matter for generating new living things:

> For in the wide wombe of the world there lyes,
> In hatefull darknes and in deepe horrore,
> An huge eternal *chaos*, which supplyes
> The substaunces of Nature's fruitfull progenyes.
>
> (iii. vi. 36

Later he does localize Chaos when Agape visits the Fates:

> By wondrous skill and many hidden wayes
> To the three Fatall Sisters house she went.

> Farre under ground from tract of living went,
> Downe in the bottom of the deepe *Abysse*,
> Where Demogorgon, in dull darknesse pent,
> Farre from the view of gods and heavens blis,
> The hideous *Chaos* keepes, their dreadfull dwelling is.
>
> (IV. ii. 47)

When Duessa visits the House of Night, 'most auncient grand-mother' of all the gods, she addresses Night,

> Which wast begot in Daemogorgons hall,
> And sawst the secrets of the world unmade.   (I. v. 22)

The 'world unmade' is primordial matter as it existed before the world was formed and as the residue of it still exists in Chaos.

In terms of the Venus–Adonis myth, the boar should represent Mars, a rival for Venus' affections, or winter, since the days shorten when Adonis must leave to visit Proserpina in the underworld; this view considers Adonis a mythical representation of the sun (*Var.* iii. 255). Since, however, the garden is one of generation, the hostile force should be representative of destruction. Greenlaw speculates that the boar might represent Chaos,[1] and Mrs. Bennett notes the possibility that its cave is the same as the cave of Chaos and Demogorgon.[2] The significance of Spenser's use of 'Abysse' seems to have escaped notice. For this shows that he related the Biblical account in Genesis to the classical sources and was thinking in terms of Christian mythography. It forms a definite connecting link with hexameral literature and gives some insight into his method of work.

There is further indication of a link between the boar and Chaos. In Psalm 80: 13 (79: 14 in the Vulgate) we read: 'Exterminavit eam aper de silva, et singularis ferus depastus est eam.' ('The boar from the forest hath destroyed it, and a singular wild beast hath devoured it.') 'It' is the vine of Judah. The boar was interpreted by the Church Fathers to mean the devil.[3] He is therefore the same as the 'old dragon' who is locked in the 'abyss'. He dwells in *silva*; and both *hyle* and *silva* represent the primordial matter of Chaos.

---

[1] 'Spenser and Lucretius', *Studies in Philology*, xvii (1920), 454.
[2] Josephine Waters Bennett, 'Spenser's Garden of Adonis', *PMLA* xlvii (1932), 51.
[3] Eucherius, in *PL* l. 751; Bruno, in *PL* cxlii. 306.

In Alanus's *Distinctiones* we find under *bestia* a rendering of Revelation 11 : 7 unlike that of the Vulgate. Alanus quotes: 'Bestia egrediebatur de abysso quae universa devoravit.'[1] ('From the abyss there went out a beast which has devoured the universe.') This passage further emphasizes the beast as a destructive force.

In an old but excellent book, Richard Payne Knight regards Adonis as the sun, a generative force, and the boar as an anti-generative or destroying attribute. He equates Venus and Adonis with Isis and Osiris, and the boar with Typhon, whom he considers to be identical with Typhoeus.[2] Since Spenser uses these various deities, we may assume his knowledge of them from contemporary handbooks. Typhaon (or Typhon) and Echidna are parents of the Blatant Beast (VI. vi. 11) and of Orthrus (v. x. 10). Typhoeus is described as being in hell (I. v. 35) after begetting twin giants, Argante and Ollyphant, by forcible rape of his own mother Earth (III. vii. 47).

Plutarch, in his essay *Isis and Osiris*, discusses the allegorical meaning of Typhon. Typhon once came near to destroying the world and the ocean as well, and slew Osiris; but Isis, the principle of generation, overcame him and restored Osiris. Typhon was vanquished but not annihilated by Isis. He is imprisoned, but sometimes escapes and works havoc until captured again (ch. 43). He and Osiris are the bad and the good parts of the World-Soul and of the World-Body. In the soul, Typhon is that part which is impressionable, impulsive, irrational, and truculent. In the body, he is the destructible, diseased, and disorderly part; unseasonable weather, eclipses of the sun and moon, are outbursts and unruly actions of Typhon (ch. 45). Hesiod identifies him with Chaos and Tartarus (ch. 53), others with violent lust as opposed to true love (ch. 59). Some feign that his soul is divided among all beasts, signifying that all irrational and brutish nature belongs to the evil deity (ch. 73).[3]

Natalis Comes explains Typhon as originally a dragon or a dragon-like king of Egypt. He is the cause of violent subterranean winds and fires, of drought, and of infectious air.[4]

---

[1] *PL* ccx. 720.

[2] *The Symbolic Language of Ancient Art and Mythology* (New York, 1876), p. 87. It is quoted, with further discussion, by E. B. Hungerford, *Shores of Darkness* (1941), p. 221.

[3] In Plutarch's *Moralia*.

[4] Cf. Comes's *Mythologiae*, VI. xxii; p. 349.

As the principle of destruction in the universe, Typhon is there-fore associated with the 'old dragon' of Revelation 17: 8, proto-type of Spenser's dragon in *The Faerie Queene*, 1. xi, and with the 'boar from the forest' of Psalm 80: 13, and with the boar who is the enemy of Adonis. This boar was sometimes identified with the Calydonian boar[1] who devastated the fields and who in Ovid's lines is a perfect example of the destructive boar from the forest:

> Silva frequens trabibus, quam nulla ceciderat aetas,   (329)
> incipit a plano, devexaque prospicit arva. . . .
> Hinc aper excitus medios violentus in hostes   (338)
> fertur, ut excussis elisus nubibus ignis.
> Sternitur incursu nemus: et propulsa fragorem
> silva dat. . . .
> Ira feri mota est: nec fulmine lenius arsit: (355)
> emicat ex oculis spiratque e pectore flammas. . . .
> Vulnera fecissent, nisi setiger inter opacas   (376)
> nec iaculis isset, nec equo loca pervia, silvas.
>
> *(Metamorphoses*, viii)

(A forest thick with trees, which no age has ever felled, begins from the plain and overlooks the sloping fields. . . . From here the boar, excited and violent, is borne into the midst of his enemies like fire struck out from the riven clouds. The grove is beaten down by his rush, and the falling forest gives a crashing noise. . . . The wild beast is moved to wrath no less burning than lightning: he darts sparks from his eyes and breathes out flames from his breast. . . . They might have wounded him had not the monster withdrawn into *a dark forest*, a place impenetrable to horses and spears alike.)

These several examples illustrate the 'boar from the forest' as an agent of destruction dwelling in *silva*, or primordial matter, and suggest that the cave in the Garden of Adonis is still another equivalent of Chaos, like the other caves already mentioned.

The account of Chaos as a great empty realm adjoining Tar-tarus seems to have become conventional. In Ovid's *Metamor-phoses*, x. 30, Orpheus has come to Pluto 'per Chaos hoc ingens vastique silentia regni', which is translated by Arthur Golding (1565) as follows:

> . . . by this howge *Chaos* now
> And by the stilnesse of this waste and emptye Kingdome.

---

[1] Cf. George Chapman, *Epicede*, ll. 627–8.

In Lucan's *Pharsalia*, Pompey's wife Cornelia determines to follow her husband in death:

> Iam nunc te per inane chaos, per Tartara, coniunx,
> si sunt ulla, sequar. (ix. 101–2)

(And now through empty Chaos and through Tartarus, if any such places exist, I shall follow you, husband.)

In Statius' *Thebaid*, the Prophet calls Chaos a part of Pluto's realm (viii. 52). In the first region of Hades, he advances 'per inane' (85) and calls upon 'inane chaos' (100) to bear witness to his guiltlessness in entering Hades.

The emptiness of the caverns of Chaos may seem puzzling. Each one is 'inanis et vacua'. An early Latin translation of the Greek Septuagint, followed by Ambrose and Augustine, renders the phrase as 'invisibilis et incomposita' in Genesis 1: 2.[1] As Plato says, matter in its first state is only potentiality, for nothing can appear to the human senses without form.[2] A shapeless lump of clay will have the form of a shapeless lump of clay if we see or feel it. Its 'shapelessness' is only relative, for nothing perceptible can be entirely shapeless. Duns Scotus says that there are actually three stages in what is called first matter: (1) potentiality, with no tangible or visible existence; (2) a stage of substance capable of being transmuted by angels and other agents besides God; (3) propinquous matter, which has already assumed a certain general form—like the shapeless lump of clay—and is the *prima materia* underlying all generable things. He identifies *hyle* as the second stage of matter.[3] Bernardus Silvestris adopted the same scheme but separated *hyle* from *silva*, using *silva* for the third stage.[4]

This theory of the several stages in first matter may explain why parts of the Chaos are 'empty' while other parts have forests and beasts; the latter are not completely formless but are emerging from formlessness, the 'griesly shade' from which they make their way into life (*FQ* iii. vi. 37). Yet the first stage of potentiality is not 'empty' in the sense of complete nothingness; it is perhaps

---

[1] For Ambrose, see below, p. 87; Augustine, *De Genesi ad Litteram*, in PL xxxiv. 247.

[2] Cf. Bennett, 'Spenser's Garden of Adonis', *PMLA* xlvii. 65.

[3] Duns Scotus, *Summa Theologica*, Q. 66, A. 2, ed. J. Montefortino (Rome, 1901), iii. 404.

[4] Cf. Sara de Ford, 'Bernardus Silvestris: A Translation, Interpretation, and a Study of Certain Relationships', Yale Dissertation, 1942, p. 242.

like energy awaiting conversion into mass before it can be tangible and visible. The third stage, or *silva*, is the substratum which immediately underlies the fluctuating forms and substances of the visible world.

WATERS

As might be expected, Spenser's landscape is varied with bodies of water: lakes, fountains, streams, and the sea. By far the largest number of these occur in Book II: Idle Lake, in which Phaedria plies her little boat (vi. 10); the 'standing lake' in which Maleger is destroyed (xi. 46); the sea over which Guyon and the Palmer are borne to Acrasia's isle (xii. 2–37); the fountain of the chaste nymph, which caused Mortdant's death (ii. 40–55); the fountain and pool at the Bower of Bliss (xii. 60–8). These make a most impressive array of allegorical waters. In Book I we have the fountain of sloth where Redcross is disarmed and captured by Orgoglio (vii. 1–7) and the Well of Life in which he is revived after his first day of battle with the dragon (xi. 29). In Books III and IV we have the various uses of the sea and streams associated with Florimell and Marinell, particularly the great assemblage of the marine gods at the marriage of the Thames and the Medway (IV. xi). Book V has the river which flows under Pollente's bridge (ii. 12, vi. 36), the sea around the islands of Amidas and Bracidas (iv. 7–20), and the egalitarian giant's parable of the mutual encroachments of sea and land (ii. 37–9). Book VI has the spring frequented by nymphs and fairies at the foot of Mount Acidale (x. 7). Book VII has the personification of streams in the Faunus episode, with an appreciative notice of the 'wholsom waters' and fountains around Arlo Hill (vi. 38–9).

Since water is a cleansing agent and is used in Christian baptism, we are likely to assign it that symbolism in all cases. Yet a little thought will suggest that this cannot be true. The rivers of Hades—Styx, Acheron, Phlegethon, Cocytus—could hardly be used as symbols of virtue; and, in fact, they are not. Dante uses them in the *Divine Comedy* to represent the punishment of various sins. We must make the distinction between clean water and polluted water, for the latter may cause evils rather than cure them. One of the Church Fathers, Rabanus Maurus, interprets *aqua* as the pleasure of the flesh.[1] Among the various interpretations given

---

[1] *PL* cxii. 861.

in Alanus's *Distinctiones* under *aqua* are (1) the sacrament of bap-tism, (2) the lustful desires of depraved man, and (3) primordial matter, since moisture is prominent in the matter of every corporal thing.[1] All these interpretations find echoes in Spenser's work.

Clearest of all the watery symbols is the Well of Life. To make sure that the meaning is not missed, Spenser refers to the renewed strength of Redcross's 'baptized hands' after his exposure to the well (xi. 36). This is the water named by Christ to the woman of Samaria, the 'living water' from 'a well of water springing up into everlasting life' (John 4: 10, 14). The Vulgate uses *fons aquae* and thus suggests the baptismal 'font' in the midst of the church.

Presumably, this is also the 'living well' in which Fradubio and Fraelissa must be bathed before they can change from the shape of trees into their former shapes (i. ii. 43). This feature may have been suggested by Ariosto, who describes Astolfo as the man changed to a tree through the enchantments of Alcina. He is re-stored by Melissa to his former shape and makes a journey to the underworld, where he becomes grimy and dirty. Upon emerging, and before climbing the mountain to the terrestrial paradise, he cleanses himself by bathing in a fountain (*OF* xxxiv. 47). Por-cacchi comments in his 'Allegory' of this canto: We are shown that no Christian can rise from this centre [earth] of vice and sin to that peak of eternal blessedness if he does not first cleanse his soul of all earthly concupiscence with the Sacraments of the Church, by confession, taking communion, and putting away wholly every hostility and brutality which infects and contaminates all things in this vale of misery.' The sacrament of Holy Commu-nion involves the use of water, but apparently Porcacchi feels that it involves renewal of vows made at baptism and thereby justifies the use of the Well of Life as a figure for either sacrament.

The Fountain of Sloth, as Padelford calls it (*Var.* i. 437), is con-trasted with the Well of Life. The latter quickens Redcross's energies; the former slows them down. All who drink of that fountain grow faint and feeble, their blood chills, and their normal powers of resistance fail. Redcross drinks of the fountain after taking off his 'whole armour of God' and just before his dalliance with Duessa (vii. 1–7); hence he is unprepared for the battle with Orgoglio, which immediately follows. The fountain seems to sig-nify the relaxing of vigilance and cessation of effort which causes

[1] *Distinctiones*, in PL ccx. 704.

one to slacken in the warfare of the soul. The suggestion for the fountain probably comes from Proverbs 25 : 26 : 'A righteous man falling down before the wicked is as a troubled fountain, and a corrupt spring.' This seems to fit Redcross, whose fall is the occasional lapse of the righteous man, not of the chronic evil-doer. The 'wicked' before whom he falls down is Orgoglio, or the sin of pride.

The contrasting fountains in Book II are the fountain of the chaste nymph (ii. 9) and the 'lascivious' fountain beside Acrasia's bower (xii. 60), which could be called the fountain of the unchaste nymph. Alastair Fowler points out a probable source for these in Trissino's epic *La Italia*, in which appear the fountain of Sinesia (conscience) and the fountain of Acratia (concupiscence).[1]

When Guyon and the Palmer find Mortdant dead and Amavia dying beside him of a self-inflicted wound, they seek to learn the circumstances. Amavia relates Acrasia's seduction of Mortdant and her own success in winning him back. At parting, Acrasia gave Mortdant a cup of wine to drink and pronounced this charm :

> Sad verse, give death to him that death does give,
> And losse of love to her that loves to live,
> So soon as Bacchus with the Nymphe does lincke.

(II. i. 55)

When Mortdant unsuspectingly drinks from the fountain of the chaste nymph, he falls down dead. 'Bacchus' had been the wine of Acrasia's cup; the 'Nymphe' had been the pure water of the fountain which would tolerate no pollution. The clash of these incompatible elements within his body killed him.

Does Spenser perhaps suggest that reformation which is too sudden or too extreme can be dangerous? His allegorical intent could be like that in Hawthorne's *The Birthmark*, where insistence on complete perfection brings death to the occupant of an imperfect world. If the poison had been eliminated gradually from Mortdant's system, he might then have profited from the pure waters, but the sudden and violent clash was more than he could endure.

The first line of Acrasia's charm concerns the name Mortdant (death-giving). The second line concerns 'her that loves to live'

---

[1] Fowler, *Spenser and the Numbers of Time*, p. 94. Fowler identifies the pure fountain as the water of baptism, in *HLQ* xxiv. 103, and *RES*, N.S. xi. 145–6.

and suggests that Amavia's name is shortened from Italian 'Ama vita' ('Love life!'). We should notice that Spenser similarly shortens Mortdant's name, sometimes writing it as Mordant. In the Argument at the beginning of the canto, Spenser's words attribute their deaths to 'Pleasures poisoned baites', or Acrasia's enchantments. In the charm, Acrasia pretends that Mortdant gives death to her by leaving her; the charm will give death to him; his death means loss of love to Amavia, who is pictured as a lover of life. In a sense, Mortdant gives death to Amavia also, for grief for him causes her to die.

The lascivious fountain in Acrasia's garden, with the pool in which two naked maidens disport themselves, is obviously a fountain of concupiscence. It and the maidens are drawn from Armida's fountain in *Gerusalemme Liberata*, xiv. 74 and xv. 55–66 (Upton). As this fountain of Tasso kills by causing excessive laughter, it probably has some influence on Spenser's Idle Lake (II. vi. 10), where Phaedria, or immodest mirth, plies her little boat. Though Spenser does not seem to picture Phaedria as vicious, he does make her appear again as a temptress on Guyon's journey toward Acrasia's isle (II. xii. 17). The implication is that leaders of 'the gay life' are more careless and more likely to sink into vice than sober, industrious characters are.

Idle Lake is featured in a Renaissance painting by Andrea Mantegna, *Wisdom Overcoming the Vices* (*c.* 1490). Wisdom is Minerva, with helmet, shield, and spear, assisted by Diana and Chastity. They put to rout Venus and the Vices, who are standing in a stagnant pool bearing the inscription 'Otia si tollis, periere Cupidinis arcus' ('If you overcome idleness, Cupid's bows have perished'). The Vices are Sloth, Hate, Suspicion, Avarice, Dalliance. At the left of the picture is a person changed into a tree, with the head still recognizable. Chastity is pictured as semi-nude, with many children (usually the icon for Charity). Cupid sports at the edge of the picture, while three Virtues watch from the clouds above.[1]

Acrasia's pool is like the one defined in Alanus's *Distinctiones* under *lacus* as 'profunditas carnalium concupiscentiarum' ('a deep of carnal concupiscences'), which is based on Psalm 40: 2 (39: 2 in the Vulgate): 'Eduxit me de lacu miseriae et de luto faecis' ('He

---

[1] Reproduced in Jean Seznec's *Survival of the Pagan Gods* (New York, 1953), p. 111.

brought me out of the lake of misery and the mire of filth').[1] The pool seemed to be of clear water, but this was only an illusion. It shares the quality of Acrasia's bower. When Guyon and the Palmer tore down the bower 'and of the fayrest late, now made the fowlest place', they merely revealed the true nature of what was already there. Like Duessa's 'beauty', the fairness of bower and pool is an illusion, a mask concealing what is filthy and ugly, a truth which some of Acrasia's devotees are unable to face.

The 'standing lake' into which Maleger is thrown (II. xi. 46) presents the most interesting study of all, for there is some question of what it represents; and this of course involves the question of what Maleger represents. Woodhouse, in his article on nature and grace, cited above,[2] considers Maleger to represent original sin and the lake to represent the water of baptism that washes such sin from the human soul. This interpretation of the lake has caused qualms among other critics. Kathleen Williams accepts it reluctantly, finding it oddly out of keeping.[3] Lyle Glazier sees the 'standing lake' used in a pejorative sense, which could hardly apply to baptism.[4] The allegory seems curiously twisted. The waters of baptism cleanse and strengthen by being applied to the body of the person baptized, as with Redcross in the Well of Life. But Arthur never touches the water of the 'standing lake' at all; he stands on the bank while he hurls Maleger into it. Maleger is not to be cleansed or strengthened; he is to be destroyed. Who then is baptized? If this is internal warfare, we might postulate externally a person from whose soul the devil, or sin, is expelled by heavenly grace. But still the image is not one of washing and cleansing, as it is with the Well of Life. Therefore, while admitting that Woodhouse could be right—and Alanus's *Distinctiones* give baptism as a meaning of *stagnum* (lake)[5]—it is well that we explore other possibilities which may be more in keeping with the circumstances of the action.

First, there is the question of what Maleger is. His name seems a contraction of Latin *male aeger* (badly sick), denoting physical

---

[1] *Distinctiones*, in PL ccx. 827.
[2] See p. 56 n. 4.
[3] *Spenser's World of Glass* (Berkeley, Cal., 1966), p. 70.
[4] 'Spenser's Imagery', p. 88. See above, p. 22 n. 2.
[5] *Distinctiones*, in PL ccx. 954.

illness. Spenser also seems to indicate this meaning in introducing
II. xi:

> What warre so cruel, or what siege so sore,
> As that which strong *affections* doe apply
> Against the *forte of reason* evermore,
> To bringe the sowle into captivity?
> Their force is fiercer through *infirmity*
> *Of the fraile flesh*, relenting to their rage,
> And exercise most bitter tyranny
> Upon the partes, brought into their bondage:
> No wretchednesse is like to sinfull vellenage.

A number of commentators[1] take this statement literally instead
of metaphorically. Literally, infirmity of the flesh is bodily illness;
metaphorically, it is incontinence or evil, or even the devil that
causes evil. The 'affections' are the forces of incontinence, and it
is harder for a person during sickness to keep his self-control. His
lack of strength gives a sense of Impotence, and his sense of frus-
tration results in Impatience, who are the two hags that assist
Maleger. The tiger, Maleger's steed, is a favourite image of flesh-
devouring cruelty, an enemy of the physical body.

Maleger's ability to rebound from the earth whenever he is
thrown against it reflects the Hercules–Antaeus story;[2] but its
meaning is probably the Elizabethan belief that recurrent attacks
of disease were caused by exhalations from the earth which
poisoned the air. In Shakespeare's *Timon of Athens*, Timon ex-
claims:

> O blessed breeding sun, draw from the earth
> Rotten humidity. Below thy sister's orb
> Infect the air. (IV. iii. 1–3)

The sister is the moon, below which is the realm of mutability,
in which all things are subject to decay. 'Rotten' should be read
as 'rotting'. The sun's rays breed vaporous exhalations from
marshy ground and fill the air with infection. This theory of
disease is ultimately traceable to Lucretius' *De Rerum Natura*, vi.
1090–1102.

---

[1] *Var.* ii. 343; Nelson, *The Poetry of Edmund Spenser*, p. 197.
[2] *Var.* ii. 347. Fulgentius and Boccaccio regard Hercules' victory over Antaeus
as an allegory of the conquest of appetite born of the flesh. Ripa says that Hercules
kills bodily appetite by holding it against his breast, the seat of wisdom, thus
raising it above the earthly things which nourished it (Kathleen Williams, *Spenser's
World of Glass*, p. 69).

That disease (Maleger) should succumb to heavenly grace (Arthur) seems to indicate a belief in faith healing. This is evident to some degree in Christian doctrine, as evidenced by prayers for those who are ill. Thus, while Arthur is curing disease of the body, Guyon is curing what Hughes calls 'a disease of the sensual nature' by disenchanting Acrasia's bower.[1] Yet Arthur's victory seems too momentous to apply to physical illness alone, and Maleger is too sinister a figure to represent merely a bout with malaria or pneumonia. As 'infirmity of the fraile flesh', he makes much harder the battle against the affections, which are themselves the seeds and first beginnings of vices (above, p. 64). But there is the further analogy of sickness of the body with sickness of the soul, when one does not necessarily give rise to the other. Such sickness may be a distemperature of one faculty or appetite, but it may extend vice to a contamination of the whole soul. In such a case, vice becomes a living death, according to Francesco Piccolomini (vi. 19; p. 351A); and such a characterization is applicable to Maleger. As the great dragon of i. xi represents spiritual death in matters of faith and doctrine, Maleger represents spiritual death from the subjection of the soul to passions and lusts of the body.

We now return to the 'standing lake' into which Maleger was cast and from which he did not return. This may well represent Alanus's third interpretation of water as primordial matter, in which case Maleger is thrust back into formlessness, as the 'old dragon' was chained in the abyss and the great boar was imprisoned in his rocky cave; for Maleger is another agent of destruction. Alanus, under *lacus*, says that a lake sometimes represents a cavern, as the lions' den in Daniel was a 'lacum leonum', and sometimes represents hell, as it is a place of depth and darkness.[2] But the lake is better explained by reference to Luke 8 : 31–3, when Christ commanded the devils to leave the man whom they possessed: 'And they besought him that he would not command them to go out into the deep. And there were a herd of swine feeding on the mountain : and they besought him that he would suffer them to enter into them. And he suffered them. Then went the devils out of the man, and entered into the swine : and the herd ran violently down a steep place into the lake, and were choked.' This is from the Authorized Version (1611). Earlier versions

---

[1] Hughes, 'Spenser's Acrasia and the Circe of the Renaissance', *Journal of the History of Ideas*, iv (1943), 398.　　　　　[2] *Distinctiones*, in *PL* ccx. 827.

give 'deep' and 'lake', except Wyclif, who writes 'hell' and 'pool'. The Greek gives 'abysson' and 'limnen', while the Vulgate gives 'abyssum' and 'stagnum'. A later Latin version, by Castalio, gives 'Tartara' and 'lacum'. Most English versions—all that I have observed—before the Authorized read 'headlong' instead of 'down a steep place'. This reading is important, for after Maleger's death the hag Impatience 'hedlong her selfe did cast into that lake' (II. xi. 47). This verbal clue repeats the image of the swine rushing 'headlong' into the lake and suggests that this is indeed the original of Spenser's 'standing lake'.

Saint Ambrose, in his *Hexameron*, I. viii. 32,[1] comments on this passage in explaining the 'abyss' of Genesis 1 : 2. In his quotation from Genesis, he gives the Vulgate's 'inanis et vacua' (without form and void) as 'invisibilis et incomposita'. He states that, in the account of the Gadarene swine, Christ showed the abyss to be a place of waters when the demons asked him not to force them to return to the abyss. He allowed them to enter a herd of swine, which ran off the cliff into a lake (*stagnum*) and were drowned, preventing the demons from having their wish. The lake was therefore 'the incomposite form and species of the world' ('erat ergo haec mundi incomposita species et forma'). In this chapter and the one before, he makes clear that he does not consider *incomposita* to mean pure potentiality; for him, first matter or *hyle* was already a tangible substance, invisible only because there was no light by which to see it. He was quoting an early Latin version of the Bible and was not himself the translator (above, p. 79).

Here, then, we find the lake as another figure of formlessness. As physical illness hastens the disintegration of the body, illness of the soul hastens the soul's disintegration likewise. The soul recedes toward deformity and ugliness and finally toward the complete extinction of that which made it divine. As a parallel with the 'old dragon' of the abyss, we might consider Maleger to be the devil, but he is the devil in a special sense. A modern psychologist might call him the agent causing disintegration of the human personality. Some implication of this kind seems to be part of Spenser's meaning. Maleger may also be 'the body of this death', as St. Paul describes original sin (below, p. 111).

There remains in Book II the sea voyage to Acrasia's isle made by Guyon, the Palmer, and the Boatman (xii. 2–37). The voyage

[1] Ambrose, in *PL* xiv. 141.

is patterned upon Ulysses' voyage to Circe's isle *after* his return
from the underworld.[1] Some of the hazards encountered by Guyon
are borrowed from a later stage of Ulysses' journey, from Circe's
isle to Calypso's isle. The Bower of Bliss seems to be a blend of
Calypso's grotto with its fountains of clear water and Circe's palace
with its artificial splendours, though a good deal of this blending
must be attributed to Tasso, whose garden of Armida Spenser
follows rather closely (*GL* xvi. 9–18). In the *Letter to Raleigh*, he
says that in Ulysses Homer presented the pattern of a virtuous
man, in Agamemnon of the *Iliad* the pattern of a good governor.
Ulysses is therefore a model to be used in *The Faerie Queene* as
exemplifying the private moral virtues. The custom of moralizing
the classical epics and myths was fairly common,[2] and Spenser
has given his own moralized version of Ulysses' trials as part of
Guyon's quest.

Guyon is accompanied by the Palmer, who acts as pilot, and the
Boatman, who plies the oars. The Boatman comes near to being
the true hero of the voyage, for he supplies the force needed to
escape the various dangers. He is pictured as old, but strong and
calm. He represents the irascible faculty at its best, disciplined
under the guidance of the rational faculty, who is the Palmer, or
prudence. One furnishes the emotional impetus to accomplish
great things; the other furnishes the wisdom to guide the impetus
aright. Together they represent the perfect union of strength and
judgement.[3] They join in avoiding or foiling the perturbations
of the concupiscible faculty, or Acrasia herself. We recall that
Acrasia's prototype Armida is explicitly identified by Tasso as the
concupiscible faculty (above, p. 25).

The voyage is indebted to Ariosto and has a good deal in common with Ruggiero's flight by boat from the palace of Alcina to
that of Logistilla. Here Ruggiero is saved by the pilot, who is also

[1] Guyon also made his voyage after emerging from the underworld of Mammon's
cave.

[2] Cf. Hermeias' allegory of the Trojan War: Troy is matter, the Trojans are
forms residing in matter; the Greeks are rational souls coming from the intelligible
world into matter, yet fighting each other about Helen, who is intelligible beauty.
(Note in Porphyry's *Select Works*, ed. Thomas Taylor the Platonist [London, 1823],
p. 293.)

[3] Cf. B. Nellish, 'The Allegory of Guyon's Voyage: An Interpretation', *ELH*
xxx (1963), 89–106. Nellish calls the Boatman 'the active principle, the very spirit of
perseverance, will, spirit, or courage' (pp. 95–6); but he does not define him as the
irascible faculty.

the oarsman. He is 'un vecchio nocchiero' ('an old pilot') who rejoices that Ruggiero is escaping the wiles of Alcina; he is both benign and discreet, wise and experienced. He praises Ruggiero for leaving Alcina before drinking of her poisoned cup, talks seriously with him about his future virtuous studies with Logistilla, and finally protects him from Alcina's pursuing ships by making him dazzle the seamen's eyes with his bright shield, which is ordinarily kept covered (above, p. 32). Here Spenser has allotted to two characters, Palmer and Boatman, the qualities which Ariosto combined into one (*OF* x. 43–50). In the 'Allegory' of Canto x Porcacchi identifies the pilot as Perfect Judgement, who always approves virtuous deeds as well done.[1]

In the latter part of this same canto, Ruggiero on his winged horse rescues Angelica from a sea monster after the manner of Perseus rescuing Andromeda. In the edition of Venice, 1570, a woodcut at the beginning of Canto x illustrates the scene. Ruggiero is attacking the monster. Angelica, nude, is tied to a rock in the distance. On the opposite shore a woman, clothed, cries out and waves her arms in anguish as a boat passes by. She has no counterpart in the text, but she might well be the source of Spenser's 'dolefull mayd' on the shore,

> That with great sorrow and sad agony
> Seemed some great misfortune to deplore,
> And lowd to them for succour called evermore. (II. xii. 27)

There is no counterpart to the 'dolefull mayd' in the *Odyssey*. This canto from Ariosto is echoed elsewhere in Spenser (below, p. 182 n. 1).

Acrasia's isle and other islands near by in the sea are 'wandring islands' which float from place to place and do not remain fixed. Spenser intends this fact as evidence of moral instability, as shown by the Boatman's warning (*FQ* II. xii. 11). To Lois Whitney's account of the various floating islands which might have influenced Spenser (*Var.* ii. 356), we may add one from Giraldus Cambrensis's *Itinerarium Cambriae*, describing such an island near Mount Snowdon, in Wales, where there are two unusual lakes:[2]

In the highest peaks of these mountains, however, are found two

---

[1] Douglas Bush, *Mythology and the Renaissance Tradition*, p. 110, identifies the Palmer as Reason and sees in him a resemblance to the pilot in Ariosto.

[2] The other lake is unusual because it contains one-eyed fish. See Giraldus's *Opera*, vol. vi, p. 135, in *Rerum Britannicarum Medii Aevi Scriptores* (1868).

lakes not unworthy of one's admiration. For one has a wandering island (*insulam erraticam*) frequently wandering to and fro (*errabundam*) by force of the impelling winds to opposite parts of the lake. Here shepherds are sometimes struck with wonder at their pasturing flocks, being suddenly translated to distant parts.

For it could have happened that a certain part of the bank, once torn away, restricted and bound together by root-bonds of willows and other shrubs naturally growing there, gradually after a time through sedimentation sustained an increase in size. And since it is impelled swiftly toward various banks by the violent force of the winds, which are found almost continually in so lofty a place, the island is not permitted to fix firm and deep tap-roots growing downward. (II. ix)

The same account is given more briefly in Giraldus's *Descriptio Kambriae*, I. v, a book which Carrie Ann Harper thinks was a source of Spenser's knowledge of history.[1] It therefore seems likely that the Welsh 'insula erratica' helped to supply details for the Wandring Islands of Spenser.

The river beneath Pollente's bridge in Book v should next receive attention. The bridge is narrow and full of dangerous trapdoors, through which the combatants on the bridge often fall into the stream beneath.[2] Pollente is accustomed to this and has a horse which is skilful in swimming, giving him an advantage when the battle is continued in the water. Nevertheless, Artegall succeeds in killing him after a fierce battle on the bridge and in the river. Afterwards, Talus breaks down the door of Pollente's castle, seizes his daughter Munera in spite of her attempts to 'buy him off', and hurls her from the same bridge into the river. He destroys the castle, repels the crowd of Pollente's followers, and enables Artegall to abolish the 'wicked custome' of charging exorbitant tolls for crossing the bridge (v. ii). Later, Britomart kills two of Dolon's sons on this same bridge (v. vi. 36–9).

Pollente is a type of the robber baron; his name signifies power (Lat. *pollens*) and suggests the arrogant exercise of unrestrained power. His ill-gotten gains are all received and stowed away by his daughter Munera (rewards), who should thereby represent avarice; but her attempt to bribe Talus with gold suggests the added meaning of bribery and political corruption. Most research

[1] C. A. Harper, *The Sources of the British Chronicle History in Spenser's* Faerie Queene (Philadelphia, 1910).

[2] This bridge is reminiscent of the 'knife-edge' bridge Al-Sirat across the abyss of hell, in Muslim mythology (*Var.* v. 213).

on this episode has concerned the political situation and the attempts to prevent the corruption of public officials in sixteenth-century England and Ireland.[1] Such a meaning is undoubtedly present in this most political of all the books of *The Faerie Queene*; but it does not help us very much in interpreting the moral allegory.

We may first approach the river and bridge through their sources in Ariosto, for they are unquestionably derived from the bridge of Rodomonte in the *Orlando Furioso*. This proud Saracen knight is perhaps the villain of the epic, which concludes with his death at the hands of Ruggiero. His toll-bridge was constructed across 'a foaming river' (*OF* xxix. 33) in order to finance a memorial to the virtuous Isabel, whom he had mistakenly slain. It was six feet wide, with no protective railings. He first fights the crazed and naked Orlando; both fall into the flood and both escape without fatality (xxix. 40-8). He next fights Brandimart, the beloved of Fleur-de-lys. Again both riders and their horses are precipitated into the river, where Rodomonte's knowledge of the currents and shallows gives him the victory; but, with unexpected chivalry, he spares Brandimart's life at the request of Fleur-de-lys (xxxi. 65-76). Finally, he encounters Bradamante, a female knight, and is overthrown on his own bridge. Chagrined at defeat by a woman, he releases his prisoners and retires to a forest cell; yet perversely he falls in love with his conqueror and seeks a way to win her love (xxxv. 34-56).

The battle between Artegall and Pollente utilizes the first two of Rodomonte's battles of the bridge: the encounter on the bridge, the fall into the river, the swimming contest of both horses and men. But, whereas Rodomonte's battles end without fatality, Pollente is beheaded by a blow from Artegall's sword as he tries to climb out of the river:

> But Artegall pursewd him still so neare,
> With bright Chrysaor in his cruell hand,
> That, as his head he gan a little reare
> Above the brincke, to tread upon the land,
> He smote it off, that tumbling on the strand
> It bit the earth for very fell despight,
> And gnashed with his teeth, as if he band
> High God, whose goodnesse he despaired quight,
> Or curst the hand which did that vengeance on him dight.
>
> (v. ii. 18)

[1] *Var.* v. 170, 173-4.

His 'blasphemous head' is erected on a pole as a warning to others who may be tempted to use great power unjustly (stanza 19).

The manner of Pollente's death takes a hint from the death of Rodomonte at the very end of the *Orlando Furioso*. Baffled by his frustrated love for Bradamante, he challenges her newly wedded husband Ruggiero to single combat. He is overthrown by Ruggiero but refuses to yield, upon which Ruggiero stabs him:

> Alle squallide ripe d'Acheronte,
> Sciolta dal corpo più freddo che ghiaccio,
> Bestemmiando fuggì l'alma sdegnosa,
> Che fu sì altiera al mondo e sì orgogliosa.   (xlvi. 140)

(To the squalid banks of Acheron, freed from the body already cold as ice, loudly swearing, fled the angry soul that was in the world so haughty and so proud.)

The details of Rodomonte's death appear also in the deaths of the Saracen brothers, Cymochles and Pyrochles, at the hands of Prince Arthur. When Cymochles is first wounded.

> Horribly then he gan to rage and rayle,
> Cursing his gods, and him selfe damning deepe.
> (*FQ* II. viii. 37)

When the fatal stroke cleaves his head,

> He, tombling downe on ground,
> Breathd out his ghost, which to th'infernall shade
> Fast flying, there eternall torment found
> For all the sinnes wherewith his lewd life did abound.
> (stanza 45)

When Pyrochles is disarmed and held prostrate on the ground, he

> Did not once move, nor upward cast his eye,
> For vile disdaine and rancour, which did gnaw
> His hart in twaine with sad melancholy,
> As one that loathed life, and yet despysed to dye.
> (stanza 50)

He is offered his life if he will yield, but he harshly refuses, upon which the Prince beheads him (stanza 52). So Rodomonte refused to yield and forced Ruggiero to kill him. In each case the victor had wrestled the loser to the ground and lay upon his body to keep him from rising.

Corflambo, who swears by 'Mahoune', is thereby identified as a Saracen. His death at the hands of Prince Arthur is likewise reminiscent of Rodomonte's death:

> But ere his hand he could recure againe,
> To ward his bodie from the balefull stound,
> He [Arthur] smote at him with all his might and maine,
> So furiously, that ere he wist, he found
> His head before him tombling on the ground.
> The whiles his babling tongue did yet blaspheme
> And curse his god, that did him so confound;
> The whiles his life ran foorth in bloudie streame,
> His soule descended downe into the Stygian reame.
>
> (IV. viii. 45)

Spenser's several examples all show resemblances to each other and to Ariosto, demonstrating how great an impression the death of Rodomonte had made upon him. The violence, the loud blasphemies which seemed to continue even after death, the flight of the soul to the rivers of hell—all these details derive from the short statement of Ariosto. Where Rodomonte goes to the River Acheron, Corflambo goes to the River Styx. Pollente, whose death closely resembles that of Corflambo, was slain in his own river, which becomes his river of death and offers a tentative parallel to Styx and Acheron in the other two accounts.[1]

Spenser's descriptive details of Pollente's river are few but significant. The river is described by Florimell's dwarf Dony as 'both swift and dangerous deepe withall' (v. ii. 8). When Munera is cast into the river by Talus, she is drowned 'in the durty mud' (stanza 27). When Artegall and Pollente fight in the river,

> Ne ought the water cooled their whot bloud,
> But rather in them kindled choler new.   (stanza 13)

This is the most significant detail of all. The property of the water in this river is to kindle and enhance wrath, not to assuage it; consequently, it is a River of Anger.

In Dante's *Inferno*, the River Styx is the place of punishment for the angry, who constantly fight and belabour each other in the mud and filth of the stream. The waters of Styx flow from the River Acheron, which is the first stream to be reached as one

---

[1] Upton cites the forester's death in *FQ* III. v. 22 as an imitation of the death of Rodomonte (*Var.* iii. 245).

enters hell and over which Charon's boat is the only means of passage. In this respect Dante follows Virgil, who pictures Acheron as 'turbidus hic coeno' ('turbid here with mud'; *Aeneid*, vi. 296), with a shore 'informi limo' ('formless slime'; 416), and as 'tristique palus inamabilis unda' ('a hateful marsh with sad wave') which is near the winding River Styx (438–9). Dante, in the *Inferno*, pictures Acheron as a 'trista riviera' ('sad-river'; iii. 78) leading to eternal darkness (87), a 'livida palude' ('livid marsh'; 98) with brown waves (118). As Dante enters the Circle of the Avaricious, he passes a depression, 'lacca . . . dolente ripa' ('lake . . . dolorous shore'; vii. 16–17) and on the other side of the circle finds a boiling spring of black water that pours down through a cleft to a lower circle and there forms the Stygian marsh or lake when it has descended 'al piè delle maligne piazze grige' ('to the foot of the malignant grey places'; 108).

At this point, it is well to remember that Dante is still standing in the Circle of the Avaricious (and Prodigal), by the boiling fountain, and is overlooking the waters of Styx some distance below, in the Circle of the Angry. Thus, these waters are associated with both circles. For Spenser, they are suitable vehicles of punishment for both Munera (avarice) and Pollente (arrogant anger). The 'durty mud' of Spenser's river is a feature of Virgil's Acheron and of Dante's Styx, where souls victimized by anger fight each other in the mire (110). These souls have surrendered to anger (116); the smoke from its fire makes them sad or sullen ('tristi'), as they had been in life (121). They are choked by the filth of the river as anger had choked their rational processes in life (129).

As Phlegyas ferries Dante and Virgil across the 'sucide onde' ('filthy waves'; viii. 10), they are accosted by Filippo Argenti, 'quei fu al mondo persona orgogliosa' ('who was in the world a proud person') and whose shade is still 'furiosa' in the underworld (46–8). Virgil makes this comment and adds: 'How many up there think themselves great kings, that shall lie here like swine in the mire!' (viii. 49–50). Dante's emphasis is upon arrogant wielders of power who freely indulge their anger towards others; these illustrate the same vice as Rodomonte and Pollente. The reader should notice that the souls of Rodomonte and Filippo Argenti are severally described as *orgogliosa*. What this would convey to Spenser is clear from his giant Orgoglio, who is angry, arrogant, violent, tyrannous, and 'puffed up' with pride (*FQ* i. viii).

While Spenser's Munera is guilty of avarice, her principal crime is bribery, the corruption of public officials by the use of money. Dante holds this crime in particular abhorrence and punishes its practitioners with immersion in a river of boiling pitch (xxi. 17). Across this river is a great bridge, from which the guardian demons hurl sinners down into the black waves (43). The bridge is repeatedly stressed (37, 64, 70, 89), and the difficulties of crossing it in the face of demons may have allied it in Spenser's mind with Ariosto's bridge. Likewise, the merciless cruelty of the demons towards the sinners may in part account for Talus's mutilation of Lady Munera before he hurled her from the bridge (*FQ* v. ii. 26). The boiling pitch of Dante's stream is sufficiently like the boiling mud of Styx and the formless slime of Acheron (Virgil) to unite all these viscous rivers in Spenser's mind and to cause their union into one river where several forms of crime are punished.

Pollente's river and bridge appear later in *The Faerie Queene*, v. vi. 36–40, occupied this time by two sons of Dolon, whose art was to entrap unsuspicious travellers by courteous words, then to destroy them by such devices as the trapdoor which dropped the guest-room bed into a dungeon (stanza 27).[1] Fortunately, Britomart was not in the bed when it dropped, and she thus escaped capture. The next day, when she sees Dolon's sons on the bridge, she charges them, hurling one into the stream and killing the other with her spear. Her victory is reminiscent of Bradamante's overthrow of Rodomonte. The allegory here may involve two more of Dante's infernal bodies of water: Phlegethon, the river of blood in which murderers are punished (xii. 47), and the lake of filth in which deceitful flatterers are immersed (xviii. 104–36). Britomart's victory would indicate that true chastity is invulnerable to flattery and to violence—the same meaning is represented by the Lady in Milton's *Comus*.

If Spenser's blending of these lakes and rivers into one seems too improbable, we should recall Dante's explanation that the four rivers Acheron, Styx, Phlegethon, and Cocytus are all one, proceeding from the tears of a great statue in Crete and utilizing the same water in different levels of hell as it flows downward

---

[1] In *Arthur of Little Britain*, at the house of Sir Robert the Scot, Arthur's bed falls through the floor, putting him and his squire into a dungeon. An ill-favoured 'villain' whom Arthur has befriended rescues them from the dungeon (ch. 60).

(xiv. 97–120). To add the river of pitch and the flatterers' lake of filth would not do violence to Dante's central conception. The rivers of the *Inferno* are really one stream in which or beside which are punished five specific sins: avarice, anger, bribery, flattery, murder; and apparently these are the five sins which are punished in Pollente's river.

The other two uses of water in Book v of *The Faerie Queene* concern the erosion of the land by the sea in some places and the building up of land by sedimentation in others. The egalitarian giant, the 'leveller', considers the eminence of the land in some places an instance of guilty inequality, whereas Artegall pronounces the law of compensation: things lost in one place are restored in another (v. ii. 37–9). In Canto iv he is called upon to decide a dispute by these principles. Bracidas's island has gradually been washed away and added to his brother Amidas's island, but a chest of treasure belonging to Amidas's wife has been lost at sea and washed up on Bracidas's shore. Amidas claims it, but Artegall pronounces that what the sea brings belongs to the finder.

The meaning of these passages seems not to go beyond the explicit one: the mutability of all things, and the law of compensation. We may note the emotional response to these figures in Shakespeare's Sonnet 64:

> When I have seen the hungry ocean gain
> Advantage on the kingdom of the shore,
> And the firm soil win of the watery main,
> Increasing store with loss and loss with store.

Again, King Henry IV, deserted by Northumberland, cries out:

> Oh God! that one might read the book of fate,
> And see the revolution of the times
> Make mountains level, and the continent,
> Weary of solid firmness, melt itself
> Into the sea! And other times to see
> The beachy girdle of the ocean
> Too wide for Neptune's hips, how chances mock,
> And changes fill the cup of alteration,
> With divers liquors!   (*2 Henry IV*, III. i. 45–53)

Shakespeare stresses the feeling of weary puzzlement with the constant mutations of the world, the transiency of life, and the unpredictability of the future. Spenser stresses the same theme of mutability, the constant change and flow of nature, without the emotional overtones of pessimism. In this regard, he is perhaps more in accord with the source of the image in Ovid's *Metamorphoses*, xv. 262 f., which Golding translates as follows:

> Even so have places oftentymes exchanged theyr estate,
> For I have seene it sea which was substanciall ground alate,
> Ageine where sea was, I have seene the same become dry lond.
> (xv. 278–80)[1]

Since Ovid's lines occur in the midst of a long list of changes illustrating the mutability of things, Spenser's lines may be taken as an advance statement of his theme in the 'Cantos of Mutabilitie'.

Finally, we come to what may be called Spenser's geographical allegories of English and Irish rivers. The first allegorizes the union of the Thames and the Medway rivers at a point east of London (*FQ* IV. xi). Here Spenser takes obvious delight in marshalling a vast array of classical sea-gods, river-spirits from abroad, and similar spirits from English and Irish rivers. His four stanzas naming the fifty daughters of Nereus are made up of proper names and bits of description. Since Spenser refers to the marriage of Peleus and Thetis in VII. vii. 12, it seems likely that his source for his pageant of sea-deities is the poem by Jean Lemaire de Belges on the subject of this marriage. Jean lists a sizeable pantheon of ancient deities, accompanied by such personifications as Discord, Labour, Envy, and others.[2]

A similar allegory, lacking the pomp and display of the first, is found in the Faunus episode of *The Faerie Queene*, VII. vi. 38–55, which uses the myth of Actaeon as a vehicle for the jealousies and unions of several Irish streams.

Spenser obviously enjoys these exercises in mythologizing after the manner of Virgil and Ovid, particularly the celebrating of the junction of two streams as a marriage or union. The lost 'Epithalamium Thamesis' must have been such a poem. But there seems to be no moral allegory behind the physical allegory. Characters associated with these river-marriages, such as Proteus,

---

[1] For the passages from Ovid and Golding, and for a related passage in John Gower's *Vox Clamantis*, see H. E. Rollins's notes to Sonnet 64 in the *Variorum Shakespeare*.

[2] In his *Illustrations de Gaule, et Singularitez de Troye*, bk. i, ch. 28.

Marinell, Nature, and Mutability, have a significance for the moral allegory; but the events themselves seem to be constructed as personifications of the landscape and its physical features, with no moral purpose to be served.

The spring by Mount Acidale (VI. x. 7) will be discussed in Chapter IX. Another landscape feature of *The Faerie Queene*, the garden, will be discussed in Chapter XI.

V

The Moral Allegory of Holiness

WE turn now from general considerations to the analysis of individual books. Book I, the Legend of Holiness, affords a very interesting study in the use of derived materials. Basically, Redcross and Una derive from Malory's account of Beaumains (or Gareth) and Linet, particularly in Spenser's account of the beginning of the quest, in his *Letter to Raleigh* (above, p. 34). However, the damsel's scorn is omitted, and Una's character is more attractive than that of her prototype. On the level of external allegory, the characters and the narrative are largely imitated from the Revelation of St. John. On the level of internal allegory, the action is mental and concerns the struggle between faith and doubt, or between true and false doctrine, in the mind of an individual person.

SPENSER AND THE REVELATION OF ST. JOHN

It has long been recognized that Spenser made numerous borrowings from the Revelation of St. John in Book I of *The Faerie Queene*. The *Variorum* edition conveniently lists those observed by Upton and other commentators. In a useful study, Josephine Waters Bennett has suggested that the Revelation not only furnished Spenser with particular passages but largely determined the structure of Book I.[1] Her important contribution is not the discovery of new borrowings, though she observes several, but her exposition of the Revelation from the Protestant point of view. From several English commentaries and from glosses in the Geneva Bible, she shows that the latter half of the Revelation was interpreted in the sixteenth century as an allegory of the Protestant conflict with the Roman Church, and concludes that this fact has an important bearing on Book I, which is now generally believed to involve a similar allegory.

[1] *The Evolution of* The Faerie Queene (1942), ch. ix.

To be convincing, Mrs. Bennett's suggestion needs the support of more numerous and impressive parallels than have yet been adduced. Also, the pattern or plan of Spenser's borrowings is left rather vague. In considering these, we should remember that the Revelation itself borrows very extensively from the Old Testament and that commentators regularly noted the relationship of various texts in different parts of the Bible.[1] It is not enough, then, to consider the Revelation alone in studying Spenser's imagery; one must examine other Biblical passages to which he would have been referred. In addition to doing this, I have examined the Latin commentaries of a number of the Church Fathers with a view to discovering any significant interpretations which may throw light upon Spenser's allegory.[2] In a recent study of sixteenth-century Protestant polemics, D. Douglas Waters has extended the usual political interpretation of Duessa as the Roman Church or papacy to include 'the pope's Mass' or 'Mistress Missa' as a personified object of satire.[3]

The latter half of the Revelation, from chapter 12 on, presents a conflict between the forces of evil and the forces of good in connection with events preceding the Last Judgement. The forces of evil are represented by the Great Dragon, the Beast from the Sea, the False Prophet, and the Babylonian harlot; the forces of good by the Woman clothed with the Sun, the Archangel Michael (usually interpreted as Christ, the Bride of the Lamb, and Christ) himself. There is a further contrast between the cities of Babylon and Jerusalem, signifying the congregations of the wicked and of the good, respectively. All of these find parallels in Spenser's allegory and exercise a controlling influence upon it. Though he has changed his characters and situations to accord with the conventions of medieval romance, they are clearly traceable to their Biblical prototypes as interpreted in the commentaries. Besides the political allegory of the conflict between the Roman and the reformed Churches, he has used the moral allegory of the restoration to Eden as representative of man's spiritual regeneration.

[1] For the reader's convenience I quote textual and numerical references from the Authorized Version (1611), after making sure that the significant phrases were available in earlier versions.

[2] These are conveniently listed under 'Apocalypse' in the indexes to Migne's *Patrologia Latina* ccxviii. 667.

[3] *Duessa as Theological Satire*, Columbia, Mo., 1970.

To begin with an admitted parallel, we know that Spenser patterned Duessa after the Babylonian harlot or 'great whore' of Revelation 17. Duessa is called a 'scarlot whore' (viii. 29); like the harlot, she bears a golden cup in her hand (viii. 14, 25) and rides upon a seven-headed beast. The stripping of Duessa after her champion Orgoglio is killed is traced by Upton to the statement in Revelation 17: 16 that the harlot shall be made desolate and naked; and Mrs. Bennett thinks Spenser's details derive from Ariosto.[1] For another significant parallel, however, we may turn to the denunciation of Babylon in Isaiah 47, where we find not only the stripping but also the sorceries and enchantments which Spenser attributes to Duessa:

Come down, and sit in the dust, O virgin daughter of Babylon; sit on the ground: there is no throne, O daughter of the Chaldeans: for thou shalt no more be called tender and delicate.
. . . Uncover thy locks, make bare the leg, uncover the thigh, pass over the rivers.
Thy nakedness shall be uncovered, yea, thy shame shall be seen . . .
But these two things shall come to thee in a moment in one day, the loss of children, and widowhood: they shall come upon thee in their perfection for the multitude of thy sorceries, and for the great abundance of thine enchantments. . . .
Stand now with thine enchantments, and with the multitude of thy sorceries, wherein thou hast laboured from thy youth.

(verses 1–3, 9, 12)

The unpleasant details of Duessa's appearance (viii. 46–8) are in part drawn from Ariosto (above, p. 59), in part from a similar passage in Isaiah 3, where the prophet declares that God will strip away the finery of the daughters of Jerusalem because of their pride and wantonness:

Therefore the Lord will smite with a scab the crown of the head of the daughters of Zion, and the Lord will discover their secret parts. . . .
And it shall come to pass, that instead of sweet smell there shall be stink; and instead of a girdle a rent; and instead of well set hair baldness; and instead of a stomacher a girding of sackcloth; and burning instead of beauty. (verses 17, 24)

---

[1] *Evolution of* The Faerie Queene, p. 116.

Spenser has expanded the description; but the scabby head, baldness, and foul smell appear to be reminiscences from this passage.

The figure of Babylon seems also to have been Spenser's major
source for the character of Lucifera, who dwells in the House of
Pride. As I have shown elsewhere, her name and some hints for
her character are drawn from Natalis Comes;[1] but her character
is elaborated far beyond these hints. As the primary source for
Duessa is the Babylonian harlot, the type of lust, so the primary
source for Lucifera is the 'daughter of Babylon', the type of pride.
For each of his two characters Spenser draws details from both
images of Babylon, but in one case his emphasis is upon lust,
while in the other it is upon pride.

The word 'Lucifera' is obviously the feminine form of 'Lucifer',
a name which occurs only once in the Scriptures, where it is applied to Nebuchadnezzar, the king of Babylon (Isa. 14: 12). Considering 'Lucifer' as a name applied to the king of Babylon, it is
logical that 'Lucifera', the feminine form of his name, should be
applied to the feminine personification of his city, so widely
known as an example of pride. Spenser must have known the
usual identification of Lucifer with Satan;[2] but, granting this
identification, it was still appropriate that Babylon should be personified as Lucifera, Satan's feminine counterpart. In the medieval
commentaries, just as Jerusalem symbolizes the Church, the bride
of Christ, so Babylon symbolizes the congregation of the wicked,
the spouse of the Devil.[3] It is therefore quite fitting that Satan
should be Lucifera's companion as she rides forth in her chariot
(iv. 36).

We may first observe how the figure of Babylon determines the
imagery of Lucifera seated upon her throne, with a dragon beneath her feet. In Revelation 12 the Great Dragon is expelled from
heaven, dragging a third part of the stars with him. Since he is
referred to in verse 9 as 'that old serpent, called the Devil, and
Satan', his fall is assumed to be the same as those of Satan (Luke
10: 18) and Lucifer. Further identification of Lucifer with the
Great Dragon is suggested by Jeremiah 51: 34, 'Nebuchadrezzar
the king of Babylon hath devoured me . . . he hath swallowed me

[1] 'Spenser's Lucifera and Philotime', *Modern Language Notes*, lix (1944), 413–15.
[2] Gregory, *Moralium*, xxiii. vi; Haymo, PL cxvi. 791–2; Primasius, PL lxviii.
898D.
[3] See below, p. 107.

up like a dragon'. I suggest that Lucifera's dragon is one of several incarnations in which the devil appears in *The Faerie Queene*, and that this comes about through the identification of Lucifer with the king of Babylon and with the Great Dragon, or Satan. Lucifera seated above her dragon is basically the same image as Duessa seated upon her beast, both stemming from the Babylonian harlot and the beast of Revelation 17. Bishop Haymo explains of this beast that it is really the devil, while the harlot represents all sinners, and that just as the Church is founded upon Christ, so the congregation of the wicked is founded upon the Devil; hence Babylon is presented as mounted upon the beast.[1] Spenser identifies this beast with the Great Dragon by drawing from the latter descriptive details for Duessa's beast (vii. 18). Lucifera's beast is also a 'dreadfull dragon', and Lucifera herself represents 'all the multitude of the proud', as Augustine interprets the Babylonian harlot.[2] Her personal appearance is imitated from the harlot. She is adorned 'with royall robes and gorgeous array. . . . In glistring gold and perelesse pretious stone' (iv. 8), while the harlot is 'arrayed in purple and scarlet colour, and decked with gold and precious stones and pearls' (Rev. 17: 4). Since purple and scarlet are traditional colours of royal robes, the resemblance is apparent. However, Spenser calls her a 'mayden queene' in imitation of the 'virgin daughter of Babylon' in Isaiah 47: 1, and her throne may be a reminiscence of the same verse.

The figure of the Babylonian harlot undergoes another transformation in Spenser's procession of the seven deadly sins (iv. 16–38), where Lucifera, herself representing pride, rides forth in a chariot drawn by six beasts, whose riders are the six other deadly sins. We have just seen that Spenser identifies the harlot's beast with the seven-headed dragon of Revelation 12; and concerning the dragon several commentators advance a moral interpretation. Richard of St. Victor identifies the dragon's seven heads with the seven deadly sins, and the ten horns with the 'Decalogue of the impious', the reverse of the Ten Commandments.[3] St. Bruno gives the following account:

For the great red dragon is the devil, who in the shape of a serpent first deceived man and who now appears red because of the blood of the martyrs, which he ceases not to shed. Here, however, he is said to have seven heads; namely the seven capital sins, which were born from

[1] *PL* cxvii. 1142C. [2] *PL* xxxv. 2449. [3] *PL* cxcvi. 799D.

Mother Pride, and from which as from beginnings all other sins are born. For these [seven] are vainglory, envy, wrath, sloth, avarice, gluttony, and lust. The ten horns are indeed all other sins, which are derived from these heads and which, since they are many, he seeks to express by that number in which all numbers are contained. For number does not progress beyond ten, but that number revolved upon itself completes all other numbers.[1]

The fact that Lucifera's appearance is drawn from the Babylonian harlot suggests that her advisers and their beasts may in some way be indebted to the beastly heads which represent the deadly sins. For the grotesque details of his procession, Spenser has used other sources,[2] but the inception of his idea of connecting the harlot with the deadly sins may well have come from the commentaries, where the connection was already made. Perhaps he may also have recalled Dante's transformation of the harlot's beast in Canto 32 of the *Purgatorio*, where the chariot which represents the Church puts forth seven beastly heads, usually interpreted to mean the seven deadly sins. Upon the chariot seat appears a shameless harlot, and beside her a giant who exchanges lustful kisses with her (the papacy and Philip IV of France).

Forgetting Dante's political allegory, we may note his remarkable transformation of the imagery of Revelation 17. The harlot is the same, but her beast is the monstrous perversion of a chariot. It is still a chariot, but from it grow the seven heads of the Biblical beast, representing the seven deadly sins. We can see how this image may have suggested a chariot for Lucifera, drawn by the other deadly sins.

If Spenser used Dante's imagery as a source for Lucifera, he may also have used it as a source for Duessa, since both are imitated from the Babylonian harlot. Duessa's beast is taken directly from the Biblical images, but her companion Orgoglio may well have been suggested by the giant in Dante. The exchange of lustful kisses suggests the amour of Duessa and Orgoglio, to which there is no specific Biblical parallel; the harlot of Revelation 17 does not have a masculine companion.[3]

Besides drawing details from the harlot's beast and the Great

---

[1] *PL* clxv. 668A.   [2] *Var.* i. 217–23, 404–16.

[3] See below, p. 207. We may also note that Alciatus in Emblem 6 pictures the harlot Babylon mounted on her seven-headed beast and bearing the golden cup in her hand, under the emblem 'Ficta Religio' ('Feigned Religion') (*Emblemata* [Lyons, 1614], p. 45). Minos's commentary is *not* directed against the papacy.

Dragon, Spenser has used the Beast from the Sea in Revelation 13 as a source for the wounding of Duessa's beast by Prince Arthur.[1] The Beast from the Sea was regularly identified by the commentators as Antichrist, the false Christ who should appear in the last days to persecute Christians and draw them from the true faith (Matt. 24: 24, 1 John 2: 18). Augustine thinks he represents the pagan rulers who formerly persecuted the Church but in later times represents the heretics within the Church.[2] Richard of St. Victor identifies him with the 'cruel princes of the pagans'.[3] These are perhaps sufficient hints to equate him with the 'Paynim King' against whom the Faerie Queene is to fight a great battle near the end of Spenser's epic (xi. 7). Sixteenth-century Protestants interpreted Antichrist as the Pope of Rome and the wounded head of the Beast from the Sea as the effect of the Protestant Reformation. The Beast received his authority from the Great Dragon, or the Devil (Rev. 13: 2), and his demand that all peoples should worship him was taken to mean the claim of papal supremacy.[4]

In Revelation 13, following the Beast from the Sea there emerges the Beast from the Land, which has two horns in imitation of a lamb. This beast is later identified as the False Prophet (19: 20), whom I take to be the original of Archimago. That enchanter's name may be interpreted either as Arch-magician or Arch-image. In both interpretations it is applicable to the False Prophet, who causes people to worship the Beast from the Sea by drawing down fire from heaven and performing other strange enchantments. He fashions an image of the Beast and insists that all must worship it; those who refuse are persecuted and killed. He causes the image to speak as though alive and works many other miracles to seduce men from the true faith. His very appearance is a hypocritical disguise, imitating the appearance of the Lamb of God and of the true apostles who were sent forth 'as lambs among wolves' (Luke 10: 3). He is the fulfilment of Christ's warning against 'false prophets, which come to you in sheep's clothing, but inwardly they are ravening wolves' (Matt. 7: 15) and of St. Paul's caution against 'false apostles, deceitful workers, transforming themselves into the apostles of Christ' (2 Cor. 11: 13).

---

[1] Cf. Bennett, *Evolution of* The Faerie Queene, pp. 109, 114.
[2] *PL* xxxv. 2442. [3] *PL* cxcvi. 818c.
[4] See Jan van der Noot, *The Theatre for Voluptuous Worldlings* (1569), f. 24; also Bennett, *Evolution of* The Faerie Queene, pp. 110–12.

In explaining the political allegory students of Spenser have found difficulty in attaching Archimago's activities to any one person and have generally concluded that he represents the subversive activities of the Catholic party in general. This multiple interpretation coincides closely with that usually given of the False Prophet. St. Martin identifies him with 'the multitude of the disciples of Antichrist',[1] Richard of St. Victor with 'the chorus of false teachers';[2] and others give similar explanations. Van der Noot declares that he represents 'all manner of false prophets and ungodly teachers', and that in the sixteenth century these are the friars, monks, canons, and priests of the Roman Church.[3] In using Archimago to represent all this group, Spenser is imitating the Revelation, where one False Prophet is used to personify the many 'false prophets' who are foretold in earlier books of the Bible.[4]

Certain of Archimago's activities are suggested by those of the False Prophet. Both fashion false images as a means of deception, the False Prophet deceiving mankind with an image of Antichrist, Archimago deceiving Redcross with an image of Una. As the False Prophet puts on the disguise of a lamb in imitation of Christ, so Archimago disguises himself in the armour of Redcross, the true follower of Christ. Archimago's imprisonment in the dungeon (I. xii. 36) and subsequent escape therefrom (II. i. 1) are probably suggested by the False Prophet's imprisonment in the pit and lake of fire and his supposed emergence therefrom with Satan and Antichrist shortly before the second resurrection.[5]

Mrs. Bennett has sought to identify Una with the Woman clothed with the Sun (Rev. 12), pointing out that her flight into the wilderness parallels Una's retreat into the wilds.[6] Since the Woman is persecuted by the Great Dragon, who is finally thrown out of heaven by Michael,[7] we have a close parallel with Una's exile from Eden until Redcross overthrows the dragon who has usurped her place there. The Woman clothed with the Sun is variously identified as the Virgin Mary, the mother of Christ,[8] and as the Church,

---

[1] *PL* ccix. 398–9.   [2] *PL* cxcvi. 853A.

[3] *Theatre for Voluptuous Worldlings*, ff. 33–4.

[4] See Matt. 24: 11, 24; 2 Pet. 2: 1; 1 John 4: 1.

[5] The False Prophet will presumably reappear in the reign of Antichrist before the second resurrection. Most commentators agree that Antichrist will reappear though the Revelation mentions only the return of Satan at that time. Cf. Haymo, *PL* cxvii. 1187C.   [6] *Evolution of* The Faerie Queene, p. 109.

[7] Most commentators assume that here Michael allegorically represents Christ.

[8] See Haymo, *PL* cxvii. 1081–3; Augustine, *PL* xxxv. 2441.

the bride of Christ;[1] some commentators also identify her with the bride in Canticles.[2] It is important to realize that the Woman clothed with the Sun, the bride of the Lamb in Revelation 19, and the bride in Canticles were considered to be the same, for Spenser has drawn details for Una from all three sources. Also, since Una is the antitype to Duessa, the allegory identifies her with the Woman clothed with the Sun. In summarizing the allegory of the Revelation, Richard of St. Victor comments as follows:

> These are two cities, one of the devil, the other of God, dissident from the very beginning, never having peace between themselves. These are two women, of whom we read that one is clothed with the sun and that the other sits upon a scarlet beast. For the total mass of the evildoers and the universal sum of the good are two cities and two women. They are cities because they are enriched by the numerous multitude of their citizens. They are women because, being coupled to their husbands, Babylon to the devil and Jerusalem to Christ, they are made fruitful of a multiple progeny.[3]

The antithesis between the Babylonian harlot and the Woman clothed with the Sun suggests that, as Duessa is copied from the former, Una may be indebted to the latter, who is here definitely identified as the bride of Christ.

When Una appears unveiled for her bridal day (xii. 21–3), Spenser's description draws upon the Biblical images. Upton has noticed that the whiteness of her raiment recalls Revelation 19: 8, and that the phrase 'withouten spot' comes from Canticles 4: 7, 'Thou art all fair, my love; there is no spot in thee'. Una's 'blazing brightness' and 'sunshyny face' may owe something to the Woman clothed with the Sun. Her earlier adventures show a significant indebtedness to Canticles 5, in which occurs the only reference to the bride's having worn a veil:

> I opened to my beloved; but my beloved had withdrawn himself, and was gone . . . I sought him, but I could not find him; I called him, but he gave me no answer.
> The watchmen that went about the city found me, they smote me, they wounded me; the keepers of the walls took away my veil from me.
>
> (verses 6–7)

---

[1] Ibid. See also Primasius, *PL* lxviii. 872–4; Martin, *PL* ccix. 365; Bruno, *PL* clxv. 667–70; Anselm, *PL* clxii. 1543–5.

[2] Through her identity with the Virgin. See Rupert, *PL* clxviii. 889; Alanus de Insulis, *PL* ccx. 95B; Paschasius, *PL* cxx. 106D; Bernard, *PL* clxxxiii. 1009D; Bruno, *PL* clxv. 717B.   [3] *PL* cxcvi. 887B.

Here may be an important suggestion for Spenser's plot. The bride awakes after dreaming that she hears the lover's voice and opens the door, but she finds that he is gone, upon which she goes out to seek him and inquire for him. This affords a parallel to Redcross's desertion of Una while she slept, her sad awakening, and her journey in search of him (ii. 6–8). The bride's encounter with the watchmen suggests an incident of Una's journey, Sansloy's attempt upon her chastity, when he uses force upon her and snatches away her veil (vi. 4–6).

We have now demonstrated Una's indebtedness to the bride of Christ, who figuratively represents the Church. This coincides with the usual interpretation of Una as the Church of England, as opposed to the false Church of Rome; more particularly, Una represents Elizabeth in her capacity as head of the Church. Furthermore, the bride is identified with the Virgin Mary, who also represents the Church, a fact which accounts for the stress laid upon Una's virginity and which fits in well with England's love for the Virgin Queen. The use of Una to represent the Church may also explain her identification with truth, since Paul tells us that the Church is 'the pillar and ground of the truth' (1 Tim. 3 : 15).

Only one major character remains to be interpreted, the Redcross Knight, who, if Spenser has followed consistently the pattern borrowed from the Revelation, should correspond to the figure of Christ. The picture of Christ in Revelation 19 is that of a knight, mounted upon a white charger, attacking and overcoming in turn the Babylonian harlot, Antichrist, the False Prophet, and the Great Dragon. Spenser's identification of his knight is made in the second stanza of the first canto. The knight wears upon his breast a 'bloodie crosse', suggested by the Biblical knight 'clothed with a vesture dipped in blood' (verse 13). Spenser says of his knight: 'Right *faithfull true* he was in deede and word.' In the Revelation, the knight 'was called Faithful and True, and in righteousness doth he make war' (verse 11). Also, this Biblical knight 'had a name written, that no man knew, but he himself' (verse 12). Following this lead, Spenser withholds from the reader for a time the name of the Redcross Knight.

As Spenser tells us in his *Letter to Raleigh*, the arms of Redcross are the 'whole armour of God' mentioned in Ephesians 6. In this account the shield is the shield of faith. Elsewhere Spenser refers to it as a 'sunne-bright shield' (xi. 40). This phrase recalls Prince

Arthur's shield of diamond, which is so bright as to dazzle Orgo-glio and which is called a 'sunshiny shield' (viii. 19–20). Dodge suggests the indebtedness of this shield to the magical shield in the *Orlando Furioso* (xxii. 81–6), because they similarly dazzle op-posing fighters;[1] but Ariosto's shield is not of diamond. For this feature Spenser is probably indebted to the diamond shield in Tasso,[2] who identifies it in his explanation of the allegory as 'the special safeguard of the Lord God'. It is likely that both Spenser and Tasso had in mind Psalm 84: 11, 'For the Lord God is a sun and shield', and that Spenser recalls the Biblical image in both the silver shield of Redcross and the diamond shield of Arthur.

In studying the pattern of Spenser's allegory as adapted from the Revelation, we should remember that the victories of the knight on the white horse over the harlot, Antichrist, the False Prophet, and the Great Dragon, as well as the subsequent mar-riage of the Lamb, all accompany the first resurrection, which is to be followed by the millennium. It is important to bear this fact in mind in order to grasp Spenser's meaning. For the general dis-position of the medieval Church was to follow St. Augustine in denying the existence of the millennium as a period of corporal delights at some time in the future. Rather it refers to the present happiness of those who have been baptized into Christ's church. Augustine interprets Christ's words in John 5: 24–5 and 5: 28–9 as referring to the two resurrections; the statement that 'the hour is coming, and now is' indicates that the first resurrection has already begun and must therefore be a rising from spiritual death through belief in Christ. Augustine is uncertain whether the second resurrection, in which bodies as well as souls shall rise, would actually occur in 1000 A.D., or whether the millennial figure is used as a round number, the solid quadrate or cube of 10, signi-fying eternity.[3] Commentators after 1000 A.D. naturally adopted the second explanation.

It thus follows that Christ's victory as described in the Revela-tion is an allegorical portrayal of his earthly ministry. Now, while Spenser's basic moral allegory in Book 1 is that of a Christian's progress through the spiritual perils of this life, he uses the fami-liar idea of Christ's ministry as the pattern of the Christian's

---

[1] *Var.* i. 259. [2] *Gerusalemme Liberata*, vii. 82. Cf. pp. 32, 89.
[3] *De Civitate Dei*, xx. vi–vii. The *Catholic Encyclopedia*, s.v. 'Millennium', gives this view as the present opinion of the Church.

career. And, as in the Revelation, this pattern is presented in the form of a knightly quest. The parallel is developed in Redcross's final battle with the dragon in Eden, a battle which corresponds to the victory of Christ over the Great Dragon as described in the Revelation. But if this is true, Professor Courthope declares, Spenser has been guilty of careless workmanship, for he has given us no clue to his meaning in his description of the dragon.[1] The details of his dragon are found in the medieval romances concerning St. George but not in the Revelation; his dragon is neither red nor seven-headed, as is the Biblical one.

To discover a clue we must observe that Spenser's method is copied from the Bible, that his dragon Errour, Lucifera's dragon, Duessa's beast, and the dragon in Eden represent the devil, or Evil Principle, in various forms. Similarly, the Bible presents several beasts who are interpreted to represent the devil. Besides the Great Dragon of Revelation 12 and the harlot's beast of Revelation 19, there are the ten-horned beast of Daniel 7 and the Leviathan of Job 41, as well as several others. Having used the seven-headed beasts of Revelation as a pattern for Duessa's beast, Spenser models his dragon in Eden after the more terrifying descriptions in Daniel and Job. The iron teeth of his dragon are found in Daniel (7: 7, 19). The burning eyes, smoking mouth and nostrils, close-fitting scales, invulnerability to wounds, enormous size, and overwhelming power are reminiscent of the Leviathan.[2] The commentators leave no doubt that this 'king over all the children of pride' is the same as the Great Dragon.[3] In rendering this passage, Origen translates 'Leviathan' as 'the apostate dragon'.[4] Isaiah declares that 'in that day the Lord . . . shall punish Leviathan and . . . slay the dragon that is in the sea' (27: 1), an apparent prophecy of Christ's victory over the Great Dragon and the Beast from the Sea. Since the Leviathan and the beast in Daniel are definitely identified with the Great Dragon, Spenser was free to use their descriptions for his dragon; and since these descriptions are so like the dragon of the romances, he was able to give a recognizable picture of the devil within the framework of the St. George story.

[1] *Var.* i. 377.

[2] Upton notes Job 41: 15, 'His scales are his pride', as a parallel but fails to observe the other resemblances. For these, read verses 14–29.

[3] Gregory, *Moralium*, xxxiii. ix; Herveus, *PL* clxxxi. 165–6.

[4] *De Principiis* i. v, in *Ante-Nicene Fathers* (Buffalo, 1886), iv. 259.

Admitting that Redcross's victory over the dragon in Eden corresponds to the defeat of the Great Dragon in the Revelation, we have still to interpret it in terms of Christ's earthly ministry. I judge that the particular significance of Redcross's triumph is the victory over death. As Christ began his ministry with victory over sin and ended it with victory over death, so Redcross begins his quest by defeating the dragon Errour and ends it by conquering the dragon in Eden. Spenser identifies this dragon with death in xi. 49, where the 'ever damned beast' cannot approach the Tree of Life because 'he was deadly made'. It was the dragon who brought death into Eden (stanza 47), exiling mankind thence, and only by his overthrow can man be restored to the joys of Eden, equivalent of the millennial reign and the happiness of those spiritually re-born in Christ.

It should be observed that the three-day period of Redcross's fight with the dragon resembles the period of Christ's victory over death. Christ began his struggle with death on Good Friday and arose from the dead early in the morning of the third day. Redcross struggles with the dragon for two days and achieves victory early in the morning of the third day. The analogy between Christ's victory over physical death and the Christian's victory over spiritual death is too well known to require elaboration. In Redcross's triumph Christ's victory represents the Christian's deliverance from original sin, 'from the body of this death', in the words of St. Paul (Rom. 7: 24).

During the period of Christ's entombment, he not only conquered death in his own person but visited the lower world to deliver the souls of the just who had died before his first advent. The Gospel of Nicodemus[1] is the major source of this 'harrowing of hell' tradition, later popularized by the medieval miracle plays. According to this gospel, after Christ's entrance into the grave, he descended to hell, burst asunder its brazen doors, overcame and bound Satan, and brought forth the souls of the patriarchs and other good men of former times. He led them to the paradise of Eden, where they will rest until the second resurrection, after which they will ascend in the flesh to the holy city of God. Spenser evidently has this imagery in mind. After the dragon's death Una's parents emerge with their retinue from the brazen doors of their castle and return to their former home in Eden. They

---

[1] *Ante-Nicene Fathers*, viii. 435–58.

represent Adam, Eve, and the patriarchs, symbolizing the human race, delivered by Christ from hell and the jaws of death, and returning to the paradise of Eden, which represents the spiritual bliss of those who abide in Christ.

For his own purposes Spenser has slightly altered the details of the Gospel of Nicodemus. The battle takes place, not in hell, but in Eden itself. He was able to make this change because the scriptural account in Genesis 3 does not specifically say that the Serpent was expelled from Eden along with Adam and Eve. Spenser's authority is probably Revelation 12 : 9, where Michael expels the Great Dragon from heaven. This is interpreted to mean Christ's expulsion of Satan from the hearts of the faithful, and also his expulsion of the wicked from the midst of his Church. Heaven here represents the Church.[1] The Garden of Eden and its companion garden in Canticles were also sometimes interpreted to mean the Church;[2] politically, Spenser uses Eden to represent England.[3] By placing the battle in Eden, Spenser is able to represent at the same time Christ's victory over death for the salvation of all believers and the restoration of truth (Una) to the Church by the overthrow of false doctrine. The political allegory is usually taken to mean the restoration of royal supremacy in the English Church to Queen Elizabeth, after it had been surrendered to the papacy by Philip and Mary.[4]

There may also seem to be a difficulty in that the brazen tower of Una's parents does not represent hell, since they enter it for protection against the dragon, not for service to him. The tower represents the Limbo of the Fathers, in which the souls of the patriarchs were preserved until Christ's earthly incarnation. Dante follows Aquinas in making this Limbo the topmost circle in the cavern of hell.[5] Its inhabitants are subject to the death of the unbaptized but not to the torments of the wicked. They are thus part of Satan's kingdom of death but are protected against his persecutions. Since one must pass through Limbo to reach the lower regions of hell, the doors of hell and the doors of Limbo are the same. It is these brazen doors which Christ burst asunder to

---

[1] Haymo, *PL* cxvii. 1085–6; Primasius, *PL* lxviii. 874D.

[2] Alanus de Insulis, *PL* ccx. 812–13; Rabanus Maurus, *PL* cxii. 1022A.

[3] See Josephine Waters Bennett, 'Britain among the Fortunate Isles', *Studies in Philology*, liii (1956), 114–40.

[4] *Var.* i. 472.

[5] *Inferno*, iv; *Summa Theologica*, pt. iii (Supplement), Q. 69, A. 5.

deliver mankind from death. It is these brazen doors from which Una's parents emerge to return to Eden.

Christ's victory over death involves his victory over hell. The gates of hell are interpreted to mean the gates of death.[1] The 'jaws of death' and the 'mouth of hell' are equivalent terms, made so because 'the grave' and 'hell' are frequently equivalent in the Old Testament, both being used to translate 'Sheol'.[2] In the Revelation the fourth horseman, Death, is accompanied by Hell (6: 8); at the final judgement Death and Hell give up their dead and are cast together into the lake of fire (20: 13–14).

Spenser clearly intends to use this association. In describing the dragon's head he writes:

> for his deepe devouring jawes
> *Wyde gaped*, like the griesly *mouth of hell*,
> Through which into his darke *abysse* all ravin fell.　(xi. 12)

'Abyss' is the word used in the Vulgate for the 'bottomless pit' (Rev. 20: 1, 3). Spenser's words are borrowed from Isaiah 5 : 14; 'Therefore gapeth hell, and openeth her mouth marvellous wide.' This is the reading of all sixteenth-century versions except the Genevan but was not adopted in the Authorized Version, with the result that a highly popular Elizabethan phrase is not clear to modern readers. I have suggested elsewhere that this verse from Isaiah is the source of the 'hell-mouth' portrayals in medieval miracle plays and in pictorial art of the Renaissance.[3] Hell-mouth is usually represented as a monstrous beastly head with its jaws stretched wide; in a number of pictures it is a brazen head in imitation of the brazen gates of hell.[4]

Spenser thus makes the dragon's mouth resemble the mouth of hell. This gives significance to the final combat when the dragon attempts to swallow up the knight but receives his death wound instead; even so hell and death sought to swallow up Christ but were overcome by him instead. In the Vulgate's description of the Leviathan occurs the reading, 'Quis revelabit faciem indumenti

[1] Psalm 107: 16, 18. See also Origen's *Commentary on Matthew*, XII. xiii, in *Ante-Nicene Fathers*, ix. 457.

[2] See any concordance which gives readings from both the Authorized and the Revised Versions.

[3] 'Biblical Echoes in the Final Scene of *Dr. Faustus*', *Studies in English* (University of Kansas Press, 1940), p. 7.

[4] Several of these pictures are reproduced in Grillot de Givry's *Witchcraft, Magic, and Alchemy* (London, 1931).

eius? et *in medium oris eius quis intrabit*?'[1] ('Who will reveal the face of his garment? And into the midst of his mouth, who will enter?') This reading may have determined Spenser's handling of the scene. For it is Christ who dared to enter into the jaws of death and the mouth of hell, and to conquer them for the salvation of the human race as the climax of his earthly ministry; so must the Christian be willing to dare who would conquer sin and death. Spenser has thus given to the battle of St. George and the dragon a profound allegorical meaning.

We have already observed Spenser's use of Babylon the harlot as a source for his imagery but have not discussed his use of Babylon the city. His introduction of the New Jerusalem in the tenth canto suggests that he may employ its opposite, Babylon, the fall of which is pictured in Revelation 18. These two cities play a prominent part in the Bible and among the commentators, who generally agree that one represents the followers of Christ and the other the followers of Satan, wherever they may be found. Allegorically, the names do not designate particular cities in particular places, but rather the congregations of the good and of the evil throughout the whole earth. Augustine explains that Jerusalem means 'vision of peace', while Babylon means 'confusion'.[2] Jerusalem is the City of God (Ps. 46: 4); Babylon is the City of Destruction (Isa. 19: 18). There are two Jerusalems. The 'beloved city' of Revelation 20: 9 is the Church of Christ on earth, while the New Jerusalem of Revelation 21 is the Church of Christ in heaven. Sometimes the two are not clearly distinguished, since one obviously provides the entrance to the other.

Spenser has introduced Babylon, or the assembly of the wicked, in the castles of Lucifera and Orgoglio, while the earthly Jerusalem is represented by the house of Coelia, whose name signifies 'heavenly'. The key to his plan is found in the Sermon on the Mount. His name for the heavenly city, 'the City of the Great King', is taken from Matthew 5: 35, where it is applied to Jerusalem and is in turn borrowed from Psalm 48: 2. His contrast between the two cities is based on Matthew 7: 13–14:

Enter ye in at the strait gate: for wide is the gate, and broad is the way, that leadeth to destruction, and many there be which go in thereat.

---

[1] Job 41: 4 in the Vulgate, corresponding to 41: 13 in the Authorized Version, which gives a different reading.
[2] *PL* xxxv. 2451.

Because strait is the gate and narrow is the way, which leadeth unto life, and few there be that find it.

Here 'destruction' suggests the City of Destruction, the assembly of the wicked who travel the way to hell, while 'life' represents the eternal life of the heavenly city. The explanation is made more definite by van der Noot's comment:

Here you may see and iudge of God, and the deuil, Christ, and Antechrist, the kyngdome of God, and of Sathan, the Churche of Christe, and the synagoge of *Rome*, or the assemblie of the reprobate, the broade waye, and the straite gate, heauen and hell, eternall lyfe and euerlastyng death.[1]

The approach to Lucifera's House of Pride is 'a broad high way' kept bare of vegetation by the multitudes of feet that travel it (iv. 2). This is of course the 'broad way' which leads to destruction. Also, in Matthew 7 : 26 occurs the parable of the House built upon the Sand. Spenser identifies this house with Lucifera's palace, which is built 'on a sandie hill' (iv. 5). According to Bishop Haymo, the House built upon the Sand is an image of Babylon: 'There are two cities of this world, Jerusalem and Babylon, whose kings are Christ and the devil; one is founded upon the firm rock, the other upon the sand.'[2]

The resemblance of Orgoglio's castle to Babylon is found in viii. 35–6. The rich array, royal arras, gold, and great store of all commodities are suggested by the riches of Babylon in Revelation 18 : 11–16. The blood of the innocents and martyrs comes from 17 : 6, in which the harlot Babylon is drunk with the blood of the martyrs. The altar from beneath which the spirits of the martyrs cry for vengeance is taken from Revelation 6 : 9–11. In the Revelation this is the altar before the throne of God, but it is mentioned again in 14 : 18, when an angel appears from it to cry out for the 'harvest of the world' involving the destruction of Babylon.

In the approaches to Coelia's house and to the heavenly city, the 'strait gate' and the 'narrow way' are stressed repeatedly. In x. 5 one must stoop low to enter the door, which is a 'streight and narrow way'. Stanza 10 is little more than a paraphrase of the two Biblical verses already quoted from Matthew, contrasting the 'narrow path' and the 'broad high way'. Redcross proceeds by

---

[1] *Theatre for Voluptuous Worldlings*, ff. 92–3. Italics not mine.
[2] *PL* cxvii. 1139D.

a 'narrow way' to Mercy's hospital (stanza 35), by a 'painfull way'
to the hermit's chapel (stanza 46), and then sees 'a little path, that
was both steepe and long' which leads on to the heavenly city
(stanza 55). The entrance to Coelia's house is 'warely watched
night and day, For fear of many foes' (stanza 5). This derives from
Nehemiah 4 : 9, where the author states that when numerous foes
conspired to fight Jerusalem and halt its rebuilding, 'Nevertheless
we made our prayer unto our God, and set a watch against them
day and night, because of them.' The parallel further identifies
Coelia's house as the earthly Jerusalem, or the Church of Christ
on earth.

In Redcross's journey from Coelia's house to the hermitage of
Heavenly Contemplation, he leaves behind Una, or truth, and receives Mercy as his guide. This arrangement was probably suggested by Proverbs 16 : 6 : 'By mercy and truth iniquity is purged',
by Psalm 25 : 10 : 'All the paths of the Lord are mercy and truth',
and by the numerous other instances in which the two words
occur together. Mercy and truth share the task of bringing the
sinful soul to repentance and guiding his feet into the right path.

The tenth canto contains several other Biblical echoes not usually observed. Una's kiss (stanza 29) is the holy kiss of greeting
in the early church.[1] The phrase 'thou man of earth' addressed to
Redcross (stanza 52) comes from Paul's sentence, 'The first man
is of the earth, earthy' (1 Cor. 15 : 47). Since Paul is differentiating
between natural bodies of flesh and spiritual bodies which will exist
after the resurrection, Spenser's phrase simply means that Redcross will see heaven while still in his fleshly body. The injunction
to 'fast and pray' (stanza 52) is distinctly Biblical. The 'highest
mount' which he then ascends (stanza 53) is of course the mount
to which the angel carried John to show him the New Jerusalem
(Revelation 21 : 10). It is the mount of vision; St. Bruno calls it
'that ecstasy and excess of mind into which we can ascend on no
other than spiritual feet'.[2] Redcross's wish to remain on the
mount or else to begin at once his journey to the heavenly city
(stanza 63) is recalled from two wishes expressed by Peter. The
first was expressed on the Mount of Transfiguration when he ex-
claimed, 'It is good to be here', and wished that he might remain
(Matt. 17 : 4). The second was expressed at the Last Supper when

---

[1] Rom. 16 : 16, 1 Cor. 16 : 20, 2 Cor. 13 : 12, 1 Thess. 5 : 26, 1 Pet. 5 : 14.
[2] *PL* clxv. 720–1.

Peter wished to die with Christ and accompany him to paradise but was told: 'Whither I go thou canst not follow me now; but thou shalt follow me afterwards' (John 13 : 36). The terms of the refusal are much the same as those given to Redcross.

John's vision of the New Jerusalem also furnishes two details for Spenser's description of Eden, the Well of Life and the Tree of Life (Rev. 22 : 1-2). The Tree is the heavenly counterpart of the Tree that flourished in Eden, while the River of the Water of Life is the same as the well of living water offered to the woman of Samaria (John 4: 14), the fountain[1] of water which sprang up in Eden (Gen. 2 : 6), and the river which flowed from the fountain (2 : 10).

Spenser's reference to Redcross's 'baptized hands' (xi. 36) suggests that the Well of Life represents the holy water of baptism. Most of the commentators give this interpretation of the 'water of life' in the Revelation;[2] Augustine calls it the baptismal font in the midst of the church.[3] Further proof is afforded by the comparison of Redcross's emergence from the Well to an eagle's renewing its youth in the sea (stanza 34). The Biblical references to the eagle's rejuvenation are Psalm 103 : 5 and Isaiah 40 : 31. Bishop Haymo comments significantly on both of these passages. Of the first he says:

The nature of the eagle is such that in old age its beak and claws grow so large that it is unable to refresh itself with food. And indeed it then ascends toward the sun, until its feathers are burned away by the heat, and thence it falls into living water. Emerging therefrom, it pares down its beak and claws on a rock and, afterward taking food, renews its youth. So we, filled with many sins, when we are held in the old age of Adam [original sin], draw near to Christ, who is the true sun, by whose warmth and infusion of grace our sins are burned away. And thereafter we are laved with the waters of baptism, whereupon we break and dash to pieces our curved beak, that is, our evil habit of mind, on the rock, that is, Christ; conforming ourselves to him, we throw off that old age and renew our youth.[4]

This is an account similar to that observed by Professor Padelford in the medieval *Physiologus*.[5] In his comment on Isaiah 40: 31

---

[1] 'Mist' in the Authorized Version, *fons* in the Vulgate. See above, p. 81.
[2] Anselm, *PL* clxii. 1583C; Martin, *PL* ccix. 413B.
[3] *PL* xxxv. 2459.
[4] *PL* cxvi. 539C. [5] *Var.* i. 303.

Bishop Haymo gives a different significance to the eagle's rejuvenation:

And thus its hair, its feathers, and its whole body are renewed. So the redeemed, who have here experienced attrition by mortifying themselves, shall be renewed through incorruption, contemplating Christ the sun of justice, as the eagle gazes at the sun with unwavering eyes.[1]

The phrase concerning attrition, 'se attriverunt mortificando seipsos', has reference to the expiations of penance, which subdue the lusts of the body and strengthen the contemplative powers of the mind. By such a contemning of the body, Spenser's seer Heavenly Contemplation has gained powers of spiritual vision 'as eagles eie, that can behold the sunne' and looks directly upon the brightness of God (x. 47).

Spenser's Tree of Life is indebted to the Tree in Revelation 22: 2, which bears both fruit and 'leaves . . . for the healing of the nations'. This double function of fruit-bearing and healing is evident in Spenser's Tree. Spenser's fruit is red, the colour of Christ's blood, and accordingly represents the Eucharist, the body and blood of Christ in the sacrament of the Lord's Supper. This accords with the commentators, who represent the Tree either as Christ or as the Cross on which Christ's body was broken and his blood was shed.[2] The Tree in the Revelation grows on both sides of the river; on the near side it represents the body and blood of Christ given for our refreshment in this life, but on the far side it represents the direct contemplation of Christ which we shall enjoy in paradise.[3]

The healing balm which flows from Spenser's Tree suggests the sacrament of Extreme Unction, administered to those in peril of death. In this sacrament the limbs are anointed with a healing oil both to strengthen the body and to heal the wounds of the mind. We have reason to believe that it was used in the English Church of Spenser's day. Without naming it, Richard Hooker recommends it for those at point of death:

God forbid we should think that the Church doth sin in permitting the wounds of such to be supplied with that oil which this gracious Sacrament doth yield, and their bruised minds not only need but beg.[4]

---

[1] *PL* cxvi. 915A.
[2] Augustine, *PL* xxxv. 2459–60; Martin, *PL* ccix. 413C; Haymo, *PL* cxvii. 1211D.
[3] Anselm, *PL* clxii. 1583D; Richard of St. Victor, *PL* cxcvi. 876A.
[4] *Laws of Ecclesiastical Polity*, v. lxviii. 11.

The reference to oil identifies this sacrament as Extreme Unction. Hooker's phrase 'gracious Sacrament' reminds us of Spenser's 'gracious ointment' which flows from the Tree (stanza 48), 'gracious' meaning 'grace-imparting' in both instances.

The flowing of healing oil or balm from the Tree of Life is not Spenser's invention but derives from the Gospel of Nicodemus. There Adam prompts his son Seth to tell how, when Adam lay near death, Seth visited Eden and begged that Michael, the guardian of the gate, would give him some oil from the Tree of Life in order to heal his father. Michael replied that the request could not be granted and that Adam must die, but that after 5,500 years from the creation of the world the Son of God should come into the earth and raise up Adam with oil from the Tree of Life.[1]

This concludes my observations of the Biblical influences on Book I. Those influences are pervasive and decisive throughout the book. The Revelation of St. John and related passages in other parts of the Bible provide Spenser's basic pattern and much of his imagery. In addition to using the Biblical pattern as a moral allegory of man's spiritual regeneration through Christ, he accepts the political explanation common among Protestants of his time and sets the whole in a framework of chivalric romance. The result is a mosaic of extraordinary richness, of which the religious element is a more important part than has generally been perceived.

THE INTERNAL ALLEGORY

To distinguish between external allegory and internal allegory in Book I will involve wide differences of interpretation. A turning point in the book comes when Redcross in a moment of weakness has sexual relations with Duessa. They yield to the temptation of lust. But, if they are both impulses within a man's soul, there can be no fornication between them except in a figurative sense. Kathleen Williams comments as follows on this aspect of Spenser's narrative: 'The knights and ladies of the world of romance embody right and wrong relationships within the inner world of man . . . The union of male and female in marriage was endlessly likened to unions of might and passivity, mind and imagination, spirit and flesh in the individual personality.'[2]

---

[1] *Ante-Nicene Fathers*, viii. 436, 449.

[2] *Spenser's World of Glass*, p. 41. The second sentence is quoted from M. A. N. Radzinowicz.

In such a vein, Shakespeare's Richard II rationalizes while in prison:

> My brain I'll prove the female to my soul,
> My soul being the father, and these two beget
> A generation of still breeding thoughts,
> And these same thoughts people this little world.
>
> (*Richard II*, v. v. 6–9)

The 'little world' is his prison cell but also suggests the microcosm of his body. The passage illustrates exactly the process of internal allegory.

If the Redcross–Duessa amour is only figurative, can it represent the temptation of lust? It is the union of holiness with deceit (vii. 1), resulting in the enslavement of holiness to pride. Whatever the sin committed, it is not one of fleshly lust. Externally, a man might feel inordinate pride in a number of things: wealth, good looks, physical prowess, mental acuteness. Deceit is more likely to ensnare a person through his mental processes, making the wrong appear right, than through other channels. In Book 1 the mental processes seem to be misled in terms of religious doctrine. 'Errour' is the term regularly used for false doctrines of theology. In spite of Una's misgivings, Redcross assaulted and killed the dragon Errour, triumphing over the more obvious pitfalls in the rationalizations of theology and thereby becoming over-confident. Externally the man substituted his own intellectual rationalizations for the tenets of revealed religion. Through this pride of intellect, he was led astray from true doctrine into acceptance of false doctrine.

In Dante's *Purgatorio*, Dante is reproached by Beatrice with an error of this kind:

> E volsi i passi suoi per via non vera,
> imagini di ben seguendo false.　　　(xxx. 130–1)

(And he turned his steps through a way not true, following false images of good.)

He had lost the 'diritta via' (direct way) in the 'selva oscura' (dark wood) at the beginning of the *Inferno* (above, p. 61). In the *Convito*, he indicates that he entered the untrue way by following Lady Philosophy (ii. 13) to the neglect of true religion. He had forgotten Beatrice, now a spirit representing heavenly wisdom; but she had nevertheless effected his rescue.

At first the angelic Beatrice appears to Dante wearing a white veil (*Purg.* xxx. 31) but later puts the veil aside and allows him to see her bright face (67). This may have had some influence on Spenser's portrayal of Una, who appears veiled to Redcross until their betrothal in Canto xii, when she reveals to him

> The blazing brightnesse of her beauties beame,
> And glorious light of her sunshyny face.   (stanza 23)

We can understand better the allegory of the veil from St. Paul's comments on the veil which Moses wore after returning from Mount Sinai and the presence of God, lest the brightness of his face injure the eyes of his audience (Exod. 34: 33–5). Paul uses this veil allegorically in reference to the Hebrews' failure to accept Christ as the Messiah: 'But even unto this day, when Moses is read, the veil is upon their heart. Nevertheless, when it shall turn to the Lord, the veil shall be taken away' (2 Cor. 3: 15–16).

This verse clarifies the significance of Una. The object of her quest is to reveal herself to those who are qualified to see. The veil is there for Redcross because of his inadequacy, not because Truth (Una) wishes to remain unrevealed. She longs as fervently as he for the time when the veil may be thrown back and they may meet face to face. But it is useless, perhaps dangerous, to reveal her beauty until he is prepared to see it. Holiness must achieve a state nearer perfection before it can comprehend the full measure of truth. Before that time it sees truth, but only imperfectly.

When Redcross is surprised by Orgoglio, he seizes his weapons but has no time to don his armour or to get his shield (vii. 8). For this armour Spenser refers us in the *Letter to Raleigh* to Ephesians 6: 13–17 for the armour of the Christian man. Most important of all, St. Paul declares, is the shield of faith 'wherewith ye shall be able to quench all the fiery darts of the wicked'. But Redcross cannot reach his shield and is therefore overthrown by Orgoglio. Externally the man loses his faith as he proudly asserts the superiority of his own intellect over Christian teachings.

Like Beatrice, Una takes the initiative in rescuing the man that she loves. She procures the aid of Prince Arthur, or heavenly grace:

> Ay me! how many perils doe enfold
> The righteous man, to make him daily fall,
> Were not that Heavenly Grace doth him uphold,
> And stedfast Truth acquite him out of all.   (viii. 1)

We have already noticed how the Biblical uses of 'mercy and truth' affect the allegory in the House of Coelia (above, p. 116). The combination of heavenly grace and truth comes from the Gospel according to St. John: 'And the Word was made flesh and dwelt among us ... full of *grace and truth*. ... For the law was given by Moses, but *grace and truth* came by Jesus Christ' (1 : 14, 17). Una's liberating function is further determined by St. John's words: 'Ye shall know the truth, and the truth shall make you free' (8 : 32). Spenser, in adapting these passages, has specified heavenly grace because he intended to use natural grace as Timias, Arthur's squire and appropriate companion (II. xi. 30).

Redcross had almost fallen victim to pride at Lucifera's house but was saved by a warning from Una's Dwarf (caution or prudence), who had discovered the castle dungeons full of prisoners and corpses (I. v. 45). After Redcross's imprisonment by Orgoglio, the Dwarf bears the news to Una and thus initiates a rescue (I. vii. 20). As Redcross is separated from Una by the machinations of Archimago, he is led into pride by Duessa. These two, hypocrisy and deceit, work through illusions and enchantments, perplexing the mind by indirections and false appearances. In external allegory they represent deceivers of every kind, with specific application to the Roman Church. In internal allegory they must represent man's capacity for self-deception, the false rationalizations and easy excuses which he tends to give himself to justify improper belief or conduct. If long continued, these produce an excessive pride in his own cleverness; and in such an atmosphere holiness must be submerged if not completely destroyed. For it to emerge again, pride must be replaced by humility through the agency of heavenly grace and truth. The first delivers man from pride; the second saves him from despair (ix. 52). Holiness can then pass through the gate of Humility into the house of Virtue. Externally the man regains a proper perspective on things.[1]

In internal allegory the Saracen brothers challenge Holiness directly, not by subtle wiles. Sansfoy, a tendency toward atheistic disbelief, is slain by Holiness. Duessa changes her loyalty from one to the other, illustrating how self-deception allows a person to rationalize expediency. Sansjoy, sanctimonious or 'long-faced'

---

[1] An excellent example of this self-righteous self-deception is Karsten Bernick, in Ibsen's *Pillars of Society*.

religion, is conquered by Holiness in the House of Pride; but he is saved by Duessa through a trip to Aesculapius in Hades. In the historical allegory Duessa clearly represents the papacy (above, p. 101), so it seems likely that Sansjoy represents the celibacy of the Roman clergy or the strict discipline of such orders as the Carthusians. The third brother, Sansloy, is internally the impulse towards lawless violence; externally he may represent the iconoclasts, the Anabaptists, and other extremists of the Protestant cause, whose recklessness obscured their view of the truth (Una).

In the episode of Fradubio and Fraelissa, who have been changed to trees by Duessa's enchantments, we again have sexual imagery used to represent the workings of the mind. Upton identifies the pair as Brother Doubt and Frailty (Ital. *fralezza*).[1] In the internal allegory self-deception perplexes the mind with unresolved doubt and frail irresolution, which stand rooted to the spot because they can never decide which way to go. They must remain so until they are bathed in a 'living well', upon which their enchantment by Deceit will end (above, p. 81). When holiness (Redcross) is reinvigorated by the Well of Life (xi. 29), we rather expect that doubt and irresolution will be purged also, and the whole mind of man directed to more positive action.

After Una is separated from Redcross, she is beguiled by Archimago wearing armour like that of Redcross. He is attacked and almost slain by Sansloy, who likewise fails to recognize him (1. iii. 26–39). Una is thus saved from Archimago but is immediately seized by Sansloy. Her lion escort attacks Sansloy but is slain by him (1. iii. 41–2). She is saved by the appearance of satyrs and fauns, who frighten away Sansloy. The 'woodborne people' worship her. Sir Satyrane, who is half satyr and half human, helps her to escape from the satyrs and challenges Sansloy to battle when he is again encountered. Una escapes while they are fighting. Archimago, hidden, rejoices to see them fighting each other.

Internally all these characters are impulses or faculties of the soul. The satyrs and fauns represent affections of the concupiscible appetite as existing in a 'state of nature' or primitive innocence, when no moral opprobrium attaches to sexual activity of any kind. When the moral world impinges upon them, allowing them to see truth, they instinctively recognize its superiority and worship it as godlike. The normal world of the satyrs is that into which

[1] *Var.* i. 205.

Hellenore sinks when she becomes a nymphomaniac (III. x. 51), the world of amorality. Satyrane has a satyr father and a human mother; he thus stands between the concupiscible and the rational, sharing the natures of both. His father has trained him to conquer all the beasts of the forest. He is the irascible faculty subduing the concupiscent affections in the service of truth, a virtue of the rational faculty (above, p. 30). But he also subdues vices of the irascible faculty, of which Sansloy, the lawless impulse of the mind, is one.[1]

Like the amour of Redcross and Duessa, Sansloy's attempted rape of Una is figurative only, in terms of internal allegory. 'Lawless lust' seizes truth, but this is not concupiscent violence. It is the element of reckless impatience in the mind that demands immediate action, even though one may act on false premises. It is unlike hypocritical self-deception, which builds up a web of artificial rationalizations to justify ill actions by making them seem good. Thus, Sansloy and Archimago both seek to capture truth and destroy holiness, but they use different methods, and these methods bring them into conflict with each other. Sansloy almost kills Archimago before recognizing him as an ally; that is, the mind's lawless impulse sweeps aside subtle evasions and indirections in favour of direct action, though the action which it takes is wrong.

One might postulate a number of external situations to fit this internal allegory. The iconoclasts, or image-breakers, of the sixteenth century ransacked churches and destroyed 'graven images' to show their anti-papal zeal; but this zeal was misdirected, and they were self-deceived. They pursued holiness but performed lawlessness. Usually mob violence of any kind is a similar instance of mistaken idealism. Each reader will find other applications of the allegory for himself.

The lion that serves Una seems to be another instance of the irascible faculty, which normally aids reason in controlling the concupiscent appetites but may also join with those appetites upon occasion in battling against reason. When the lion rushes upon Una to devour her, he is serving the concupiscent appetite of hunger; but, when he recognizes her natural superiority and decides to protect her, the irascible faculty returns to its true

---

[1] This division of functions within the irascible faculty is again illustrated in the Salvage Man's attack on Turpine (below, pp. 181, 183).

allegiance to the rational faculty and turns against the concupis-
cent appetites, or other harmful beasts of the forest. Marsilio
Ficino states this interpretation in his 'Argument' to Book ix of
Plato's *Republic* (in reference to *Republic*, 588–9):

> Next consider that figure of the soul's nature. In which, under the
> name of a multiple beast, consider the nature of concupiscence; under
> the figure of a lion, the vigour of the irascible nature; under the form
> of a man, reason. And see how expressly he depicts the life of the
> ambitious, unjust, or lustful man as a life of miserable servitude.
> Again, take the formula, by which you are able to interpret the crossing
> of souls into beasts, as meaning that they are said to migrate into the
> affections and habits of beasts rather than into the bodies of beasts as
> such.[1]

Like Pyrochles and Turpine, Sansloy is a vicious excess of the
irascible faculty and is opposed to the controlled indignation
which is the true nature of that faculty; hence his conflicts with
the lion and Satyrane. The cause of truth (Una) may be served by
controlled indignation but not by reckless violence and thought-
less anger.

When Archimago and Duessa persuade Guyon to challenge
Redcross (ii. i. 1–33), the implication seems to be that the zeal of
holiness is made to appear fanatical and intemperate, like the
recklessness of Sansloy. But the difference is quickly perceived
by Guyon, and the two knights are united as friends, illustrating
Francesco Piccolomini's statement that two virtues may clash
momentarily but are basically harmonious (above, p. 33).

In the final canto, when Una reveals her face to Redcross by
laying aside her veil, truth and holiness are united. Externally, the
Christian has finally rejected false doctrine (Duessa, Archimago),
accepted true doctrine (Una), and has achieved a more nearly
perfect measure of holiness thereby (above, p. 121).

ADDENDUM: ARTHUR AS GIANT-KILLER

In Book i, Arthur's greatest exploit is the slaying of Orgoglio.
The manner of this conquest is interesting. Avoiding the giant's
first blow, which buries his club in the ground, and taking advantage of his struggle to remove the club, Arthur steps in and cuts

---

[1] Plato, *Opera Omnia*, tr. Ficino (1551), p. 642.

off his left arm. After a further exchange, Arthur cuts off his right
leg. When the giant falls to the ground, Arthur cuts off his head
(viii. 10, 22, 24).

In the chronicles, King Arthur's most picturesque adventure is
his slaying of the great giant of Mont-Saint-Michel in Brittany, after
the latter had abducted King Hoel's sister (or daughter) Helen.[1]
This suggests the slaying of another giant by another Arthur, also
in Brittany. In *Arthur of Little Britain*, the prose romance translated by Lord Berners, Arthur conquers a giant, first striking off
one arm and then thrusting the giant through the midriff.[2] In
Stephen Hawes's *The Pastime of Pleasure*, the knight Grand Amour
kills a three-headed giant, first cutting off one leg and then all three
heads. Spenser seems to have combined these two accounts into
one, making Arthur cut off the giant's arm, leg, and head, in that
order. Also, when Grand Amour fights a seven-headed giant, he
dodges the stroke of the giant's axe, which buries itself three feet
in the earth from the force of the giant's blow. The resemblance
to Orgoglio's club is apparent.[3]

After Orgoglio is beheaded, Spenser writes:

> But soone as breath out of his brest did pas,
> That huge great body, which the gyaunt bore,
> Was vanisht quite, and of that monstrous mas
> Was nothing left, but *like an emptie blader was.*   (viii. 24)

These lines reflect De Guileville's description of Pride in *The
Pilgrimage of the Life of Man*. She is pictured as a swollen and
puffed-up woman, borne on the back of another woman (lines
13972–84), who carries a mirror (14002). Pride is a daughter of
Lucifer (14030). When she looks angry, men think that she might
bind the skies:

> Al ys but smoke, al ys but wynd,
> Lyk a *bladdere* that ys blowe,
> Wych, with-Inne a lytel throwe,

---

[1] This exploit is mentioned by Geoffrey of Monmouth, John Hardyng, and
Pierre de Langtoft, among others. The same incident is told by Malory, *Le Morte
D'Arthur*, bk. v, ch. 5.

[2] For a discussion of *Arthur of Little Britain* see Sarah Michie in *SP* xxxvi (1939),
105–23.

[3] EETS, o.s., no. 173, lines 4408–16, 4821. Other uses by Spenser of Hawes's
Pastime of Pleasure are discussed in *Var.* i. 414–18.

Pryke yt with a poynt, a-noon,
And ffarwell, al the wynd ys gon,
That men ther-off may no thyng se. (14162–7)[1]

De Guileville's Pride is only an inflated bladder, like Orgoglio.
She is a daughter of Lucifer, suggesting Lucifera, Spenser's other
representation of pride.

[1] From the translation by John Lydgate, EETS, e.s., nos. 77, 83, 92.

VI

The Moral Allegory *of* Temperance

HE battles of temperance are embodied in Guyon, who also
represents the companion virtue of fortitude (above, p. 15).
He is a fairy knight, not a mortal visitor to Fairyland like
Redcross, Britomart, Arthur, and Artegall. He bears on his shield
a picture of Gloriana, the Faerie Queene, and thus gives to Prince
Arthur his first glimpse of that idealized lady (II. ix. 2). For a time
he and Arthur become companions on the quest, and together
they rout the besiegers of Alma's castle. The most dramatic single
victory of the book is given to Arthur, who defeats Maleger after
Guyon's departure. Guyon's crowning victory is his resistance to
and overthrow of Acrasia, who weaves strong spells and enchantments.

GUYON AND INTERNAL ALLEGORY

Guyon, as the virtue of temperance within the soul, acts primarily
on the defensive. He does pursue his sworn purpose to subdue Acrasia, who has caused the deaths of Mortdant and Amavia
(above, p. 82); but even in this victory he is largely on the defensive, resisting her enchantments and sexual blandishments. His
contests with the Saracen brothers Pyrochles and Cymochles are
defensive, as are his rejections of the various temptations in
Mammon's cave. It is reserved for Arthur to slay the Saracen
brothers, as he also destroys Maleger.

As one would expect in a work on temperance, the internal
struggle is the struggle for self-control, the victory over self,
and the conquest of one's own appetites. A. C. Hamilton interprets
Guyon and the Saracen brothers as partly internal, partly external,
allegory. Guyon is a man. Pyrochles and Cymochles are inward
impulses or urges which he must fight. Acrasia, however, is external temptation, meaning that she must be an actual woman who
ensnares many men into sexual incontinence, and whom Guyon
successfully resists.[1]

[1] Hamilton, *The Structure of Allegory in* The Faerie Queene, p. 101.

We can perhaps get a more logical analysis if we consider all the characters as impulses within the soul. The virtue of temperance is reinforced and counselled by prudence in the person of the Palmer; but for a time the two are separated when Phaedria refuses to ferry the Palmer across Idle Lake in her little boat. Externally, this may mean that a man imprudently exposes himself to the temptations of 'immodest mirth' (Phaedria) by attending a 'wild' party, where he is led into 'loose desire'. He resists the temptation, as the internal clash between Guyon and Cymochles would suggest; but he abandoned prudence (Palmer) by attending the party in the first place.

Guyon must fight most of his battles on foot, for quite early in the action he loses his horse Brigadore, stolen by Braggadocchio while Guyon is aiding Amavia (iii. 3). The horse is not recovered until v. iii. 34, when he and Guyon recognize each other at Marinell's tournament. At the same time that Guyon reclaims his horse, Artegall reclaims from Braggadocchio his shield, which the latter had borrowed in order to claim victory in the tournament. On this occasion the false Florimell disappears after indicating her preference for Braggadocchio. Finally, the pretender is 'uncased' by Talus, much like Duessa in Book I, and flees from the sight of men.

Brigadore's name means 'golden bridle', but there is no general agreement on his allegorical significance. Hamilton notes that 'the horse is traditionally linked with the passional element in man, and therefore with the body'.[1] Yet it would be difficult to think of temperance's separating itself from the human body, as Guyon and Brigadore are separated. For internal allegory both of them should be impulses of the mind. The separation of the knight from his horse may well be imitated from Stephen Batman's *The Trauayled Pylgrime* (1582), a work which influenced extensively Spenser's allegory in Book II.[2] There the horse Will escapes from the knight Youthful Courage to run about in the Field of Worldly Pleasure. Can Brigadore represent the will in man's soul, as Guyon represents the virtue of temperance? This seems quite probable, since the will is the force that drives man to action.

---

[1] Ibid., p. 217.
[2] For other influences of this work upon Spenser see Katherine Koller, 'The Trauayled Pylgrime by Stephen Batman and Book Two of *The Faerie Queene*', *Modern Language Quarterly*, iii (1942), 535–41.

When the affections gain control of the will, they can defy reason, its usual governor, and can have their own way. But in this case Brigadore is captured by Braggadocchio, who is therefore Guyon's rival for control of the will. Braggadocchio, as an internal impulse of the soul, must obviously be the urge toward boastfulness and pretence, as opposed to moderation in speech and manner. Braggadocchio gets control of the will; externally, the man becomes boastful and arrogant in manner, though in matters of personal morality he still remains temperate. When, internally, temperance and justice join to show him the absurdity of his pretences, his will returns to the control of temperance, and he drops his boastful manner.

This interpretation is made more likely by the common image of the 'bridled' or 'unbridled' horses as representative of controlled or uncontrolled passions. The original of these is probably the pair of horses in Plato's *Phaedrus*, 246, interpreted by Francesco Piccolomini as the irascible and concupiscible faculties (ix. 21; p. 499B). The image reappears in Iago's reference to 'unbitted lusts' and in Angelo's remark, 'Now I give my sensual race the rein', a definite surrender of the will to the sensual affections.[1]

The most significant experiences of Guyon occur in connection with Mammon's cave, which is his principal place of testing. The most puzzling aspect of Mammon's realm is the presence therein of the Garden of Proserpine, with its black fruit and its tree of golden apples overhanging the waters of Cocytus (vii. 56). The association may stem from a confusion of Plutus, the god of money, with Pluto, king of the underworld and husband of Proserpina. Such a confusion occurs in Stephen Taylor's *A Whippe for Worldlings, or The Centre of Content*. The same passage uses the name 'Braggadocho's' as a stock name for showy boasters and reminds us of Spenser's Braggadocchio.[2] Since Plutus is the equivalent of Mammon as a money-god, his identification with Pluto would serve to connect Mammon with the Garden of Proserpine.

This garden may owe something to the Garden of Time in *The Trauayled Pylgrime*. There the golden apples shine like those in the Garden of the Hesperides. But this is the Garden of Time and

---

[1] Shakespeare's *Othello*, i. iii. 336; *Measure for Measure*, ii. iv. 160. Cf. my book *Shakespeare's Derived Imagery*, ch. 6.

[2] *A Whippe for Worldlings, or The Centre of Content*, London, 1586.

therefore of Death, for all things subject to time are likewise subject to death. They may be fittingly ruled by Proserpina, queen of the dead. As Proserpina had unwittingly bound herself to remain in Hades by eating fruit there, Guyon would likewise sentence himself to the place of death if he should eat of the golden fruit.[1]

Yet another possible link between Mammon and the golden apples is provided by Jan van der Noot's discussion of misers (of whom Mammon is a type):

> Some other become thorough riches, like vnto the Dragon which kept the Golden apples of the Orchard of *Hesperide*, whereof he himself had no commoditie, neyther suffred any other to enjoy any part of it. Tertullian sayeth, that riches resemble and are muche lyke vnto the Apples of *Sodome* and *Gomorre*, which seemed goodly and faire to the eye, but being once touched, fell and straightway turned into dust and ashes.[2]

A marginal note refers to chapter 29 of Tertullian's *Apology*. Spenser must have known van der Noot's book, for he translated the poems which were included in it. Since the apples of Sodom and Gomorrah represent the sterility and barrenness of riches, it may well be that they have influenced the apples which appear in Mammon's cave.

Henry Lotspeich has noted the way in which Virgilian figures of allegory line the corridor leading into Mammon's cave and the way in which the classical Hades has been adapted to the anteroom of a Christian hell (*Var.* ii. 251). We should again note that the period of Guyon's sojourn in the cave is three days, just as Redcross's struggle against the dragon in Eden lasted for three days. In Book I the three-day period represents the time between Christ's entombment and resurrection, during which he 'harrowed hell' and brought forth the souls of the patriarchs from Limbo to their promised paradise (above, p. 111). Guyon is made to repeat another part of Christ's experience, the three days of temptation in the wilderness after he was weakened by forty days of fasting. Spenser has transferred the underground setting from one

---

[1] Cf. Ovid, *Metamorphoses*, v. 538.

[2] *A Theatre for Voluptuous Worldlings* (1569), f. 8. Italics not mine. Frank Kermode relates the golden apples to the 'forbidden fruit' in the Garden of Eden and therefore to forbidden knowledge ('The Cave of Mammon', in J. R. Elliott, *The Prince of Poets* [New York, 1968], p. 267). This would require a migration of the Tree of Knowledge from its place in Eden.

story to the other: Redcross does not descend into the earth, but Guyon does.

Christ's entry into the wilderness is reflected in Guyon's approach to the region of Mammon's cave:

> he traveild through wide wastfull ground,
> That nought but desert wildernesse shewed all around.   (vii. 2)

In this wilderness, Guyon encounters Mammon and the temptations begin. Frank Kermode has pointed out this Biblical parallel but does not develop the temptations in quite the way that I understand them.[1]

Spenser has changed the order of the temptations as listed in the Bible, giving first the temptation of wealth and power, second the temptation of fame, and finally the temptation of hunger. The characteristic feature of the first temptation is that it involves worship of the tempter. Matthew writes of it as follows: 'Again, the devil taketh him up into an exceeding high mountain and sheweth him all the kingdoms of the world, and the glory of them; And saith unto him, All these things will I give thee, if thou wilt fall down and worship me' (4: 8–9). Before entering the cave with Guyon, Mammon says:

> Wherefore, if me thou deigne to serve and sew,
> At thy commaund, lo! all these mountaines bee;
> Or if to thy great mind, or greedy vew,
> All these may not suffise, there shall to thee
> Ten times so much be nombred francke and free.   (vii. 9)

Mammon continues by offering him 'crownes and kingdomes . . . glory and renowne' (stanza 11). We should notice the use of 'mountains' in the two accounts and the requirement of worshipping the tempter in each case.

The second temptation is more subtle, for no mention is made of worshipping the tempter. The appeal is made to the desire for fame and public recognition of one's superiority, to one's desire 'to be as gods'. It was this phrase which deceived Eve into eating the forbidden fruit in the belief that it would bring her godlike wisdom (Gen. 3 : 5). Christ was tempted to a public display of his

---

[1] The parallel with Christ's temptation in the wilderness, suggested by Frank Kermode (op. cit.), is reviewed at length in Alpers's *Poetry of* The Faerie Queene, pp. 235 ff. Neither Kermode nor Alpers explains Guyon in terms of internal allegory.

godhood as follows: 'Then the devil taketh him up into the holy city, and setteth him on a pinnacle of the temple, and saith unto him, If thou be the Son of God, cast thyself down: for it is written, He shall give his angels charge concerning thee: and in their hands they shall bear thee up, lest at any time thou dash thy foot against a stone. Jesus said unto him, It is written again, Thou shalt not tempt the Lord thy God' (Matt. 4: 5–7). Mammon's version of this temptation is to offer Guyon his daughter Philotime in marriage.[1] She controls the great chain, or Ladder of Ambition, up which men mount to fame. She is also a goddess 'worthie of heven and hye felicitie'. The implication is that marriage to her would make Guyon as one of the gods, as his reply to Mammon indicates:

> 'Gramercy, Mammon,' said the gentle knight,
> 'For so great grace and offred high estate,
> But I, that am fraile flesh and earthly wight,
> Unworthy match for such immortall mate
> My selfe well wote, and mine unequall fate.   (vii. 50)

Guyon adds politely that he is already betrothed to someone else and hence is not eligible as a suitor for Philotime's hand.

The third temptation is that of hunger. In the Biblical account Satan merely suggests that Christ miraculously change stones into bread to assuage his hunger. In Spenser's account Mammon urges Guyon to eat of the golden fruit in the Garden of Proserpine (vii. 58, 63), fruit for which Tantalus is vainly reaching in an attempt to assuage his hunger. Guyon refuses. The precise significance of the golden apples is elusive; but, since they are there to be eaten, they are obviously parallel to the Biblical temptation of hunger.

Finally, when Satan departed and Christ's ordeal was over, 'angels came and ministered unto him' (Matt. 4: 11). When Guyon emerges from Mammon's cave and faints from hunger and shock, an angel guards him until the arrival of the Palmer (viii. 1–8), the only episode of the kind in the entire poem.

Considered as internal allegory, Guyon is the internal virtue of temperance resisting internal visions of wealth and splendour. When he faints upon emerging from the cave, the virtue of temperance is on the verge of overthrow. Externally the person does

---

[1] For Philotime's name see my article 'Spenser's Lucifera and Philotime', *MLN* lix (1944), 413–15. Also above, p. 14.

not faint, but his sense of moderation is finally conquered by his desire to be rich and famous. Yet God's providence (the angel) prevents him from embarking on his new course of wealth-worship until his natural prudence has had time to reassert itself, indicated by the arrival of the Palmer. In his agitated state of mind, the person is more subject than usual to violent anger and to hedonistic temptations (Pyrochles and Cymochles) but is saved from these by his sense of religion and the divine grace residing within his soul (Arthur). With the overthrow of his impulses toward anger and voluptuousness, the person's normal equanimity and sense of moderation gradually return; that is, Guyon regains consciousness and strength.

ACRASIA

In Chapter IV we have already discussed at some length Alma's castle and the surrounding forest as figures for the human body, and no further comment seems to be needed here. We have also discussed the fountain in Acrasia's garden, but some further notice should be given to Acrasia herself. Her name occurs in the *Nicomachean Ethics*, VII. i. 4, in a series of three terms: *akrasia, malakia, tryphe*, rendered into Latin by Du Val as *incontinentia, mollitia, luxus* (incontinence, softness, ease).[1] *Tryphe* may be the source of Tryphon, the leech who heals Marinell's wound in the house of Liagore (III. iv. 43).

Spenser has indicated Acrasia's nature in describing 'Mordant and Amavia slaine With Pleasures poisoned baytes' (II. i. Arg.). In moralizing upon their deaths Guyon remarks: 'The strong through pleasure soonest falles, the weake through smart' (i. 57). As Mordant the 'strong' was killed by Acrasia's poisoned cup, we must consider that she represents pleasure.

Since Spenser later makes Pleasure an approved citizen of the Garden of Adonis (III. vi. 50), it is necessary to determine why she is considered to be evil in one case and good in the other. The answer seems to be that pleasure as a normal accompaniment of sexual activity leading to the generation of offspring is regarded as good because it accords with nature. But pleasure which is a revelling in physical sensation for its own sake is dangerous and

[1] Merritt Y. Hughes has noticed the appearance of *akrasia* in this passage ('Spenser's Acrasia and the Circe of the Renaissance', *JHI* iv [1943], 390).

becomes vicious when it overcomes rational considerations; it is not in accord with nature but becomes an artificial stimulation of the senses. Hence, the Bower of Bliss is constructed by art as well as by nature, whereas Venus' bower in the Garden of Adonis is constructed entirely of surrounding and overshadowing trees, that is, by nature alone.[1]

This distinction seems to be made by Tasso in the last canto of *Gerusalemme Liberata*. Armida and her garden (*GL* xiv. 61–76) are very clearly the model for Acrasia and her garden. There the concupiscible faculty (Armida) has seduced the irascible faculty (Rinaldo) away from its allegiance to the rational faculty (Godfredo). Rinaldo, however, returns to his true allegiance and helps to capture Jerusalem (civil happiness). At the end of the epic Armida comes to the Christian camp and begs Rinaldo to accept her again as a lover. He does so, but now he is the dominant partner. He does not return to her garden, but she remains with him and subject to him, as he is subject to Godfredo (xx. 136). This places the several faculties in their proper relationship, with the concupiscible subject to and not dominant over the other two faculties. Tasso does not comment on this reunion of Rinaldo and Armida in his *Allegory of the Poem*, but its significance may be deduced from the identifications which he makes earlier.

It should be remembered that Guyon and the Palmer do not kill Acrasia. They tear down her bower, bind her, and bring her away. The tearing down of the bower is the soul ridding itself of its subservience to sexual excitement and reducing that impulse to its proper place in the order of things. Its proper place is not a position of dominance in the soul; only when pleasure is dominant is it poisonous.

This is the interpretation usually applied to Circe and Ulysses. Love of her changes other men to beasts, but not him. He remains as her lover for a year after their first meeting, but he is the dominant partner, not she; that is, reason does not succumb to sexual pleasure. When she is dominant, she is destructive. When she is dominated, she still gives pleasure but is constructive in helping Ulysses prepare for the continuation of his journey.

The question of pleasure in the sexual relation and its proper stress or lack of stress was a matter of much concern to the

[1] C. S. Lewis makes this point in *The Allegory of Love* (Oxford, 1936), pp. 324–6.

early Fathers of the Church. It was made so by the Latin wording of the Vulgate, in Genesis 2 : 8, which reads 'paradisus voluptatis' (paradise of pleasure) instead of 'a garden eastward in Eden' (Authorized Version). Since the garden was made for Adam and Eve, and since they had been commanded to 'increase and multiply', it seemed almost essential that the 'pleasure' of the garden be regarded as sexual pleasure. Before the Fall of man, through his disobedience to God, sexual pleasure was innocent. Augustine states that, had man remained innocent, he would have reproduced his kind without any ardour of lust, without any labour and pain of child-bearing on the part of the mother. Eventually, he would have been translated to a higher state of being without undergoing the pangs of death.[1] Augustine is supported in this theory by Gregory the Great, the Venerable Bede, and Peter Lombard.[2] The last of these adds that, since the Fall, from the lustful concupiscence of the parents at its conception, the child's flesh is polluted by sin; this pollution is cleansed by baptism.[3] Thomas Aquinas expanded upon the earlier statements, declaring that in a state of innocence coition was regulated by reason. It excluded both ardour of desire and restlessness of mind; and for that very reason the pleasure of the senses was greater, not less, than in more exciting illicit amours.[4]

The conclusion of these passages seems to be that in all physical union since the Fall there is a measure of lustful concupiscence involved, though this is less true in some instances than in others. Aquinas, in stressing the greater pleasure of coition controlled by reason, obviously has in mind the serenity of love within the marriage bond as contrasted with the excitements and apprehensions of illicit love. Spenser agrees with him in this, finding in married love the supreme expression of romantic happiness.

Augustine says explicitly that, since the Fall, a measure of 'lust' is necessary to secure the generation of offspring. There are two ways of serving lust. One, though tainted by the Fall of man, is nevertheless laudable. This is the lust—or desire—exercised within

---

[1] Augustine, *De Genesi ad Litteram*, IX. iii (PL xxxiv. 395).

[2] Gregory, PL lxxix. 620; Bede, *Quaestiones super Genesim* (PL xciii. 271); Peter Lombard, *Sententiae*, II. xx. 1 (PL cxcii. 692).

[3] Peter Lombard, *Sententiae*, II. xxxii. 3 (PL cxcii. 727).

[4] Aquinas, *Summa Theologica*, pt. I, Q. 98, A. 2. Duns Scotus in his *Summa Theologica* makes a similar statement (ed. Montefortino, Q. 98, A. 2; vol. iii, p. 886).

the marriage bond. The other, lust indulged outside marriage, is wicked and miserable.[1]

Thus, as Peter Lombard says, man's fallen nature is such that some measure of blame attaches even to the generation of legitimate offspring,[2] but this fault of the human condition is a general fault; and within its framework the restrained exercise of pleasurable desire may be praiseworthy. Adam's fall infected the substance of which he was made, the *limus terrae*, or slime of the earth, according to the Vulgate reading (Gen. 2 : 7). Spenser uses this 'slime' repeatedly. Alma's castle, the body of man, is made of Egyptian slime (II. ix. 21). Marinell's goddess-mother Cymodoce faints when he is wounded and would have died if any 'mortal slime' had entered into the composition of her body (III. iv. 35). King Kimbeline had reigned in Britain at the time of Christ's birth:

> What time th'Eternall Lord in fleshly slime
> Enwombed was, from wretched Adams line
> To purge away the guilt of sinfull crime.   (II. x. 50)

Here the 'fleshly slime' is the womb of the Virgin Mary. Later the earth which should 'germinate' a Saviour (Isa. 45 : 8 [Vulgate]) was likewise interpreted allegorically as the womb of the Virgin.[3] But, since Christ was not born from coition of his mother with an earthly father, there was no lustful pleasure involved in his conception and no pain for his mother at his birth;[4] the pain of childbirth was Eve's punishment for her share in the Fall (Gen. 3 : 16). Spenser repeats this interpretation in the birth of Belphoebe and Amoret from the nymph Chrysogone:

> Unwares she them conceivd, unwares she bore:
> She bore withouten paine that she conceiv'd
> Withouten pleasure.   (III. vi. 27)

From these illustrations, we can see the significance of pleasure in the sexual relation. It is a driving force inculcated in mankind

---

[1] Augustine, *Contra Julianum Pelagianum*, v. xvi. 62 (*PL* xliv. 818).

[2] Some later writers deny that coition for the generation of children within the marriage bond has any measure of sin at all. See Peter Comestor, *Historia Scholastica*, ch. x (*PL* cxcviii. 1064); Vincent de Beauvais, *Speculum Naturale*, xxxi. iv, in *Opera* (1624), vol. i, p. 2293B.

[3] Alanus de Insulis, Sermon vii (*PL* ccx. 217B).

[4] Aquinas, *Summa Theologica*, pt. III, Q. 35, A. 6. For other sources see the *Catholic Encyclopedia*, 'Virgin Mary', xv. 464H.

with a view toward perpetuation of the race. It smacks of original sin because the birth–death cycle itself is a result of the original Fall. But human beings must live according to that cycle, generating new bodies as habitations for the heavenly souls that are sent to occupy them. As a promoter of such generation, pleasure is good, for it serves the purposes of nature in an imperfect world. But, if undisciplined and uncontrolled, pleasure exalts the earthly or fleshly part of man above his heavenly part, the rational soul, subjecting the immortal to the mortal, the superior to the inferior, the imperishable to the perishable. In such cases, pleasure must be conquered lest both body and soul fall to complete destruction or to the level of mindless animals who have no immortal souls.

Since Acrasia's name signifies incontinence, it would seem that her opposite should be continence; yet Guyon is called temperance. Quoting Aristotle, Francesco Piccolomini points out that these terms are two degrees of the same thing: the battle to control concupiscent desires. In the continent man, the struggle still goes on, and the issue is in doubt; in the temperate man, the victory is largely won, though not yet complete (ii. 10, p. 100D; iii. 14, pp. 157–8).

Thomaso Porcacchi sees an allegory of this difference in Canto viii of the *Orlando Furioso*. Both Astolfo and Ruggiero seek the palace of Logistilla, or Virtue. Astolfo is the temperate man, Ruggiero the continent man. The first is accompanied by Melissa (divine grace) and makes a quick journey, without impediments, arriving at an early hour (*OF* viii. 18). The second arrives after much fatigue and sweat, having been impeded by a servant (fear), a bird (strong appetite), a dog (pain), and a horse (excessive merriment). He accomplishes the journey, but it is a difficult one and takes a long time.[1]

The goal of the continent man is to reach a state of temperance, where such journeys towards virtue are progressively more easy, for the really severe tests cannot be won by the ill-prepared. Guyon's successes are matched by those of his feminine counterpart Britomart, or chastity. The state of continence is exemplified by Scudamour and Amoret, for whom the battle is much harder than for Guyon and Britomart. Guyon overcomes Acrasia and Britomart overcomes Busyrane; but Scudamour cannot pass

[1] In his 'Allegory' to Canto viii (*Orlando Furioso* [Venice, 1570]). Cf. above, p. 59.

through the fire at Busyrane's house when Britomart goes through safely. Amoret resists Busyrane but cannot overcome his enchantments, but Britomart overcomes him and forces him to undo the charm which binds Amoret. Scudamour and Amoret have other significances, but they both exemplify the continent person in whom the struggle against concupiscence is still sharp and the issue doubtful.

Francesco Piccolomini pursues further the question of incontinence. In the continent man the appetites of sense are in accord with right reason. But when sense subdues reason and reason follows sense, approving only what is pleasant to sense, the man is vicious and incontinent. Again, men govern themselves in terms of love for themselves; they choose between two kinds of pleasure. One indulges the external man in sensual pleasures and represents incontinence. The other subjects the external man to the internal man, the inferior to the superior, and achieves a constitution of the parts of the soul which is harmonious with nature. Only this second kind of pleasure can be called true delight (vii. 18; p. 375D). Francesco thus repeats Aquinas's view of the pleasure involved in sex relations (above, p. 136).

To subdue one's physical desires is harder than to overcome anger or grief. Francesco writes:

Aristotle agreed with Heraclitus in *Nicomachean Ethics* II. iii, saying, 'It is more difficult to resist pleasure than wrath.' And Seneca affirmed that 'he rules a great power who commands himself, and he who conquers desire is stronger than he who overcomes an enemy'. And Solomon said that 'he who conquers his own soul is stronger than he who conquers cities'.   (iv. 50; p. 230c)

Spenser writes on the same subject:

> A harder lesson to learn continence
> In joyous pleasure then in grievous paine:
> For sweetnesse doth allure the weaker sence
> So strongly, that uneathes it can refraine
> From that which feeble nature covets faine:
> But griefe and wrath, that be her enemies,
> And foes of life, she better can restraine;
> Yet Vertue vauntes in both her victories,
> And Guyon in them all shewes goodly maysteries.
>
>   (II. vi. 1)

Here again we have Guyon portrayed as an exemplar of both temperance and fortitude, which control lust and wrath respectively; and, of the two, temperance is the more difficult. In overcoming Acrasia, Guyon passes his supreme test, bringing to the soul a harmonious relationship in which the pleasures of the body serve to inspire and not to obscure the rational nature of man.

VII

The Moral Allegory of Friendship, Chastity, and Love

BOOKS III and IV of *The Faerie Queene* constitute an analysis of love and friendship as these motives operate within human society and within the human soul. The subject is not completed within the two books but extends into Book v, occupying Cantos iii, v, vi, and vii of that book. There are five major plots to be considered: Cambell–Triamond, Belphoebe–Timias, Britomart–Artegall, Amoret–Scudamour, and Florimell–Marinell. In addition, five major characters are carried over from the first two books: Redcross, Guyon, Satyrane, Archimago, Duessa. Arthur also reappears but with a relatively minor role.

FRIENDSHIP

Both Aristotle and Francesco Piccolomini think of friendship as a term including romantic love. Friendship between men is illustrated by the story of Cambell and Triamond, who are the titular heroes of Book IV but play a relatively minor part in it. In them, friendship is bolstered and strengthened by romantic love, since Cambell and Triamond marry each other's sisters.

The *philia* of Aristotle and *amicitia* of Francesco, when not referring to affable and friendly manners, involve an element of love which makes friendship a closer attachment than ordinary friendliness. Though Aristotle dismisses the topic rather quickly (*Nic. Eth.* ix. ii–iii), Francesco devotes an entire book to friendship (bk. vii), in which he stresses the element of love, supporting his views with quotations from Plato's *Symposium*. He states that friendship may exist between men, or between women, or between man and woman (vii. 20; p. 378B). He notes the affinity of such words as *amabile, amor, amicus, amicitia*; and he adds to these *desiderium* (desire), *dilectio* (esteem), and *benevolentia* (good will) (vii. 2; p. 357C). He defines friendship as follows: 'Friendship is

the mutual, open, and confirmed love of upright men, rising from
a recognition of uprightness and leading to a conjunction of
honest life' (vii. 3; p. 359A). Again he writes: 'Friendship is love;
desire is an affection and companion of love. We seek to follow
an object and enjoy it; most fully, however, we enjoy with
friendly probity, in conjunction of life, actions proceeding from
virtue, as though rays from the sun' (vii. 4; p. 360A). Desire is not
excluded from upright love but cannot be the sole element in it.
Where friendship is based solely on pleasure or solely on utility,
it cannot be strong and lasting, says Aristotle. Such friendship
can exist between two persons who are bad, between one good
and one bad person, or between persons who are neither bad nor
good (*Nic. Eth.* VIII. iv. 2). These unions are easily dissolved by
calumny and suspicion, which can be withstood only by the friendship of good persons. Spenser illustrates this in the Duessa–Ate
and the Paridell–Blandamour friendships, the second of which
breaks up in a quarrel over the false Florimell, a quarrel further
stirred up by Ate but pacified by the Squire of Dames. Spenser
makes this comment upon them:

> So well accorded forth they rode together
> In friendly sort, that lasted but a while,
> And of all old dislikes they made faire weather;
> Yet all was forg'd and spred with golden foyle,
> That under it hidde hate and hollow guyle.
> Ne certes can that friendship long endure,
> How ever gay and goodly be the style,
> That doth ill cause or evill end enure:
> For vertue is the band that bindeth harts most sure.
>
> (IV. ii. 29)

The episode seems clearly designed to illustrate the dictum of
Aristotle.

At the beginning of Canto ix, Spenser makes the following
comment upon the Amyas–Placidas–Paeana story:

> Hard is the doubt, and difficult to deeme,
> When all three kinds of love together meet,
> And do dispart the hart with powre extreme,
> Whether shall weigh the balance downe; to weet,
> The deare affection unto kindred sweet,
> Or raging fire of love to woman kind,
> Or zeale of friends combynd with vertues meet.

But of them all, the band of vertuous mind,
Me seemes, the gentle hart should most assured bind.

(IV. ix. I)

As indicated by Heffner and DeMoss, this stanza has a general indebtedness to Aristotle.[1] For example, the 'raging fire' of love is that based upon pleasure, without the added mutual respect that is based on virtue. It is that desire which Francesco Piccolomini calls the companion of love rather than love itself (above, p. 142). The posing of the additional question of preferability between family ties and friendship is suggested by Francesco's chapter, 'Whether Friendship is to be preferred to Affinity and Conjunction of Blood' (vii. 16; pp. 373–4). It is a natural instinct, he writes, to prefer our relatives by blood and to help them, since in benefiting our family we are partly benefiting ourselves. But, while nature binds brothers together, virtue binds friends, together with choice and free will, which are preferred before nature and bind more strongly than nature. A good friend may be more congenial than a brother, and in an absolute sense friendship is to be preferred to blood relationship. But a connection by blood is a certain natural friendship, and it is possible for blood relatives to be joined by moral friendship also. Best of all is the friendship of brothers, when nature, fortune, and virtue happily conspire to join them by blood and by a common outlook on things.

Spenser has illustrated this passage in the three sons of Agape: Priamond, Diamond, and Triamond; these were triplets, born at a single birth, and all three loved the exercise of arms (IV. ii. 42):

These three did love each other dearly well,
And with so firme affection were allyde,
As if but one soule in them all did dwell,
Which did her powre into three parts divide.   (stanza 43)

With the successive deaths of Priamond and Diamond at Cambell's hands, the tripartite soul is reunited in Triamond, making him equal to Cambell in prowess, therefore a brave foe and a worthy friend.[2] While all three lived, their 'firme affection' proceeded from their common birth and their common interest in warfare.

In connection with friendship, we have Spenser's portrayal of the goddess Concord holding the balance between Love and Hate

<hr>

[1] *Var.* iv. 213, 296.   [2] Cf. C. G. Smith in *Var.* iv. 328–30.

(IV. x. 31–5). Its inclusion may be partly indebted to Francesco's association of concord with friendship: 'Concord is the consent and agreement of many persons on one subject; it is broader than Friendship. Where Friendship is, there is Concord, but the reverse is not always true. Yet the best concord arises from Friendship and is as though its "affection" and fruit' (vii. 2; p. 358B).[1]

Spenser's use of the goddess Concord and his use of the three sons of Agape, in both instances to illustrate friendship, suggest an indebtedness to the *Emblemata* of Andreas Alciatus. Emblem 40 bears the motto 'Insuperabilis Concordia'. The picture shows a crowned warrior with one head and body but with three faces, six arms, and six legs. The three left hands balance a shield, the lower side of which rests on the ground. The three right hands hold a spear, a short sword, and a mace or sceptre. The poem underneath reads:

> Tergeminos inter fuerat concordia fratres,
>   Tanta simul pietas mutua, & vnus amor:
> Inuicti humanis vt viribus ampla tenerent
>   Regna, vno dicti nomine Geryonis.

(Among triplet brothers there had been so much concord, together with mutual piety and one love that, unconquered by human power, they might hold ample kingdoms, being called by the single name of Geryon.)

In the gloss of Claudius Minos, we are told that the ancients fashioned the three-formed image of Geryon because 'common opinion asserted that only one soul and one will were in the king, although there were three persons'. Spenser says that the three sons of Agape seemed to have one soul which was divided into three parts. Curiously enough, he seems to have used the picture accompanying Emblem 40 as a model for his description of the giant Gerioneo, in v. xi, thus employing the emblem twice to secure quite opposite effects.[2]

THE TOURNAMENT OF LOVE

The four couples, Belphoebe–Timias, Britomart–Artegall, Amoret–Scudamour, and Florimell–Marinell, represent various

---

[1] Cf. *Nic. Eth.* VIII. i. 4, IX. vi. For other resemblances, see *Var.* iv. 226–8.

[2] 'Alciatus, *Emblemata* (edn. of Lyons, 1614, pp. 177–8). Editions with Minos's commentary appeared as early as 1573.

aspects of romantic love. The internal struggle is usually in the mind of a woman, but sometimes in the mind of a man. The problems involved concern physical love and its moral implications. The wooing of Belphoebe ends in 'platonic' love, without physical coition. The other three love-affairs end in marriage and represent the triumph of virtuous love. In contrast to these, we have a moral *exemplum* in the person of Hellenore, who falls from a virtuous marriage when seduced by Paridell and falls yet further to become a nymphomaniac among the satyrs. When given an opportunity to return to her husband Malbecco, she will not accept it.

Books III and IV revolve largely around the activities of the Knights of Maidenhead. The term is used for maidenhood, just as 'womanhead' is used for womanhood in reference to Amoret (III. vi. 28). But Spenser is aware of 'maidenhead' in its anatomical sense, referring to the hymen as the sign of a girl's virginity. The various struggles occur within her soul between the forces persuading her to surrender her virginity and those which persuade her not to surrender it. The latter are the Knights of Maidenhead.

This allegory was probably suggested by the *Roman de la Rose*, in which the Rose is the 'virgin flower' of woman. Its anatomical significance is unmistakable at the end of the poem, when the lover successfully plucks the Rose after being aided by Venus. The castle which shelters the Rose is therefore the woman's body, and its defenders are her mental impulses which persuade her against surrender: Daunger (disdain), Shame, Fear, and Wicked-Tongue. This last partakes of external allegory, representing the fear of gossip or slander from without, a fear that is quieted by False Appearance (Faux-Semblant) which conceals the proposed amour. The lover receives hope from Fair Welcoming (Bel Accueil), the woman's natural cordiality and friendliness. The overcoming of her mental resistance is represented in the storming of the castle by the forces of Venus and Cupid.[1]

In Spenser's treatment of this subject, the attack and surrender do not necessarily involve illicit love. The surrender is usually envisaged as coming after marriage, and the campaign is to bring the girl to marriage and a subsequent surrender of virginity. The

[1] For Spenser's use of the *Roman de la Rose* and the tradition which it established see *Var.* iii. 211, iv. 221.

opponents of Maidenhead are not necessarily vicious, though some of them may be, for they include Cambell and Triamond on the one hand, Paridell and Blandamour on the other.

The great tournament arranged by Satyrane, with Florimell's girdle as the prize, is a full-scale portrayal of this struggle (IV. iv). Satyrane leads the Knights of Maidenhead in a three-day clash with the challengers. Spenser introduces various knights not mentioned elsewhere in order to give the effect of a crowded pageant. Some of their names have little significance, but others have more.

We have already identified Satyrane as the irascible faculty within the soul (above, p. 30). He opens the tournament by encountering Bruncheval (Fr., dark horse). The two champions strike so hard that they knock each other senseless. The allegorical meaning probably stems from Plato's *Phaedrus*, 246, where the white horse represents the irascible faculty and the dark horse the concupiscible faculty (above, p. 130). The dark horse only appears here, but the white horse appears in the person of Florimell's palfrey (below, p. 147). Here Bruncheval represents the concupiscible faculty, with its natural appetite for sexual experience, which the irascible faculty (Satyrane) seeks to subdue. The battle is inconclusive.

The next champion of Maidenhead is Ferramont (Iron Mountain), who seems to be a symbol of steadfastness. He is assailed in turn by Blandamour and Paridell, the seductions of fickle and insincere love (above, p. 31) and easily overthrows both of them. But he cannot hold his ground against Triamond (friendship), who unhorses him and then defeats in turn Devon, Douglas, and Paliumord. Satyrane, reviving, returns to the fight and severely wounds Triamond but the next day is himself overthrown by Cambell, the other example of friendship. Cambell is overcome by a host of Satyrane's comrades but is rescued by the wounded Triamond, and the two friends end the day in triumph.

On the final day Satyrane overcomes all challengers until he meets a Salvage Knight, who is Artegall in disguise. The unknown knight overthrows Satyrane, Sangliere (the boar), and Brianor. Artegall continues by overthrowing seven more knights and seems about to conquer the Knights of Maidenhead single-handed. Then Britomart rushes forth and in succession overthrows Artegall, Cambell, Triamond, and Blandamour. Since she does not take off her helmet, no one knows her identity. When she refuses the prize for the third day's victory, it is awarded to the disguised Salvage Knight Artegall, but he has already departed (IV. V. 21).[1]

Returning to the external situation of the woman in whose soul these combats take place, we find her steadfast in her resistance to lascivious impulses (Blandamour, Paridell). But when true friendship (Triamond) asks her love, she finds it difficult to refuse. Her irascible faculty (Satyrane) revives, and she struggles against the claims of friendship but is on the verge of yielding. After a night's sleep, her irascible faculty and power of resistance are again strong, but these are soon overthrown by her sense of justice (Artegall). She feels that she *owes* her love to the friend who has done so much for her. But then her moral principles (Britomart) come to the rescue. Unchaste conduct is not required of her to requite an imagined obligation or to reward a friendship or to satisfy a temporary passion. For example, if she is wooed by a married man whom she cannot legally wed, she rejects the idea that she should become his mistress, even though she may like him very much.

Having used Plato's 'dark horse' in Bruncheval, Spenser uses its companion, the 'white horse', in Florimell's steed. The white palfrey bears Florimell away from everyone, both friends and enemies. But when she secretly leaves the Witch's house, her horse is tracked and finally caught by the tireless beast that feeds on women's flesh. Florimell escapes by sea, but the beast devours her horse. He is interrupted by Satyrane, who beats him into submission but cannot kill him; he is tamed and muzzled with the Girdle of Chastity, which Florimell had dropped. We have earlier pointed to Satyrane and the beast as the irascible faculty subduing the concupiscible faculty (above, pp. 30, 58). But Florimell's palfrey may also represent the irascible faculty from another point of view, that which aids virtue by flight. Francesco Piccolomini has noted the principles of pursuit and flight in the development of affections and perturbations (above, p. 33). Satyrane aids Beauty by pursuit; the palfrey preserves Beauty by flight. Both are parts of the irascible faculty and both seek to save Beauty from the concupiscible faculty.

[1] This episode may derive from a tournament described in Henry Goldwell's *Shews, devices, Speeches before the Queen* (1581). The Queen's seat is called the Fortress or

BELPHOEBE AND TIMIAS

In *A Treatice of Morall Philosophye*, William Baldwin defines chastity: 'Chastitie and puritie of lyfe, consisteth eyther in sincere virginitie, or in faithefull matrimonie. The first degree of chastitie, is pure virginitie; ye second faithful matrimonye' (f. 163ᵛ).[1] Spenser thus advises young ladies:

> To youre faire selves a faire ensample frame
> Of this faire virgin, this Belphebe fayre,
> To whom, in perfect love and spotlesse fame
> Of chastitie, none living may compayre:
> Ne poysonous envy justly can empayre
> The prayse of her fresh flowering maydenhead:
> Forthy she standeth on the highest stayre
> Of th'honorable stage of womanhead,
> That ladies all may follow her ensample dead.   (III. v. 54)

In her representation of virginity, Belphoebe represents the 'highest stayre' or first degree of chastity and womanhood. Yet Spenser must not be taken as urging all ladies to remain virgins for ever; he is urging them to remain virgins until they have married. Their chastity is then that of the second degree, of 'faithfull matrimonie'. Those who undertake the 'maiden pilgrimage'[2] for religious or patriotic or idealistic reasons are deserving of special honour; and foremost among these was Queen Elizabeth. Her continued virginity seems to have inspired a secular cult of virginity paralleling the religious adoration of the Virgin Mary. Or, rather, it intensified such a cult; for the virgin goddess Diana had always been honoured in a different way from the virgin goddess Vesta. The first was a free spirit who enjoyed the arduous life of a hunter. The second preserved the sanctity of the home, and her altar fires were tended by maidens who took the vows of perpetual virginity. Elizabeth was regularly portrayed as Diana, and Spenser makes Belphoebe a foster-child of Diana, who adopted her when Venus adopted her twin sister Amoret (III. vi. 28).

Castle of Perfect Beauty. Twenty-one knights enter the lists as defenders. 'And afterwards in the middest of the running, came in *Sir Henry Lea*, as vnknowen, and when he had broken his sixe staues, went out in like maner againe' (Bii). Italics not mine.

[1] *A Treatice of Morall Philosophye* (London, 1567).
[2] Theseus' phrase in *A Midsummer Night's Dream*, I. i. 75.

In both cults, the emblem of virginity is the Rose or 'vir[
flower' representing the hymen; and this image is expanded well
beyond its physical meaning. St. Bernard called virginity 'the
flower of the garden',[1] and Rabanus Maurus called it 'the ornament of the world' (*decor mundi*).[2] Spenser writes of it:

> That daintie rose, the daughter of her morne,
> More deare then life she tendered, whose flowre
> The girlond of her honour did adorne. (III. v. 51)

God brought this flower from paradise and rooted it in earthly
flesh for the greater glory of womankind:

> In gentle ladies breste and bounteous race
> Of woman kind it fayrest flowre doth spyre,
> And beareth fruit of honour and all chast desyre.
> (stanza 52)

The preservation of virginity does not mean that Belphoebe is
immune to romantic love. On the contrary, she has great treasures
of love, for true love does not have to express itself in physical
coition in order to exist, at least not in Fairyland. In the medieval
Irish story of Teague's voyage to Fairyland, Teague learns that
there lovers take their delight in looking at each other without
any 'impurity or fleshly sin whatever'.[3] Timias is not able to love
in this way until he loses Belphoebe and suffers intensely from her
absence. When she accepts him again into her favour, he learns to
be happy with a 'platonic' relationship, since this is the only one
that she will permit.

Viewed as internal allegory, the love of Belphoebe and Timias
represents the association of virginity with grace and honour. As
Francesco Piccolomini interprets the moderate desire of honour,
it becomes almost the same as modesty (above, p. 14). Spenser
writes of Belphoebe:

> In so great prayse of stedfast chastity
> Nathlesse she was so courteous and kynde,
> Tempred with *grace* and goodly *modesty*,
> That seemed these two vertues strove to fynd
> The higher place in her *heroick mynd*. (III. v. 55)

---

[1] Bernard, in *PL* clxxxiii. 1009D.   [2] Rabanus Maurus, in *PL* cxii. 929C.
[3] Meyer and Nutt, *The Voyage of Bran* (London, 1895), vol. i, p. 204.

Grace and modesty are suitable companions of virginity, all three contributing to the charm of youthful girlhood, and likewise of maturer spinsterhood. Belphoebe's 'heroick mynd' reflects Francesco's classification of virginity as heroic temperance (above, p. 9). Since she represents heroic temperance, she is first introduced to the reader in Book II, the Legend of Temperance; since she represents a form of chastity, she reappears at length in the next book, the Legend of Chastity; since the grant of her 'favour' to Timias represents a sublimation of romantic love, she likewise appears in Book IV, the Legend of Friendship.

BRITOMART AND ARTEGALL

Britomart and Artegall are predestined to wed. He does not know this, but she does, first from Merlin's magic mirror and then from Merlin's own lips. Their son-to-be, Aurelius Conan, will seize the crown of Britain as his right and will fight great wars against the Saxons (III. iii. 29), continuing the tradition of King Arthur.[1] Britomart's career as an Amazonian warrior comes at the suggestion of her nurse and squire Glauce, and is an excuse to visit Fairyland, where Artegall is living. Since Artegall does not know the true secret of his descent from a royal line of Celtic kings, Britomart has the historical mission of bringing him back to Britain. Her marriage will be a matter of national duty as well as personal preference.

Yet Artegall has another historic mission to fulfil, this time in the service of Gloriana. He must save the lady Eirena (Erin or Ireland) from the clutches of Grantorto (Spain) and, almost incidentally, defeat the enemies of Burbon (Henri IV of France). Thus Artegall lives in two centuries, the sixth and the sixteenth, in one as an actual personage of history, in the other as a reincarnation after the lapse of a thousand years. He is a 'hero' in the timeless land of spirits that Francesco Piccolomini and Plutarch locate in or near the Island of Britain (above, p. 49).

Artegall's relations with Britomart are marked by unusual episodes. They first meet at Satyrane's tournament, where Artegall is in disguise and therefore cannot be identified by the device on his shield. In the jousting, Britomart defeats him without

---

[1] For discussion see Rathborne, *The Meaning of Spenser's Fairyland*, pp. 226–30.

knowing who he is. In their later encounter, her helmet is knocked off and Artegall is so struck by her beauty that he can fight no more. Instead, he seeks her hand in marriage and finally wins her consent to a betrothal; then he departs with a promise to return within three months (IV. vi. 43). In terms of internal allegory, these clashes mean that the impulse towards chastity seems to conflict with the impulse towards justice in a person's soul. Francesco had said that two virtues might seem to clash when they were imperfectly understood, but that there could be no lasting opposition between two virtues, since their natural condition was harmonious (above, p. 33). Under what external conditions would justice involve unchastity or chastity involve injustice, or seem to do so?

One such example has been given early in this chapter: a girl's feeling that she owes a male friend her sexual favours in return for his kindnesses. In Shakespeare's *Measure for Measure*, Isabella is asked to surrender her chastity in order to save her brother's life. In Heywood's *A Woman Killed with Kindness*, Susan Mountford feels that she must surrender her chastity in order to save her brother's honour. In these instances justice seems to demand the surrender of chastity, but the conflict is more apparent than real. Francesco also observes that a refusal to love one who loves you is a kind of injustice (VII. vii; p. 363B). The method of returning love must be limited by other commitments; e.g. Belphoebe accepts only a 'platonic' relation with Timias. This observation may have helped to determine Spenser's choice of justice as a suitable mate for chastity.

It is harder to explain Britomart's clash with Guyon. In their joust he is violently overthrown (III. i. 6); i.e. chastity defeats temperance. But how could these two conflict within the human soul? It seems a contradiction in terms to speak of a person as temperately unchaste or moderately unchaste. But can a person be intemperately chaste? This is a possibility, that a person can be so militant or pugnacious in the exercise of a virtue that he or she exceeds the bounds of moderation and becomes offensive to other people through a too well advertised goodness. We are reminded of the Athenians who banished Aristides because they were so weary of hearing him called 'the Just'.[1]

The quarrel between Guyon and Britomart is composed by the

---

[1] Plutarch, *Lives*, 'Aristides', Modern Library Edition, p. 396.

Palmer (prudence) and Arthur (heavenly grace). Spenser then shows the proper relation of the virtues:

> Thus reconcilement was betweene them knitt,
> Through goodly temperaunce and affection chaste . . .
> In which accord the Prince was also plaste,
> And with that golden chaine of concord tyde.   (stanza 12)

This emphasizes the close natural affinity of temperance and chastity, listed by Francesco as companion virtues (above, p. 9).

Further questions arise. Artegall is a Knight of Maidenhead (v. iv. 34), yet at Satyrane's tournament he fought in disguise against the Knights of Maidenhead. We then come to the crucial question of his subjection to Radigund. Radigund is a female warrior who has vowed revenge on the whole masculine sex through chagrin at the rejection of her love by Bellodant (wargiving). Her method of revenge is the same as Omphale's treatment of Hercules; she dresses the knights in women's clothes, compels them to do household chores, and hangs any that refuse (v. iv. 30–2). Her hatred of men is based on thwarted love, and she falls in love with her prisoner Artegall, but her messages are falsified by her maid Clarin, who loves Artegall herself. Artegall is stronger than Radigund but could not fight her after taking off her helmet and seeing her beauty; hence he must fulfil his contract to obey her commands. His own sense of justice renders him powerless; but Britomart, when fighting for his release, has no such inhibition. When she has laid Radigund prostrate, she strikes again and kills her. She releases Artegall and the other prisoners:

> So there a while they afterwards remained,
> Him to refresh, and her late wounds to heale:
> During which space she there as princes rained,
> And changing all that forme of common weale,
> The liberty of women did repeale,
> Which they had long usurpt; and them restoring
> To mens subjection, did true justice deale.   (v. vii. 42)

These lines leave little doubt concerning Spenser's opinion of dominant women. Radigund seems to be a kind of rabid suffragette who crusades for 'equality' but seizes superiority, almost a Strindbergian heroine. Yet her mind was twisted by her hatred, and she was not comfortable in her superior role, for her dominance was unnatural. She hated the natural and normal limitations of her sex and in this was unwomanly.

The full title of Jesus College, Cambridge, is 'the college of Jesus, the Blessed Virgin Mary, St. John the Evangelist, and St. Rhadegund', as the patent was issued to John Alcock in 1497. St. Rhadegund was included in this exalted company because Jesus College was built on the site of the ancient nunnery of St. Rhadegund, and the present college chapel was the church of the nunnery.[1] We should expect Spenser to be interested in antiquities of this kind and perhaps in Rhadegund herself.[2] J. H. Walter has noted the resemblance of the names Radigund and Rhadegund and has examined the life of St. Rhadegund. He notes that she married, but refused to consummate her marriage by coition with her husband. He speculates as to whether this fact can shed any light on the allegory.[3] Actually, it furnishes the key to the characters of Radigund and Britomart.

In her early adventures Britomart is so successful that she might well have become like Radigund, for she overthrows every male knight against whom she lifts her spear. She is militant chastity, chastity on a heroic scale. In her encounter with Guyon she may even be intemperate chastity. Her clashes with Artegall (justice) are then explained if the external situation is that of a wife who denies her husband marital privileges or of a girl who extends the period of her engagement to an excessive length before marriage. Then justice might reasonably join friendship in opposition to the Knights of Maidenhead, thinking that even chastity can be somewhat excessive under the circumstances.

Just before her great battle with Radigund, Britomart visits the Temple of Isis, which is to be her place of perfecting the virtue of chastity. Isis is normally regarded as a goddess of fertility, though Spenser here lists Osiris and Isis as representing justice and equity (v. vii. 2–3). In the midst of the temple are Isis and

---

[1] John Steegman, *Cambridge* (New York, 1941), pp. 11–12, 62.

[2] Rhadegund (or Radegunde), a princess of Thuringia, was forced to marry Clotair I, who had conquered her country. After he had put her brother to death, she left him and became a nun, later abbess, in a convent in Poitiers. Her life was written in Latin prose by Venantius Fortunatus (*Catholic Encyclopedia*: 'Fortunatus', vol. vi, p. 149).

[3] '*The Faerie Queene*: Alterations and Structure', *MLR* xxxvi (1941), 51. Quoted in Donald Cheney's *Spenser's Image of Nature*, p. 161. Cheney thinks that Spenser's reference to Hippolytus (v. viii. 43) may likewise deprecate an excessive commitment to chastity (p. 161).

Osiris represented as a silver statue; Osiris is a crocodile at the feet of Isis. Britomart falls asleep by the altar and dreams that the crocodile begs to have coition with her, that she consents, and that she afterwards gives birth to a lion. Perplexed by the dream, she asks one of the priests to interpret it. He explains that the crocodile represents Artegall, who will restore her to the crown of her country. She will marry him and bear a lion-like heroic son. The implication is that she should submit herself to marriage and motherhood, after her many quests and adventures abroad.

Thus the situation is explained. Chastity that takes the vow of perpetual virginity (Belphoebe) will always protect the maidenhead or 'virgin rose' from violation. But chastity that looks towards faithful matrimony should unite with justice within the woman's soul and should not prolong capriciously the period of virginity under the pretence that such a delay is virtuous. The wife or wife-to-be owes a duty to her husband. In this and in other matters, the acceptance of a husband in marriage involved, for Spenser, a submission to the husband's will. Britomart's wound by Radigund (viii. 33) signifies a momentary yielding of chastity to an anti-masculine bias, a bias quickly overcome by more truly feminine impulses.

In terms of internal allegory, Radigund's amorous advances to Artegall are only figurative. Female domination seeks the support of justice, pretending that this is the correct order of marriage. But actually it 'imprisons' justice because it is essentially unjust. True chastity in the soul deliberately destroys the impulse toward female domination and unites with justice in determining on wifely submission. The wedding of justice (Artegall) and chastity (Britomart) is not the external marriage. It is the union of impulses within a woman's soul that determines her to be a true and loyal wife.

Aristotle says that justice or its opposite is usually concerned with our actions or attitudes towards other people. But, metaphorically speaking, there is an internal justice needed between different parts of our own nature; e.g. between the rational and the irrational impulses of the soul, or between two impulses when one seems to be thwarted by the other. It is such justice that exists between a master and a servant or between husband and wife (below, p. 174). Artegall's relations with Britomart and Radigund are a representation of this internal justice, whereas Artegall's other actions and decisions represent external justice in the attitudes of a man towards other men.

AMORET AND SCUDAMOUR

Amoret is womanhood, sister of Belphoebe, or maidenhood. As Belphoebe represents love without coition, Amoret represents love with coition, the physical side of wedded love. Amoret, perfected in womanhood in the Temple of Venus, was brought out by Scudamour, whose name means 'shield of love' (*escu d'amour*) and who carries a picture of Cupid on his shield, which he won by his journey to the temple. This Temple of Venus is presumably in the Garden of Adonis, where Amoret had been placed in III. vi; but it was not mentioned in the earlier description. The temple was not part of Spenser's original plan. The quest of Scudamour, as described in the *Letter to Raleigh*, is to release Amoret from the enchanter Busyrane. Scudamour fails to penetrate the fire around Busyrane's castle, but Britomart penetrates it, undoes the charm, and rescues Amoret. This seems to be the obvious climax of the story as Spenser originally planned it. Amoret's story was to be concluded with the end of Book III. Instead of the last three stanzas which end the book, in the 1590 edition Spenser had five stanzas describing the reunion of Amoret and Scudamour. They proceed at once to passionate embraces, in Britomart's presence:

> At last she came unto the place, where late
> She left Sir Scudamour in great distresse,
> Twixt dolour and delight halfe desperate
> Of his loves succour, of his owne redresse,
> And of the hardie Britomarts successe:
> There on the cold earth him now thrown she found,
> In wilfull anguish, and dead heavinesse,
> And to him cald; whose voices knowen sound
> Soone as he heard, himself he reared light from ground.

> There did he see, that most on earth him joyd,
> His dearest love, the comfort of his dayes,
> Whose too long absence him had sore annoyd,
> And wearied his life with dull delayes:
> Straight he upstarted from the loathed layes,

And to her ran with hasty egernesse,
Like as a deare, that greedily embayes
In the cool soile, after long thirstinesse,
Which he in chace endured hath, now nigh breathlesse.

Lightly he clipt her twixt his armes twaine,
And streightly did embrace her body bright,
Her body, late the prison of sad paine,
Now the sweet lodge of love and deare delight:
But she, faire lady, overcommen quight
Of huge affection, did in pleasure melt,
And in sweet ravishment pourd out her spright:
No word they spake, nor earthly thing they felt,
But like two senceless stocks in long embracement dwelt.

Had ye them seene, ye would have surely thought,
That they had beene that faire hermaphrodite,
Which that rich Romane of white marble wrought,
And in his costly bath caused to be site:
So seemd those two, as growne together quite,
That Britomart, halfe envying their blesse,
Was much empassiond in her gentle sprite,
And to her selfe oft wisht like happinesse:
In vaine she wisht, that fate n'ould let her yet possesse.

Thus doe these lovers with sweet countervayle
Each other of loves bitter fruit despoile.
But now my teme begins to faint and fayle,
All woxen weary of their journall toyle:
Therefore I will their sweatie yokes assoyle,
At this same furrowes end, till a new day:
And ye, faire swayns, after your long turmoyle,
Now cease your worke, and at your pleasure play:
Now cease your worke; tomorrow is an holy day.

(stanzas 43–7)

Opinions differ as to whether the passionate embrace portrayed in these lines indicates actual coition. C. S. Lewis thought that the comparison to a hermaphrodite indicated the true union of man and wife in 'one flesh' (Gen. 2 : 24), unlike the casual indulgence of Paridell and Hellenore, 'a wanton payre Of lovers loosely knit' (III. x. 16).[1] The 'bitter fruit' of love, of which the lovers 'despoile'

---

[1] Lewis, *Spenser's Images of Life*, p. 38.

each other, would seem to be a reference to coition, real or anti-
cipated, and to the pleasures of physical love.

Here the successful culmination of the quest involves Amoret's
ability to unite freely and pleasurably in sexual relations; consequently, Busyrane must represent some inhibition that had prevented her from doing this. Internally this scene represents the
union of womanhood with the desire of physical love; externally
it is a woman overcoming her frigidity or similar inhibition and
so desiring instead of fearing sexual relations. But the internal
preparation is not itself an act of coition even when described as
such; it is the preliminary step to the external sexual union which
will follow. This external union will be preceded by marriage if
marriage does not already exist, for Spenser at all times insists
upon Amoret's chastity.

It must be repeated that, in this view, Scudamour and Amoret
are not externally the lovers who are to be married. Both of them
are impulses within the soul of a woman contemplating marriage
and the sexual union which is to follow. But their figurative embrace is described so vividly that they seem to be real people.
Also, Spenser did not take the precaution of describing them as
married people, an oversight which put their union into the same
class as that of Redcross and Duessa. The Redcross–Duessa union
had been plainly evil, but that of Scudamour and Amoret is the
fulfilment of a virtuous quest; it is both witnessed and envied
by the excessively virtuous Britomart, apparently reversing all the
moral precepts which Spenser had earlier been imparting. The
vividness of his description of an erotic scene between two un-
married lovers, while the virtuous guardian of chastity watched
approvingly, was difficult to accept; it was as though Acrasia
and Verdant had suddenly become heroic objects of the poet's
admiration.

As internal allegory this scene represents the birth and growth
of a woman's desire for physical union with her future husband.
We may assume that some readers failed to see the internal
allegory or possibly disapproved even if they did see it. We have
noted in the preceding chapter the varying attitudes towards
pleasure in the physical side of marriage. To some persons strong
physical desire might seem unwomanly, even within the marriage
bond. Spenser rejects this conception absolutely. Like Aquinas, he
believes that physical pleasure in marriage is greater than that of

furtive illicit amours or casual encounters (above, p. 136). When directed toward its proper object, it is so strong that it raises a person to a vision of heavenly love and the love of God.[1] It is essentially the love which Juliet felt towards Romeo: she longed passionately for the union of their wedding-night and later rejected as a kind of profanation the suggestion that she should turn her love towards someone else.[2]

We know that, after the publication of the first three books of *The Faerie Queene* in 1590, Spenser was vigorously criticized for writing of love in the way he did; for he answers the criticism in the Proem to Book IV and attributes it by implication to Lord Burleigh:

> The rugged forehead that with grave foresight
> Welds kingdomes causes and affaires of state,
> My looser rimes (I wote) doth sharply wite,
> For praising love, as I have done of late,
> And magnifying lovers deare debate;
> By which fraile youth is oft to follie led,
> Through false allurement of that pleasing baite,
> That better were in vertues discipled,
> Than with vaine poemes weeds to have their fancies fed.
>
> Such ones ill judge of love, that cannot love,
> Ne in their frosen hearts feele kindly flame:
> Forthy they ought not thing unknowne reprove,
> Ne naturall affection faultlesse blame,
> For fault of few that have abusd the same,
> For it of honor and all vertue is
> The roote, and brings forth glorious flowres of fame,
> That crowne true lovers with immortall blis,
> The meed of them that love, and do not live amisse.
>
> (stanzas 1–2)

Here Spenser reflects Francesco Piccolomini's statement that love is the soul, spirit, and life of honour (vii. 13; p. 369B). Spenser goes on to show that the love of friends, like that of Socrates and Critias, may produce great achievements. He thus subtly shifts his ground from love as a sexual union to the broader definition including friendship, in order to refute 'these Stoick censours'.

---

[1] Cf. Spenser's *Fowre Hymnes*.
[2] Shakespeare, *Romeo and Juliet*, III. ii. 10–16, v. 235–40.

He will not try to please them but will write for Queen Elizabeth, who does understand love and is 'the Queene of love, and prince of peace from heaven blest'. This extravagant line envisages Elizabeth as combining the qualities of Christ, Venus, and the Virgin Mary, perhaps relating her love to the love of God. The following and final stanza of the Proem urges Cupid to visit the Queen and seems to urge her towards marriage. At this date (1596) the foremost candidate for such a marriage was the Earl of Essex, who became Spenser's patron some time after the death of the Earl of Leicester in 1588. Spenser's friend Raleigh was already married and thus a candidate for 'favour' but not for matrimony.

That the original ending of Book III was in fact the target of criticism by Burleigh and others seems to be indicated by the fact that Spenser omitted it in the second edition (1596). Instead of being reunited with Scudamour, Amoret finds that he has disappeared. Furthermore, Spenser retells the story of Amoret to assure the reader that she and Scudamour had been *married* after he brought her out of Venus' temple (IV. i. 2). But the marriage was unconsummated because she was stolen away by Busyrane from the wedding festival. Amoret remains a companion of Britomart until she is kidnapped by Lust. She is rescued through the joint efforts of Timias and Belphoebe, then is protected by Prince Arthur, who leaves her temporarily in order to settle the quarrel of six knights: Scudamour and Britomart against Druon, Paridell, Blandamour, and Claribell (above, p. 31). Arthur, who does not know Scudamour, fails to mention Amoret's presence near by but listens with the others to Scudamour's 'flashback' account of finding Amoret in the Temple of Venus. One might expect Arthur to give the joyous news of Amoret's nearness immediately after Scudamour's narrative; but this account, if intended, was reserved for Book VII. Spenser ends Canto x abruptly after Scudamour's speech and turns with Ariosto-like suddenness to the story of Florimell, who had languished in Proteus' dungeon for seven months and fourteen complete cantos (IV. xi. 4). How much further the story of Amoret would have been developed, we can only speculate; for that portion of Book VII was never written, or at least was never published.

Scudamour's winning of Amoret in the Temple of Venus is rather like the lover's storming of the castle in the *Roman de la Rose*.

Scudamour must defeat the twenty knights who guard the bridge before he can arm himself with the Shield of Love. He then encounters Doubt, Delay, and Daunger before he can enter Venus' garden and then her temple. Venus smilingly approves his seizure of the half-reluctant Amoret. In the *Roman de la Rose*, the lover is opposed by Daunger, Fear, Shame, and Wikked-Tonge (Chaucer's spelling), but is aided in his conquest by Venus (cf. above, p. 145). The obstacles in each case are impulses within the girl's mind. In Spenser, Scudamour and Amoret are likewise impulses within the girl's mind as her 'womanhood' becomes associated with physical desire; externally, the girl is falling in love.

The virtuous union of 'womanhood' with physical love in a woman's soul was inhibited in Book III by Busyrane and in Book IV by Lust, the first of whom was overcome by Britomart (chastity) and the second by Belphoebe (virginity). Accordingly, we may investigate the place of the two evil impulses in the internal warfare of the soul.

Lust is much the easier to interpret. He represents sensual appetite at its lowest, desiring the excitement of orgasm with no concern for the partners that help him to attain it. He is quite content with the old hag in his cave rather than the more beautiful Amoret and Aemylia,[1] and he sometimes obtains the desired effect by masturbation (IV. vii. 19–20). If indulged without restraint, these sensual impulses will reduce a person to the level of beasts, as they did Hellenore. But opposed to these sensual impulses are the woman's native modesty and grace (Timias) and her inclination to preserve her virginity (Belphoebe). These save her womanhood from the destructive effects of sensuality. But womanhood does not emerge unscathed. It is badly bruised by the violent handling of lust and is wounded by its would-be rescuer, modesty and grace (Timias). This wound seems to indicate the woman's shame at having felt and almost yielded to such sensual temptations. Only through the agency of heavenly grace is her wounded self-esteem healed, for Arthur gives Amoret the

---

[1] The old hag on whom Lust satisfies his desires has a counterpart in *The Story of England* (c. 1338) by Robert Mannyng of Brunne. In Mannyng's account of the duel between King Arthur and the giant of Mont-Saint-Michel, Bedivere learns of the death of Hoel's daughter Helen from an old woman who is forced to stay near the giant in order to satisfy his lust. Warned by her, Bedivere leaves but returns with Arthur, who kills the giant (ed. Furnivall, 1887, in *Rerum Britannicarum Medii Aevi Scriptores*, pp. 426–35).

'pretious liquor' (Holy Communion) which restores her to health (IV. viii. 20). Externally, the woman feels herself once more a child of God, no longer an outcast, and is able to bear with greater equanimity the evil aspersions of Sclaunder (stanza 35).

The interpretation of Busyrane is more difficult. His name seems to be derived from Busiris, an oriental king noted for his enjoyment of his victims' sufferings as they were mutilated or dismembered. He is shown with his dismembered victims in Emblem 41 of *The C Hystoryes of Troye* (above, p. 39) as a warning to good knights against excessive cruelty. (To save money, the printer used the same woodcut in Emblem 81, on Calcas.) Busyrane employs excessive cruelty and also physical mutilation—he has taken Amoret's heart from her breast and pierced it with a dart. Dorothy Atkinson cited a conjurer Artidon who has opened his breast to show his wounded heart to the captive woman whose love he seeks.[1] But, while this image may contribute to the general notion of exposing the heart, it is obviously quite different from the picture of Busyrane piercing Amoret's heart to force her to accept his love. The suggestion for this image comes from Francesco Piccolomini. In discussing the iconography of the Greeks, Francesco says: 'Indeed, learned men formed an image of Vice bearing in one hand a sword, in the other a crown; so that whoever should overcome Vice should be honoured with a crown, but whoever should succumb to him should be transfixed with a sword, even to the inmost depths of the heart' (ix. 47; p. 540D).

This passage occurs on the same page as Francesco's discussion of Ate as the goddess of calamity, a character whom Spenser has used in Book IV of *The Faerie Queene* as a mischief-maker who seeks to alienate Scudamour from Amoret. Francesco continues the passage with a discussion of the four evil states of the soul: incontinence, vice, beastliness, and ignorance. Like Hercules, we should arm ourselves against these with continence, civil virtue, heroic virtue, and wisdom, to expel from the soul these 'monsters' and to banish far away these plagues, deformities, and impotences (pp. 540–1).

[1] 'Busirane's Castle and Artidon's Cave', *MLQ* i (1940), 185–92. The romance, translated from the Spanish, is *The Mirrour of the Princely deedes and Knighthood, etc.* Like Scudamour, Rosicleer is the Knight of Cupid and bears Cupid's picture on his shield. Like Britomart, he passes the enchanted fire to rescue Artidea for her lover Lurizo from the castle of Artidon, the enchanter.

The quotation above, concerning the transfixed heart, suggests that Busyrane is a form of vice to which Amoret has partially yielded, though not entirely so; for she remains true to Scudamour, at the cost of excruciating suffering. Yet she has not the power to throw off the enchantment and break the charm; she can only suffer. Nor can Scudamour enter the castle or break the charm. Only Britomart succeeds in doing these things.

We must ask what vice Busyrane may represent. His abduction of Amoret on her wedding night has suggested to most modern interpreters that he represents a physical shrinking from coitus, that Scudamour's rough wooing as the hour of love approaches has upset and frightened Amoret.[1] Mentally she desires love, but physically she shrinks from it. The situation is that of the new bride in Tennessee Williams's play *Period of Adjustment*. This theory is strengthened by the Masque of Cupid, which pictures all the tyrannies and unhappiness of love, and by the similar wall decorations of Busyrane's palace. Yet these various afflictions of love are all illusions, 'phantasies In wavering wemens witt' (III. xii. 26), promoted by the enchantments of Busyrane.

Altogether, Busyrane seems too sinister a figure to represent merely a bride's nervous qualms before her first sexual experience. The extreme cruelty involved, Amoret's intense suffering, and the transfixed heart betoken a vicious persecution. Busyrane seeks not only to alienate Amoret (womanhood) *from* virtuous physical love (Scudamour) but *also* to win her *to* his ~~also~~ brand of love, which involves vice. There are other clues. The hot fire around Busyrane's palace burns with a murky smoke, not with a clear flame. Busyrane sits before the brazen pillar to which Amoret is bound, 'figuring strange characters of his art', drawing strange pictures with her heart's blood. He is the enemy of normal physical love, for his fire burns Scudamour and repels his attempt to enter the palace. Only Britomart (chastity) is able to endure the flame and to enter there.

All of these signs point to Busyrane as representing some form of sexual perversion, or perhaps various forms of it. The transfixed heart of Amoret is sufficient to identify her persecutor as the Vice of Francesco's account. The murky smoke (III. xi. 21) con-

---

[1] Spens, *Spenser's* Faerie Queene, p. 105; Parker, *The Allegory of* The Faerie Queene, p. 174; Hamilton, *The Structure of Allegory in* The Faerie Queene, pp. 154–5; Roche, *The Kindly Flame*, p. 83; Williams, *Spenser's World of Glass*, p. 107.

trasts with the 'kindly flame' of true love (IV, Proem. 2). The 'strange characters' drawn by Busyrane suggest unnatural love (III. xii. 31). The desperate struggle of womanhood (Amoret) to remain true to normal physical love (Scudamour) despite the attraction of a latent Lesbianism or homosexuality (Busyrane) would account for Amoret's intense suffering. And it better justifies the sinister portrayal of Busyrane, for it is difficult to see how a bride's nervousness could constitute a vice at all.

This interpretation is confirmed by Prudentius' *Psychomachia*, in which the author sets up various combats between virtues and their opposite vices: Faith versus Worship of Pagan Gods, Patience versus Wrath, Humility versus Vanity, Sobriety versus Luxury, Charity versus Avarice. The opponent of Chastity is Sodomita Libido, or Sodomy. This identification of Chastity's logical opponent as Sexual Perversion may well have suggested Spenser's use of Britomart as the conqueror of Busyrane.[1]

A further suggestion for this element of the allegory may have come from the highly influential *De Planctu Naturae* of Alanus de Insulis, mentioned by both Chaucer and Spenser.[2] Alanus's work is remembered for its vivid personification of Nature; but it is actually a tract against various kinds of unnatural love. These perversions are condemned as evil because they contravene the laws of Nature.

The emotional struggles of Amoret do not imply that the woman in whose soul she resides is actually guilty of masturbation, fornication, and sexual perversion, but only that she feels strong impulses towards them. In this same soul are Belphoebe, Britomart, and Arthur (virginity, chastity, and heavenly grace), who combat and subdue her lawless sexual impulses and enable her to perfect her womanhood in the true happiness of married love (Scudamour). Amoret's ability to wear the Girdle of Chastity (IV. v. 19) suggests that the woman's vices are unrealized impulses rather than overt actions. Nevertheless, the struggle against these impulses towards aberrations and sensuality is a difficult one, and only when the victory is won is she prepared to be a happy bride.

---

[1] Joshua McClennen lists these combats from Prudentius' *Psychomachia*, without connecting them to their counterparts in Spenser ('Allegory and *The Faerie Queene*: A Study of Spenser's Use of Moral Allegory', Harvard Dissertation, 1940, p. 87).

[2] Chaucer, *Parlement of Fowles*, l. 316; Spenser, *FQ* VII. vii. 9.

FLORIMELL AND MARINELL

The first appearance of Florimell comes near the beginning of Book III. Arthur, Timias, Guyon, and Britomart are travelling together:

> At length they came into a forest wyde,
> Whose hideous horror and sad trembling sownd
> Full griesly seemd: therein they long did ryde,
> Yet tract of living creature none they fownd,
> Save beares, lyons, and buls, which romed them arownd.
>
> All suddenly out of the thickest brush,
> Upon a milkwhite palfrey all alone,
> A goodly lady did foreby them rush,
> Whose face did seeme as cleare as christall stone,
> And eke through feare as white as whales bone:
> Her garments all were wrought of beaten gold,
> And all her steed with tinsell trappings shone,
> Which fledd so fast that nothing mote him hold,
> And scarse them leasure gave, her passing to behold.
>
> (III. i. 14–15)

She is pursued by a mounted 'griesly foster' or forester, who seeks to defile her with 'beastly lust'. The three men immediately spur their horses after her, Timias in pursuit of the forester, Arthur and Guyon desiring Florimell herself. She seems to them 'the fairest dame alive'; only Britomart was not moved to 'follow beauties chace'. Arthur separates from Guyon and chooses the right path, but he cannot catch Florimell, who flees 'through thick and thin, through mountains and through playns' (iv. 46). From her dwarf Dony, he learns that she excels

> In stedfast chastitie and vertue rare,
> The goodly ornaments of beautie bright;
> And is ycleped Florimell the Fayre.
>
> (v. 8)

Though Mother Parker defines Florimell as innocence, and Miss Rathborne as civility,[1] most critics agree that she represents beauty.

The *Orlando Furioso* opens with the flight of Angelica on horseback, a headlong rush very much like the flight of Florimell. Angelica is called *bella*, or Angelica the Beautiful (i. 15). Roche

---

[1] Parker, *The Allegory of* The Faerie Queene, p. 158; Rathborne, 'The Political Allegory of the Florimell–Marinell Story', *ELH* xii (1945), 279–89.

cites Sir John Harington, translator of the *Orlando Furioso*, as saying that Angelica represents beauty.[1]

Roche also follows earlier critics in finding a parallel between the two Florimells and the two Helens of Euripides' play *Helena*.[2] As the most beautiful woman in the world, Helen was doomed by Venus to marry Paris in fulfilment of Venus' promise when he awarded her the golden apple as the prize of beauty. But Juno took pity on Helen and substituted an image of Helen made of vaporous air. This false Helen eloped with Paris, waited in Troy until the war was over, was reclaimed by Menelaus, and has wandered with him for seven years while he is trying to reach his home in Sparta. Driven ashore in Egypt, he conceals her in a cave while he visits the royal palace to spy out the land. In this palace is the true Helen, virtuous and chaste, whom Juno had entrusted to Proteus, king of Egypt. Proteus had protected and concealed her until his death, but now his son Theoclymenus demands her hand in marriage. She and Menelaus recognize each other, and a messenger brings the news that the false Helen had disappeared before his eyes after explaining the imposture. The king's sister Theonoe helps the newly united pair to escape from Egypt.

The two Florimells seem obviously indebted to the two Helens. Spenser has assigned to Proteus the actions of Proteus' son as well; for Proteus, in *The Faerie Queene*, first protects Florimell from the old fisherman and then demands her hand in marriage. Also, the two Helens and the two Florimells seem to represent chaste and unchaste beauty. Florimell's imprisonment of seven months in Proteus' cave may correspond to Helen's stay of seven years in Proteus' palace after the end of the Trojan War, during which time she had no news of Menelaus.

Florimell also owes something to Florence, the beloved of Arthur in *Arthur of Little Britain*. The two names suggest a common Latin derivation, *flori* being the combining stem of *flos* (a flower) while *florens* is a participle (flowering). Florence is admired by so many knights at a tournament that, to secure privacy, she sets up an image of herself in a pavilion, where it is seen and mistaken for the real Florence by most of the knights.

---

[1] Roche, *The Kindly Flame*, p. 15: 'In the hard adventures of Angelica, we may note how perilous a thing beautie is if it be not especially garded with the grace of God, and with vertue of the mind' (Harington).

[2] Ibid., pp. 152–7. Additional documentation of the legend is supplied by Roche. Cf. *Var.* iii. 270, v. 190.

Later the fairy queen Proserpina consents to impersonate Florence, whom she closely resembles. She is wooed by the Emperor, goes through the betrothal ceremony and part of the wedding; but at the touch of the wedding-ring she suddenly vanishes. The time gained by her imposture enables Arthur to come to the rescue of Florence, who has returned to her home in the Cleere Tower.

The presence of Florimell at a tournament at which the false Florimell also appears may be due to the influence of the episode of Florence and Proserpina. Also, Florence's eagerness to see Arthur, whom she is destined to marry, and her rejoicing that he is so goodly a personage may be reflected in Britomart's reaction to the praises of Artegall (III. ii. 11) and to her first sight of him (IV. vi. 29).[1]

In the possession of a goddess mother who seeks to save him from a foretold danger, Marinell is reminiscent of Achilles.[2] Euripides mentions that Achilles had been a suitor of Helen, who had chosen Menelaus instead. This reference suggests that Marinell stems from Achilles and Menelaus combined into one, a suggestion strengthened by the fact that a suitor of the false Florimell, Paridell, is described by Spenser as a descendant of Paris of Troy (IV. ii. 11).

These three prototypes of Florimell—Angelica, Helen, Florence—support the usual opinion that she represents beauty. The characterization of Florimell as beauty is part of the moral allegory, which in this story blends readily with the physical allegory (below, p. 228). The beauty of Florimell is transient earthly beauty, 'the ineffable sadness of all transitory loveliness of the earth', as Janet Spens calls her. She and Marinell represent 'the world of sense at the point where it is about to be transmuted into the world of soul'.[3] It is through such fleeting earthly beauty that we come to understand and aspire to heavenly beauty, as Spenser tells us in the *Fowre Hymnes*. Through Florimell the Fair on earth, we learn to comprehend Sapience in heaven.

Marinell's name is the French diminutive of *marin* (the sea), and Spenser's comment upon the sea sets forth its wonderful fecundity (IV. xii. 1–2). Natalis Comes had interpreted the large number of Neptune's sons as signifying the fertility of the sea (below,

---

[1] Cf. Sarah Michie, '*The Faerie Queene* and *Arthur of Little Britain*', *SP* xxvi. 105–23.

[2] *Var.* iii. 240.

[3] Spens, *Spenser's* Faerie Queene, p. 84.

p. 229). Accordingly, Marinell may be taken to represent fertility, and his ultimate union with Florimell is that of fertility with beauty.

In the world of sense, Marinell represents careless and lavish fecundity, with no intrusion of moral considerations. He feels no passion because he knows no restraint. Like the sea, he is fecund but cold. He is indifferent to Florimell (beauty) because to him love is not associated with aspiration. All this is changed when he is wounded by Britomart (chastity), who represents the intrusion of the moral world upon his consciousness. As a figure in internal allegory, he represents amoral sexuality as an attitude within a person's soul. This amorality is overcome by an impulse to chastity which triumphs so completely that normal sexual impulses almost disappear. They are revived by Tryphon (easy living), but the person's standards have changed. He is now responsive to beauty (Florimell) and finds that sex now is the basis for a mutual union of souls, not merely for a careless union of bodies. The effect upon Marinell is like that of Una upon the satyrs (above, p. 123); it introduces an element of the ideal which until then the beholders had not known.

Finally, the allegory of Marinell and Florimell was powerfully influenced by the Plato–Socrates–Diotima account of the birth of love from Porus (plenty) and Penia (poverty, need, privation) in the garden of Jove (*Symposium*, 201–12) as it was explained by Francesco Piccolomini. Like Plato, Francesco views romantic and conjugal love as a part of friendship (vii. 20; p. 378B). He comments further: 'Plato in the *Symposium* says with Diotima that the lover wishes to procreate from the beautiful something for his eternity; with Aristophanes, however, he says that the lover seeks union with the beloved.' The connection of lover and beloved is expressed through the fable of the androgynus (vii. 4; p. 360A, C). In the discarded stanzas of the 1590 edition of Book III, Spenser uses the image of the androgynus or hermaphrodite to describe the union of Scudamour and Amoret (above, p. 156).

In Chapters 5 and 14 of book vii, Francesco has two lengthy discussions of Diotima's fable. In the first, he declares that plenty is called the father, poverty or privation the mother, of love. Poverty or privation pertains to matter and is returned to it, which is said to be as a mother (*mater-ia*). Plenty is the object which, like a father, fulfils the desire of matter (vii. 5; p. 361B).

In chapter 14, Francesco debates which is nobler, the lover or the beloved:

Sometimes Plenty is found in the lover alone, as God, because he is good, creates the sum of things and, because he is good, perfects it by loving. . . . Similarly, a fecund man loving a girl into whom he effuses seed and fecundity that thence she may receive matter for forming offspring, is said to excel her . . . for the man loves from the internal plenty of his fecundity, while the woman loves on account of her need (*inopiam*). Thence it is said in [Aristotle's] *Physics*, i. 81, that the woman seeks the man as matter seeks form. Or else this fecundity is principally and truly in the thing beloved, as when the creature loves the creator: and then the beloved is preferred. Or, again, this fecundity is in each one; and then both excel by reason of fecundity and are deficient by reason of poverty (*indigentia*). And this happens when two friends love each other, drawn by mutual virtue; for in each is considered a fecundity proceeding from proper virtue and a certain poverty of common life and of other things accompanying human frailty. These things are true of every love, whether honest or useful or delectable. . . . Plato considered the lover as excited by the shadow of beauty shining in matter and elevated by the fury of love to the essence of the beautiful. Contrariwise, Aristotle judged that true forms are found in matter and thinks more lightly of love's fury as destitute of reason and ideas. Thence it is clear in what way good and plenty produce love in a more eminent degree than need does; the good as good is fecund and communicable by its nature; thence seeking to be propagated, it bears most eminent love, such as that by which God loves the world.   (vii. 14; p. 371C, D)

Earlier in the same chapter he quotes Plotinus and the Academics on the awakening of love by the beauty of the beloved, and the soul's progress to a recognition of ideal beauty. He adds: 'Plato in the *Symposium* says in the speech of Diotima: "Love is a desire of immortality; it is not a desire of the beautiful, but of generation and birth in the beautiful, by which birth the lover may be preserved immortal"' (p. 370D). The sense of these words is well expressed in the first lines of Shakespeare's first sonnet:

> From fairest creatures we desire increase
> That thereby beauty's rose might never die.

The Porus–Penia theme is the major ingredient of the Marinell–Florimell relationship. Marinell owns the Rich Strand, and all the wealth of the world comes pouring in upon him. He represents plenty. Florimell, whom all others desire, desires only Marinell, and he is not even aware of her love. She obviously represents privation or need. When Marinell learns that she loves him and has suffered so much for this love, he begins to love in return out of pity and a desire to satisfy Florimell's need:

> His stubborne heart, that never felt misfare,
> Was toucht with soft remorse and pitty rare;
> That even for griefe of mind he oft did grone,
> And inly wish that in his power it weare
> Her to redresse: but since he meanes found none,
> He could no more but her great misery bemone.
>
> Thus whilst his stony heart with tender ruth
> Was toucht, and mighty courage mollifide,
> Dame Venus sonne, that tameth stubborne youth
> With iron bit, and maketh him abide,
> Till like a victor on his backe he ride,
> Into his mouth his maystring bridle threw,
> That made him stoupe, till he did him bestride:
> Then gan he make him tread his steps anew,
> And learne to love, by learning lovers paines to rew.
>
> (IV. xii. 12–13)

Thus, Marinell's first sentiment is one of pity, a wish to satisfy Florimell's need. This sympathy gradually turns to love as Marinell himself becomes aware of a need for the kind of chaste love that Florimell offers, something over and beyond bodily pleasure and casual sexuality. His sense of need is for that 'birth in beauty' described by Diotima as a means of assuring his immortality. This desire for immortality is expressed not only in the production of children but also in noble deeds and memorable actions to which friends, married or otherwise, inspire each other. Thus it is that, in the tournament which celebrates his wedding, Marinell surpasses all his previous efforts with deeds of such valour that all watchers stand in amazement (v. iii. 8).

In this way Spenser illustrates Francesco Piccolomini's comment that lovers experience a mutual need and a mutual plenty which supplies each other's need. Florimell supplies Marinell's need for a 'birth in beauty', but beauty itself experiences a need to be awakened into reproducing itself; physically, the female cannot do this without the agency of the male. Hence Francesco's quotation from Aristotle that woman seeks man as matter seeks form.

In beginning his chapter 'Plato's Opinion Concerning Beauty' (viii. 34; p. 432B), Francesco writes: 'Among the gifts of Nature and the goods of the body conspiring to constitute the highest good of a man living this life, there is also named Beauty, which is accompanied by Grace.'

This hint was sufficient to make Spenser place Florimell upon Mount Acidale, where she was brought up by the Graces (IV. v. 5). There she inherited the Girdle of Chastity, which Venus discarded when she deserted her husband Vulcan for the love of Mars. This girdle's name, Cestus (or Caestus), superficially resembles Latin *castus* (chaste) and was appropriate for Venus 'what time she used to live in wively sort' (stanza 3). It is the symbol of wedded love. We may also note that Alanus de Insulis explains that Latin *cingulum* (girdle) represents chastity; for, just as a girdle restricts the flowing of garments, so chastity restricts and bridles the flux and motion of concupiscent desires.[1] Spenser has made his allegory of beauty–fertility–immortality into an enthusiastic praise of wedded love.

If Florimell and Marinell are viewed in terms of internal allegory, as impulses within the soul of the individual man or woman, the question posed is: With what other impulse of the soul is the perception of earthly beauty most fittingly allied? There are several candidates. Beauty might seem to belong with heavenly grace as representing God-in-Man (Arthur), or with the virtuous and temperate life (Guyon), or with the irascible faculty that subdues disordered lusts (Satyrane), or with the infinite variety of all nature (Proteus), or with the urge towards generation of life (Marinell). The last is deemed the most suitable companion of beauty, for it assures the continuation of beauty in other lives and other minds long after the original exemplar has disappeared. But first the impulse to generation needs the discipline of chastity (Britomart) to limit and direct it toward the greatest measure of human happiness. Only when it is so limited is fertility a fit companion of beauty, for only then does it look upon the generative function as part of man's relationship with God. When this internal union of beauty with chaste fertility has been achieved within the soul, the man or woman concerned is prepared for Christian marriage.

[1] *Distinctiones*, in PL ccx. 740.

VIII

The Moral Allegory of Justice

ARTEGALL represents justice, as we know from the heading of Book v, a book devoted primarily to his exploits. But he had already appeared in Books III and IV as a foil to Britomart, who seeks him as her prospective husband. In Satyrane's tournament he fights in disguise and is finally overcome by Britomart. In their second encounter, when her helmet is knocked off, he gasps in admiration and can fight no more. This treatment of Artegall as a romantic figure has its logical conclusion in his defeat and imprisonment by Radigund and in his release by Britomart, whose role as rescuer is parallel to Arthur's rescue of Redcross from Orgoglio. These actions of Artegall in connection with Britomart seem of a different kind from his other administrations of justice throughout Book v (above, pp. 154–5).

Aristotle acknowledges that justice may be classified in several ways. He first recognizes distributive and commutative justice, which deals with the correct apportionment of honours, wealth, and other awards among various individuals; then corrective justice, which punishes wrongdoers and corrects their wrongdoing (*Nic. Eth.* v. ii. 12–13). Spenser has sought to illustrate these kinds of justice. Artegall's arbitration of the quarrel of Amidas and Bracidas over the ownership of wealth washed up by the sea is a good example of distributive justice (*FQ* v. iv. 4–20). His award of the surviving lady to the weak squire who opposed Sir Sanglier is another example of distributive justice, though the punishment of Sir Sanglier, who is forced to bear with him the head of his slain wife, is an example of corrective justice (v. i. 14–29). Perhaps Artegall's rejection and overthrow of the giant who espoused egalitarianism of landscape and of people may be considered an instance of commutative justice, which aims at an exchange rather than a distribution (v. ii. 29–50).

The examples of corrective justice are seen in Sanglier, Pollente, Munera, Braggadocchio, Guile, the enemies of Burbon, and Grantorto, to name only those 'corrected' by Artegall. In administering corrective justice, he is greatly aided by his squire Talus, an iron man wielding an iron flail, tireless and swift, and irresistible by ordinary human force. This character is one of Spenser's most interesting creations and hardly deserves B. E. C. Davis's description of him as a 'grotesque automaton' who has no place 'upon the shores of old romance'.[1] Talus is found in the *Minos*, attributed to Plato, and is described as a judge in Crete who brought to the people the laws engraved on brazen tablets. Apollonius of Rhodes altered this description to portray Talus as actually made of brass, and numerous references in classical literature confirm the description.[2] Erasmus, in his *Adagia*, under *Chalcenterus*, applies this word to those who tirelessly endure great labours 'as if they had bowels of brass, as was fabled concerning Talus, the guardian of the island of Crete'.[3] Again, under *Risus* he cites Talus as a man of brass who killed many people in Sardinia and laughed at the heaps of dead surrounding him.[4] B. E. C. Davis[5] notes that in *Huon of Bordeaux* the castle of Dunother is guarded by two men of brass who wield iron flails. Since these men are nameless, and since Spenser had read this romance (*FQ* II. i. 6), it seems likely that Talus' flail is recollected from this source, though similar figures occur in *Arthur of Little Britain*. Spenser may have changed Talus' body from brass to iron because he serves Artegall during the Iron Age. He had served Astraea, goddess of Justice, and had been left behind for Artegall when Astraea abandoned the Earth during the Iron Age (v. i. 12).

Padelford notes that Talus represents the law as the embodiment and executor of justice.[6] Perhaps he should have gone a step further and identified Talus with Talio, the *lex talionis* or *ius talionis*. The visual likeness of the two names makes an identification possible. Talio is the Latin word used by translators to render Aristotle's *antipeponthos* (*Nic. Eth.* v. v. 1), meaning reciprocity and signifying a reciprocal suffering. It is the root word of 're*tali*ation', a term which expresses very well the essence of Talio.[7] Francesco Piccolomini tries to reconcile Aristotle's

---

[1] *Var.* v. 298. [2] *Var.* v. 165–6.
[3] Erasmus, *Adagia* (Frankfurt, 1670), p. 696.
[4] Ibid., p. 620. [5] *Var.* v. 298. [6] *Var.* v. 277.
[7] Cf. Marsilio Ficino, *Com. in Plotinum*, III. 'De Prouidentia', xiii: 'Ideoque delicta quae prouidentia in una non punit uita, in alia uita talionis poena punire' ('Therefore the sins which providence does not punish in one life, it will punish in another life by the penalty of Talio'). In *Opera Omnia* (edn. of Basel, 1561), p. 1694.

conflicting statements concerning it. In the *De Republica*, ii. 1, and earlier in the *Eudemian Ethics*, he had said that the equality of Talio preserves states. But in the *Nicomachean Ethics*, v. v, he seems to deny this, writing that Talio is not consonant with either public or private justice (Intr., ch. 13; p. 15D). But he does not completely condemn the law of Talio in this last quotation, for he explains that he condemns it when practised with an arithmetic equality ('tit for tat') but not when practised with geometric proportion. Thus, he does not condemn the law itself but the manner of its use by the ancients (p. 16C). A French translator of Aristotle into Latin, Guillaume Du Val, explains in his introductory comments that Talio is a certain reciprocal suffering involving the proposition that a person should suffer exactly as much as he has caused others to suffer, or pay back exactly as much as he has taken away. Moses seems to have approved Talio when he said: 'An eye for an eye, and a tooth for a tooth.' But Talio is not perfectly applicable to either distributive or corrective justice; e.g. it may be right for a magistrate to strike a prisoner, but not for the prisoner to strike him back.[1] Justice in Talio, or retaliation, consists in a proportion appropriate to the circumstances, not in an exact reciprocity for the injury caused. Thus an element of mercy or equity enters to modify the rigid code of Talio.

Talus administers justice, but it is a harsh and ruthless justice— 'strict justice', perhaps we should call it. It represents the law of Talio. The proportionate reciprocity advocated by Aristotle is represented by Mercilla, who is forced to administer punishment but does so regretfully and would mitigate it if she could. It will be noticed that, after Talus visits Mercilla's court with Artegall, his enforcements of justice are much less harsh than formerly, for he is restrained by Artegall.

In this connection we may note the clash of Artegall with Arthur when each knight thinks he is defending Samient against a 'paynim' (v. viii. 9–14). The episode suggests that the ways of heavenly grace at times seem unjust, as in Christ's parables of the workers in the vineyard and the prodigal son. In the first, the owner of the vineyard pays the same wage to those who began work late in the day as to those who began early; in the second, the faithful elder son is indignant that the prodigal should be received with so much attention by their father. These benevolences are

---

[1] Aristotle, *Opera* (Greek and Latin), 2 vols. (Paris, 1619), vol. ii, p. 11.

manifestly unjust if viewed by the strict law of Talio. If viewed as an allegory of men's return to God, they express joy at the return of each sinner to the fold of Christ's flock and are not incompatible with justice. So Arthur (heavenly grace) and Artegall (justice) come to 'faire accordaunce', embrace lovingly, and swear to 'maintaine mutually' each other's cause. They are brought to this stage by Samient, whose name may signify 'togetherness' (Dutch *samen*). As internal allegory, the clash further illustrates Francesco Piccolomini's statement that virtues may seem to 'fight' each other when they are imperfectly understood but that their natural state is one of harmony (above, p. 33).

At the end of Book v of the *Nicomachean Ethics*, Aristotle raises the question of whether a man can exercise injustice towards himself. Ordinarily, he cannot.

> In a metaphorical and analogical sense, however, there is such a thing as justice, not towards oneself but between different parts of one's nature; not, it is true, justice in the full sense of the term, but such justice as subsists between master and slave, or between the head of a household and his wife and children. For in the discourses on this question a distinction is set up between the rational and irrational parts of the soul; and this is what leads people to suppose that there is such a thing as injustice towards oneself, because these parts of the self may be thwarted in their respective desires, so that there may be a sort of justice between them, such as exists between ruler and subject.
>
> (*Nic. Eth.*, Loeb edn., v. xi. 9)

This internal justice between different parts of the soul is a natural subject for internal allegory. Thus the clash between Britomart and Radigund involves two conceptions of the proper role of femininity in society, and Britomart's victorious union with Artegall asserts the husband's right to be the head of his household. In this sense Britomart and Radigund are conflicting impulses within the mind of a woman. Artegall, her sense of justice, dwells within her mind also and is the final determinant that causes her to submit to the will of her husband.[1]

T. K. Dunseath has pointed out that Artegall's various mis-

---

[1] See above, p. 154. The dual role of Artegall in external allegory and internal allegory may account for the appearance of conflict between Artegall's duties as an incarnation of justice and his obligations as a knight, or as a human being, as observed by Judith H. Anderson, '"No Man It Is" : The Knight of Justice in Spenser's *Faerie Queene*', *PMLA* lxxxv (1970), 65–77.

adventures are a means of resolving discords within himself in preparation for his role as a just and even-handed judge.[1] This conclusion belongs in the realm of external allegory, considering Artegall as a man, not as an impulse within the mind. Since justice consists in right conduct towards others, it naturally involves a large measure of external allegory and a number of people. The enemies of justice resort to extortion (Pollente), bribery (Munera), brutal force (the Soudan), and fraud (Malengin). These are the methods of injustice and must be conquered before any equitable administration of justice is possible.

To Arthur falls the task of defeating the Soudan, who battles in support of the wrong (Adicia). When he fails to come at the Soudan because of the armoured chariot from which the latter fights, he dazzles the Soudan's horses by uncovering his diamond shield (v. viii. 37). This seems to represent the direct interposition of God in human affairs, imitating Tasso's diamond shield which was 'the special safeguard of the Lord God' (above, p. 32). Like Duessa's seven-headed beast, the Soudan's horses are the instruments of evil, and their ruler is defeated by the failure of his instruments.

This episode can also be interpreted in terms of internal allegory. We may assume that a man is so committed to a wrong point of view (the Soudan and Adicia) that even the modicum of heavenly grace (Arthur) within his soul is powerless to dissuade him from the wrong course. His mind is closed to any valid arguments. Nothing will move him but a direct revelation of the power of God. The light of the diamond shield is like the light that dazzled Paul on the road to Damascus and supersedes all efforts to move the man by appeals to logic and reason. Through awe and fear, he recognizes in a burst of insight the error of his way.

In the last three cantos of Book v, the historical or political allegory is so completely dominant that there seems to be little room for moral interpretation, except in so far as the Spanish cause is always wrong and the English cause is always right. Gerioneo and Grantorto are representations of the Spanish threat as it existed in the Netherlands and in Ireland, and as it was combated by Leicester (Arthur) and Lord Grey of Wilton (Artegall). Yet Spenser's two knights represent other leaders as well, notably

[1] *Spenser's Allegory of Justice in Book Five of* The Faerie Queene (Princeton, 1968).

the Earl of Essex and Sir John Norris.[1] Here, as elsewhere, Spenser uses composite figures who represent several persons or qualities at the same time.

Because of the double capacity in which Artegall appears, the representations of justice in action are less extensive than those of the other major virtues in action.

[1] *Var.* v. 324–35. For Artegall as Sir John Norris see Bennett, *The Evolution of* The Faerie Queene, pp. 191–5. For Prince Arthur as both Leicester and Essex see Alastair Fowler, 'Oxford and London Marginalia to *The Faerie Queene*', N & Q viii (1961), 416–19.

IX

The Moral Allegory of Courtesy

As a study in allegorical technique, Spenser's sixth book displays the most interesting problem in *The Faerie Queene*. He faced the task of presenting courtesy as a virtue which was not merely a superficial veneer of good manners but which yet must be presented through one's conduct towards other people. Courtesy becomes a virtue only in the exercise, for we can hardly think of a person as showing courtesy if he never sees or speaks to anyone else. Similarly, affability and urbanity, two major ingredients of courtesy, express one's manner towards other people and have to be externally expressed. They do not fit well into the pattern of internal allegory, though they are outward manifestations of impulses within the soul. They are the conversational virtues and promote agreeable social relations.

Francesco Piccolomini mentions yet another conversational virtue, one concerned with the content rather than with the manner of a person's utterance. This virtue he calls integrity or candour or veracity, the habit of speaking the truth, and he groups it with affability and urbanity (iv. 28–9; pp. 200B, 203–5). This virtue is also characteristic of Calidore, but it is not truth in the sense that Una represents that virtue. She is the hidden truth which one must seek behind the veil of illusory appearances. Calidore does not represent the search for truth but the honest expression of opinion in the course of communication with others. In this sense he represents the Aristotelian virtue of verity, together with affability and urbanity.

CALEPINE, MIRABELLA, AND INTERNAL ALLEGORY

We have already observed the gentleness and mildness which are usually characterized as mansuetude (above, p. 8). To reveal more fully the operation of this virtue, Spenser has recourse to a remarkable device, the use of a double. Calidore and Calepine are two sides of the same coin, one representing Spenser's ideal gentleman in his daily contacts with other people and in his mission to suppress libellous slander, the other representing the internal disposition of this same gentleman and his struggle to maintain a proper balance of virtues within his own soul. Calidore's experiences occupy Cantos i and ii and half of iii, after which he withdraws in favour of Calepine, to return at the beginning of Canto ix. Calepine and related characters of the internal allegory thus occupy five and a half cantos of the book, but he never meets Calidore after their first encounter. Yet there are certain parallelisms in their adventures. Calepine kills a bear; Calidore kills a tiger. Calepine rescues his lady from cannibals; Calidore rescues his from brigands. In each case Calepine's victory comes first, as though a prototype of that which Calidore is to achieve in the external world. Spenser seems to illustrate Francesco Piccolomini's dictum that, before a man can hope to win victories over others, he must first conquer himself (v. 35; p. 296c).

Francesco presents mansuetude as being associated with clemency and lenity (iv. 29; p. 202D). Its deficiency is too great a slowness to wrath or a complete absence of wrath; for at times a man ought to be moved to righteous indignation (i. 27; p. 75D). The excess of mansuetude is wrath, not in the violent fits of *furor*, but wrath as a habit of mind. Among those having this fault Francesco includes the *pikroi*, who are bitter and implacable and who remain angry for a long time; and the *chalepoi*, who are difficult, hard, savage, and rough. Those are so called who are angered more seriously, more implacably, and for a longer time than is proper to the circumstances, and who may not be placated (iv. 29; p. 202D). These Greek terms are clearly applicable to Sir Turpine, who is harsh and cruel to all knights errant because one such knight had formerly 'wrought him fowle despight' (iii. 40). Spenser identifies Turpine's brand of wrath as rancour (vi. 43). Turpine's name comes from Latin *turpis*, meaning base, dishonourable, shameful, disgraceful, adjectives which Spenser repeatedly applies to Turpine. He thus makes a clear distinction between the noble indignation of his virtuous knights and the ignoble cherishing of a grudge or other revengeful feeling.

It seems likely that Calepine's name is borrowed from the *chalepoi* (χαλεποί, pronounced *calepoi*).[1] Singular forms of the word

---

[1] Aristotle uses the term with the same meaning in *Nic. Eth.* IV. v. 12, his chapter on mansuetude or gentleness. He uses *pikroi* in IV. v. 10.

are *chalepos* and *chalepon*; the noun for hardship or suffering is *chalepa*. Spenser is apparently thinking of Calepine as the endurer and recipient of harsh and savage treatment rather than the performer of it. In this sense, Calepine is one who is mistreated by the *chalepoi*. This would accord with mansuetude, which is not an aggressive virtue but consists in a mild reaction to the aggressiveness of others.[1]

In Book VI Timias reappears surprisingly, since his story had apparently ended with his reconciliation with Belphoebe in Book IV, and since he does not appear in Book V to accompany his master Prince Arthur. But, as a representative of natural grace, his presence is called for. Francesco states that in the actions of others towards us, whether injurious or beneficial, our response should be corrected by mansuetude, to which grace is joined (iv. 28; p. 200A). Hence mansuetude (Calepine) and grace (Timias) are natural allies within the soul of a man who is oppressed or persecuted; they prevent too violent a response. When his natural grace of manner (Timias) and his peace of mind (Serena) are upset by false slander uttered against him (the bite of the Blatant Beast), they are both calmed by his prudence (the Hermit), which helps him to regain his poise and self-control.

A further ingredient of courtesy is nobility, and Spenser believes that this quality belongs to those of 'gentle' blood. Calidore is of 'gentle' birth (iii. 2). So is the Salvage Man, who had grown up in the woods like a wild beast but was of 'gentle' birth, a fact which is displayed in his kindness to Serena and Calepine (v. 2). Spenser may have been indebted to Francesco for these portrayals. Nobility is an inherited virtue, the latter declares, and noble men will procreate upright sons (iv. 16; p. 186D). A certain external image of nobility may attend men of great wealth and may delude the eyes of the common people, but the true test of nobility is whether it fights strongly against vices. The riches of Midas are not more noble than the poverty of Socrates or Aristides. Wealth, however, may enhance nobility if properly used as an instrument of virtuous actions (viii. 15; p. 408B). There is a certain inborn natural nobility which is instinctively honoured by the generality of men. For example, Romulus, the founder of Rome, was brought up among shepherds;

---

[1] For an alternative explanation of Calepine's name see Cheney, *Spenser's Image of Nature*, pp. 201–3. Cf. also Arnold Williams, *Flower on a Lowly Stalk* (1967), p. 70.

and, because he excelled in martial qualities, he soon had the other shepherds submitting to him. Similar accounts may be read of Cyrus the Great and others (viii. 18; p. 411c).

Spenser would have remembered that Romulus was in the first place suckled by a she-wolf, and Francesco's citation of him may have furnished some hints for the Salvage Man. Savage men were already a traditional element of literature; but Spenser's stress on the inheritance of noble instincts by such a one follows closely Francesco's line of reasoning on the subject.

Quoting Bernheimer's *Wild Men of the Middle Ages*, Donald Cheney remarks that Hercules was sometimes identified with the 'wild man' or 'savage man' of medieval tradition.[1] His club and lion's skin might suggest such a primitive man. But figuratively Hercules slaying monsters represents man's conquest of concupiscent vices within himself (above, p. 26). This equates him with the irascible faculty, which fulfils this function within man's soul, and suggests that Spenser's Salvage Man is a representation of the irascible faculty, along with Sir Satyrane, Una's lion, and Guyon's boatman.

Spenser may well have found both the Salvage Man and the Hermit in contemporary masques presented before Queen Elizabeth. Bush mentions a wild man appearing in such a masque in 1574.[2] In 1575 a 'hombre salvaggio' appeared in the entertainments at Kenilworth Castle in honour of Queen Elizabeth.[3] In 1591, at Cowdray in Sussex, 'a wilde man cladde in Iuie' welcomed the Queen to an oak-tree adorned with the coats-of-arms of the Sussex gentry, assuring her that these 'heartes of Oke' would always be her loyal servants.[4] At Woodstock, in 1585, Queen Elizabeth was welcomed by a Hermit, who told of a past experience in the Temple of Venus, and by the Queen of the Fayry, who arrived in a chariot or 'wagon of state'.[5] This association of the

---

[1] Cheney, pp. 104 ff. Cf. also Herbert Foltinek, 'Die Wilden Männer in Edmund Spensers *Faerie Queene*', *Die Neuren Sprachen* (1961), 493–512. Radulphus de Coggeshale's medieval *Chronicon Anglicanum* gives accounts of four savage men and children who at different times were discovered in England (edn. of 1875, pp. 117–21, in *Rerum Britannicarum Medii Aevi Scriptores*).

[2] Douglas Bush, *Mythology and the Renaissance Tradition*, p. 82. Cf. *Var.* iv. 203–4.

[3] Robert Laneham's *Letter*, in *Pageants at Kenilworth, 1575* (Philadelphia, 1822), pp. 19–21.

[4] *The Speeches and Honorable Entertainment giuen to the Queenes Maiestie in Progresse, at Cowdrey in Sussex, by the right honorable the Lord Montacute* (August 1591).

[5] *The Queenes Maiesties Entertainement at Woodstocke* (London, 1585).

Hermit with the Fairy Queen may have suggested Spenser's Hermit, who had been a doughty knight and a man of the world before retiring to a life of contemplation (v. 37, vi. 4).

Calepine, in his two encounters with Turpine, seeks to propitiate the latter with conciliatory words and even begs his gatekeeper for overnight harbourage in tones of 'submission base'. Calepine fears for the life of the wounded Serena and calms any anger that he may have. When Turpine attacks him the next morning, Calepine seeks to avoid him and even hides behind Serena, but is badly wounded nevertheless. Then he sees the Salvage Man, unarmed, rush in upon Turpine and put him to flight. Calepine is healed in the Salvage Man's bower and profits by his example, for he kills with his bare hands the bear that is carrying off a child, and this is a preparation for his single-handed rescue of Serena from the cannibals. We may say that the vicinity of Turpine's castle was Calepine's place of testing, the Salvage Man's bower was his place of perfecting, and the rescue of Serena was his climactic test.

Serena's troubles begin when she suffers the poisonous bite of the Blatant Beast. The Salvage Man cannot cure her wound but escorts and protects her after Calepine gets lost while chasing the bear. He thus repeats the action of the lion and of Satyrane in escorting Una through the dangers of the forest after Redcross's disappearance. Serena and her guide are joined by Arthur and Timias, the latter also suffering from the bite of the Blatant Beast. After all medicines fail, the Hermit cures the wounds of Serena and Timias with this prescription:

> First learne your outward sences to refraine
> From things that stirre up fraile affection;
> Your eies, your eares, your tongue, your talke restraine
> From that they most affect, and in due termes containe. . . .
>
> Abstaine from pleasure, and restraine your will,
> Subdue desire, and bridle loose delight,
> Use scanted diet, and forbeare your fill,
> Shun secresie, and talke in open sight:
> So shall you soone repaire your present evill plight.   (vi. 7, 14)

The Hermit seems to be another representation of prudence, which Francesco called a companion of all the virtues (above,

p. 13). His admonitions are much like those of the Palmer in Book II.

We may think of Serena's place of testing as the forest, where she suffers the bite of the Blatant Beast, the indignities of Turpine, and the loss of Calepine. Her place of perfecting is the Hermit's cottage. Her final great test is the ordeal of capture by the cannibals, which she endures successfully.[1]

The internal allegory is somewhat as follows: Serena is serenity or peace of mind, which accompanies a mild disposition or mansuetude (Calepine). Mansuetude opposes within the soul the impulses toward rancour and revengeful anger (Turpine) and is not misled by false blandishments (Blandina). But mansuetude is the mean between rancorous anger and abject submission, not the extreme of abject submission itself, and therefore has a capacity for righteous indignation. This lesson is learned from association with the irascible faculty (Salvage Man) and thenceforward marks the actions of mansuetude. Francesco expresses the relation between the two by saying that mansuetude is the mean rightly controlling the irascible faculty so that, in being aroused to wrath, it constantly chooses as it ought (iv. 29; p. 203B). This means a measured response of righteous indignation, not anger uncontrolled. Grace (Timias) may join in opposing or controlling wrath and is then itself controlled by mansuetude or clemency (ibid.).

This same passage states that grace has yet another function in the soul, that of opposing ingratitude. In this case it is not controlled by mansuetude, but partly by justice, partly by magnificence. Spenser has represented ingratitude by Mirabella (Ital., beautiful sight). She had treated her many lovers with scorn and disdain, taking pride in the number of her conquests; finally Cupid had sentenced her to be persecuted by Scorn and Disdain until she could help as many lovers as she had harmed. When Arthur hears this account, he declares that Cupid's sentence was just (viii. 23) and offers to release her from Disdain, whom he has overcome (stanza 29), but the lady feels that she must carry out

---

[1] Serena tied to the stake by a band of cannibals (viii. 45–50) has some indebtedness to Angelica tied to a rock by a band of savages (*OF* x. 98–9). In each case the woman, though facing imminent death, is concerned about the immodest exposure of her naked body. Cf. Cheney, *Spenser's Image of Nature*, p. 105, for comment on a similar scene in Boiardo.

her penance. Earlier Timias had attacked Disdain, who had captured him. He is now released by Prince Arthur (stanza 27).

In the first place Mirabella had represented ingratitude towards her many wooers, for failure to love one who loves you is a form of injustice (above, p. 151). Now her servants Disdain and Scorn represent ingratitude as they torment her during every step of her journey. The forces opposing ingratitude are justice (Cupid's sentence), grace (Timias), and magnificence (Arthur), the three opponents named by Francesco. Again, Francesco states that disdain (*aspernatio*) is opposed by the moderate desire of honour (i. 22; p. 68c), which is the alternative significance of Timias in Spenser's symbolism, and by magnanimity, which may indicate that here Arthur represents this virtue also (above, p. 6).

After the persecution of Calepine by Turpine, the latter is sought out and punished by Arthur, who is now accompanied by the Salvage Man in lieu of his wounded squire Timias. Arthur pursues Turpine right into his castle and would have killed him but for the interposition of Blandina. Turpine balefully suborns two young knights to murder the Prince, but Arthur is vigilant, kills one of the attackers, and spares the other on condition that he will help to ensnare Turpine. This young knight is Enias, whose name in Greek means the reins or the bridle. When Enias brings Turpine to see the dead Prince (his death has been reported) they find Arthur asleep, and Turpine tries to bribe Enias to murder him, but the young man abhors such treachery. As the Salvage Man returns from a foraging expedition after food, Arthur awakes, sees Turpine, seizes him and hangs him up by the heels.

Internally Turpine is a rancorous and revengeful disposition which upsets peace of mind (Serena) and irritates a normally mild temperament (Calepine). It is accompanied by a pretended pity and concern (Blandina) and uses Iago-like deceit. This self-destructive mood is very hard to displace from the mind; its defeat by the irascible faculty (Salvage Man) merely puts it to flight for a time. Only heavenly grace (Arthur) can subdue the appetite for revenge, and even then not fully. Turpine is baffled but not destroyed; rancour is controlled but could blaze up again.[1]

---

[1] For an interesting comparison of Rancour and Furor as two undesirable forms of wrath see Pierre de la Primaudaye's *Suite de l'Académie française* (Paris, 1580), ch. 55, pp. 185–6. (This is Part ii of *The French Academie*.)

When Arthur and Enias meet Mirabella and Timias as they travel captive to Scorn and Disdain, Enias asks Arthur's permission to fight Disdain. The permission is granted. Enias attacks but falls from the reflex action of his own blow. Disdain puts his foot on Enias' neck and orders Scorn to tie him up, just as he had earlier tied Timias. Arthur intervenes, disables Disdain, and unties Timias, while the Salvage Man rescues Enias from Scorn (viii. 27–8). Timias and Enias are therefore parallel and are probably companions in their service to Arthur. They have both opposed Disdain and they are both opposed to Turpine, though neither has actually fought against Turpine.

The probable explanation of Enias is found in Francesco Piccolomini's classification of virtues. In discussing hate as pertaining to the irascible faculty, he considers the question of elements opposed to wrath within the soul:

> First, by reason of its universal latitude, to Wrath are opposed Grace and Indulgence, as Aspasius has shown in [his commentary on] *Nicomachean Ethics*, II. iii. (i. 11; p. 54B)

> Grace, according to Aspasius, is opposed to Wrath in a certain manner. Where Wrath proceeds from an injury, Grace and Ingratitude are concerned with the benefit [or its opposite] received; or if Wrath is definitely seeking revenge, Grace is inwardly indulgent [and forgiving]. (iv. 29; p. 203A)

Here are named three attitudes or impulses within the soul that counteract the impulse towards wrath. They are mansuetude, grace, and indulgence. The first two are represented by Calepine and Timias. The third should be represented by Enias, if Spenser is following Francesco as closely as he has done elsewhere. Spenser has chosen Enias as a name for indulgence because 'giving the rein' proverbially signifies a freeing from restraint, as in Angelo's 'Now I give my sensual race the rein'.[1] It is not complete freedom, for in the image of the bridled horse the rein and bridle may be used to reassert control as long as the horse wears them; but it is a relaxation of the strict control involved in 'keeping a tight rein'. As between master and subject, more tolerance is shown, discipline becomes less harsh, and greater autonomy is granted. The master thus disarms the subject's wrath and reduces his own tendencies to anger by an attitude of conciliation.

---

[1] Shakespeare's *Measure for Measure*, II. iv. 160. Cf. above, p. 130.

In vindictive anger, Disdain seems to have the same persistent quality that Turpine has, except that he affects a lofty contempt instead of rancorous hatred. We might say that he represents cold anger. Both Timias and Enias attack him, and both are defeated. Only heavenly grace (Arthur) can overcome the cold contempt of Disdain and the smouldering wrath of Turpine within the soul; for such inveterate attitudes of mind are the hardest of all to change.

When we externalize the actions of Calepine and Turpine, we must visualize a man with a grievance which torments him. Most probably it is a slanderous piece of gossip that annoys him, for his peace of mind (Serena) has been wounded by the Blatant Beast. In spite of his vindictive anger (Turpine), he seeks to maintain his native kindness and gentle temper (Calepine). But the effort is difficult, and he almost loses his self-control. His determination to discipline and control his feelings stems from his irascible faculty (Salvage Man), which temporarily subdues his vindictiveness and restores his mild demeanour. But his peace of mind (Serena) is still disturbed by the unavenged slander, and his native poise or grace (Timias) is also disturbed; externally, his manners become aggressive and his voice becomes harsh. Finally, his prudence (the Hermit) dictates that he must deliberately avoid worry, 'tranquillize' himself, go on a diet, avoid secret brooding, etc. At the same time he prays for Christian charity, and heavenly grace (Arthur) subdues the vindictive anger within his soul. His peace of mind is restored, as well as his native grace of manner.

Yet this exercise in self-control has been only a preparation, for a new crisis assails him with far worse perturbations (cannibals) than any he has known. His peace of mind (Serena) is again endangered, but his equanimity has been strengthened by the earlier experience. His mild temperament is unimpaired and quiets all the clamorous perturbations that would disturb his peace of mind; this is Calepine's victory. The man emerges from his second emotional crisis with a calm acceptance of what he cannot help.

There are paradoxical elements in this interpretation. Calepine's slaying the cannibals presents the most violent action in the book, yet this action represents the non-violent calming of aroused emotions. In the Salvage Man's attack on Turpine, the irascible faculty is calming the man's anger, not exciting it. Calepine's slaying of the bear represents the suppression of a violent perturbation to keep a mild and unruffled temper. His earlier pusillanimous conduct before Turpine represents externally the man's unsuccessful attempt to keep his temper, until his irascible faculty as disciplinarian of affections and perturbations aids him in the task of self-control.

Mirabella offers a somewhat different situation, one concerning the soul of a woman. Mirabella is the element of beauty within the soul of a woman who makes many 'conquests' but treats her suitors with scorn and disdain; these outward manners reflect the same qualities within the woman's soul, where they serve the element of cruel and capricious beauty (Mirabella). Externally the woman herself then falls in love with a man who treats *her* with scorn and disdain; and these qualities within her soul are now turned against her own beauty which has so little effect on the man that she loves. Internally her natural grace (Timias), her newly indulgent feeling towards others (Enias), and her sense of religion (Arthur) try to combat her despairing self-contempt; but they fail because of her conviction that it is right that she should suffer. Her hopeless love for her scornful non-lover becomes a kind of expiation for her former cruelties, and she now seeks to help others who suffer the pangs of love. Only thus can she eventually gain release from self-contempt and restore her self-respect.

CALIDORE AND THE BLATANT BEAST

The externalization of Mirabella resembles the situation of Briana, whose love for Crudor enables him to amuse himself by forcing her into discourteous actions (i. 13–15). After Calidore kills her seneschal Maleffort (Fr., evil strength), Briana treats him with 'womanish disdaine' (i. 30) until the arrival of Crudor (Lat., cruelty) to challenge him. After defeating Crudor, who begs for his life, Calidore reproaches him for unknightly pride and cruelty and grants him his life on condition that he thenceforth shows friendly courtesy to all knights and ladies, and that he begins by wedding Briana, who loves him (i. 40–3). This unexpected requital of her disdain by the granting of her dearest wish so transforms Briana that she becomes gracious, generous, and happy;

and Crudor himself undergoes a similar transformation, regarding Calidore as a friend.

This little allegory is intended to show that courteous actions will beget courtesy in others; a modern play on the same subject is Jerome's *The Passing of the Third Floor Back*. The basic rationale of courtesy is stated by Calidore in his homily to Crudor:

> In vaine he seeketh others to suppresse,
> Who hath not learnd him selfe first to subdew;
> All flesh is frayle, and full of ficklenesse,
> Subject to fortunes chance, still chaunging new:
> What haps to day to me to morrow may to you.
>
> Who will not mercie unto others shew,
> How can he mercy ever hope to have?
> To pay each with his owne is right and dew.
> Yet since ye mercie now doe need to crave,
> I will it graunt, your hopelesse life to save.   (i. 41–2)

Courtesy involves kindness and forbearance, which are akin to mercy; and a man should show mercy to others because he may need mercy himself at some future time. Thus, courtesy is considerably more than polite manners. It involves a spirit of generosity—Lat. *generosus* means a gentleman—towards other members of the human race and self-conquest in refraining from humiliating or injuring other people.

This theme of self-conquest is expressly stated in the first two lines of the passage just quoted. But self-conquest is necessarily a victory in terms of the *psychomachia*, or internal warfare. While Calidore's words to Crudor suggest that such a self-conquest should take place within Crudor's soul, it is possible to regard both Calidore and Crudor as impulses within another soul, in which the impulse towards civility and courtesy overcomes the impulse towards capricious cruelty and sadistic enjoyment. The battle determines the outward demeanour of the person concerned, who will express either courtesy or cruelty, but not both. Yet both of these internal impulses are known primarily through their outward manifestations, when a person shows courtesy or cruelty towards other people; and they thereby illustrate the interplay of internal allegory with external allegory. Briana, Maleffort, and the cutting of beards and hair seem part of the external allegory—the outward discourtesies result from inward cruelty.

Calidore's emphasis upon self-conquest suggests that this may be an element in his own mission. We have noted how the victories of Calepine, the Salvage Man, and Arthur in Book VI are exercises in self-control fought out on the level of internal warfare. Since Calidore exemplifies tact and courtesy toward other people, he is necessarily a part of the external allegory. But one's manner towards others is so much a product of one's state of mind that it must be closely related to the internal struggle of the soul. The object of Calidore's quest, the Blatant Beast, appears in both the external and the internal allegory. Calidore pursues him through the world, but the beast wounds both Serena and Timias, who are figures in the internal warfare of the soul.

We are accustomed to think of the beast as slander, which Calidore as a true knight seeks to combat wherever it is found. To put down slanderous aspersions by others, Calidore must either fight them or show their claims to be false. Yet none of these procedures seems to involve the self-conquest upon which he had discoursed to Crudor. Self-conquest appears again in the advice given by the Hermit to Timias and Serena, the three who represent prudence, grace, and peace of mind. Though given in terms of internal allegory, this advice concerns the regulation of the external body and the bodily senses:

> First learne your outward senses to refraine
> From things that stirre up fraile affection;
> Your eies, your eares, your tongue, your talke restraine.
>
> (vi. 7)

One should not look for, read, or listen to disquieting gossip; nor should one lend one's tongue to repeat irresponsible rumours. This suggests that self-conquest in the courteous man may consist in controlling his own tongue. Since the tongue merely utters what the mind thinks, its control is a matter of internal warfare; but, since its effects are felt in their impact upon other people, it is also a part of external allegory.

In so far as Calidore's pursuit of the Blatant Beast represents self-conquest, it is a man's effort to control his own tongue, to prevent it from speaking impulsively, maliciously, or falsely. Only after subduing his own tongue can he effectively 'suppresse' other malicious tongues. We may draw this conclusion from a comparison of the Blatant Beast with descriptions of the tongue by Spenser and others.

In Canto i, the beast is called 'a monster bred of hellish race' begot of Cerberus and Chimera, who wounds, bites, and torments wretched men 'with vile tongue and venemous intent'. In Canto vi, he is called a 'hellish dog' begot of Typhaon and Echidna, with rusty iron teeth that make incurable wounds:

> A wicked monster, that his tongue doth whet
> Gainst all, both good and bad, both most and least,
> And poures his poysnous gall forth to infest
> The noblest wights with notable defame. (vi. 12)

After conquering the beast, Calidore muzzles him so that he no longer can utter his blasphemous detractions and so cows him that he follows on the leash like a frightened dog (xii. 36). Yet he is not tamed and soon breaks loose again.

In Sonnet 80 of the *Amoretti*, Spenser informs us that he had recently completed Book vi of *The Faerie Queene*. In Sonnet 85, he denounces an anonymous gossip who has stirred up Elizabeth Boyle against him:

> Venemous toung, tipt with vile adders sting,
> Of that selfe kynd with which the Furies fell
> Theyr snaky heads doe combe, from which a spring
> Of poysoned words and spitefull speeches well,
> Let all the plagues and horrid paines of hell
> Upon thee fall for thine accursed hyre,
> That with false forged lyes, which thou didst tel,
> In my true love did stirre up coles of yre.

Here the tongue is not the poet's own, but that of someone else; it is the *lingua calumniatrix* mentioned by Erasmus (*Var.* vi. 384).

Poisonous serpent-tongues appear in the mouth of the Blatant Beast (xii. 28). The image, however, is Biblical:

> They have sharpened their tongues like a serpent: adders' poison is under their lips. (Ps. 140: 3)

> Their throat is an open sepulchre; with their tongues they have used deceit; the poison of asps is under their lips; whose mouth is full of cursing and bitterness. (Rom. 3: 13–14)

The obvious source of the 'adders sting' seems to be in the first of these passages. A longer discourse on the tongue is found in the Epistle of St. James:

> If any man among you seem to be religious, and bridleth not his tongue, but deceiveth his own heart, this man's religion is vain.
>
> (1 : 26)

> And the tongue is a fire, a world of iniquity: so is the tongue among our members that it defileth the whole body, and setteth on fire the course of nature, and is set on fire of hell. For every kind of beasts, and of birds, and of serpents, and of things in the sea, is tamed, and hath been tamed of mankind: but the tongue can no man tame; it is an unruly evil full of deadly poison.   (3 : 6–8)

We can assume that the Biblical passages gave rise to various sermons and homilies,[1] but I have observed none so picturesque as the commentary on an emblem of Alciatus in the variorum edition of 1621. The commentary is supposedly a synthesis of the comments of earlier scholars, specifically Claudius Minos and Franciscus Sanctius (Sanchez).

The particular emblem is no. 11, 'Silentium'. The illustration shows a man with his fingers to his lips, enjoining silence. The poem reads:

> Cum tacet, haud quicquam differt sapientibus amens:
>   Stultitiae est index linguaque voxque suae.
> Ergo premat labias, digitoque silentia signet,
>   Et sese Pharium vertat in Harpocratem.   (pp. 65–6)

(When he is silent, the fool differs not at all from wise men. The index of his folly is his tongue and his voice. Therefore let him compress his lips and signify silence by his finger and turn himself into Pharian Harpocrates.)

The notes explain that Harpocrates was an Egyptian god of silence, while Pharos was the lighthouse at Alexandria that sent its rays broadcast over the surrounding sea and land. The commentator further explains that the tongue is the index of the mind and brings out thoughts as an obstetrician brings the child forth

---

[1] Without particularizing, the *Catholic Encyclopedia*, under 'Silence', mentions 'innumerable' tracts on the perils of the tongue and the need for a Rule of Silence (xiii. 790).

from the womb.[1] Impure thoughts produce a monstrous offspring
in impure words of the tongue:

In such manner as one touched by leprosy breathes contagion and
infects by the breath, so does the depraved will or affection through the
sting of the tongue. The blow of a scorpion or viper is not so noxious;
a certain poison is under the lips, but through the channel of the
throat from the root of life [the stomach?], where first it appears.
Accordingly, the tongue is the index of the mind, which, if it is ruled by
the bridle, demonstrates health; if unbridled and voluble, it demonstrates sickness. When it bitingly attacks others like a mad dog, what
indication of a tranquil mind is that, pray? It spreads the seeds of
discord and the causes of war, obscures a clear name with foul smoke
and befogs a shining fame, blabs out in public what ought to be kept
secret and greatly increases an exaggerated falsehood, dissimulates
and colours the truth, invents, forms, and elaborates what happened
in no place and at no time, vows in curses and kills with execrations,
reviles the holy Deity of heaven who should be adored, accustoms
itself to perjuries, favours falsehood and detests its opposite. Does not
such a mind breathe the privies of Avernus and the filthy pits of
Acheron, and manifest itself by its index, the tongue? Which bites,
stings, murmurs, snarls, howls, groans, hisses, cries shrilly and loudly,
cries thunder and lightning, sets up and knocks down, collects and
scatters, wounds and cures, whenever it pleases, or whenever its
interior power or motion dictate. He is almost miraculous who,
moderate in these things, neither hearkens to the dictates nor follows
the power of the tongue, having confined this plectrum of nature and
bound it to the command of Queen Prudence, by whose command it
should move and direct itself. We are sometimes led astray by the
lubricity and agile flexion of this member; it slides away like an eel or
lamprey that is caught and held between the fingers, and commits an
injury before reason notices it. It outflies the dart in swiftness, nor is
its onset known except by the wound already inflicted; it may not be
intercepted in course when already fired from the bow of the mind.
O carnage of this dart, how unforeseen you are and swifter than
the East Wind! . . . For silence obtains so much of authority and
ornament that it may give a reputation for prudence to an undisciplined
and untaught man if he shall have known how to control the vice of
garrulity.[2]

[1] This image is probably influenced by Socrates' description of himself asking
questions as a midwife helping ideas to be born (Plato, *Theaetetus*, 150).
[2] Alciatus, *Emblemata*, with commentaries of Claudius Minos and Franciscus
Sanctius, and notes of Laurentius Pignorius. Ed. by Joannis Thuilius. 'Patauii apud
Petrum Paulum Tozzium', 1621, pp. 66–7.

The 'hellish' nature of the 'mad dog', the violent execrations and curses, accord with Spenser's description of the Blatant Beast. The need to bridle him is similarly stressed. Calidore's quest and capture of the beast then represent a person's effort to control his own tongue, in so far as the quest is part of the internal struggle of the soul. Externally, the quest involves a man's outward demeanour—a sharp tongue is incompatible with courtesy—and also his attempts to discredit slanderous rumours circulated by others.

CALIDORE AND THE GRACES

As Calidore's first place of testing is the House of Briana, his second is the House of Melibee. Melibee, the foster-father of Pastorella, is an admirable figure and entertains Calidore hospitably. The latter faces a difficult problem of tactful courtesy, for he loves Pastorella and wishes to woo her. Yet he must not violate Melibee's hospitality or presume upon his own superior social station, which is obvious to all those around him. Likewise he is a rival of Coridon for Pastorella's love, yet he does not wish to humiliate Coridon or take an unfair advantage of him. When Calidore wins the wrestling match and is awarded the crown of victory, he gives it to Coridon as one more deserving of it, thereby restoring the shepherd youth to cheerfulness (ix. 44). To pursue his purposes while remaining friendly with his 'inferiors' and avoiding any hint of supercilious condescension was a difficult task, which Calidore successfully performed. Nor was it the result of an insincere pose; his manner which disarmed hostility resulted from a genuine respect for the feelings of others.

Following Spenser's normal pattern, the place of perfecting for Calidore comes in Book vi, Canto x, at Mount Acidale, where he sees the dance of the Graces. The various sources of Acidale refer to it as a fountain, not as a mountain. Boccaccio gives Acidalia as a name for Venus and explains it as follows:

> Acidalia is a name given to Venus, either from the Acidalian fountain which is consecrated to Venus and the Graces in Orchomenus, a city of Boeotia, where formerly foolish people thought that the Graces, sisters of Venus, bathed; or because she may be the occasion of sprouting many cares—I venture that we know with how many cares she occupied lovers—and the Greeks call cares Acidas (*akides*).[1]

---

[1] *Della Genealogia de gli Dei* (Venice, 1627), f. 51ᵛ (Italian version). Cf. *Var.* vi. 247. For extensive documentation of the Graces see D. T. Starnes, 'Spenser and the Graces', *Philogical Quarterly*, xxi (1942), 268–82.

Natalis Comes also mentions this fountain:

First of all mortals, King Eteocles of the Orchomeni built a temple to the Graces; for the ancients said that these often went alone to the Orchomeni, to the Acidalian fount to bathe, as witness Strabo, Book ix.[1]

Comes regards the Graces as patronesses of agriculture, bringers of peace and plenty.

Spenser places this fountain at the foot of Mount Acidale, which is in reality no more than a mound. He is perhaps thinking of this as a parallel to the haunt of the Muses on Mount Helicon, from which flow the springs of Helicon. His description of the fountain follows:

> And at the foote thereof, a gentle flud
> His silver waves did softly tumble downe,
> Unmard with ragged mosse or filthy mud;
> Ne mote wylde beastes, ne mote the ruder clowne
> Thereto approach, ne filth mote therein drowne;
> But *nymphes and faeries* by the bancks did sit,
> In the woods shade, which did the waters crowne,
> Keeping all noysome things away from it,
> And to the waters fall tuning their accents fit.　　(x. 7)

The top of the mount is the place of the dance for the nymphs and fairies, and here Venus often comes with the Graces to disport herself in the dance (stanza 9).[2]

That the nymphs of classical mythology were regarded as the fairies of Elizabethan folklore is made evident in Arthur Golding's translation of Ovid's *Metamorphoses*, where he regularly renders *nymphae* as 'fairies'. The association of nymphs with the Graces in the dance is based on three passages from the *Odes* of Horace:

> Jam Cytherea choros ducit Venus, imminente Luna:
> 　Junctaeque Nymphis Gratiae decentes
> Alterno terram quatiunt pede.　　(Book i, no. 4)

(Now Cytherean Venus leads off the dance by moonlight; and the comely Graces, in conjunction with the nymphs, shake the ground with alternate feet [tr. Smart].)

[1] Comes, *Mythologiae*, iv. xv: 'De Gratiis' (edn. of 1616, pp. 222–3).
[2] In a short poem by Faustus Sabaeus occur these lines:
> Nudus Acidaliis Amor excerpebat in hortis
> Pallentes violas, purpureasque rosas.
(In Acidalian gardens, naked Love was gathering pale violets and crimson roses.)
(Ranutio Ghero, ed., *Delitiae CC Italorum Poetarum*, pt. ii (1608), p. 556.)

Fervidus tecum puer et solutis
Gratiae zonis, properentque Nymphae.   (Book i, no. 30)

(Let there come hasting with you your impetuous boy and the loose-girdled Graces and the Nymphs.)

Gratia cum Nymphis, geminisque sororibus audet
Ducere nuda choros.   (Book iv, no. 7)

(A Grace, with the Nymphs and her twin sisters, dares to lead the dance naked.)

The last two passages are quoted by Natalis Comes.[1] While various commentators have referred to these lines from Horace, none has adequately stressed the association of the Graces with the nymphs for purposes of the dance. Spenser uses this association in making the Graces appear in the dance of the fairies. In the centre he places Colin Clout's beloved as the fourth Grace. Around her revolve the three Graces, and around these a hundred fairies, or minor graces.[2] The first Horatian passage, including Venus with the Graces and nymphs, suggests that upon occasion Venus herself would be the central figure of the dance; but the third quotation omits Venus, naming only the nymphs and the three Graces. Accordingly, Colin Clout's love as a fourth Grace takes the place which would normally be occupied by Venus in the dance. Colin Clout, the piper, apparently sits between the inner and the outer circles.

Both Natalis Comes and Francesco Piccolomini mention the tradition that there was a fourth Grace—Comes names her as Suadela (persuasion)—but both accept the more common view that the Graces were only three in number.[3] Spenser, therefore, had some authority for expanding the number of Graces in order to include his lady love.

C. S. Lewis[4] points out that the nudity of the Graces and their

---

[1] *Mythologiae*, iv. xv; p. 222.

[2] The hundred maidens in the outer ring may have numerological significance, for 100 is the square of the perfect number 10 and is often used to represent the whole, or the sum of things (below, p. 274). The three Graces in the inner circle correspond in number to the Trinity, and the one in the centre to Unity, a symbol for God. Cf. 'The Cosmic Dance' in E. M. W. Tillyard's *Elizabethan World Picture* (London, 1943), ch. 8; Fowler, *Spenser and the Numbers of Time*, pp. 222–6; Harry Berger, Jr., 'A Secret Discipline', in William Nelson, *Form and Convention in the Poetry of Edmund Spenser* (New York, 1961), pp. 63–75.

[3] Comes, *Mythologiae*, iv. xv, p. 222; Francesco, viii. 38, p. 438c.

[4] *Var.* vi. 250.

fellow dancers creates an effect of innocent beauty quite unlike the lascivious nudity of the bathing maidens in Acrasia's garden (ii. xii. 63). This earlier use of nude maidens in a fountain may have decided Spenser against the use of a similar scene in the Acidalian fount; instead, he chose to represent the dance of the nude maidens. In descriptions of the three Graces commentators generally interpret their nudity as representative of sincerity of mind and purity of heart. In Alciatus's emblem on the Graces (no. 163), the editor of the variorum edition comments:

They also say that the Graces bathe in the Acidalian fount, which is in Orchomenus, a city of Boeotia . . . since it is necessary that their benefactions be pure and have nothing sordid, without any hope of reward. . . . He offers two causes why the Graces are depicted as nude. First, because for acquiring love and grace it is necessary that the heart itself should appear clear and pure and without any veil of falsehood. Likewise, in setting forth benefits, it is necessary on both sides that nothing be 'double' or hidden, but all clear and simple.[1]

Here are named two ways in which the Graces are interpreted. In one way they are concerned with the giving and receiving of benefits, as stated in Seneca's *De Beneficiis*.[2] Tact and courtesy are required of both the giver and the receiver. It is in this connection that Latin *gratia* and Italian *grazie* are used to mean 'Thank you'. The other interpretation considers the Graces as the aids of Venus in exciting love, and grace as a quality allied to beauty, but not the same thing as beauty. We have already noted that Florimell, or beauty, was reared among the Graces on Mount Acidale; i.e. grace is the perfection of beauty (above, p. 170). It is likewise to be judged the perfection of courtesy, the quality which elevates polished manners into true courtesy and therefore perfects the virtue of Calidore.

We have already seen how the conferring of divine gifts equates heavenly grace with magnificence in the person of Arthur (above, p. 8) and how natural grace is represented by Timias (above, p. 15). It is difficult to define grace as applied to human personality, for it appears in outward manners but stems from internal virtues. Francesco gives three chapters to the study of grace (viii. 36–8) and makes some observations about it which are useful in understanding Spenser.

[1] Alciatus, *Emblemata*, no. 163: 'Gratiae', (edn. of 1621), pp. 688–9.
[2] *Var.* vi. 251.

Grace applies first to the giving of benefits without expectation of reward, of which God's gifts to man are the most eminent examples. Secondly, grace applies to charm and comeliness (*lepor et venustas*) and is necessarily bound up with beauty; in this sense the Graces are called handmaids (*ancillae*) of Venus. Thirdly, grace is assumed for the sake of loving, making the beloved object pleasing to the lover. One may judge that there are three choruses (*chori*) of Graces, each one threefold, and from these arises one Grace the most absolute and most gracious of all; and this Grace is the companion of beauty (viii. 36; pp. 435–6).

These passages seem to postulate nine Graces, like the Nine Muses or the 'trinal triplicities' of Spenser's hierarchy of angels.[1] Two pages later, however, Francesco observes that there are normally three Graces named, though some observers confuse them with the Seasons (*horae*) and think there are four. But, he observes further, Venus may be assumed to have many Graces as attendants and handmaidens (*plures . . . Gratias asseclas et ancillas*) (viii. 38; p. 438B). These accounts would allow Spenser considerable flexibility in his handling of the dance of the Graces.

As Calidore watches the dance, he is puzzled as to the identity of the dancers:

> Whether it were the traine of Beauties Queene,
> Or nymphes, or faeries, or enchaunted show,
> With which his eyes mote have deluded beene.   (VI. x. 17)

Here he again associates the nymphs and fairies with each other and with Venus and her followers.[2] His description of the fourth Grace, Colin Clout's love, as the most perfect of them all is reminiscent of Francesco's description of the 'most absolute and most gracious' Grace that arises from the three choruses of Graces. Spenser writes:

> All they without were raunged in a ring,
> And daunced round; but in the midst of them
> Three other ladies did both daunce and sing,
> The whilest the rest them round about did hemme,
> And like a girlond did in compasse stemme:

---

[1] Spenser, 'An Hymne of Heavenlie Love', l. 64.

[2] Spenser makes the nymphs and fairies sing by the Acidalian fount (*FQ* VI. x. 7). Francesco states that grace, which is allied to beauty, may be shown in words and songs as well as in physical appearance and actions (viii. 38; p. 439D).

And in the middest of those same three was placed
Another damzell, as a precious gemme
Amidst a ring most richly well enchaced,
That with her goodly presence all the rest much graced.

(stanza 12)

But she that in the midst of them did stand
Seem'd all the rest in beauty to excell.   (stanza 14)

Such were the goddesses which ye did see;
But that fourth mayd, which there amidst them traced,
Who can aread what creature mote she bee,
Whether a creature, or a goddesse graced
With heavenly gifts from heven first enraced?
But what so sure she was, she worthy was
To be the fourth with those three other placed.   (stanza 25)

For which the Graces, that here wont to dwell
Have for more honor brought her to this place,
And graced her so much to be another Grace.   (stanza 26)

Francesco notes two opinions concerning the parentage of the Graces: first, that they are the daughters of Jove and Eurynome; second, that they are the daughters of Venus and Bacchus. The first theory is more appropriate, he thinks, if we think of the graces in terms of the conferring of gifts and benefits. The second is more appropriate if we think of grace as joined with beauty (viii. 38; p. 438D). Grace is not the handmaid but rather the life and spirit of excelling beauty. The graces show themselves in gestures, motions, actions, speech, and laughter, and are the 'salts' of action. Grace is a certain external light of reason and congruent dexterity rising from a right constitution of soul and body, and following perfect beauty. Neither grace nor beauty can be perfect without the presence of the other (viii. 37; p. 437C).

We have already noticed dexterity and the 'salts' of conversation as a part of urbanity (above, pp. 12–13), and something of the same idea is apparent in that grace which is the companion of beauty. We have already noticed Spenser's union of beauty and grace in the person of Florimell, who was reared on Mount Acidale among the Graces (above, p. 195). But Spenser's choice of Jove and Eurynome as the parents of the Graces[1] shows that, as the

---

[1] This parentage of the Graces is given by Hesiod (*Var.* vi. 253).

perfecters of courtesy, the Graces are more to be considered in the light of giving and receiving benefits. Francesco quotes Seneca concerning this aspect of the Graces, that they are always cheerful and laughing, as befits the giving and receiving of benefits (e.g. the Christmas spirit). They are young, because the memory of benefits does not grow old. They are virgins, because benefits are incorrupt and sincere. They are unclothed, because benefits are not bound or restricted. They are clear and open, because benefits are willing to be seen; i.e. there is nothing covert or secret about them (viii. 38; p. 438c).

Spenser describes the three Graces as follows:

> These three on men all gracious gifts bestow,
> Which decke the body or adorne the mynde,
> To make them lovely or well favoured show,
> As comely carriage, entertainement kynde,
> Sweete semblaunt, friendly offices that bynde,
> And all the complements of curtesie:
> They teach us, how to each degree and kynde
> We should our selves demeane, to low, to hie,
> To friends, to foes; which skill men call civility.
>
> Therefore they alwaies smoothly seeme to smile,
> That we likewise should mylde and gentle be,
> And also naked are, that without guile
> Or false dissemblaunce all them plain may see,
> Simple and true, from covert malice free:
> And eeke them selves so in their daunce they bore,
> That two of them still froward seem'd to bee,
> But one still towards shew'd her selfe afore;
> That good should from us goe, then come, in greater store.
>
> (VI. x. 23–4)

Spenser has slightly altered the description of the Graces in order to make their qualities the perfection of courtesy. For example, Francesco shows the Graces laughing because the exchange of presents or other benefits makes cheerful both the givers and the receivers. Spenser makes them smile as an incentive to mansuetude, the virtue represented by Calepine. In most representations of the three Graces, two are pictured as facing the reader, while one is turned away from the reader. Francesco explains this as meaning that no person can be happy in every respect; some element of good fortune will always be turned away from him (viii. 38; p. 439B). Servius had explained it as meaning that gifts which we might give would be repaid to us twice over.[1] This is repeated in the gloss to Alciatus's emblem on the Graces.[2] Spenser has reversed this, having two of the Graces facing away from the reader, as a sign that we ought to give more than we receive. He may have had some authority for this change. In an edition of Vicenzo Cartari's *Imagini de gli Dei delli Antichi*, Padua, 1626, the three Graces are shown riding with Venus in her chariot (p. 432). Two Graces at the rear of the chariot stand with their backs to the reader. The third Grace, with her back towards the other two, faces the reader, as does Venus, who stands in the front of the chariot.[3] The artist was probably only striving for a symmetrical arrangement of this picture, for in a later picture of the three Graces (p. 455) they are portrayed in the usual manner, two facing the reader, one with face and body averted.

The inscription under this second illustration affords a close parallel to Spenser's use of the Graces: 'Images of the three Graces, goddesses of beauty and grace; goddesses also of gratitude and of benefit, named Euphrosyne or Jollity (*giocondità*), Aglaia or Comeliness (*venustà*), and Thalia or Gaiety (*piacevolezza*): goddesses of conversation, sociability, and friendliness, and of that cheerful life which men desire to live.'

It is this quality of grace that adds the touch of perfection to Calidore's inward spirit and outward manner. He is able to complete his conquest of the Blatant Beast; that is, to restrain his own tongue from unkind or hasty remarks, and by his friendly demeanour to disarm the sharp tongues of others. This marks the triumph of courtesy as the great harmonizer in human society.

[1] *Var.* vi. 254.

[2] Alciatus, *Emblemata* (edn. of 1621), p. 688.

[3] The illustrations are different in various editions of Cartari and Alciatus, and I cannot be sure that Spenser had seen this picture of the Graces. Its existence suggests that he may have seen it or another one like it.

X

Studies in the Historical Allegory

S PENSER's clearest use of historical allegory occurs in Book v of *The Faerie Queene* and has been adequately discussed by earlier scholars; consequently, I shall not discuss it here. In two other instances, it seems to me that something may be added to existing scholarship, and a discussion of these two is the substance of this chapter.

CLEOPOLIS AND PANTHEA

In Cleopolis, the City of Glory, stands Panthea, a shining tower of glass or crystal. Spenser does not record the precise use of this building; one may suppose it to contain memorials of knightly deeds performed in the service of Gloriana. Inevitably, one looks for possible actual or literary models for the city and the tower.

In 1514 Quintianus Stoa published a Latin poem *Cleopolis*, in praise of the city of Paris.[1] From this Spenser may have borrowed the name of his city in Fairyland; and, since Elizabeth styled herself Queen of France, he may have included France as a legitimate part of her realms as allegorized in his poem. However, he probably envisioned other cities as contributing details to his imaginary ideal city. Isabel Rathborne convincingly demonstrates that Troy, Rome, and London (Troynovant) were probable sources of Cleopolis,[2] and these three are mentioned in the dialogue of Britomart and Paridell (III. ix. 33–46), which sets forth numerous details of British history. Yet, though Cleopolis is the scene of Gloriana's court, Spenser seems to say expressly that it is not the city of London. Paridell speaks of Brutus, the traditional founder of the kingdom of Britain:

> His worke great Troynovant, his worke is eke
> Faire Lincolne, both renowmed far away,
> That who from east to west will endlong seeke,
> Cannot two fairer cities find this day,
> Except Cleopolis. (III. ix. 51)

---

[1] Rathborne, *Meaning of Spenser's Fairyland*, p. 22.   [2] Ibid., pp. 105–7.

This seems to say that Cleopolis is fairer than either London or Lincoln and therefore cannot be either of them.

The answer may be that London and Westminster are separate entities and were so in Spenser's time. To this day, when Londoners speak of 'the City', they mean the area around the Tower of London and St. Paul's Cathedral, not including the West End or Westminster Abbey. It might therefore be possible for Spenser, a native of London, to think of 'the City' as Troynovant and of Westminster as Cleopolis, in which case Westminster Abbey would probably correspond to Panthea, the 'tower of glass' and temple of Honour.

The possibility remains that Cleopolis is a composite of several earthly cities, or rather that it is an ideal city of Glory with several —or perhaps many—earthly prototypes. If this is accepted, the most likely candidate is Glastonbury, in Somerset. For Glastonbury, the ancient Avalon or Isle of Apples, is traditionally and indisputably the one spot in the British Isles which is a part of Fairyland. It was formerly one of several islands in the midst of a shallow lake—the others are Meare, Wedmore, Athelney, and Beckery—and was the ancient Celtic paradise for the souls of warriors slain while defending their country. It was also the haunt of fairies, and particularly of the fairy queen. Here came Ogier the Dane to dwell with Queen Morgan le Fay; returning to the normal world, he found that his short visit to Avalon had covered two hundred years of earthly time. In her chapter 'The Fayerye', Miss Rathborne gives this and other evidence of Avalon's associations with the fairyland of medieval romance.[1]

The alternative Celtic name for Avalon was Ynisvitrin, or Isle of Glass, and Glastonbury was popularly believed to mean City of Glass.[2] This would not quite correspond to Cleopolis, which is not of glass but contains Panthea, a tower of glass or crystal. We find, however, in John Leland's *Assertio* concerning Prince Arthur the statement that in the Saxon tongue *Glas* or *Gles* means glass, but that *bury* refers to a *castrum* or castle, not to a city, as is usually supposed.[3] This brings a castle of glass much closer to Spenser's tower of glass and equates Glastonbury with Panthea.

---

[1] Ibid., pp. 195–201.

[2] *Encyclopedia of Religion and Ethics*, ed. J. Hastings, vol. ii, p. 690. References are given to Chrétien's *Erec*, 1933–4, and Geoffrey's *Vita Merlini*, 41.

[3] *A Learned and True Assertion of the original, Life, Actes, and death of the most Noble, Valiant, and Renowned Prince Arthure, King of great Brittaine* . . . (1582), ch. 11.

Leland quotes Geoffrey of Monmouth's description of Avalon, which Richard Robinson, Leland's translator, renders as follows:

> The Isle of *Apples*, which called is fortunate,
>   Of effect hath name, for it bringes forth all things:
> The seeded ground no neede of Plowmen hath,
>   All tillage wantes, saue that which Nature bringes.
> Of it owne accorde it beares both Grapes & Corne,
>   And apples grow in woods, first grafts being pruned & shorne.[1]

The first line identifies Avalon with the Fortunate Isles of ancient myth, perhaps including Avalon's neighbouring islands, since the term is given in the plural. These may also be the islands of the Daemons and Genii—or fairies—the Sporades which Plutarch placed in or near Britain, according to Francesco Piccolomini (above, p. 49). Mrs. Bennett has traced the ancient tradition of Britain among the Fortunate Isles,[2] but Geoffrey seems to limit the term to Avalon and the islands surrounding it. Avalon has the usual features of earthly paradises: mild climate, fruits and grain ripening without tillage, as given also in Ovid's description of the Golden Age.[3]

As a fairyland of fame, Glastonbury also has strong claims. From the waters surrounding it, Prince Arthur received his magic sword Excalibur, and hither he returned to be treated for his fatal wound. The fairy 'ladies of the lake' received him into their barge for transport to Avalon, and popular fable pictured him as still alive, waiting for the time of his destined return.[4] With the discovery of his tomb near St. Joseph's Chapel in Glastonbury in 1179, the hope for his literal return was dispelled. Sixteen feet down, in a casket of alder wood covered with a flat stone, were found the bodies of Arthur and Guinevere. The golden hair of Guinevere still gleamed in full beauty but fell into dust at the first touch of the delver's hands. A leaden tablet affixed to the under side of the stone identified the tomb as that of Arthur. The tablet was removed, and Leland declares that he had seen it with his own eyes, but he neglects to state where it was kept. The grave was moved, by order of Henry II, to a more respectable position in the new abbey, and later by Edward I to the central aisle of the

---

[1] *A Learned and True Assertion*, f. 21.

[2] Josephine Waters Bennett, 'Britain among the Fortunate Isles', *SP* liii (1956), 114–40.   [3] *Metamorphoses*, i. 89–112.

[4] Rathborne, *Meaning of Spenser's Fairyland*, p. 182.

great chapel.[1] There it can still be seen, despoiled of its inmates by some irreverent hand, a pathetic memorial among the other ruins of Glastonbury.

Glastonbury is also identified with the beginnings of the English Church. Hither came Joseph of Arimathea in A.D. 53 with a small band of followers, to preach the gospel of Christ. King Arviragus, second son of Cymbeline, gave him the Isle of Avalon for the building of his church. Not many years before, Joseph had begged from the Romans the body of Christ, had wrapped it in clean linen, and had laid it in the rock sepulchre planned for himself (Matt. 27: 57–60). With him he brought to Glastonbury the Holy Grail, or communion cup used at the last supper of Christ and the Apostles. His staff, thrust into the earth, took root and produced the flowering thorn which blossoms at Christmastide as well as in late spring. An early English life of Joseph concludes with a woodcut in which he lies with his head resting on his left hand, while from his bosom grows a tree bearing future bishops and kings who do homage to the Virgin and Child standing in the midst of the tree.[2] This seems to view Joseph as a founder of the English State as well as the English Church, perhaps because Arthur himself on his mother's side was descended from Joseph's nephew Helarius.[3] When King Lucius brought from Rome the two Christian missionaries Faggan and Duvyen in A.D. 187, he granted to them the Isle of Avalon formerly occupied by Joseph.[4] Lucius' reign is marked by the large-scale conversions of Britons to Christianity. From the British Church came St. Helen, daughter of the king of Colchester, wife to the emperor Constantius and mother of Constantine the Great, who was crowned at York as Emperor of the West and later became emperor of the entire Roman Empire, which he brought into the fold of the Christian Church. Helen herself visited Jerusalem, rediscovered the Holy Sepulchre, and arranged for its preservation, thus repeating Joseph's pious action of three centuries before. From Glastonbury St. Patrick went forth to convert Ireland to Christianity, then returned to spend his last

---

[1] Leland's *A Learned and True Assertion*, ch. 15.

[2] *Here after foloweth a treatyse taken out of a boke whiche somtyme Theodosius the Emperour founde in Jherusalem in the pretorye of Pylate of Joseph of Armathy* (n.d.). Printed by Wynkyn de Worde.

[3] Leland, *A Learned and True Assertion*, in Robinson's *Introduction*.

[4] John Hardyng's *Chronicle*, ed. Henry Ellis (London, 1812), pp. 88–90.

days as Abbot of Glastonbury, dying in 493. From the Irish Church came St. Columba and afterwards St. Aidan, who converted the Scots and Northern Saxons. Thus the church at Glastonbury could fairly claim to be the parent of the English Church. Great things had proceeded from small beginnings in Avalon.[1]

Miss Rathborne has suggested that Spenser's Fairyland is designed to honour not only the ancient British (Celtic) kings, but the Saxons and Normans as well.[2] This would accord with the history of Glastonbury, which received great honour from kings of all three nationalities. Here were buried Joseph of Arimathea, Sir Galahad, and King Arthur. In 719, King Ina (or Iwe or Ivor)[3] built at Glastonbury the great Church of St. Peter and St. Paul. After this was plundered by the Danes, it was refounded in 946 as an abbey by St. Dunstan, the Saxon cleric who became Abbot of Glastonbury and afterward Archbishop of Canterbury. Here were buried the Saxon kings Edmund, Edgar, and Edmund Ironside. Shortly after the abbey was remodelled in 1184, it was destroyed by fire, and upon its ruins was erected by Henry II the noble edifice whose ruins mark the spot today. Henry died before the work was finished, and it lapsed for a hundred years but was eventually completed in 1303. Any or all of these great structures could have served as a model for Spenser's Panthea, or temple of Honour and Glory, though historically the career of Arthur antedates them all.

Perhaps the spirit of Glastonbury is best expressed in another early biography of Joseph (1520), this time in verse:[4]

> Than hyther into brytayne Joseph dyd come
> And this was by kyng Aueragas dayes
> So dyd Joseph and also Josephas his sonne
> With many one mo as the olde boke says
> This kynge was hethen & lyued on fals layes
> And yet he gaue to Joseph aulonye
> Nowe called Glastenbury & there he lyes
> Somtyme it was a towne of famous antyquyte. . . .

[1] Much of this information is found in *Glastonbury: The Isle of Avalon*, an illustrated guide supplied by the Avalon Press, Glastonbury.

[2] Rathborne, *Meaning of Spenser's Fairyland*, p. 179.

[3] Chroniclers differ as to this king's name and as to whether he was Celtic or Saxon.

[4] From a life of Joseph of Arimathea, published by Richard Pynson in London in 1520.

Heyle tresour of Glastenbury moost imperyall
In sauour smellynge swete as eglantyne
Now shall thy name flourysshe ouerall
Jhesu for thy sake the bell of mercy doth rynge.
Great cause hath Englande (Laus deo to synge
God and Joseph to prayse w^t all our dylygence
That many men delyuereth out of mournynge
By our lordes fauour grace & magnyfycence. . . .

Now holy Joseph pray for vs to our lorde
To send vs peas and perfyte charite
And among the comyns welth and concorde
And that our ryche men may vse lyberalyte
Whiche than shall towarde the deyte
Where aungelles to Jhesu do great reuerence
Vnto the whiche god bryng bothe you & me
Of his fauour grace and magnyfycence.[1]

THE HISTORICAL ALLEGORY OF BOOK I

As already noted in Chapter V, the allegory of Book i clearly involves the conflict between Una as the 'true Church' or Church of England and Duessa as the 'false Church' or Church of Rome. The first represents 'one-ness', or the unity of the Church of Christ; the second represents 'two-ness', or division, duplicity, and schism. From Spenser's point of view, the papacy was the divisive force that split the Church by its departure from the principles of true religion; the reformed Church, or the Anglican portion of it, was the original Church, adhering to the principles taught by Christ and the early Apostles.

The various historical allegories proposed are summarized in the *Variorum Spenser*, i. 449–95.[2] Sir Walter Scott and Thomas Keightley saw in Book i an allegory of the history of the Church from its beginnings. Later scholars—Whitney, Buck, Winstanley, Padelford, Greenlaw—interpret Book i in terms of sixteenth-century English history, Miss Winstanley seeking to limit the

---

[1] These stanzas have the construction and rhyme scheme of the Spenserian stanza, except for the lack of a final Alexandrine. Cf. p. 224 n. 1. Spenser uses this form in *The Shepheardes Calender*, 'November', ll. 1–8.

[2] I have used as sources for historical facts the English histories of T. F. Tout and John Richard Green, Gibbon's *Decline and Fall of the Roman Empire*, and the Funk & Wagnalls *Encyclopedia* (1912).

allegory to Henry VIII's reign, Padelford extending it to include Mary's reign as the period of Redcross's sojourn in the dungeons of Orgoglio. He interprets the final battle with the dragon as the events of Elizabeth's reign involving Mary Queen of Scots.

These explanations all possess a good deal of logic but leave unexplained several important points which should have a significance in the historical allegory. These are:

1. Redcross's origin. He supposes himself to be a fairy knight but springs 'from ancient race of Saxon kinges'. He is a changeling, brought to Fairyland by the fay who stole him, and hidden in a furrow of the fields until a ploughman found him (i. x. 64–6).
2. Duessa's parentage. She is the daughter of Deceit and Shame, granddaughter of Night (i. v. 26–7) in terms of the moral allegory. In terms of the historical allegory, she claims to be the true faith or Fidessa,

> sole daughter of an emperour,
> He that the wide west under his rule has,
> And high hath set his throne where Tiberis doth pas. (ii. 22)

In pretending that she is betrothed to Redcross, she calls herself

> The wofull daughter and forsaken heyre
> Of that great Emperour of all the West. (xii. 26)

3. Una's parentage. Her father is king of Eden (xii. 26). In more fortunate days, her father and mother had spread their rule over all the territory watered by the rivers Phison, Euphrates, and Gehon (vii. 43). These are three of the Biblical rivers that flow from the Garden of Eden (Gen. 2: 10–14). The parents are now shut up in a castle for safety from a great dragon.
4. Identity of the dragon. The huge dragon was 'bred in the loathly lakes of Tartary'. He has besieged Una's parents for four years and has slain many would-be rescuers (vii. 44–5).

We may consider first the dragon in terms of historical allegory. Padelford's connection of it with events involving the Queen of Scots seems unlikely, since Mary is personified as Duessa in v. ix. 38 and would probably be nearer to Duessa in Book 1 if she is there involved at all. Nor are Duessa and Archimago (the papacy and the Roman clergy) involved in Redcross's struggle against the dragon, as we should expect them to be if the dragon represents plots of the Roman Church. We should consider possible alternatives.

In Dante's figurative description of the Church as a chariot, we have already noticed the harlot seated upon the chariot and the giant beside it as possible prototypes of Duessa and Orgoglio, particularly since the chariot puts forth seven beastly heads (the deadly sins) and Duessa rides upon a seven-headed beast (above, p. 104). But there is more to the vision than this. Before its transformation, the chariot is twice attacked by an eagle (Roman emperors); then a dragon appears underneath, transfixes the chariot with his sting, and tears away a portion of the floor. This dragon is interpreted to mean Mahomet,[1] who in Christian eyes was a schismatic who seduced a portion of the Christian Church. This hint may well have been used by Spenser. The dragon in Eden was 'bred in the loathly lakes of Tartary'. Tartary has regularly been interpreted as Tartarus, the dragon as the devil, who shall be cast into the lake of fire in hell.[2] The image does not exactly fit, since the devil was not 'bred' in hell but is to be punished there. Nevertheless, this meaning was probably intended as part of the moral allegory; but it seems to have little relevance for the historical allegory. If Spenser follows Dante's lead, however, the dragon's birth in Tartary does have a real significance. In 1065, Jerusalem was captured by the Seljuk Turks, who were supposed to have come originally from Tartary.[3] Their cruel persecution of Christian pilgrims to the Holy Land led to the First Crusade, resulting in the capture of Jerusalem by the Christians in 1099. It was reconquered for the Saracens by a Kurdish chieftain, Saladin, in 1187; Saladin's father had worked for the Seljuk Turks. In the Third Crusade Richard the Lion-Heart secured free access of Christian pilgrims to the Holy City in 1190; one over-enthusiastic English chronicler, John Hardyng, declares that he captured the city.[4] In 1228, the German Emperor Frederick II regained the city from Saladin's successors by a treaty

[1] So identified in the notes of Henry Cary, Thomas Okey, and E. H. Plumptre, following earlier commentators.

[2] *Var.* i. 255.

[3] J. F. Michaud, *The History of the Crusades*, tr. W. Robson (New York, 1859), vol. i, pp. 31–2, 34.

[4] Hardyng's *Chronicle*, (edn. of 1812), pp. 265–6.

which guaranteed Muslims free access to *their* holy places in the city. In 1244, a band of Khorasmians from Tartary, who had been displaced by Jenghiz Khan, captured Jerusalem and began persecuting Christian pilgrims. In 1270, Prince Edward of England, later Edward I, landed in Palestine, relieved the city of Acre from a siege, and penetrated inland as far as Nazareth, where he forced a ten-year truce in the fighting.[1] It therefore appears that Spenser could have made a distinction between the different groups of the infidels. The Arabs, who had captured Jerusalem four centuries before the First Crusade, had not refused visiting rights to Christian pilgrims. Though the Saracens were not Christian, they are pictured in Malory as being chivalrous and sometimes virtuous.[2] But the Seljuk Turks and the Khorasmians were not so; they appeared to be oppressive monsters of cruelty. Accordingly, they could be represented as a dragon bred in Tartary, whence they originally came. Dante had already supplied the image of Mahomet as a dragon attacking the Church. Spenser may be using Tartary as an ambivalent term, meaning Tartarus or hell in the moral allegory and the land of Tartary in the historical allegory.

The clues are too slight for us to regard this theory as more than speculation unless other elements of the allegory accord with it. Accordingly, we may now consider the identity of Redcross in terms of the historical allegory. J. E. Whitney says of him: 'St. George is *Fidei Defensor* not representing Henry VIII alone, but rather the sovereigns of England, who bear the title of Defender of the Faith.' Whitney then interprets the allegory in terms of Henry VIII and his successors.[3] The interpretation is not convincing in its present form; but suppose that we include earlier as well as later sovereigns of England. The descent of Redcross from Saxon kings must mean that the line represented goes back to a point before William the Conqueror. If Redcross is not limited to one particular person, he may well represent the whole line of English royalty, or the English Crown. This would make him

---

[1] Gibbon, *Decline and Fall of the Roman Empire*, ch. 59 (London: Chandos Library edn., n.d.), vol. iii, p. 490. (References are to this edition.) The Khorasmians were not Muslims, but they had seized Jerusalem from the Christian rulers and had persecuted Christian pilgrims to the Holy Sepulchre.

[2] For example Sir Priamus in *Le Morte D'Arthur*, v. x, and Sir Palomides in VIII. xxxi.

[3] *Var.* i. 455–8.

parallel to the English Church (Una), which is also considered throughout the whole of its history. Spenser is fond of these composite figures, as we have seen in the various cities which are prototypes of Cleopolis, and he may be using such figures here.

Since Spenser lays so much emphasis upon the ancestry of Arthur and Britomart, it is surprising that he did not find Redcross's origin in the line of Celtic kings. But this line had been interrupted. When King Cadwallader, who had retired to Brittany, sought to raise an army to regain his crown, an angel appeared and commanded him not to do so, since God would punish the Britons for their sins by giving their land to the Saxons, but promised that after eight hundred years the line of British (Celtic) kings should return to their inheritance. Cadwallader retired to a monastery in Rome in 680, where he died in 688. He was the last Celtic king who laid claim to all Britain, though various Welsh chieftains continued to occupy parts of the island and to fight the Saxons.[1] In so far as the royal line of England was an unbroken sequence, it began with the Saxons. Edward the Confessor, the last lineal Saxon king, was by his Norman mother Emma a first cousin once removed to William the Conqueror and had promised the crown of England to William as the nearest heir. On strict principles of primogeniture, William's claim was superior to that of Harold, who was Edward's brother-in-law but had no blood relationship to the royal family.

We may now look at the relation of the British Crown to the several Crusades; for to English chroniclers the relationship seemed much closer than we generally realize. The Turks seized Jerusalem in the year preceding the Norman conquest of England. The necessity of a Crusade was preached by Peter the Hermit. The leader elected to head the expedition, with the title of King of Jerusalem, was Robert Curthose, Duke of Normandy and eldest son of William the Conqueror. Upon the death of his brother William II and the accession of Henry I, Robert left the expedition in order to return and claim the English throne, but he failed of this objective and also lost his dukedom of Normandy. John Hardyng moralizes that this was Robert's punishment

[1] Hardyng, *Chronicle* (edn. of 1812), p. 178; David Powel, *The historie of Cambria, now called Wales* (London, 1584): 'The beginning of the Principalitie and government of Wales', pp. 1–5. This work was revised from that of Humphrey Llwyd. Each division of the book is paged separately.

for deserting the cause of Christ to promote his personal interests.[1]

Robert had left command of the expedition to Godfrey of Boulogne, who completed the conquest of Jerusalem in 1099 and who might be regarded as Robert's deputy. Godfrey's title of King of Jerusalem descended to Henry II of England by way of his father Geoffrey of Anjou. When Jerusalem was again in imminent danger of capture in 1183, Baldwin IV sent the Patriarch of Jerusalem to Henry, bearing the royal staff of office and the royal robes, to urge Henry to accept the title and the responsibility of saving the Holy City.[2] This Henry would not do, but his son Richard the Lion-Heart pursued the claim with great valour and gained visiting rights for Christian pilgrims, though not the city itself. When Frederick II, Emperor of the Holy Roman Empire, gained the city by treaty in 1228, the English felt that they had a part in the conquest. Frederick's wife was a sister of Henry III of England. His predecessor, the Emperor Otto, was a grandson of Henry II of England, whose own mother had been Empress by her first marriage, to Emperor Henry V. After the death of Frederick II's son, a brother of Henry III of England, Richard of Cornwall, was elected emperor; but the choice was never ratified by the Pope, so Richard used the title King of the Romans. These close links with Frederick II would associate the English Crown with his successful Crusade, in which 60,000 English soldiers took part.[3] The final effort of Prince Edward in 1270 achieved only partial success but appeared to the English as a great victory, since he forced a truce in the fighting. Edward was accompanied by his younger brother Edmund, and these two brothers became the ancestors of the two parents of Henry IV. All his life Henry IV planned a Crusade to the Holy Land but was never able to embark upon it. Later sovereigns maintained an interest in Jerusalem. John Hardyng, in the Proem to his *Chronicle*, analyses the claim of the Duke of York, Edward IV's father, to the crown of England and also to the crown of Jerusalem. And we find Mary Tudor, among her other titles, styling herself Queen of Jerusalem.[4]

[1] Hardyng, *Chronicle* (edn. of 1812), pp. 245–6.   [2] Ibid., p. 259.

[3] The reported and probably excessive figure (Gibbon, ch. 59, vol. iii, p. 485).

[4] In the dedication to Queen Mary of Robert Record's *The Castle of Knowledge* (1556), she is called 'Queen of England, Spain, both Siciles, Fraunce, Jerusalem, and Ireland'.

It therefore seems possible that Spenser has planned an allegory of the English Crown's relations to the Crusades and the attempts to expel the cruel tribes of Tartary from Jerusalem. Perhaps some of the episodes may be attached to particular individuals, but the allegory is best interpreted as a composite view of English royalty in its relation to the Holy Land. In 1581 appeared Tasso's romantic epic of the First Crusade, with its accompanying moral allegory. Fired by this beautiful poem, *Gerusalemme Liberata*, Spenser may have decided to give his own version of the Crusades as a supplement to his moral allegory.

The purpose of Redcross's quest is to rescue Una's parents from the dragon. Since Una represents the English Church, her parents are assumed to be the primitive Church in Jerusalem; the castle in which they take refuge could be any of the fortified towns along the coast of the Crusader kingdom. These, notably Acre, were besieged at various times but did not finally succumb until 1291, twenty years after Edward's expedition.[1]

Redcross, or the English Crown, is himself the prize in a contest between Una and Duessa, or the English Church and the Roman Church. Propagandists of Elizabeth's reign carried on a spirited campaign to prove the English Church equal to the Roman Church in age and in spiritual authority. They accepted its founding in A.D. 53 by Joseph of Arimathea. Since the Roman Church claimed to be founded by St. Peter, one Christopher Carlisle analysed the dates from history and from the Scriptures to 'prove' that Peter could not have settled in Rome.[2] In any case, argued the English clergy, Christ's words to Peter, 'Upon this rock I build my church', did not give Peter authority over the other Apostles but only singled him out for special honour. The Pope was the Bishop of Rome and no more. His assumed authority

---

[1] The Crusaders officially survived in the Knights of St. John of Jerusalem, or Knights Hospitallers, who surrendered Acre in 1291 and sailed for Cyprus. From 1310 to 1523 they held the Island of Rhodes, then spent seven years in Crete, and in 1530 received the Island of Malta, which they controlled until 1798. Conceivably, Spenser may have considered Malta the castle in which Una's parents survived and have hoped for yet another Crusade, supported by Elizabeth of England.

[2] Christopher Carlisle, *A Discourse . . . that Peter was neuer at Rome. Furthermore, that neither Peter nor the Pope is the head of Christes Church. Also an interpretation upon the second Epistle of S. Paul to the Thessalonians, the second Chapter* (London, 1572). A second edition appeared about 1580. This may have been the Captain Christopher Carlisle who was present with Spenser in Bryskett's Irish cottage in 1582-4 (*A Discourse of Ciuill Life*, pp. 5-6).

over other sees of the Church was a usurped authority based on no traditional right. Even less valid was his claim to temporal authority by which he presumed to set up and depose kings and princes. This 'power of the sword' was claimed by Pope Boniface VIII about 1300. John Jewel, Bishop of Salisbury, pointed out in 1562 that Pope Clement had denied that the Bishop of Rome had such power.[1]

Spenser's Duessa bases her claim to be Fidessa, or the true faith, on the fact that she is the sole daughter and 'heyre' to the Emperor of the West. Her claim to be the heir as well as the *sole* daughter almost certainly refers to the Donation of Constantine, a document which gave to Pope Sylvester and his heirs complete control of Rome and all the western portion of the Empire, at the time when Constantine the Great withdrew to Constantinople. This Greek document was brought forward in 1440 and was examined by various scholars, who declared it a forgery. However, it persisted and was the primary basis of the Pope's claim to temporal authority. The Donation was published in English in 1534, together with the lengthy opinion of Laurentius Valla and a shorter one by Nicholas, Cardinal of Cusa, pronouncing it a forgery.[2] Constantine indeed gave money and lands for churches in and near Rome, and these were mentioned by several popes; but there is a complete absence of any references to temporal dominion by the popes except in the Donation itself. Also, Constantine appointed his son Constantine as Emperor of the West, which he would not have done if temporal sovereignty had been alienated to the popes. With the deaths of Constantine II and Constans in the West, the empire was reunited under Constantius, Emperor of the East, and the Churches of both Rome and Constantinople recognized his authority over them.

Constantine the Great was first crowned at York, in England, in A.D. 310, as Emperor of the West, the title which his father Constantius had held before him. His subsequent campaigns to gain Rome and later the Eastern Empire were marked by two things: they were successful, and they were made under the sign of the Cross. The Greek historian Eusebius heard from Constan-

---

[1] Jewel, *Apologia Ecclesiae Anglicanae* (1562) (unpaged). Later editions appeared in 1584 and 1588.

[2] The Donation of Constantine appeared in English about 1534, as *A Treatise of the Donation gyuen vnto Syluester, Pope of Rhome*.

tine's own lips of his vision of the Cross bearing the motto 'In hoc signo vince' ('In this sign, conquer'), which appeared to him the night before his battle with Maxentius for possession of Rome; subsequently, the banner of the Cross was always borne before Constantine into battle.[1] Thus, Constantine was the proto-Crusader who went from Britain to the East to destroy paganism. In him the circle was complete: Jerusalem, Glastonbury, York, Rome, Constantinople, Jerusalem. His faith was derived from his British mother Helen, and hers from the Church founded by Joseph of Arimathea. Apostles had gone out from Jerusalem to all parts of the world; but to the British Church was reserved the glory of giving to Christianity its world-wide triumph. Such was the myth, hardly dimmed by such spoil-sports as Polydore Vergil, who maintained that Helen was not a British woman and who minimized the effect that Britain had upon her son.[2]

Like Redcross, Constantine was also a dragon-slayer. When a great dragon menaced the city of Rome, Constantine followed him into his den and destroyed him there, then closed the mouth of the den with an immovable wall of brass. He was honoured by Pope Sylvester for this act of bravery.[3]

To England, then, it seemed presumptuous that the papacy (Duessa) should assert dominion over England on the basis of a commission from Constantine. If anything, the English Crown and the English Church should have dominion over Rome, a claim actually made by King Arthur as a successor of Constantine the Great.[4] Both rulers had fought the 'Saracens'.[5] At the very least, the two Churches should be co-equal. Both were daughters of the parent Church at Jerusalem, but the Roman Church had built up a specious pretence of being the sole repository of temporal power and the superior authority in spiritual power.

[1] Eusebius states, in his *Life of Constantine*, that Constantine had personally told him of this episode. See Gibbon, ch. 20, vol. i, p. 549.

[2] Polydore Vergil, Italian born, was attacked by Holinshed, David Powel, and others, for exposing the 'myths' about Constantine and Arthur in his *Historiae Anglicanae* (Basel, 1534). He thought that Constantine's mother was born in Bithynia.

[3] Andrew Wyntoun's *Chronicle* narrates how Constantine assailed the dragon and 'brist yt', then closed its den with a wall of brass (Scottish Text Society, vol. l [3], p. 424). John Capgrave assigns this exploit to Pope Sylvester (*The Chronicle of England*, ed. F. C. Hingeston [London, 1858], p. 78).

[4] Hardyng, *Chronicle* (edn. of 1812), p. 141.

[5] 'A Short English Chronicle' (Lambeth MS. 306), in *Three 15th Century Chronicles* (Camden Society Publications, Vol. 28); *King Arthur* (London: Wynkyn de Worde, 1529), bk. v, chs. 10 and 11.

In Canto ii, Duessa further declares that her father, the Western Emperor, had betrothed her to a mighty king, who was slain by his foes before the marriage took place, and his body was hidden away by them. She was searching for his corpse when Sansfoy found her and compelled her to accompany him, though he could never seduce her virtue (ii. 23–5). The meaning probably is that Constantine the Great set up his son Constantine II as Emperor of the West to be the consort of the Church of the West. But Constantine II was slain almost immediately by his brother Constans, who in his turn was slain by the rebel Magnentius. There was no further Emperor of the West for some time, the title and authority reverting to Constantius, Emperor of the East. In English eyes, there it should have remained: one emperor and one Church. Charlemagne was a usurper. His father Pepin first induced Pope Zecharias in 751 to crown him King of the Franks, then rewarded Zecharias by giving him all Italy as a temporal possession and expelling the Eastern emperors from their seat at Ravenna. Thus Pepin and Zecharias were two thieves rewarding each other, and Charlemagne was their heir.[1] But in this exchange Pepin had accepted his crown from Zecharias, thus acknowledging the supremacy of pope over emperor, whereas until then the early Church had always accepted the supremacy of emperor over pope. By the teaching of the early Church, the sovereign in his regulative and order-keeping capacity could dictate the personnel but not the doctrine of the Church. Thus, in the Acts of Supremacy declaring Henry VIII and Elizabeth 'supreme head' of the English Church, the English were returning to the principles of Constantine and his successors. The Roman Church, claiming to derive its authority from him, was insisting on division or 'two-ness' by maintaining an authority independent of the Eastern emperors, and this divisiveness was the direct cause of the conquest of Constantinople by the Turks in 1453.[2] Spenser did not believe that Duessa (the papacy) really wanted a 'husband' to whom she would owe wifely obedience. She preferred to sell herself as a harlot to the strongest man available, using him to bring others into subjection to her power, after which she would turn on her lover

---

[1] See Tyndale (below, p. 220). A later work by Thomas Bell, *The Downefall of Popery* (London, 1608), pp. 7–17, repeats the charge of conspiracy against Pepin and Zecharias.

[2] Cf. Tyndale, below, p. 220.

and subdue him. She craved power and would use any means to get it. She saved Sansjoy and Redcross from death, not out of pity, but to increase the number of her subjects. She might need to use them later against Orgoglio.

The pride and arrogance of the Roman Church in its relations to the English Church began quite early, the English said. The first occasion came when Augustine, the Roman missionary who founded the see of Canterbury, met with the Welsh or British Christians to introduce uniformity of church discipline. The Britons rejected his proposals, which included recognition of Canterbury as the primary see of the country. Then, according to David Powel, Augustine urged the heathen Saxons to make war against the Christian Britons. Ethelred or Ethelbert, of Kent, twice defeated Brockwell, the Welsh leader. After this, 1,000 priests and monks of Bangor, with many lay brothers, came barefoot to make their submission to the Saxons and to crave their mercy. The Saxons cruelly murdered them all, and responsibility for this massacre was attributed to Augustine.[1]

Spenser takes note of this tradition in Merlin's words to Britomart:

> Whilst thus thy Britons doe in languor pine,
> Proud Etheldred shall from the North arise,
> Serving th'ambitious will of Augustine,
> And passing Dee with hardy enterprise,
> Shall backe repulse the valiaunt Brockwell twise
> And Bangor with massacred martyrs fill.   (III. iii. 35)

Augustine had his way and became primate of England with the approval of the Saxon kings. Yet still the Welsh Church struggled on, obscure and ignored, protected by the mountain fastnesses and the people of Wales. This may be the first incident in which Una (English Church), deserted by Redcross (English Crown) for Duessa (Roman Church), is saved by the 'woodborne people' (Welsh). How Elizabethans regarded this situation is described by Powel: '. . . in the yeare 540, when the right Christian faith (which Joseph of Aremathia taught in the Ile of Aualon) reigned in this land, before the proud and bloodthirstie moonke Augustine infected it with his Romish doctrine . . . In those daies the Brytaines refused the doctrine of Augustine as erronius and corrupt.'

---

[1] Powel, *The historie of Cambria*: 'A Description of Cambria', p. 15.

He then quotes a warning against 'Romish woolues' in the verses of the Welsh bard Taliesin:

> And because no man should doubt of them I haue set them here as they were written by him that made them. Whereby it may be proued, that the Brytaines the first inhabiters of this realme did abhorre the Romish doctrine taught in that time, which doctrine (I am sure) is little amended now in the Churche of Rome: and that may be to us a mirrour to see our owne follie, if we doo degenerate from our forefathers the ancient Brytaines in the sinceritie of true religion, as we doo in other things.[1]

However unfair their view of Augustine may be in the perspective of history, it was the view prevailing in 1584, when Powel's book appeared. The same arguments, including the attack on Augustine, had been expressed about 1549 in a book by R. V.: *The olde Fayth of greate Brittaygne and the newe learnynge of Inglande*, printed by Anthony Scoloker.[2] In 1586, Thomas Billson, Warden of Winchester, repeated the account of Augustine and the Bangor monks, then defended the right of the sovereign to act independently of the pope in making Church appointments. Gregory the Great had exhorted Ethelbert, the first Saxon Christian king, to spread the gospel over England as Constantine spread it over the Roman Empire. Gregory's action, writes Billson, shows the pre-eminence of the sovereign in affairs of the Church. Bishops are the fittest men to deal with spiritual matters, but under the law of the prince, not under the pope.[3]

The most serious alienation of the English Crown from the English Church came with King John's abject surrender to Pope Innocent III in 1213. John gave England to the pope, temporal as well as spiritual dominion, and received it back as a fief, agreeing also to pay an annual tribute of 1,000 marks. This condition endured for ninety-two years until 1305, when Edward I and

---

[1] Powel, *The historie of Cambria*: 'The beginning of the Principalitie and gouernement of Wales', pp. 254–5.

[2] The identity of R. V. remains unknown.

[3] *The true difference betweene Christian Subiection and vnchristian rebellion: wherein the Princes lawful power to command for truth, and indepriueable right to beare the sword, are defended against the Popes censures and the Iesuits sophismes, vttered in their APOLOGIE and DEFENCE OF ENGLISH CATHOLIKES. With a demonstration that the things reformed in the Church of England by the lawes of this Realme are truly Catholike, notwithstanding the vaine shew made to the contrarie in their late* Rhemish Testament (1585), pp. 114, 336, 341.

Philip IV of France subjected the papacy to the temporal power of royalty. Boniface VIII, who had claimed supreme power, spiritual and temporal, over all the world, was ruined before his death. The new pope, Clement V, though a Gascon, was a subject of the English king. At Philip's behest he removed the seat of the papacy to Avignon in France, where it remained during the 'Babylonian captivity'. This loss of power and flight to Avignon are probably reflected in the stripping and flight of Duessa after the death of Orgoglio. Her royal robes are removed, revealing a wrinkled hag of unimaginable filth. Then she is released.

> Shee, flying fast from heaven's hated face,
> And from the world that her discovered wide,
> Fled to the wastfull wildernesse apace,
> From living eies her open shame to hide,
> And lurkt in rocks and caves, long unespide.   (viii. 50)

However, after seventy-two years the papacy was returned to Rome. So Duessa, after a time, resumes her activities in Book IV of *The Faerie Queene*, after trying to intervene by letter in the marriage of Redcross and Una in Canto xii of Book I.

The final defeat of Duessa should also represent the repudiation of papal supremacy by Henry VIII. Here the victory may be a composite of anti-papal measures taken by Edward I, Edward III, and Henry VIII. The Act of Supremacy declaring Henry the head of the Church is represented in the betrothal of Redcross and Una. The reign of Mary Tudor is the interruption caused when Duessa sends Archimago in disguise with the letter claiming Redcross as her own. The restoration of supremacy to the Crown in 1559 is the final marriage of Redcross and Una.

In the historical allegory, one other reference point is reasonably sure. Prince Arthur's arrival represents the accession of Henry VII and the Tudor Dynasty in 1485. C. Bowie Millican has given an extended account of this motif in the literature of Tudor England. The Tudors were of Welsh descent, and their accession came 800 years after Cadwallader surrendered the crown, just as his angelic visitor had foretold. The belief that Arthur would return to save his people enjoyed a great vogue under the Tudors,[1] and it is quite likely that Henry VII named his eldest son Arthur in order to exploit this sentiment. Yet as a composite figure

---

[1] Charles Bowie Millican, *Spenser and the Table Round* (1932).

Prince Arthur may well embody both the Tudors and the real Arthur of ten centuries before.

It appears that the historical allegory of Book 1 involves two main themes: the pre-eminence of the English Crown and its wearers as Crusaders to the Holy Land, and the relation of the English Crown to the English Church and to the papacy. These themes are interwoven with each other.

Redcross wears the garb of the Crusader, with the red cross on his breast. But there is one distinctive feature about his arms: the shield is of silver. Though the knight has never fought in battle, his shield is dented with deep wounds and has therefore been used before. In the moral allegory, it is the Shield of Faith, of all who have fought the good fight and have kept the faith (2 Tim. 4: 7). This accounts for its scars but not for its silver. In John Hardyng's *Chronicle* we find the following heading of chapter 48:

How Ioseph [of Arimathea] conuerted this kyng Aruiragus, & gaue hym a shelde of ye armes that wee call sainct George his armes, which armes he bare euer after; & thus became that armes to bee ye kynges armes of this lande, long afore sainct George was gotten or borne. And as Maryan, the profounde chronicler, saith, he bare of siluer, in token of clennes, a crosse of goules, significacion of the bloodde that Christe bleedde on ye crosse, and for it muste nedes of reason be called a crosse.　　　　　　　　　　　　　(p. 84)

The term 'gules' in heraldry signifies red, and Hardyng's lines may be echoed in Spenser's words:

> But on his brest a bloodie crosse he bore,
> The deare remembrance of his dying Lord.

Spenser immediately adds that the same arms are engraved on the silver shield of Redcross (i. 2).

Hardyng explains further that these arms were later borne by King Lucius after his baptism, by Constantine the Great, and by Sir Galahad, who '. . . at Auelon found a shilde of the same armes, a speare & a sweorde, that Ioseph lefte there for hym; which armes Aruiragus, Lucyus, and Constantyne bare of siluer, a crosse of goules'.[1] Galahad founded the Knights of the Grail, honouring the cup of the Last Supper, which Joseph had brought to England from Palestine. Galahad died in Sarras, beside Egypt,

---

[1] Hardyng, *Chronicle* (edn. of 1812), pp. 99, 133.

and Sir Percival brought his heart back to Avalon, wrapped in gold. Arthur and other knights rode to Glastonbury for the burial of Galahad's heart. His shield, with St. George's arms, was hung over his tomb.[1]

Thus Galahad, the knight of purity, enters the composite picture represented by Redcross, where he joins Constantine the Great as a Crusader towards the East. He also joins Robert Curthose, Richard the Lion-Heart, and Edward I in the ranks of Crusaders. As a knight of holiness, he has additional companions in King Arviragus, King Lucius, and King Henry VIII, all of whom did much to forward the cause of the 'true Church' in England.

Archimago, the magician who separates Redcross from Una, has already been equated with the Beast from the Land, or False Prophet, in the Book of Revelation (above, p. 105). About 1548 John Bale declared that this beast represented all false prophets and ungodly preachers, both of Rome and of Mahomet.[2] Indeed, Protestant pamphleteers of the sixteenth century show a tendency to group together the papists and the Saracens as enemies of the true Church. Archimago's disguising of himself with the arms of Redcross may represent the preaching of Crusades by the popes and other members of the Roman clergy. At one time the papal legate Pelagius actually asserted the right to command the Fifth Crusade, which he led into disaster.[3] But some thought that the Roman pontiffs were really bent on weakening their royal allies, the Christian kings, and were secret allies of the Saracens. For example, Gregory IX first excommunicated Frederick II for not beginning his Crusade promptly and excommunicated him a second time for beginning it without papal permission. When Frederick regained possession of Jerusalem without war, the pope castigated him for having made any form of treaty with the Saracens. Certainly, to many observers, Gregory IX appeared more interested in 'cutting down to size' the European monarchs than he was in regaining the Holy Sepulchre, though he had preached this Crusade in the first place. At the same time as he sought to reduce Frederick's power, he was making fresh

---

[1] Ibid., pp. 135–6.
[2] *The Image of bothe churches, after the moste wonderfull and heauenlie Revelacion of Sainct John (c. 1548).*
[3] Gibbon, ch. 59, vol. iii, p. 484.

exactions of Frederick's brother-in-law, Henry III of England. Hence Archimago is recognized as a secret ally by the Saracen Sansloy when he is revealed as wearing the arms of Redcross in order to deceive Una.

Perhaps this duplicity of the papacy and the Roman clergy was best stated by William Tyndale, whose *Practyse of Prelates* was printed abroad in 1530 but not in England until 1548 and 1549, after Henry VIII's death. Tyndale's role as translator of the Bible and as martyr assured respectful attention to his words, as evidenced by the two editions in successive years. He reviews the rivalry between the churches of Rome and of Constantinople, and he comments upon Emperor Phocas's grant to Boniface III recognizing the primacy of Rome. Boniface's greed for power is compared to that of Cardinal Wolsey. Tyndale continues:

And loke how besye Mahomete was in those partyes [the East], so besye was the Pope in these quarters to inuade ye empyre (with ye helpe of his sworne bisshoppes which preached all of none other god then the Pope) whyle the Emperoure was occupyed a farre of in resistynge of Mahomete.   (Bviii)

He then reviews the seizure of power in the West by Pepin and Pope Zecharias:

And thus the Empyre was deuyded in two partes: the Pope and the french kynge partynge the one half betwene them. And as the Emperoure decayed the Pope grewe. And as the Pope grewe so the secte of Mahomete grewe for the Emperoure (halfe his empyre lost) was not able to defende him self agenst the infidels. And the Pope wold suffre no helpe hence to come for two causes: One lest the Emperoure shuld recouer his Empyre agayne and a nother because ye prelates of the grekes wold not submitte them selues vnto his godhed as the prelates of these quarters of the worlde had done.   (Ci, Cii)

Tyndale then notes Charlemagne's role in driving from Italy the Lombard King Desiderius, who favoured the 'right' or Eastern emperors, because Charlemagne wished to be emperor himself (Ciii).

After this passage, Tyndale observes the role of the Roman Church during the Gothic invasions of the Empire:

And in all this ceason whosoeur wan the maystrye him the spiritualtye receaued and him they crouned kynge and to him they claue. And what so euer any tyrant had robbed all his life that or the most parte therof must he deale amonge them at his deeth for feare of purgatorye. The spiritualtye all that season preached the pope myghtely.   (Cvii)

He then describes the emperor and the pope by a fable of the tree and the ivy. At first the ivy (papacy) serves to adorn the tree (emperor) but finally chokes it to death (Dii).[1]

Tyndale's charge that the 'spiritualtye' of Rome would ally themselves with any conqueror, regardless of his right, obviously describes the conduct of Spenser's Duessa. This raises the question of the various conquerors who may be represented in Orgoglio. In Dante's vision of the Church already described, the harlot (papacy) is accompanied by a giant (Philip IV of France) who carries her off (to Avignon). From Tyndale's remarks, the most obvious prototype of Orgoglio is Charlemagne. For the imprisonment of Redcross the Crusader in Orgoglio's dungeon, the most notable example would be the long imprisonment of Richard the Lion-Heart by the German Emperor Henry VI. (This emperor hated Richard for having befriended Henry the Lion, husband of Richard's sister and father of the next emperor, Otto.) As the proud giant conquered by Prince Arthur (the Tudors), Orgoglio should represent Richard III of England; his dungeons would then represent the Tower of London, in which Richard's two nephews were murdered. Redcross, emerging weak and sick, represents the low estate of the Crown, of royalty as an institution, not as a person. At Bosworth Field Richard's crown was discovered hanging on a thorn bush, which might also suggest its low estate. Redcross in the Cave of Despair may suggest the despair of the English people during the Wars of the Roses; the cleansing in Coelia's house suggests the returning lustre of the Crown brought about by Henry VII. (If the Crown represents the institution of royalty rather than individual persons, the Tudor kings could be represented by Arthur and also be part of the composite representation of Redcross.) Una's role in the Cave of Despair suggests that in the time of distress true religion was the comfort of the people and prevented complete destruction.

Perhaps we should add to the composite image of Orgoglio the king who helped the papacy (Duessa) to fasten its hold on the English people by 'imprisoning' the Crown. This would be

---

[1] References to edn. of Marburg, 1530.

Philip II of France, whose threatened invasion of England forced John's surrender to the papacy in 1213. After John's surrender, the pope asked Philip to call off his attempt to invade England, a request which could be reflected in Duessa's request to Orgoglio that he should spare Redcross's life.

Sixteenth-century partisans also engaged in a lively controversy as to which Church really constituted the 'old faith'. We have noticed David Powel's stress on the religion of Joseph of Arimathea as the 'old' and the doctrines of Augustine as the 'new'. The two positions are set out very well by Thomas Stapleton and Heinrich Bullinger. Stapleton, an English adherent of Rome, translated Bede's *Ecclesiastical History* (Antwerp, 1565) and set forth the Roman viewpoint in a persuasive introduction. He rebutted the argument that, for the first 600 years of its history, the Church at Rome and elsewhere followed the simple ritual of the early Christians, but that Rome thereafter made extensive innovations and abandoned the old religion. He quoted Bede to show that the early English Church had the same position as modern Rome on celibacy of the clergy, auricular confession, prayers for the dead, the Mass, pilgrimages, vestments, use of holy water, and the use of Latin in church services. He argued that the Church of England took its rise from Rome (via Augustine) and should render traditional obedience to Rome.[1]

Heinrich Bullinger was a Swiss adherent of Zwingli and a leader of the Zwinglian faction in the reformed Church. In 1581 was republished Miles Coverdale's translation of Bullinger's *The Olde Fayth*, which first appeared in 1547. After reviewing the struggles of the early Church and its brave endurance of persecution, Bullinger noted that as it became wealthy, it became less religious:

> Of this then followed it farther, that the singlenesse of faith was forgotten, newe lawes made, the olde rites and customes either peruerted, or else vtterly ouerthrowen and abused: whereby men came farre from the doctrine and Christian ceremonies, from the way of trueth into errour foolishlie, and partely into ceremonies of idolatrie. Hereof commeth it, that we haue nowe the abhominacion of the Popes power, of pardons, of Masses for the deade and quicke, of merites, power and intercession of Sainctes in heauen, of worshipping their

---

[1] The British partisans argued that the true British Church antedated the coming of Augustine.

bones vppon earth, of idolls, and vayne ornamentes, pompe and pride of the Churche, of hyred singinge and praying in the temple, and of the whole swarme of idle religions. All which thinges with other moe like fondnesse, are nothinge but newe alterations, peruertinges, and contrarie to all old ordinaunces, hauing no grounde in Gods word, and are cleane against God, though many hardnecked people are yet in a furie & braule for such thinges, and wil make all the world beleue, that this their foolishnesse, alteracion, and peruerting of Gods ordinauce is the *olde faith* . . . Neuerthelesse (as I saide afore) God always set forth his worde and doth yet. Contrarywise, the Pope with his multitude and Mahumet with his (as it seemeth and becommeth very Antichristes) have hitherto vndertaken to suppresse *the old relig[i]on*, and to set vp his owne ordinaunce (vnknowen to our fathers of olde time) to bring it in to possession, & vnder the name of God and his holy Church, to spreade it vpon all christendome. For out of the Actes and statutes of the Pope and his wanton spiritualty [i.e. priests], and out of the lawes of Mahumet, it is manifest, what the one hath taken in hand & done now more then 600. yeares, and the other vpon a 900. yeares. It is euident yet also euen now, wherto his generall counsayls and parliamentes do extende. But not regarding how he threateneth and faceth, and how he garnisheth his new and wanton religions with false (but dissembling) titles, boastinge of many hundreth yeares, many generall counsails, fathers, holy men, doctours, vniuersities, cloisters, singing, praying, fasting, almes geuing displ[a]ying, and telleth such like: All his bragging sette aside, let vs cast his relig[i]on from vs, and take vppon vs vnfainedly *the true olde religion*, which hath endured since the beginning of the worlde, by the which all holy men haue euer loued, worshipped and serued God, and knew nothing vtterly of the Popes religion.[1]

This emphasis on the older and simpler religion as being more genuine was the essence of the Anglican position. The Roman ritual had become too elaborate; it involved too much pomp and pageantry. Exasperation with these papal innovations is expressed in Peter Moone's *A Short Treatyse of Certayne Thinges Abused in the Popysh Church, Long Vsed* (1548):

> In ye stede of goddes word we had holy bread and water
> Holy palmes holy asshes, holy candles holy fyer
> Holy bones holy stones, holy crewittes at the aulter
> Holy censars holy bannars, holy crosses holy atyer

[1] From edn. of 1581, pp. 148–51.

Holy wax holy pax, holy smoke holy smyer [smear; ointment]
Holy oyle holy creame, holy wyne for veneration
Holy coope holy canepy, holy reliques in the quier
Thus gods word could not florissh ye light of our saluation.[1]

Spenser stresses the simplicity of Una's costume as compared with Duessa's scarlet gown, mitre, golden cup, and jewels. When unveiled, Una is radiant and beautiful; Duessa, when uncased, is foul and ugly. Una is the true faith, Duessa the false faith. The 'old faith' is expressed through Una's parents, the primitive Christian Church at Jerusalem, which antedates Duessa's claimed father, Constantine the Great. Besides, even this claim of Duessa's is false because the Donation of Constantine was a forgery.

A further clue to the historical allegory may be found in Meredith Hanmer's *The Great bragge & challenge of M. Champion a Iesuite, commonlye called Edmund Campion, latelye arriued in Englande* (1581). Hanmer reviews the history of the Church from its beginnings, giving a list of its enemies that may well have provided Spenser with most of his characters in Book 1:

There are heathens and infidels, that can not be numbered: The number of *Turkes* & *Saracens* is infinite: the *Arrians* deceaued thousands, and the Church of Rome at this day with the golden cup of Idolatry & abhomination, maketh drunk the inhabitants of the earth . . . And the *Pope* hath lately about 40 yeares past confirmed the sect of *Iesuits*, & sends them abroad in the euening of the world with the *Anabaptists*, & in the night season, with the enemy of God and man, to sow tares among the wheat . . . But as touching this late order of *Iesuits*, this society passeth all other sectes in Hypocrisie & outward shew of holines . . . I will at this present no more but warne thee: *Beware of false Prophets*: we are commaunded to *be wise as Serpentes, and simple as Doues.*   (Preface)

He also mentions Montanus and Manes as sowers of schism in Eastern lands, and an English sect called the Family of Love.[2]

The parallels with Spenser's enemies of the true Church are very striking. Duessa represents the Church of Rome. Archimago, who is hypocrisy and the False Prophet, represents the Jesuit Order. Sansloy, who is both an ally and a rival of Archimago, probably represents the Anabaptists, whose lawless violence and

---

[1] The reader will notice that here again we have the rhyme scheme of the Spenserian stanza, lacking the final Alexandrine. Cf. p. 205 n. 1.

[2] Cf. van der Noot's attack on the Roman clergy (above, p. 106). Italics not mine.

impatient extremism were as dangerous to the true Church as the machinations of the Jesuits; Hanmer lists the two groups together as enemies of the Church. Sansfoy may represent the Arian heresy, which caused bloodshed in the early Church and which was restrained if not destroyed by Constantine the Great.[1] The dragon in Eden represents the Turks. Sansjoy is harder to place. Hanmer mentions the Family of Love, a puritan sect which held that the elect—themselves—were exempt from the law of sin; apparently this was a rationalization of free love within their own group.[2] Spenser's view of married and monogamous love as the source of joy (above, p. 157) might have led him to regard such a group as joyless, if he is following Hanmer's list. Or, as already suggested, he may refer to the Roman rule of clerical celibacy, which was abolished in the English Church. Or he may refer to the ascetic orders, such as the Carthusians (above, p. 123). Or, not impossibly, he may include them all in a composite figure of sanctimonious and barren piety.

As protectors of the English Church (Una) when the Crown (Redcross) had deserted it for the Roman Church (Duessa), Satyrane and the lion should have historic parallels. As Satyrane, one thinks of Llewellyn of Wales, who fought King John and would not stop at the pope's bidding; or of Archbishop Cranmer, who advised Henry VIII during the separation of the English Church from the Roman supremacy. The lion, who rushed upon Una to destroy her but remained as her champion and protector, might well be Archbishop Stephen Langton, who was forced upon England by the pope against King John's wishes and then protected the Church against the exactions of both the king and the papal legate Pandulph. He secured Pandulph's recall by the pope and earlier had been a prime mover in securing John's assent to Magna Carta. But these identifications are highly speculative, for the clues do not lend themselves to an exact determination of the figures represented.

In determining the historical allegory, certain points seem reasonably clear. Una corresponds to the Church of England, which derived its authority from Joseph of Arimathea and ultimately from the primitive Church in Jerusalem. Duessa

---

[1] Hardyng states that Constantine destroyed the Arian heresy (*Chronicle* [edn. of 1812], p. 101). Cf. Gibbon, ch. 21, vol. i, p. 586.

[2] See A. L. Rowse, *The England of Elizabeth* (London, 1953), p. 458.

corresponds to the papacy, which heads the Church of Rome and which claims to derive the temporal 'power of the sword' from Constantine the Great, a false claim. Redcross corresponds to the English Crown, or spirit of England, represented by the cross of St. George, in its relations to the Crusades and its relations to the Church. Prince Arthur corresponds to the Tudor Dynasty, which began to reign in 1485. Probable but not sure is the identification of the dragon in Eden with the tribes from Tartary who occupied Jerusalem.

I have not followed Padelford in making Mary's reign the major defection of Redcross from Una. The Elizabethan pamphleteers are curiously reluctant to criticize Mary.[1] The usual line is that she was well-meaning but misguided, sincerely pious but wrong. She was a Tudor queen, the daughter of Henry VIII and the sister of Elizabeth, facts which tended to mute any really vicious criticism. Such criticism was directed against the pope and against Philip of Spain, her husband, but not against Mary. An interpretation which identifies her with the harlot Duessa is out of keeping with most criticisms of Mary Tudor, though there is no such reticence concerning Mary Queen of Scots, who is portrayed as Duessa in v. ix. 38. When Duessa's messenger returns in i. xii to interrupt the marriage of Redcross and Una, this interruption seems to be a fair equivalent of Mary's reign, for Duessa is clearly the papacy and not the English sovereign. Still, this is a matter of doubtful judgement, and Mary's reign could be included in the composite image of the English Crown's alienation from the English Church without doing any violence to my central theory. In such a case, Orgoglio would obviously represent Philip II of Spain.

Like Artegall and Calidore, Redcross must leave his new bride to do further service to Gloriana. Perhaps this service would not be finished

> Till I of warres and bloody Mars doe sing,
> And Bryton fieldes with Sarazin blood bedyde,
> Twixt that great Faery Queene and Paynim King,
> That with their horror heven and earth did ring.   (xi. 7)

Historically, this battle could be that between the Britons and the African 'paynim' Germundus, who invaded England in A.D. 590

[1] See Hartwell (above, p. 52) and Batman (above, p. 129), as examples.

to help the Saxons destroy the Christian religion. He struck the Britons the blow from which they never recovered, and drove their survivors into Wales, Cornwall, and Brittany.[1] Hardyng calls him a 'paynym' king.[2] This battle took place forty-eight years after Arthur's death in 542. Or else the usual interpretation may be the right one, envisioning, as it does, a battle between England and Spain after invasion by the Spaniards. Since the Spanish army never set foot in England, the image of 'Bryton fieldes with Sarazin blood bedyde' seems hardly appropriate to the defeat of the Armada. But Spenser probably wrote his lines shortly before 29 July 1588, the date of the Armada's defeat, at which time an actual invasion was generally expected. Because of the Moorish tradition in southern Spain, Spenser could appropriately speak of the Spaniards as Saracens. He probably expected the invaders to be conquered, as he had seen them conquered in Ireland, and looked forward to celebrating the victory in a later book of *The Faerie Queene*.

In its essentials, my interpretation of the historical allegory enlarges upon the positions of Scott and Keightley, who saw in Book i an allegory of the English Church from its beginnings. The English Church and the English Crown are seen as the rightful heirs of the Church and the Crown of Jerusalem, with claims superior to those advanced by the Roman Church. The 'taking of the Cross' by the Crusaders who opened the path to Jerusalem is the symbol of every Christian's commitment in the pilgrimage of life. Spenser's use of composite figures enabled him to represent the 'then' and the 'now', the historical and the moral, by the same allegorical figures, who must be viewed on several levels at the same time.

---

[1] Holinshed, *The First and Second Volumes of Chronicles* (1586), bk. v, ch. 18, pp. 97–8; Powel, *The historie of Cambria*: 'A Description of Cambria', p. 15, calls Gurmond a pagan African chief, but on page 6 of the following section he calls him 'an arch pirate and captaine of the Norwegians'. Spenser follows Powel's second statement (*FQ* III. iii. 33).

[2] Hardyng, *Chronicle* (edn. of 1812), p. 152.

XI

Studies in the Physical Allegory

I N a few instances Spenser allegorizes the physical processes of
nature instead of the moral nature of man. A study of these
instances is richly rewarding. In their higher reaches, physical
allegory and moral allegory tend to become one, for they both
lead the mind towards God as their source and origin. The vision
of eternity which concludes *The Faerie Queene* is both physical and
ethical. Also, since the moral nature of man adapts itself to the
facts of his physical existence, physical allegory is thereby comple-
mentary to moral allegory and may help to explain human nature.

FLORIMELL, MARINELL, AND PROTEUS

The physical interpretation of Florimell and Marinell as forces of
nature was probably suggested by Emblem 106 of Alciatus's *Emblemata*: 'Potentia Amoris'.[1] Cupid is pictured without his bow
and arrows, but holding in one hand a spray of flowers and in the
other a fish. The verse reads:

> Nudus Amor viden' vt ridet, placidumque tuetur?
> Nec faculas, nec quae cornua flectat, habet:
> Altera sed manuum flores gerit, altera piscem,
> Scilicet vt terrae iura det atque mari.

(See you not how unarmed Love laughs and looks gently? He has
neither torches nor horns which he may bend. But one of the hands
holds flowers, the other a fish, signifying that he gives laws to the land
and to the sea.)

Claudius Minos glosses *faculas* as the torches of Cupid which
fire the heart and weaken (*conficiat*) the soul of man. The *cornua*
are the ends of a bow-stick which appear like a pair of horns when
the string is fully drawn. The final line illustrates Virgil's 'Omnia

---

[1] (Emblem 107 in edn. of 1621.) Alciatus's emblem is suggested as a source by
Roche in *The Kindly Flame*, pp. 189–94.

vincit Amor' ('Love conquers all') and similar passages of like intent from Lucretius, Ovid, and Propertius, who say that Love rules both land and sea. Alciatus's stanza is traced to an epigram from Book iv of the *Greek Anthology*, which is literally translated into Latin by Minos and which differs very little from Alciatus's words. Minos identifies the spray of flowers as the rose of Cupid, which is sweet but nevertheless has thorns. The fish, identified as a dolphin, is more loving of man and represents the tranquillity of the sea after the dolphin has quieted the angry commotion of its waves.[1]

The tradition that Love, or Eros, or Cupid, gives laws to both land and sea partakes of the teaching of Hesiod, who declared that Eros was the first of the gods to rise out of Chaos and was the agency of creation for all the rest; he is at once the oldest and the youngest of the gods. Love is therefore the agent for the continued perpetuation of life through its various forms of reproduction.[2] He rules the land and the sea and causes the union of land and sea.

The function of the sea in this union is clearly explained by Natalis Comes in his chapters on Neptune and Oceanus.[3] In the first (*Mythologiae*, ii. 8), he explains that Neptune's wife Amphitrite is water, the body and matter of all moisture around or within the earth. Neptune is a spirit diffused through the universal mass of water, as though the soul of the element of water.[4] 'Ingens filiorum Neptuni numerus praeterea quid nisi maris fertilitas est?' ('Moreover, what is the great number of Neptune's sons unless it is the fertility of the sea?'). He adds that the fruitfulness of the waters is equalled by the voracity of the fish; hence Neptune's sons are called cruel.[5]

In the chapter on Oceanus (viii. 1), Comes writes:

Oceanus, who was called the father of rivers, of all things living, and of the gods . . . Orpheus seems to have thought that from this

---

[1] *Emblemata* (Lyons, 1614), pp. 372–4. Numerous editions with Minos's notes appeared from 1573 on.

[2] Hesiod, *Theogony*, 119–22. Cf. Marsilio Ficino, *Commentarium in Conuiuium* [Plato's *Symposium*], oratio 1, ch. iii: 'Origo Amoris ex Chaos': 'In all things, then, Love is the companion of Chaos, precedes the world, arouses the torpid, lightens the darkness, makes the dead to live, forms the unformed, and perfects the imperfect' (*Opera Platonis* [edn. of 1551], p. 374). Cf. the contrary effects of Vice as stated by Francesco Piccolomini (above, p. 65). Cf. p. 258 n. 4.

[3] These passages from Comes have been noted by Lotspeich (*Var.* iv. 276).

[4] Comes, *Mythologiae* (edn. of Padua, 1616), p. 88.   [5] Ibid., p. 89.

Oceanus himself both the gods of the ancients and all things had their beginning; since surely all things, before they are born or die, need moisture, without which nothing can either decay or sprout anew, as Thales thinks.[1] . . . Orpheus stated, and all the theologians of the ancients, that this same Oceanus was the beginning of birth to the gods and to [all] things; because, as Thales thinks, nothing without moisture is born or decays; and all the qualities of the elements, which they called by the names of gods, are born from moisture.[2]

It is obvious that, through rainfall, the sea provides moisture which enables the land to bear vegetation, and thus the sea may be said to impregnate and make fertile the land. I have discussed at length elsewhere the cycles of generation and corruption by which the processes of birth and death were interpreted.[3] Since spermatozoa were not recognized before the invention of the microscope (1628), the conception of life in the maternal womb was thought to be like that of spontaneous generation in nature. The menstrual flow of the mother combined with the seminal fluid of the father, and these must decay or coagulate or 'work' before new life could sprout from them in the form of an embryo. Accordingly, Comes's words on the place of the sea's moisture in the generation–corruption cycle are directly applicable to human conception and birth. The analogy of sea-foam to masculine semen appears in the mythical birth of Venus Urania from the foam of the sea; i.e. from the severed genitals of Uranus which had been thrown into the sea.

In one sense, then, the union of Marinell and Florimell represents the sea's giving moisture to the land for the production of vegetation. The moisture is not life but it awakens the seeds into life. The analogy to human and animal reproduction is readily understood. Marinell may be interpreted as fertility. His principal rival for Florimell's love is Proteus, who plays an important part in the physical allegory.

As a prophet, Proteus had predicted that Marinell should be in great danger from a woman, a prediction which caused Cymodoce (Gk., wave-receiver) to warn her son against the society of women (III. iv. 25). Proteus had rescued Florimell from the libidinous fisherman, then had wooed her for himself. When she rejects him,

---

[1] *Mythologiae* (edn. of 1616), p. 426.   [2] Ibid., p. 428.
[3] 'Hamlet's "God Kissing Carrion": A Theory of the Generation of Life' *PMLA* lxiv (1949), 507–16.

he imprisons her in a dark cave beneath his palace; she remains for seven months, the same length of time that Amoret spent in the House of Busyrane (III. xi. 10, IV. xi. 4). In each case the old man woos the girl to what would be essentially a sterile relationship, and in each case she prefers a more youthful and productive love. Proteus finally surrenders Florimell, at Neptune's command, to Cymodoce for marriage to her son Marinell.

Proteus is associated by name with two prototypes of Florimell. In the *Orlando Furioso* he is the tyrant who procures the capture of Angelica and her sacrifice to the sea-monster, from whom she is rescued by Ruggiero (*OF* viii. 52, 57). In Euripides' *Helena*, he is the benevolent king of Egypt who protects the true Helen until his death, after which his son demands her in marriage. He originally comes from Homer's *Odyssey*, iv. 460, where his ability to change his shape at will is presented.

Roche has collected a number of explanations of Proteus. He is the 'unformed matter of things' (Ponticus Heraclides), 'the beginnings of the whole of nature, changing matter by multiform species' (Orphic Hymns), 'multiform' and 'unformed matter' (Natalis Comes), 'the nature of things' (Charles Stephanus). Roche himself concludes that Proteus 'represents the whole world of mutable nature and man in so far as man's body is independent of but not opposed to his soul'.[1]

Natalis Comes quotes another Orphic Hymn on Proteus:

> Gestantem claues pelagi te maxime Proteu
> Prisce voco, a quo naturae primordia primum
> Edita sunt, formas in multas vertere nosti
> Materiam sacram prudens, venerabilis, atque
> Cuncta sciens, quae sint fuerint, ventura trahantur.

(I call you bearing the keys of the sea, great and ancient Proteus, by whom the primordial beginnings of nature were first brought forth; you know how to turn the sacred matter into many forms; you, prudent, venerable, knowing the totality of things which are, have been, and shall be.)

On the same page, Comes comments: 'All matter exists in the intellect prior to form and always seeks various forms by impulse of nature, wherefore Proteus was said to be turned into so many forms.'[2]

---

[1] Roche, *The Kindly Flame*, p. 160.
[2] *Mythologiae* (edn. of 1616), VIII. viii; p. 442.

Again, interpreting the character *ethice*, Comes suggests that Proteus may represent the clever statesman who can change his manner according to his audience and be all things to all men.[1]

Francesco Piccolomini has two observations on Proteus. The first has been already quoted:[2] 'Since man is a little world, an epitome of the great world, a marriage of divine and mortal, by the image of Proteus he has strength to receive every form and to live every life.' Francesco writes also: 'Accordingly, we gather that nothing in the sphere of mortal things is found more happy than man, and none is found more unhappy than he; wherefore Asclepius the Athenian affirmed that skin-changing (*versipellem*) human nature was fittingly signified by the image of Proteus in the Mysteries' (ix. 6; p. 476c).

From these various references it should be clear that, *physice*, Proteus represents either first matter or the adaptable quality of first matter, the ability to assume all forms. *Ethice*, he represents the versatility and variety of human nature, something like the 'infinite variety' of Cleopatra which age could not wither nor custom stale.[3] In both of these capacities he is significant for the story of Florimell.

Whether we assume that Proteus is first matter or the master artificer who gives forms to first matter, we are justified in considering the caves under his palace as the abode of first matter and in equating them with the cave under the mount in the Garden of Adonis and with the 'abyss' of Chaos which has already been discussed in Chapter IV. Thus, Florimell or beauty is imprisoned in first matter. Spenser's authority for this is Aristotle's dictum that 'true forms' are found in matter, as Francesco reports it (above, p. 168). This is equivalent to saying that beauty exists in matter, for it seems opposed to Plato's view that only the shadow of beauty exists in matter and that this incites the lover to seek the true beauty in the pattern world above.[4]

Actually these two views are not incompatible. Forms are necessarily latent in the material by which they become tangible and visible. To use our former analogy of a lump of clay to first matter (above, p. 79), we find that the sculptor can shape the clay into an ugly gargoyle or into the head of a beautiful woman. Both

---

[1] *Mythologiae* (edn. of 1616), viii. viii; p. 443.   [2] Above, p. 50.

[3] Cf. Shakespeare's *Antony and Cleopatra*, ii. ii. 240–1.

[4] See Spenser's 'Hymne in Honour of Beautie', l. 36.

forms were latent in the clay as capabilities only, but they were activated by intelligible forms visualized in the mind of the sculptor. We may say that he releases the forms imprisoned in the clay, which could never have borne these particular forms without his visionary mind and his shaping fingers. For Spenser, the sculptor's mind is analogous to the Platonic pattern world, which in Christian terms is the mind of God.[1]

Florimell, the principle of beauty or beauteous forms imprisoned in matter, is wooed by Proteus, the wonderful variety of objects and scenes in nature; but she chooses instead Marinell, the principle of fertility and reproduction. Her choice is dictated by the instinctive desire for immortality, for continuation into the future, which is the basis of human love. This is not to say that the endless variety of the physical world is un-beautiful, but only that it is not as beautiful as the vision of immortality which is the joint achievement of those who truly love (cf. above, p. 168).

The interpretation of Florimell as beauty imprisoned in first matter is supported by the forest in which we first see her (above, p. 164). It is a wide forest, full of 'griesly' horror, empty of all life except savage beasts. This is clearly the Virgilian *silva*, immense, empty except as occupied by wild beasts (above, p. 65). The word 'griesly' relates it to the 'griesly shade' of Chaos out of which new forms emerge into life (*FQ* iii. vi. 37). The beholders have only a fleeting glimpse of Florimell as she rushes out of 'the thickest brush' and quickly disappears in the distance. Yet the glimpse is enough to inspire them with longing. Since the *silva* also represents the fleshly body, this bit of action illustrates the Platonic notion that the shadow of beauty seen in earthly things inspires the soul with desire to possess it and to comprehend the essence of beauty. The savage beasts figuratively represent the vices and perturbations proceeding from weakness of the flesh, and among these the personified virtues must travel; hence the fact that Arthur, Guyon, Timias, and Britomart are proceeding together through the desolate forest.

The union of physical and moral allegory is well illustrated in the account of Florimell and Marinell. Man is a physical being

---

[1] The *logos* (thought, mind, word) is the second person of the Platonic Triad: Divine Will, Divine Mind, World-Soul, corresponding to the three persons of the Christian Trinity. The Gospel of St. John opens by identifying Christ as the Word. Cf. below, p. 282.

who performs moral (or immoral) actions. As a part of nature, he is subject to the laws of nature, and these necessarily modify his actions. For his moral nature, he does not depend on physical nature alone but seeks to draw his pattern of virtuous conduct directly from God, the creator of nature. Since God would not prescribe conduct inconsistent with his own creation, man's task becomes one of understanding physical nature correctly before drawing his own moral inferences from it.

THE GARDEN OF ADONIS

The Scholarly Background

In addition to the Garden of Adonis and the 'Cantos of Mutabilitie', Spenser's *Fowre Hymnes* may be included in the 'Platonic' portion of his works. Actually he is careful to show that the *Hymnes* contain a blending of Platonic and Christian ideas. The latest student of the subject, Robert Ellrodt, has shown that the same combination of ideas is found in the other works as well; e.g. he finds influences from St. Augustine as well as from Plato in the Garden of Adonis. He is even tempted to doubt that any first-hand influence of Plato appears in the garden, since Spenser twice confuses proper names from the *Dialogues* of Plato and seems therefore to be unacquainted with them.[1]

In the first of these instances, the reference to Socrates' drinking the hemlock in the presence of Critias, 'his dearest belamy' (*FQ* II. vii. 52), Ellrodt accepts the probable confusion in Spenser's memory of Plato's *Phaedo* with a passage from Cicero's *Tusculan Disputations* which mentions Theramenes drinking the hemlock in the presence of Critias.[2] Critias, then, he thinks, was confused by Spenser with Alcibiades, Socrates' young friend who pretended to be his 'lover'. But this seems most unlikely. Much more probably, Spenser's memory confused Critias with Crito, who was present on Socrates' last day of life—Alcibiades was not—helped Socrates with his bath, and arranged details of his burial. On the preceding day Crito had made plans for Socrates' escape from prison, but Socrates had refused to take advantage of them; these details are related in Plato's dialogue *Crito*. Plato also wrote a dialogue entitled *Critias*, in which Critias relates the account of

[1] Ellrodt, *Neoplatonism in the Poetry of Spenser* (Geneva, 1960), p. 96.
[2] *Var.* ii. 263-4.

the lost continent of Atlantis. With two names so very similar, it is not surprising that Spenser, like many later readers of Plato, confused them in his memory. Such a confusion would be evidence *for* his knowledge of the *Phaedo* rather than the reverse. His reference to 'fayre Critias' may involve a confused recollection of the *Charmides*, in which Critias introduces his youthful cousin Charmides, whom Socrates declares to be the most beautiful youth that he has ever seen and jestingly pretends a romantic attraction towards him.

The second and more serious confusion comes in the Proem to Book IV, Stanza 3 :

> Witnesse the father of philosophie,
> Which to his *Critias*, shaded oft from sunne,
> Of love full manie lessons did apply.

The reference is apparently to Plato's *Phaedrus*, 230, a passage in which Socrates discourses with Phaedrus under the shade of a plane-tree. The discourse is of love. Spenser's memory substituted Critias for Phaedrus,[1] a fact which Ellrodt thinks would show that Spenser had not read the dialogue.[2] But Spenser had an equally bad slip of memory when he inadvertently substituted Guyon for Redcross among his own characters (III. ii. 4). One might argue more cogently that his memory of the 'shade' of the plane-tree showed that he had read the *Phaedrus*. It is impossible to trace with certainty the vagaries of his memory; but one might suppose that Socrates' discourses with the youthful Phaedrus in *Phaedrus* and the *Symposium* are analogous to his discourse with Charmides and Critias—how love may be effectively combined with virtue —and that Spenser recalled the name most often used by Plato. Critias appears in five dialogues: *Charmides, Protagoras, Eryxias, Timaeus, Critias*. Since Plato does not mention Critias' subsequent bad reputation in Athens, we cannot assume that Spenser knew anything about it.

Ellrodt, like Brents Stirling before him, has over-reacted against the claims of Platonic influence made by Josephine Waters Bennett in 1932.[3] The controversy, begun in *PMLA* with Stirling's reply to Mrs. Bennett,[4] was later continued in the *Journal of*

---

[1] *Var.* iv. 164.   [2] Ellrodt, *Neoplatonism in the Poetry of Spenser*, p. 96.

[3] Bennett, 'Spenser's Garden of Adonis', *PMLA* xlvii (1932), 46–80.

[4] Stirling, 'The Philosophy of Spenser's "Garden of Adonis"', *PMLA* xlix (1934), 501–38.

English and Germanic Philology[1] in articles which appeared too late for summaries in the *Variorum Spenser*, and which should be read in their entirety. The reader will do well to consult the *PMLA* articles in addition to the *Variorum* summaries. The earlier suggestions of influence upon the Garden of Adonis from Lucretius, Empedocles, and Giordano Bruno are adequately summarized in the *Variorum*.[2]

If Mrs. Bennett was guilty of over-complicating the allegory of the Garden of Adonis, Stirling was guilty of over-simplifying it. He pointed out that the ideas concerning the union of form and matter were of general currency, as found, for example, in Arthur Golding's introductory epistle to his translation of Ovid's *Metamorphoses*. Therefore, he concluded, Spenser need not have read Plato or the Platonic commentaries at all. Ellrodt follows somewhat the same line, arguing that Spenser probably read parts of the Platonic commentator Ficino before writing the *Fowre Hymnes* but need not have read him or any of the Platonic dialogues before 1590, when the Garden of Adonis passage was printed. He even suggests that Spenser did not use the one-volume edition of Plato's complete works because of its physical weight and must have preferred lighter volumes containing individual dialogues.[3]

Though both authors carefully avoid saying that Spenser did not read Plato, their arguments constitute too much of a reaction against Mrs. Bennett's claims. Spenser at Cambridge must have been exposed to the writings of Plato. Among the entertainments for Queen Elizabeth at Cambridge in 1564 was a 'war' between Aristotle and Plato,[4] and within a few years Cambridge was to become a great centre for Platonic studies. Plato was easily available in Latin,[5] and so was the *Opera Omnia* of Ficino.[6] From

---

[1] Bennett, 'Spenser's Garden of Adonis Revisited', *JEGP* xli (1942), 53–78; Stirling, 'Spenser's "Platonic" Garden', ibid., pp. 482–6, with rejoinder by Mrs. Bennett, pp. 486–9.

[2] iii. 340–4.

[3] Ellrodt, *Neoplatonism in the Poetry of Spenser*, pp. 96–7.

[4] In Hartwell's *Regina Literata* (above, p. 52).

[5] Ficino's one-volume translation of Plato's *Opera* appeared in 1483–4, 1491, 1546, 1550, 1551, 1581. A translation by Janus Cornarius, with Ficino's Arguments and Commentaries, appeared in 1561, and one by Serranus (Jean de Serres) in 1575.

[6] Editions were printed at Basel in 1561 and 1576. Apparently the paging is identical. All references to Ficino are to the *Opera Omnia*, except when otherwise specified.

internal evidence, it is my opinion that Spenser had read from both authors, perhaps extensively. He had the linguistic ability to read them, and his several references to Plato suggest that he had the interest also. It would seem to be a rather obvious part of his university training.

In her first article Mrs. Bennett adduced an impressive number of parallels and analogues from various sources. One point at issue between her and Stirling was her belief that the Garden of Adonis contains forms only and is not the meeting-place of form and matter, which she considered a later stage in the process of generation. She was influenced by Ficino's theory of successive stages of emanations from the Creator down to the concrete world as we know it. Stirling's reply questioned this identification and sought to show that Spenser had adequate warrant without Ficino for his portrayal of the garden as the meeting-place of form and matter; the forms were already the 'substantial forms' which were to become bodies. He did not perceive that the problem arose partly from Mrs. Bennett's failure to clarify Ficino's opinion.

Mrs. Bennett in her second article protested that no Platonist or mythologist ever equated Venus with matter or made her the presiding deity of Chaos. But something like this is precisely what Ficino did do. In his *Commentary on the Symposium*, II. vii, he distinguishes between Venus Urania in the upper world and Venus Pandemos in the lower world. The latter is assigned a mother because of the etymological resemblance of *mater* and *mater-ia*. Venus' mother is matter, represented by Dione. Venus is placed in the World-Soul, the child of Jove and Dione. She is assigned a mother 'quia materiae mundi infusa cum materia commercium habere putatur'[1] ('because, infused into the matter of the world, she is thought to have commerce with matter'). Furthermore, the World-Soul, of which Venus is a part, is later declared to be the soul of first matter: 'animam mundi, id est materiae primae'.[2] In his *Commentary on Philebus*, Ficino makes it clear that Venus is not herself matter. She is a lower part of the World-Soul which desires to produce in corporeal forms the beauty which Venus Urania had beheld in the type-forms (*speciosas rerum formas*) among the divine ideas. Hence, Venus Pandemos is assigned as a father the upper part of the World-Soul called Jove, and as a mother Dione

---

[1] *Com. in Conuiuium*, II. vii; p. 379 in Plato's *Opera* (edn. of 1551).

[2] Ibid. VI. iii; p. 395.

because Venus looks back towards matter. Because the act of generation is pleasurable, and because all generation proceeds from the 'soul' which is called Venus, Venus receives her name because she is a companion of venery (sexual intercourse).[1] Accordingly, both Stirling and Mrs. Bennett are partly wrong and partly right. Venus is not identical with matter, but she operates in matter as her normal place of abode.

In her first article Mrs. Bennett wrote: 'Out of the garden the souls go down into generation, and the forms of other things go out also, to give "forme and feature" to the substance supplied by Chaos, and so "invade the state of life".'[2] This statement implies that the substance supplied by Chaos is added to the souls and forms after they have left the garden; it thus makes necessary another region in which the souls and forms are joined with the substance. Stirling objected to this postulation of yet another region or 'garden' and to localizing the garden at all. In her second article Mrs. Bennett seems to change her position somewhat; for she states that Genius clothing the 'babes' with 'sinfull mire' represents a union of form and matter just before the babes go out into the world.[3] She is not sure whether the 'clothing' takes place inside or outside the garden gate.[4] If it takes place inside the gate, then she has conceded that the garden is a place for the union of form with matter and not a place of forms only. Stirling is mistaken, however, in identifying the 'babes' and 'shapes' of stanzas 32 and 35 with the 'every substaunce' of stanza 38;[5] for the latter refers to varieties of first matter prepared for the reception of different species (below, p. 262). In their separate ways, both form and matter are 'eterne'; it is only their composites that fade and perish (below, p. 253). Spenser stresses both the continuity of form, or forms, and that of matter, or substance.

In reviewing this controversy Ellrodt does a great service in pointing out the probable influence of Christian writers, particularly St. Augustine.[6] Since stanza 34 clearly reflects Genesis 2: 5 and identifies the Garden of Eden as a prototype of the Garden of Adonis,[7] we might expect the hexameral writings to have some

---

[1] *Com. in Philebum*, I. xi; pp. 1216–17, in Ficino's *Opera*.
[2] *PMLA* xlvii. 78.
[3] *JEGP* xli. 65–6, 72.   [4] Ibid., p. 77.   [5] Ibid., p. 482.
[6] Ellrodt, *Neoplatonism in the Poetry of Spenser*, pp. 70–92.   [7] *Var.* III. 343.

influence upon Spenser's garden. Unfortunately, Ellrodt minimizes the Platonic element too far. St. Augustine himself was influenced in his views by Plato.[1] Like him, Spenser has a debt to both Platonism and Christian teaching. There is nothing inherently improbable about a Platonic influence upon Spenser and no reason to exclude it in favour of Christian influence.[2] He had both.

This sketchy summary cannot do justice to the intricate argument and massive scholarship of all three writers discussed; but I have tried to put a finger on the nub of the controversy. I shall attempt a different approach to the subject by considering the garden an allegory and trying to state explicitly what is being allegorized. Instead of beginning with the upper circles of creation and working downward, I shall begin at the bottom and work upward. Perhaps some measure of clarification will emerge.

The Anatomical Garden

When Iago speaks to Roderigo his cynical words which begin, 'Our bodies are as gardens', he is using a long-established figure of speech. He is treating it in a moral sense: the flowers and vegetables represent virtues, the weeds represent vices, etc.[3] He uses the allegory *ethice*, as Comes and Minos would say (above, p. 20). But there is another tradition which considers the allegory of the garden *physice*, in which primary emphasis is laid upon the body's generative powers. The purpose of a garden is to grow new plants from seeds, and this makes it a fit symbol for the generation and growth of all life. Consequently, the garden of the body, *physice*, represents the genital areas and more particularly the womb, in which the new growth of animal life takes place.

The garden may be another of those archetypal symbols which occur naturally and repeatedly in the human consciousness. Freud, in his *Traumdeutung* (1900), has shown that very frequently erotic dreams will mask themselves as journeys through a garden or a forest. His explanation is that the pubic hair around the

---

[1] As pointed out by Abelard, *Expositio in Hexameron*, PL clxxviii. 752–3.

[2] Besides the writings of Ficino and other commentators in Latin and Italian, Spenser had available in English Richard Stanyhurst's *Harmonia* (1570), a commentary on the *Institutes* of Porphyry. This work has many of the ideas concerning form and matter that are found in the writings of Ficino.

[3] *Othello*, i. iii. 324. See my book *Shakespeare's Derived Imagery*: 'The Unweeded Garden' (1953, reprint by Octagon Books, 1967), pp. 189–96.

genital organs naturally suggests vegetation and therefore determines the character of the dream.[1]

We note among recent critics of Spenser a disposition to see this meaning in the Garden of Adonis. Ellrodt, Roche, Nelson, Cheney, Alastair Fowler, and Rosalie Colie see an anatomical allegory in the garden.[2] The suggestive feature seems to be the *Mons Veneris* of female anatomy, which might correspond to the mount of Venus in the midst of the garden. Some also point out that myrtle-trees have an erotic association, and that these surround Venus' bower on top of the mount.[3] Roche stresses the general nature of Spenser's allegory of the Garden of Adonis:

> Spenser simply appropriated the name for his own uses. His myth is meant to symbolize creation and fertility in all its aspects. Thus the complicated arguments of Professors Bennett and Stirling about the location of the garden are beside the point [as Stirling himself said]. The garden is the world because the world is engaged in the act of creation described in the poem. The garden is a Platonic realm too because Platonic forms are engaged in the act of creation. The garden is the womb of every mother and is the growth of every living thing. It is everywhere and nowhere *in particular*. Spenser's meaning is not difficult unless we try to restrict its meaning to one particular kind of creation.[4]

The general correctness of this 'inclusive' view does not justify the final sentence. We still need to understand what the several stages in the garden mean and what is the part played by Venus and Adonis. In terms of plant life, their love seems almost like a ritual copulation performed to make the crops grow.[5] But some of the forms in the garden are made for beasts, some for birds, and some for fish, as well as some for 'reasonable sowles'. Therefore, any explanation must take account of animal and human generation, for these are included in Spenser's allegory.

Of the various authors mentioned above, Alastair Fowler has come closest to an adequate explanation, but he does not quite

---

[1] For a more complete study see Freud's *Der Traum*, ch. x: 'Die Symbolik in Traum', in *Vorlesungen zur Einfuehrung in die Psychoanalyse*, in *Gesammelte Schriften* (1924), vol. vii, p. 158.

[2] Ellrodt, *Neoplatonism in the Poetry of Spenser*, p. 88; Nelson, *Poetry of Edmund Spenser*, p. 209; Roche, below, n. 4; Cheney, *Spenser's Image of Nature*, p. 136; Fowler, *Spenser and the Numbers of Time*, p. 137; Colie, *Paradoxia Epidemica* (Princeton, 1966), pp. 336–7.   [3] For example, Fowler, p. 137; Ellrodt, p. 88.

[4] Roche, *The Kindly Flame*, p. 120. Italics not mine.

[5] J. G. Frazer, *The Golden Bough* (1914), vol. v, ch. 1, p. 5.

clarify Elizabethan opinions concerning embryology. Here we must recur to our former explanation (above, p. 230). When Aristotle, Augustine, and Ficino speak of 'seeds' in human generation, they are not speaking of spermatozoa or ova. The *rationes seminales* or seminal reasons of Augustine were most like the genes of modern embryology, for they caused the offspring to assume its special character and even to resemble one parent or the other in certain features.[1] Many seminal reasons might go into determining the aspect of a single offspring. Conception was not envisaged as a union of two cells; rather, it was a union of two forms of moist matter: the maternal menses and the paternal semen. Yet these two merely provided matter capable of generation, for obviously pregnancy did not always follow coitus. For pregnancy there was needed an energizing force or 'efficient cause', which set in motion the process of generation. Duns Scotus declared that the efficient cause was not a seminal reason but that it moved seminal reasons.[2] Ficino explained that an efficient cause was needed in order to start a living body.[3]

After coitus, according to Aristotle, the combined masculo-feminine fluids remained idle in the womb for seven days.[4] At the end of that time they began to 'work' and to decay, and from the decayed matter sprouted the new embryo. This paralleled spontaneous generation in rotting matter, the sprouting of a plant from the decay of its seed, and the sprouting of a chick from the decay of its egg. What started this process physically was the influence of the sun. Aristotle's phrase 'Man and the sun generate man'[5] was repeated over and over by Renaissance commentators. Without the generative influence of the sun, there could be no generation of life.[6]

Venus

What is the place of Venus in this sequence? The answer is found in Virgil's *Georgica* in a matter-of-fact discussion of horse-breeding.

---

[1] See below, p. 282 n. 4. For Ellrodt's discussion see *Neoplatonism in the Poetry of Spenser*, pp. 80–4.

[2] Scotus, *Summa Theologica*, Q. 115, A. 1, ed. Montefortino, iii. 1003.

[3] Ficino, *De Immortalitate Animorum* (hereafter cited as *De Immortalitate*), IV. i; p. 123. This work is the same as *Theologia Platonica*.

[4] Aristotle, *Historia Animalium*, VII. iii.   [5] Aristotle, *Physics*, II. ii.

[6] For further documentation of these points see my article mentioned on p. 230 n. 3.

When the mares are taken to the stallion, Virgil says, they should be hungry and fresh from exercise; the 'Venus' will then be planted more deeply and there is a greater likelihood of pregnancy:

> Hoc faciunt, nimio ne luxu obtusior usus
> Sit genitali arvo, et sulcos oblimet inertes;
> Sed rapiat sitiens *venerem*, interiusque recondat.   (iii. 135–7)

(This they do, that by too much idleness the use [coitus] may not be more dulled to the genital field and fertilize inert furrows; but that the genital field may thirstily seize upon the Venus and store it away within.)

Here the 'Venus' is very definitely the masculine semen, while the 'genital field' is the female genital area.

The first two lines of this quotation occur in a gloss by Claudius Minos to Alciatus's Emblem 77: 'Amuletum Veneris'. The picture shows Venus and Cupid beside the dead body of Adonis, while the boar that killed him runs away in the distance. The poem reads:

> Inguina dente fero suffusum Cypris Adonim,
>   Lactucae foliis condidit exanimem.
> Hinc genitali aruo tantum lactuca resistit,
>   Quantum eruca salax vix stimulare potest.

(Cyprian [Venus] covers with leaves of lettuce the dead Adonis, his groin pierced by the tooth of a wild beast. Hence, so much as the lettuce resists the genital field, by so much the lustful eruca is hardly able to stimulate it.)

Minos's notes explain that the eruca (colewort) is an aphrodisiac and that lettuce is supposed to have a reverse effect. We are concerned, however, only with Minos's gloss on the 'genital field':

He placed here the genital field for the masculine genitals (*virilibus*) and the *pudenda*, because they are the instruments of generation, as Virgil in *Georgica* iii:

> Haec faciunt nimio ne luxu obtusior usus
> Sit genitali aruo, et sulcos oblimet inertes.

Augustine did not disdain the same form of words in *De Civitate Dei*, bk. 18, ch. 23: 'But to the will', he says, 'those members, like all others, should be subject: and so the vessel created for this work should sow the genital field as now the hand sows the earth', etc. So the genital field is called in Greek *kepos* and in Latin *hortus* (a garden).[1]

---

[1] Alciatus, *Emblemata* (edn. of Lyons, 1614), pp. 287–8.

It is not clear whether Minos's phrase 'virilibus et pudendis' applies to the masculine genitals alone or to those of both sexes, for *pudendum* (part to be ashamed of) is usually applied to the female genitals. The doubt makes little difference, for in Minos's quotation from St. Augustine the genital field clearly refers to the female genitals. Thus the 'garden' includes both the masculine and the feminine genital areas, a point of immense importance in interpreting Spenser's Garden of Adonis.

The variorum edition of Alciatus (1621) quotes Minos's note verbatim, then adds the following:

Apuleius ex Menandro:

> Arentque sulcos molles aruo Venereo,
> Thyrsumque pangant hortulo in Cupidinis.[1]

(Apuleius from Menander: 'And let them plough soft furrows in the Venereal field and drive deep the thyrsus in the garden of Cupid.')

The thyrsus, Bacchus' ivy-wreathed staff, is here used as a phallic symbol.

As a kind of prologue to the Garden of Adonis, Spenser gives an account of the birth of Belphoebe and Amoret. They are born to the nymph Chrysogone without the agency of a father 'through impression Of the sunbeames in moyst complexion' (*FQ* III. vi. 8). Spenser continues with these words about the sun:

> Great father he of generation
> Is rightly cald, th'author of life and light;
> And his faire sister for creation
> Ministreth matter fit, which, tempred right
> With heate and humour, breedes the living wight.
>
> (stanza 9)

Stirling identifies the 'faire sister' with earth as the provider of matter, and Mrs. Bennett does the same.[2] This violates the usual mythological interpretation that the sun (Apollo) and the moon (Diana) are brother and sister. Ellrodt perceived the error[3] and is supported by Alastair Fowler. But Fowler is perplexed by the phrase 'ministreth matter fit', which he thinks must mean 'provides matter', a function usually assigned to the earth. He also

---

[1] *Emblemata* (edn. of Padua, 1621), p. 342.
[2] Stirling, *PMLA* xlix. 514; Bennett, *JEGP* xli. 69 n.
[3] Ellrodt, *Neoplatonism in the Poetry of Spenser*, p. 103.

thinks that Chrysogone must be the moon, an assumption which introduces hopeless confusion. He is puzzled because the matter of living bodies seems to have two separate sources, earth and moon.[1] The answer is quite simple. Earth (and ultimately Chaos) provides the dry matter, the basic material, in vegetation the dry seed. The moon provides the moisture which fits the matter for generation. Spenser's phrase does not mean that the moon was herself the mother. In 'Epithalamion', 385–7, Spenser implores the moon to prepare 'matter fit' in the womb of his own bride:

> Encline thy will t'effect our wishfull vow,
> And the chast womb informe with timely seed,
> That may our comfort breed.

Here the function of the moon was the same as it was with Chrysogone: to temper the basic matter in the womb with moisture and thus make it apt for generation. This tempered matter is the menses, which is produced according to the lunar cycle and therefore seems particularly appropriate to the moon.

In seeking a place for Venus in the process of generation, Fowler quotes from Ficino's commentary on Plato's *Timaeus*:

> Rightly is the sun, the father of generation, placed next to the mother of generation [the moon]: the first heat to the first moisture, the illuminator to the illuminated. . . . The sun through lunar moisture lays the foundation of generations; through the moisture of Venus, he brings to completion or sets free the forms of the creatures generated. (Sol per lunarem humorem generationes inchoat, per Venereum generabilium formas absoluit.)[2]

Perhaps the translation of *generabilium* should be 'of generable things' or 'of things capable of being generated', for Ficino does not imply that the process of generation is always completed.

In another work, Ficino remarks that the moon controls the natural spirit and Venus the genital spirit of things in the lower world.[3] In the light of information already given, the moon prepares the menses, while Venus is the addition of masculine semen to prepare the moist matter for generation into corporeal form. The efficient cause, or energizing influence of the sun, is still

---

[1] Fowler, *Spenser and the Numbers of Time*, p. 140.

[2] Ibid., p. 141; Ficino, *Com. in Timaeum*, Appendix, ch. xx; p. 1468.

[3] *De Vita Coelitus Comparanda*, ch. vi; p. 537. Cf. p. 254 n. 1.

needed. Ficino had also stated: 'A certain universal virtue of the sun may not produce this man, who is a particular effect, except through another man as though a particular and proper cause.'[1] This is tantamount to saying that the energizing power of the sun is transmitted through masculine semen, along with its other qualities. This was the usual interpretation of Aristotle's statement that 'man and the sun generate man'. But Ficino seems to feel that there may be occasional exceptions. He remarks on the powers of the moon: 'Although, if the moon like to Venus, directly equal in moisture and almost as warm, should be properly mixed with Jove or the sun, you almost have Venus already.'[2] In discussing the birth of vegetation, he remarks that the Venereal moisture seems unnecessary, that the sun (Phoebus) and the moon (Diana) through heat and moisture are sufficient for generation if they are aided by Jove (the World-Soul). He then adds: 'Accordingly, why not for "planting" (as I may say cynically) man may we not use [operate] by benefit of the moon and of Jove and of Phoebus? For we always use for this a certain office of Venus. But I might have said more correctly that those others are always used. For to me Venus herself *is* Diana.'[3] These lines indicate that in some instances of human generation the Venereal moisture in masculine semen is not necessary, that the power of the sun may be applied directly to the matter tempered by lunar moisture. This is just the explanation that Spenser gives of the conception of Belphoebe and Amoret in the womb of Chrysogone.

Natalis Comes identifies Venus as follows: 'For Venus is nothing else than the hidden desire of coitus instilled by nature for purposes of procreation ... She is said to have been born from the foam of the sea, since the genital semen of animals is only a foam of the blood.'[4] Comes adds that Priapus is usually named as a child of Venus and Adonis. He is called the god of gardens, has unusually large genital organs, and represents genital semen.[5] Comes thinks that Adonis represents the power of the sun, since, 'without the power of the sun, Venus is nothing'.[6] What he means is that masculine semen has no energizing power without the influence of the sun. Mrs. Bennett notes this last passage and also

---

[1] *De Immortalitate*, xv. xi; p. 350.
[2] *De Vita Coelitus Comparanda*, ch. vi; p. 538.   [3] Ibid., ch. xxv; p. 569.
[4] *Mythologiae* (edn. of Padua, 1616), iv. xiii; p. 211.
[5] Ibid. v. xv; p. 285, and x; p. 542.   [6] Ibid. iv. xiii; p. 213.

mentions Cornutus's identification of Aphrodite (Venus) with *spumantia* (foam), which is the seed of animals.[1] It can thus be seen that, even at this level, Venus is both literal and metaphorical. Literally she is the fluid emitted during coitus; metaphorically she is the desire caused in part by a superabundance of that fluid. Upon this base are built the various allegorical meanings attributed to her.

Since Venus is mythologically a goddess, we naturally attribute to her the feminine role in procreation. Once we realize that she, partly, at least, represents the masculine role, the various personifications become clearer. The double sex of Venus (*FQ* IV. x. 41) would seem to be a reference to her as the masculo-feminine fluid resulting after coitus has taken place. This is the 'matter' associated with Venus. If we follow Virgil, we say that she *is* this prepared matter; if we follow Ficino, we say that she is *in* this matter; if we follow Comes, we say that she and Adonis produce this prepared matter (Priapus). The moon plays a major role in preparing the feminine matter in the womb before coitus; Venus is added as a result of coitus.[2] In Ficino's view she sets free (*absoluit*) the forms of generable things (cf. pp. 244, 254). This sounds as though they are forms 'imprisoned' in matter or latent there, and that Venus releases them by preparing them to be activated. The efficient cause is still needed to set the process of activation in motion.

Adonis

We cannot understand the process of generation without determining Adonis' part in it. Mrs. Bennett has noted the identification of Adonis as the sun, as stated in Natalis Comes and others;[1] and this is probably one aspect of him, for he does seem to correspond to the efficient cause in the process of generation as we have outlined it. Yet he must represent something more:

> All be he subject to mortalitie,
> Yet is eterne in mutabilitie,
> And by succession made perpetuall,
> Transformed oft, and chaunged diverslie:
> For him the father of all formes they call;
> Therfore needs mote he live, that living gives to all.
>
> (III. vi. 47)

[1] *JEGP* xli. 70.

[2] Though the moon does not have the genital power of Venus, she is sometimes pictured as supervising the 'mixing' of fluids, the resulting conception, and the foetal life within the womb (Ficino, *De Vita Coelitus Comparanda*, ch. vi; p. 537).

These lines hardly seem descriptive of the sun, who is one of the 'changeless' heavenly bodies. As we search for a possible clue, we find one in the *Anticlaudianus* of Alanus de Insulis, a poetic allegory of Nature's attempt to make a perfect man. Having decided to undertake the task, Nature sends Prudence into the heavens to secure from God a perfect soul. Prudence beholds the mysteries of flowing and changing forms. Among other things, she learns

> Cur formae species purgata serenat Adonim.[1]

> (Why species purged of form reveals Adonis.)

When Prudence brings the completed soul to Nature, the latter begins construction of a suitable body, lavishing upon it all the treasures of form:

> Spirat in hac forma Narcissus, et alter Adonis
> Spirat in hac specie.[2]

(Narcissus breathes in this form, and another Adonis breathes in this species.)

In these two quotations Adonis is identified with species, the type-form which endures though the individual body perishes. It is quite likely that Spenser took his identification directly from Alanus.

Once we know that Adonis represents the principle of species, we can see his place in the scheme of generation. For many centuries man solaced himself with the thought that the species is eternal, though the individual perishes. Only with the nineteenth century and the discovery of extinct species in fossil forms, did man recognize that entire groups could die, that the maintenance of species was not divinely ordained. Spenser lived before the recognition of this melancholy truth.

Ficino's words on immortality of the species bear a striking resemblance to Spenser's line, 'And by succession made perpetuall'. Ficino writes:

> Sic homo tanquam diuinus humanam *speciem* seruat quadam *successione perpetuam*.[3]

(So man, as though divine, preserves by a certain succession the human species perpetual.)

---

[1] *PL* ccx. 544B. Editions of the *Anticlaudianus* appeared in Basel, 1536, and in Venice, 1582.

[2] Ibid., p. 550B.   [3] *Epistolae*, Bk. iv: 'Matrimonii Laus', p. 778.

Res quidem corporeae ex materia formaque compositae, unitatem *speciei perpetuam successione* conseruant.[1]

(Certainly corporeal things composed of matter and form conserve by succession a perpetual unity of species.)

Genitalis quoque natura imaginatioque, naturae comes, sic ex potentia in actum in se rerum motionumque generandarum semina promit, ut et ordinatissima *perpetua successio* fiat, et tandem ad eadem uel similia certis temporum curriculis redeatur.[2]

(Also the genital nature and imagination, the companion of nature, so from potentiality into act bring forth in themselves seeds of things and motions to be generated, that a most orderly and perpetual succession is made and at last there is a return to the same or similar [forms] in certain courses of time.)

In this last passage, the perpetual succession is produced by genital nature and by imagination, the companion of genital nature. Ficino names Venus as the genital nature of the World-Soul (below, p. 254 n. 1). In Spenser's scheme, her companion is Adonis. Ficino's *imaginatio* may have been interpreted by Spenser as the differentiating power of species, which classifies forms according to their various types. Here Ficino does not seem to be referring to the generation of bodies, but to the production of seminal reasons into an active status: 'seeds of things and motions to be generated' but not as yet actually generated. Species and genital nature have combined, but the efficient cause is not yet active.

Postremo in fine libri notabis, *naturam* in rebus sub Luna compositis quasi, uel debiliorem, uel in loco debiliori, uel inter debiliora non conseruare *perpetuam* in singulari composito uitam: imitari tamen per continuam generationis *successionem*, qua seruat *speciem* quoad potest coelestem uirtutem, quae speciem simul indiuiduamque conseruat.[3]

(Finally, in the end of the book [Plotinus' *Enneads*] you will notice that Nature, in composite things under the moon—as if weaker, or in a weaker place, or among weaker things—does not conserve perpetual life in the individual composite; yet she imitates it through a continual succession of generation, by which she preserves species as long as she can [preserve] the celestial virtue, which conserves the species and the individual together.)

[1] *Com. in Plotinum*, IV. iii. 8; p. 1735.　　　[2] Ibid. II. ii. Introd.; p. 1604.
[3] Ibid. II. i. 8; p. 1604.

It is noteworthy that here Ficino pictures Nature as the controlling force in both the sublunar and the celestial worlds, a fact which may account for Spenser's portrayal of her in the 'Cantos of Mutabilitie', where her authority is superior to that of Jove and where she is the court of final appeal.[1]

Cum ex materia rebus *mutabilitas* accidat, profecto, nisi essent res quaedam a materia segregatae, ordo consequens *perpetuaque successio,* similium in transmutatione rerum conseruari non posset.[2]

(Since from matter mutability happens to things, actually unless there were certain things segregated from matter, a consequent order and perpetual succession could not be conserved in the transmutation of like things.)

This passage seems to say that species, the type-form which endures through a perpetual succession of individual forms, could not exist if it were a material substance, for then it would be subject to mutability. Since it is not material, it can be 'eterne in mutabilitie'; for, while it operates in matter, it is separate from matter. If we include among 'certain things segregated from matter' the 'companion' of species (genital nature or Venus), we approach Mrs. Bennett's position that neither Venus nor Adonis represents matter. They are *in* matter but must be thought of as being apart from it, like sugar in coffee, or like yeast in dough, or like the soul in the body.

In one of his letters Ficino remarks that species itself is always *eternal*.[3] Again, he calls Venus that pleasure which 'in generation makes species *sempiternal'* by inciting creatures to the act of generation.[4] The species is always true to itself; Ficino denies that the soul of a man could return in the form of a beast.[5] Species acting in matter corresponds to its exemplar in the world of ideas. Though species in matter seems to undergo changes through certain vicissitudes of the seminal reasons, still it is conserved everywhere as the same species because of the eternal perseverance of ideas in the Divine Mind and of like forms waking in the World-Soul.[6]

[1] Cf. E. C. Knowlton, 'Natura as an Allegorical Figure', Harvard Dissertation, 1918.   [2] *Com. in Plotinum,* v. ix. 4; p. 1770.
[3] *Epistolae,* Bk. xi: 'Deus nullius mali causa'; p. 939.
[4] *Com. in Philebum,* i. xi; p. 1217. Ficino uses 'eternal' to mean 'without end', 'sempiternal' to mean 'until the end of Time'. Cf. p. 291 n. 1.
[5] *De Immortalitate,* xvii. iv; p. 393.   [6] *Com. in Plotinum,* ii. i. 3; p. 1597.

In stating that species is true to its type, Ficino says: 'Praeterea nec oporteret omnem animam omnes *induere* species'[1] ('Moreover, it is not reasonable that every soul should *indue* all species'). This recalls Spenser's lines on the forms in the Garden of Adonis:

> Infinite shapes of creatures there are bred,
> And uncouth formes, which none yet ever knew;
> And every *sort* is in a sondry bed
> Sett by itselfe, and ranckt in comely rew:
> Some fitt for reasonable sowles t'*indew*,
> Some made for beasts, some made for birds to weare . . .
>
> (III. vi. 35)

Spenser's use of 'indew' could be an echo of Ficino's usage. The two passages are closely akin in meaning. Spenser's forms are separated according to their 'sort' or species, each 'sort' carefully separated from the others. Presumably, a 'reasonable sowle' could be assigned to any of the forms contained under its species but could not receive one from the various species of birds, beasts, and fish.

Adonis as the immortality of species in a world of perishable forms is also the god of reviving vegetation that had seemed to perish with the onset of winter. Sir James Frazer, in *The Golden Bough*, has treated extensively this aspect of Adonis, with documentation from classical and patristic sources.[2] Another interesting treatment of the subject is a Latin poem by the Italian humanist Pontano, 'De Hortis Hesperidum, sive De Cultu Citriorum', in which he compares an orchard of citrus trees (or lemon trees) to the Gardens of the Hesperides because both produce golden fruit.[3] Because the citrus tree is long-lived and, when destroyed, sends up sprouts from its roots, he compares it to Adonis. He gives an Ovidian-like fable of the citrus tree springing from the grave of dead Adonis after Venus had watered it with her tears (f. 139). Venus and her nymphs sing the return of Adonis in the spring (f. 142). The citrus tree has an eternal genus and an eternal species (f. 147). When the trunk has finally died, the Parcae, who administer the decrees of Fate, run their spindles backwards,

---

[1] Ibid. IV. viii. 2; p. 1755.

[2] *The Golden Bough* (1914), vol. v, chs. 1–3, 9–10: 'Adonis'.

[3] J. J. Pontanus, *Opera* (Venice: Aldus, 1513). Folio numbers from this edition are quoted in the text.

quo lucis in auras
Extinctum reuocent vitaeque ad munera Adonim
Et Veneris dulces iterum instaurentur amores.   (ff. 147–8)

(. . . by which into the airs of light they may recall extinct Adonis to the rewards of life, and the sweet loves of Venus may again be restored.)

That is, the citrus tree sprouts once again.

Ficino comments upon the relation of species to seminal reasons as follows: 'He [Plotinus] thinks the particular causes of natural things to be their seminal reasons in the vegetal nature of the World-Soul, to which always by a certain order the seminal reasons in individual species may respond. But by what pact all may sprout from the universal *seminary* of the world, he examines with many questions.'[1]

In speaking of the foetus forming in the womb, Ficino writes that species is principally conserved 'because the principal and acting force there is seminal reason'.[2] This does not mean that seminal reason initiates generation; like the genes, it guides the development of the foetus after generation has started.

Duns Scotus explains: 'For a seminal reason is either the substantial form of a seed, or a quality necessarily following its substantial form . . . For, since seminal reason is intended by the Author of nature as a way towards outward and more perfect forms, seminal reasons can be present in all mixed [composite] things.'[3] Scotus's words make clear how Spenser could represent the seminal reasons of returning vegetal souls as seeds replanted in the garden and also as forms growing in the garden (cf. p. 265 n. 5).

Thus species is closely allied to seminal reasons and their accompanying forms. The active forces in determining species are seminal reasons. Species compartmentalizes and classifies the seminal reasons so that each corporeal form produced will remain true to its type-form or species. Certain seminal reasons are appropriate for each separate species, and not for others. They keep the species true to type. Within the type-form, every individual form varies from every other, but only within limits; e.g. men are men, and not beasts; lions are lions, and not elephants; etc.

[1] *Com. in Plotinum*, II. iii. 16; p. 1638.   [2] Ibid. II. iii. 13; p. 1635.
[3] Scotus, *Summa Theologica*, Q. 115, A. 2, iii. 1004–5.

Yet neither species nor seminal reason can initiate the process of generation. That process is set in motion by the efficient cause. Physically, the efficient cause is the power of the sun. For plants this power is imparted directly to the earth. For men and animals it is normally imparted through masculine semen, where it meets with the Venereal moisture. Yet the sun, like the moon, is a physical agent of some invisible force. When Ficino calls the sun and the moon the father and mother of generation (not of forms),[1] he thinks of them as tangible and visible executors of intangible and invisible causes. As Scotus has said, the ultimate efficient cause is God.[2] Ficino declares that God diffuses the World-Soul from a centre; i.e. from the sun and moon.[3] He calls the sun the Vicar of God in generation.[4] Again, he declares that the World-Soul, everywhere living, sets forth everywhere its virtue of common (universal) life chiefly through the sun.[5] Thus, while Venus and Nature are parts of the World-Soul, the sun and moon are instruments of the World-Soul. As the sun is a physical agent diffusing the power of the World-Soul, and as Adonis represents the generative power of the sun, it follows that he must also represent that part of the World-Soul whose force is diffused through the sun's rays. This force, or efficient cause, acts in matter, producing vegetal and sensible souls of animals and men. Ficino describes this lower acting soul:

in motion and time of this kind the soul exchanges various garments in itself; which garments may not all reasonably exist at the same time, since a certain one is present, this one is past, and that one is future. Accordingly, for this reason the soul everywhere is and is not in a certain manner perpetual in mutation. . . . For that Identity pertaining to perfect and stable being does not characterize this soul-flux (*fluxui huic animali*); nor again does it undergo so great alteration that it is altered from its own nature or from itself. For what is moved everywhere by exchanging certain garments, the same is altered in appearance. And so, throwing off earlier garments but induing (*induens*) later ones, it seems to die and to be reborn; but again neither newly receiving

[1] *Com. in Timaeum*, Appendix, ch. xx; p. 1468. Cf. p. 244 n. 2.

[2] Scotus names God as the only efficient cause (*Summa Theologica*, Q. 115, A. 1, iii 1003). He does not apply the term to the agents through whom God works, as most other commentators do. Cf. p. 241 n. 2.

[3] *Com. in Timaeum*, Appendix, ch. xiii; p. 1467.

[4] *De Immortalitate*, XVIII. iii; p. 403.

[5] *De Vita Coelitus Comparanda*, ch. i; p. 532.

nor ever abandoning the property natural to itself, neither is it ever newly made nor does it perish . . . particularly because the matter in sensible things is also sempiternal.[1]

Here the vegetal-sensible World-Soul is described in much the same way as species, persisting through a variety of forms, seeming to die but only seeming, assuming new appearances as it 'indues' new garments of flesh, the substance or matter of which is likewise 'eterne' and likewise changes its form. The vegetal-sensible soul is part of the All-Soul or the World-Soul acting in matter.[2] Species is like a signet-ring that stamps a certain general form upon material substance;[3] the World-Soul is like the hand that moves the ring. It is the efficient cause or the agent of the efficient cause, acting through the power of the sun. Hence species and the vegetal-sensible World-Soul are two aspects of the same thing and are similarly described as throwing off old garments and 'induing' new ones while preserving their basic identity intact. Adonis includes the functions of them both.

Again Ficino writes:

You will observe that in our body, beyond the vital garment (*uestigium*) imprinted by the World-Soul, which is too common, there is also a vital and proper garment imprinted by our [rational] soul, and that this differs from that of the World-Soul, not changed by external causes but rather changed by means of itself. Whence it follows that, in no mutation of this kind, will it ever throw off its proper species.[4]

As stated elsewhere, Ficino believes that this second vital garment is imprinted with the arrival of the rational soul in the foetus forty-five or forty-nine days after conception (below, p. 270). The rational soul impresses its particular 'garment' on the foetus and determines its form in detail, but always within the limits of species first imprinted by the World-Soul.

The World-Soul is the same as the Holy Spirit who was borne above the waters in Genesis 1: 2 and through whom the first matter of Chaos was differentiated into genera and species.[5] The

---

[1] *Com. in Parmenidem*, ch. xcv; p. 1200.
[2] *Com. in Plotinum*, IV. ix. 3; p. 1756.
[3] Ficino uses the figure of a seal stamping forms in wax. He believes that both the matter (wax) and the type-form survive the destruction of the composite body (*De Immortalitate*, v. xi; p. 145). Cf. p. 254 n. 1 and p. 260 n. 1.
[4] *Com. in Plotinum*, VI. vii. 7; p. 1788.
[5] *Com. in Philebum*, I. xi; pp. 1216–17.

lower portions of the World-Soul, operating in matter, are Nature, Venus Pandemos, and Adonis. The last of these is both the type-form stamped by the signet-ring and the hand that impels it to stamp the forms in matter; i.e. both the species and the efficient cause. It operates by means of the seminal reasons existing within itself and within the matter to be formed.[1]

In commenting upon the parts played by the two sexes in animal and human generation, Vincent de Beauvais comments that from the masculine fluid comes the spirit-artificer—the vegetal soul—and form, while the feminine fluid provides the foundation and basic matter of generation.[2] This confirms the analysis that we have already made. The mother provides suitable matter tempered with lunar moisture, the father provides the species which determines the limits of form (Adonis). He also provides the efficient cause which begins the process of generation and establishes the vegetal-sensible soul in the embryo (Adonis). He partly provides Venus, who is not form but an impulse towards form, the added quality which makes the feminine menses able to assume form. Ficino states that Venus Pandemos 'rerum formas explicat in materia'[3] (sets forth the forms of things in matter). Perhaps we cannot do better than to use Mrs. Bennett's terminology, naming Venus as the mother of forms, since Spenser calls Adonis 'the father of all formes'.

Ficino's verb *explicat*, like his earlier verb *absoluit* (above, p. 244), carries the implication of releasing or liberating the imprisoned forms. Thus Venus operates in matter, though she is not the same thing as matter in Ficino's interpretation. He states that there are four 'lives' named for the quadruple virtue of the World-Soul: Saturnian life in the intellect, Jovial life in the intelligence, Venereal life in animal virtue already loving matter, Dionysiac life in that portion completely immersed in matter. On the lowest level the World-Soul becomes 'drunk' with matter and oblivious

[1] Ficino calls Venus the genital nature of the World-Soul (*Com. in Plotinum*, v. viii. 13; p. 1769). Nature is the vegetal life of the world, which is called 'the seminary of natural things' (ibid., IV. iv. 2. 39; p. 1747). She is like a seal stamped upon matter from an intellectual beginning (ibid., III. i. 11; p. 1693). She prepares matter which has 'life' and is apt for generation (e.g. protoplasm). Venus makes it apt for the reception of form. Adonis impels this matter towards generation and re-stamps it with the type-forms of particular species. Cf. p. 253 n. 3 and p. 260 n. 1.

[2] *Speculum Naturale*, xxxi. 33; p. 2317c in *Opera Omnia* (Duaci [Douai], 1624), vol. i.

[3] *Com. in Philebum*, I. xi; p. 1217.

to its higher estate.[1] Venus represents the first mingling of the soul with matter, the beginning of corporeality. Adonis represents the type-form (species) and the energizing force which carries forward corporeality into the actual production of living bodies. Venus is the genital nature of the World-Soul, Adonis is its active and formative nature, though each partakes in some degree of the qualities of the other. The earth and the moon (with the aid of Chaos) provide the substance for the composite bodies which Venus and Adonis are constantly bringing into life.

Form and Matter

Duns Scotus compares the Platonic and the Aristotelian positions on the nature of forms. Plato supposed a world of ideas or 'ideal' forms, changeless and eternal, which furnished the exemplary pattern of all forms generated in the lower world. Aristotle, in his *Metaphysics*, I. iii, objected to this, thinking that human beings were sufficient for generating other human beings. If there are such ideal forms, he thinks, they are of species only and would have to be shared among so many individual forms that they could not be said to generate any particular individual.[2]

Scotus himself takes the Platonic position, modified to fit Christian doctrine. The ideas or exemplars are in the 'sapience' of God, and God is the exemplary cause of all things. The exemplars are immutable and incorruptible, and in them all truths shine again.[3] The 'sapience' of the Father is the same as the Word (*Logos*) and the Son, who is the second person of the Trinity.[4]

This account looks forward to Sapience, in 'An Hymne of Heavenly Beautie', and helps us to realize the combination of Platonic and Christian thought in Spenser's poem. But Scotus warns us that there is another Sapience, not the Son of God, mentioned in Ecclesiasticus 1 : 3 : 'Before all things Sapience was created.' (The Son of God was not made or created, but *begotten*; cf. the Nicene Creed.) This second Sapience is the angelic nature, which was created before the corporeal world.[5]

---

[1] *Com. in Timaeum*, ch. xxvi; p. 684 in *Opera Platonis* (edn. of 1551).
[2] Scotus, *Summa Theologica*, Q. 44, A. 3, iii. 9–10.
[3] Ibid., p. 11.
[4] Ibid., Q. 45, A. 6, iii. 52. An excellent background for this material is provided by Herschel Baker's *Dignity of Man* (Harvard University Press, 1947).
[5] Scotus, *Summa Theologica*, Q. 61, A. 3, iii. 311.

Scotus reviews two theories of the relation of form to matter. Anaxagoras argued that *all* forms lie in matter, that generation is only the outgoing from matter of forms already existing there, and that the generating force does nothing but extract them and give distinguishing marks to things already existing. Scotus objects that so complete a generalization would never allow for the appearance of any new forms and is contrary to the theory of original creation *ex nihilo*, without any presupposed matter.[1]

Another theory, continues Scotus, which was held by Avicenna and others, is that the agent (efficient cause) creates the form outside matter and leads it into matter. The agent or acting force is entirely separate from matter and is called the giver of forms.[1]

These two theories correspond roughly to the views taken by Stirling and Mrs. Bennett with regard to forms in the Garden of Adonis. Mrs. Bennett sees Adonis and Venus as sending forms to matter; Stirling sees them as transforming forms in matter.[2] Scotus's phrase, 'the giver of forms', is suggestive of Adonis as 'the father of all formes'.

Scotus accepts Aristotle's view that the agent or acting force works only in composites, applying form to matter or supplying matter to form. The agent brings potentiality into act; this involves acceptance of Anaxagoras' theory that forms led out of matter were potentially there before.[3] In the natural world the process of formation is the mutation of existing matter, not the creation of anything wholly new. Form comes into existence in the instant when potentiality in matter becomes act.[4]

The effect of this doctrine is to rule out any conservatory of immaterial forms. It does not, however, prevent an allegorical presentation of such forms as are latent in matter. We can see how Ficino struggles with this problem. He accepts the Platonic world of ideas, as does Spenser, the 'wondrous paterne' which is 'perfect Beautie' (HB 36–40), by which Venus Urania quickens the dull earth (line 55). But on earth Venus Pandemos is infused in matter and the World-Soul is the soul of first matter (above, p. 237). This seems to be an attempt to follow Aristotle's reasoning about material forms. Ficino expresses it in various ways. The seeds of

---

[1] Scotus, *Summa Theologica*, Q. 45, A. 8, iii. 66.
[2] Bennett, *PMLA* xlvii. 57; Stirling, *PMLA* xlix. 516.
[3] Scotus, *Summa Theologica*, Q. 45, A. 8, iii. 66.
[4] Ibid., p. 67.

sprouting forms lie hidden in matter.[1] The beginning of material form is a certain life not sprouting from matter but infused in matter.[2] Forms in matter hang from forms in the World-Soul as if it were their fountain;[3] but we have just seen that the World-Soul acts in matter. Forms latent in matter, not including forms of rational souls, are brought forth in the lap of matter (*ex materiae eruit gremio*) at the very moment that their composite union of form and matter is completed.[4]

Ficino again refers to the 'lap' of matter, when he pictures Nature in 'the seminary world' adding dimension to incorporeal forms to make them corporeal bodies; for dimension involves the union of matter and form. Forms, through seminal reasons, can exist in matter even if they are not there in the manner of bodies. There is a question whether substantial forms are resolved back into first matter. Some observers think that some forms, lacking quantity, 'insinuate themselves directly into the *naked lap* of matter'.[5]

For Ficino the emergence of forms in the 'lap' of matter has its counterpart in the emergence of vegetal souls in the 'lap' of the World-Soul:

Since the whole machine [of the world] is subject to the World-Soul, nothing resists it, nothing proper to itself flows from it, nothing alien touches it. Again, the whole mass of bodies through a life infused from the soul itself now are bound together among themselves, and again are bound to the soul and straightway are subject to it; our soul indeed comes into the body as if already a member of the world and thence already 'living' in the *lap* of the whole soul, being firmly connected to it as a foetus is connected to the womb.[6]

Since 'the lap of the whole soul', or World-Soul, is productive of vegetal souls, and since forms are brought forth in 'the lap of matter', and since the World-Soul operates in first matter, we may expect a certain correspondence of the two 'laps' with each other, if indeed they are not the same. They may have some

[1] *De Immortalitate*, I. vi; p. 91.

[2] *Com. in Plotinum*, VI. i. 27; p. 1773.

[3] Ibid. v. ix. 3; p. 1770.

[4] *De Immortalitate*, xv. ii; p. 335. For other references to forms produced 'in the lap of matter' see ibid. I. iii; p. 84, and VI. i; p. 156.

[5] *Com. in Plotinum*, ii: 'De Materia', xii; p. 1650.

[6] Ibid. II. ix. 7; p. 1669.

relevance to 'Venus lap' in Spenser's 'Hymne in Honour of Love', 57–63:

> For ere this worlds still moving mightie masse
> Out of great Chaos ugly prison crept,
> In which his goodly face long hidden was
> From heavens view, and in deepe darkness kept,
> Love, that had now long time securely slept
> In Venus lap, unarmed then and *naked*,
> Gan reare his head, by Clotho being waked.

Spenser is probably following Ficino's chapter in his commentary on Plato's *Symposium*: 'Origo Amoris ex Chaos' (I. iii), which was itself suggested by Hesiod.[1] Love, says Ficino, accompanied Chaos from the beginning and satisfied the hunger of unformed matter for the ornament of forms:

> Not otherwise the matter of this world, since in the beginning unformed Chaos lay without the ornament of forms: by that love inborn to itself it directed itself into the World-Soul and proved itself obedient to it; and, by this conciliating Love, having received from the soul the ornament of all forms which are seen in the world, the world was effected out of Chaos.[2]

Here Love is pictured as inborn in the matter of Chaos, which was permeated by the influence of the World-Soul. Hence with Venus as the genital nature of the World-Soul (above, p. 254), it is logical that Love, or Cupid, should be born in his mother's lap in the matter of Chaos. This is not an unfit place for the Queen of Beauty, as Mrs. Bennett protests;[3] Venus is there as Una among the satyrs or as a missionary among the cannibals, an inspiration towards a higher order of being. Along with her son, she will 'arouse the torpid, lighten the darkness, bring to life the dead, form the unformed, and perfect the imperfect'.[4]

The pre-existence of vegetal souls in the 'lap' of the World-Soul has other counterparts in Ficino. He states that the vegetal nature of souls is an image of the World-Soul.[5] Again, he states that the vegetal 'life' of the world is alternatively called Nature and

---

[1] *Var.*: *Minor Poems*, i. 511–12.

[2] *Com. in Conuiuium*, I. iii; p. 374 in *Opera Platonis* (edn. of 1551).

[3] Cf. Stirling, *PMLA* xlix. 537; Bennett, *JEGP* xli. 68.

[4] Cf. p. 229 n. 2.

[5] *Com. in Plotinum*, IV. iv. 2. 35; p. 1746.

'the seminary of natural things'.[1] Nature and the 'seminary' (seed-plot) are also linked in Spenser's garden:

> In that same gardin all the goodly flowres,
> Wherewith Dame *Nature* doth her beautify,
> And decks the girlonds of her paramoures,
> Are fetcht: there is the first *seminary*
> Of all things that are borne to live and dye,
> According to their kynds.　　　(*FQ* III. vi. 30)

After speaking of the forms growing in the Garden of Adonis, Spenser proceeds to relate them to matter:

> Daily they grow, and daily forth are sent
> Into the world, it to replenish more;
> Yet is the stocke not lessened nor spent,
> But still remaines in everlasting store,
> As it at first created was of yore:
> For in the wide wombe of the world there lyes,
> In hatefull darknes and in deepe horrore,
> An huge eternal chaos, which supplyes
> The substaunces of natures fruitfull progenyes.
>
> All things from thence doe their first being fetch,
> And borrow matter whereof they are made,
> Which, whenas forme and feature it does ketch,
> Becomes a body and doth then invade
> The state of life out of the griesly shade.
> That substaunce is eterne, and bideth so,
> Ne when the life decayes, and forme does fade,
> Doth it consume and into nothing goe,
> But chaunged is, and often altred to and froe.
>
> The substaunce is not chaungd nor altered,
> But th'only forme and outward fashion;
> For every substaunce is conditioned
> To chaunge her hew, and sondry formes to don,
> Meet for her temper and complexion:
> For formes are variable, and decay
> By course of kinde and by occasion.　　　(stanzas 36–8)

Here Spenser has left a slight ambiguity in the third line, for it is not clear whether he refers to ' the stocke' of forms or of matter. The difficulty is more apparent than real, for both form and

---

[1] Ibid. IV. iv. 2. 39; p. 1747. Cf. p. 254 n. I.

matter go out of the garden, the matter being the 'sinfull mire' with which the babes are clothed, or its equivalent in other species. The succeeding lines suggest that the stock of matter is meant, drawn from Chaos, which supplies 'the substaunces of natures fruitfull progenyes'. This substance, which is eternal and changes only in outward form, seems to be prepared matter immediately underlying the flux of forms, perhaps the third stage of first matter as defined by Duns Scotus and Bernardus Silvestris (above, p. 79). This substance is sufficient for the needs of generation so long as there is no increase in the total number of corporeal bodies living at one time, for bodies that decay and die are kept in the supply of substance under another form. Only when the population of living bodies increases is it necessary to prepare more material from Chaos to meet nature's needs.

There is some question whether the substances of bodies actually go back into first matter, because they change instantly from one form to another. Vincent de Beauvais declares that such transition, though seemingly instantaneous, requires that the bodies pass through a stage of something unformed, of matter lacking any form yet capable of receiving all mutable forms. He adds that the 'abyss' of unformed matter in Genesis 1 : 2 may also signify spiritual formlessness.[1] His moral symbolism thus closely parallels that of Francesco Piccolomini (above, p. 65) and of Spenser, as shown at length in Chapter IV.

The nature of the substratum, or first matter, underlying the mutations of bodily forms has been a matter of speculation. We have already noted the three stages of first matter, as stated by Scotus and Bernardus Silvestris, the third stage of which has form of a kind and is the immediate substratum underlying mutations (above, p. 79). Ficino states these stages in the formation of first matter somewhat differently: (1) incorporeal potentiality, lacking form and magnitude; (2) matter extended into dimension and magnitude; (3) body, or corporeality (but still a substratum).

In the third stage, God formed this 'body'—i.e. matter so extended —into many forms, particularly of the elements and of the heavens,

---

[1] *Speculum Naturale*, II. xvii; p. 89c. Like Vincent, Ficino notes the necessity of having an incorruptible matter able to 'indue' all forms as a base (*susceptaculum*) for composite bodies (*De Immortalitate*, v. iv; pp. 136–7). This basic matter must be empty of forms in order that the 'author' may 'express' his form by 'impressing' the matter, in the manner of a notary (*obsignatoris*) using a seal (*Com. in Plotinum*, ii : 'De Materia', viii; p. 1647). Cf. p. 253 n. 3 and p. 254 n. 1.

and confirmed it in the sky in the forms of stars. Under the sky, besides the forms of the elements, he formed it into forms of vapours, stones, metals, and plants and animals. A certain unique matter was everywhere indued (*induta*) by all these forms.[1]

In two later passages Ficino develops this idea of differentiated matter yet further. As the forms of things are classified into different species, so there should be a principle of species in matter, of matter prepared to receive a particular kind of form. Since seminal reasons in matter reflect the ideas in the Divine Mind and each seminal reason responds to the idea of which it is a reflection, matter might naturally divide according to the kinds of seminal reasons inhabiting it. By so doing, it allures the kind of soul most congruent to it:

It adds up to this, that the World-Soul by divine providence has at least as many seminal reasons of things as there are ideas in the Divine Mind, by which reasons it fabricates just as many species in matter. . . . Soon, into this matter so opportunely prepared, you draw a gift (*munus*) from a unique idea, manifestly through the seminal reason of the [World-]Soul. . . . Zoroaster, then, called congruities of forms of this kind to the reasons of the [World-]Soul divine allurements, and Synesius confirmed them to be magic charms. For lastly one may believe that at a certain time all gifts directly from the [World-]Soul to a certain proper species of matter are collected together; except, fittingly, gifts only of seed from which such a species sprouted; and of conforming seeds. Thus here a man, by the acceptance of human [qualities] only, thence claims for himself, not gifts proper to fishes or birds, but gifts human and like himself.[2]

Later, Ficino varied his reasoning slightly:

Nature contains in herself more seeds of things than the [Divine] Mind contains ideas. Since indeed the virtue of *Nature* and of seed is weaker, it is not able to comprehend in one seed and to do through one what one idea possesses and is able to do. Therefore, through many seeds is distributed the vigour of a single idea, and the weakness of [their] virtue is compensated by number. By the same reasoning, *matter* is led into many forms under only one seed. Dimension, always subject to division, adds to the innumerable multitude of this world; and [so do] the varying separate motions, and the multiplex mixture of things among themselves, and the mass and the number of virtues proceeding everywhere by necessity from separate superior causes.

[1] *Praedicationes*, p. 493.　　[2] *De Vita Coelitus Comparanda*, ch. i; p. 531.

Thence, lest the [many] species of mutable things should at some time perish, the number of individuals is divinely increased beyond the multitude of permanent things *by substances (substantiis)*, now by succession, and now simultaneously.[1]

These passages are of the utmost importance for an interpretation of the Garden of Adonis. Ficino's sense of symmetry required that the world of matter should correspond in detail with the world of forms. As the divine ideas marked a differentiation into various species to be administered through the World-Soul, which yet retained its all-form, so should the ultimate first matter of Chaos be differentiated into substances while yet remaining part of the basic substratum. In the third passage quoted, Ficino uses *matter* which becomes *substances* to augment the supply beyond that first established, lest the various species of mutable things should perish. This seems to be exactly Spenser's reasoning. From Chaos comes 'matter' which supplies the 'substaunces' of Nature's offspring. Ficino includes Nature also, explaining her numerous progeny as a compensation for her and their relative weakness. The passage also makes clear how Spenser can speak of 'substaunce' in an inclusive sense and of 'substaunces' and 'every substaunce' in a differentiated sense. It is all basically one substance, or first matter; but it is differentiated to match the various species of forms. Each differentiated 'substaunce' can don sundry forms, but these forms are of one species 'meet for her temper and complexion'. All of the inclusive substance is 'eterne' and not subject to annihilation, though it is constantly altered and assumes many shapes. This basic substance supplies all species, but 'every substaunce' is limited to a single species for which it is especially tempered. We may draw an analogy to 'beef' which is differentiated into steak, roast, and hamburger, all of which may represent the same cut of beef prepared or 'tempered' in different ways.

The first creation of matter referred to in line 5 of stanza 36 refers to Genesis 1 : 1 : 'In the beginning God created heaven and earth.' The almost universal interpretation of this verse was that of creation *ex nihilo*, the emergence of the confused matter of Chaos from a state of non-being.[2] Spenser glances at this theory when he declares that the substance does not go back into nothing

---

[1] *Com. in Plotinum*, iii: 'De Providentia', xvii; p. 1697.
[2] Augustine, *PL* xxxiv. 178; Bede, *PL* xciii. 240; Comestor, *PL* cxcviii. 1056; Angelomus, *PL* cxv. 114C; Hugo of Rouen, *PL* cxcii. 1250D.

Errata
    Note 2, l. 2, read   iii, 1003.

(stanza 37). To go back into formlessness is not to go back into nothingness. Again, the 'darkness upon the face of the abyss' may have suggested the 'hateful darkness' which Spenser describes as the abode of Chaos.

We must not overlook Mrs. Bennett's contention that 'the stocke' which remains undiminished must refer to the forms in the garden, since not until the latter part of 36 stanza is any reference made to matter or Chaos. The 'For' of line 6 does seem to imply that matter goes out of the garden and must be replenished. But, as we have noted above, both form and matter must go out in the bodies which emerge from the gates. Therefore it is possible that the first creation of line 5 refers to the forms as well as to matter. If so, the line would seem to support Augustine's theory of simultaneous creation, as Ellrodt has already suggested.[1] Augustine based his theory on Ecclesiasticus 18 : 1 : 'He who lives in eternity created all things together', and on Wisdom 11 : 18 : 'Thou who madest the world of unformed matter'.[2] He applied these to Genesis 1, where the order of creation differs slightly from that in Genesis 2 : man was made after the animals in Genesis 1 but before the animals in Genesis 2. Therefore Augustine supposed the two chapters to represent separate stages of creation. In the first, God created the world and all future creatures in it in his mind, as an architect envisions a building or a sculptor a statue. His world-plan survives in his mind and is the same as the pattern world of ideas in Plato.[3] At the same time, God also created the first matter in which these forms based on the ideas would later appear. The whole vast plan was created in an instant of time, the order of the six days merely indicating a logical progression of details.[4] Later hexameral writers were disposed to allow God a little more time.[5] Augustine thought that in Genesis 2 God began the detailed stages of bringing the items he had planned into the world of material bodies, a process which is still going on.

[1] Ellrodt, *Neoplatonism in the Poetry of Spenser*, p. 77.

[2] Augustine, *De Genesi ad Litteram*, VI. vi, PL xxxiv. 343; *De Genesi contra Manichaeos*, I. v, PL xxxiv. 178. He notes that some manuscripts read 'unseen matter'.

[3] Abelard, *Expositio in Hexaemeron*, PL clxxxviii. 738A, B; Vincent, *Speculum Naturale*, I. iii; p. 19C; Ficino, *Com. in Parmenidem*, ch. xcv, p. 1198.

[4] Augustine, *De Genesi ad Litteram*, v. xi; PL xxxiv. 330.

[5] Vincent de Beauvais argues that the six days of differentiation according to genera and species were an actual interval of time. He quotes Peter Lombard to the same effect (*Speculum Naturale*, II. xiv–xv; pp. 87–8). Cf. p. 281 n. 1.

One consideration favours Spenser's use of Augustine's theory. Among the forms in the garden are 'uncouth formes, which none yet ever knew' (stanza 35). This seems to mean that new species or mutations of existing species will appear in future on earth, but that their nature is already determined; that is, their forms already exist. Or it may simply refer to the forms of individuals, in existing species, that have not yet entered the round of generation or appeared on earth. In either case, these forms have to pre-exist bodies and must exist somewhere. They may be forms latent in matter, but in order to think of their union with matter our minds have to view them as separate from matter until corporeal union occurs. We tend to abstract and localize, as when we say 'the society of scholars' or 'the underworld of criminals', though the individuals so classified may be widely separated and have no knowledge of each other. So it may be with Spenser's garden of forms; while it is described as a place, it may not be a real place in any particular locality.[1] To what 'airy nothing' has he given 'a local habitation and a name'?[2]

The Anatomical Garden Again

We have earlier noticed, under Alciatus's emblem on Venus and Adonis (above, p. 242), Claudius Minos's gloss which identifies the genital organs of both sexes as a figurative garden. He did not call it a garden of Venus or of Adonis, but we can assume that Spenser made the connection; for the 'genital field' of the poem was the genitals of Adonis, and the 'genital field' was identified as a garden. The naked babes who are clothed with flesh by Genius and are sent out into the world would seem to be children awaiting bodies of flesh; they are ultimately sent out from the womb, which is therefore represented by the garden. The generation of their bodies, which is the union of form with matter, receives its initial impulse from the union of Venus and Adonis in the matter of the womb tempered with lunar moisture. This part of the allegory is reasonably clear. But the time from generation to birth is only nine months, while some of the forms in the garden have been there for a thousand years. It is necessary to account for their presence before the act of generation takes place.

---

[1] Cf. Roche (above, p. 240) and Stirling, *JEGP* xli. 483.
[2] Cf. Shakespeare's *Midsummer Night's Dream*, v. i. 16–17.

Ellrodt suggests that the forms are the seminal reasons, or *rationes seminales*, described by Augustine, for these carry on the characteristic features of species and individuals from one genera-tion to another.[1] Thus they could include the 'uncouth formes' which have not yet appeared in the world of bodies. Ellrodt also suggests that the 'babes' could be the vegetal souls of men.[2] The two suppositions differ somewhat in that numerous seminal reasons may be needed to produce one body,[3] whereas a body has only one vegetal soul. But, as Mrs. Bennett points out, the 'babes' and the 'formes' are not supposed to be identical, for the latter are garments for the souls to wear and are not the souls them-selves.[4] Some, but not all, of the forms and shapes appear to be bred from the returning souls (babes) which are planted like seeds in the garden. We can perhaps understand the matter better if we recall the Platonic view of the soul as a kind of internal sculptor that shapes *from within* the outward form of the human body.[5] Its instruments for this shaping are the seminal reasons appropriate to it. When the bodily flesh and the rational soul have both departed from it, the vegetal-sensible soul is replanted in the garden; that is, its seminal reasons, with their accompanying forms, are reintroduced there. The soul, as such, does not remain active and there is doubt whether it retains its identity (below, p. 273); it becomes active again only when Genius collects the seminal reasons for another 'babe' to go out into the world. It grows and flourishes in the garden *through* the seminal reasons which are its component parts and the outward expression of its form (above, p. 251).

Another theory of Augustine partially explains the allegory of the garden. He believed that the first created members of each species held in themselves the seminal reasons of all later members

---

[1] Note my suggestion that the seminal reasons correspond to the genes of modern embryology (above, p. 241). They may be called 'reasons' because they are reflections of the reason, or mind, of God, in which is the pattern world of ideas. They must be distinguished from Lucretius' *primordia* (first-beginnings), which are atoms of matter. Erigena's 'primordial causes' (below, p. 296) seem to be the seminal reasons.

[2] Ellrodt, *Neoplatonism in the Poetry of Spenser*, pp. 82–4.

[3] i.e. there may be a seminal reason for the head, one for the hand, one for the foot, etc.

[4] Bennett, *PMLA* xlvii. 61.

[5] Cf. Francesco Piccolomini (above, p. 50). Aquinas states that the vegetal soul is the 'substantial form' of the living body (*Summa Philosophiae*, ed. Cosmo Alamanno [Paris, 1890], 'De Anima', Q. 52, A. 1, ii. 49).

of the species, and that each later generation similarly held the
seminal reasons of those who should come after them. He based
this belief on Hebrews 7: 9, 10, where Paul states that Levi was
in the loins of Abraham (his great-grandfather) when the latter
paid his tithes. 'Why', asked Augustine, 'not say that Abraham
himself was in Adam, and Adam in the first works of the world
when God created all things together?'[1] He supported this view
by quoting Jeremiah 1: 5: 'Before I formed you in the womb, I
knew you', a verse which suggests some pre-existent form for the
unborn child even before its conception. Augustine thought that
the seminal reasons which determined the form of Adam might
have existed in Chaos, the first beginning of the material world,
but he admitted that they might have begun when God created
Adam from the slime of the earth.[2] This was a creation of the
vegetal soul (and possibly the sensible soul); the rational soul was
added when Adam was placed in the Garden of Eden, or Paradise
of Pleasure.[3]

So far as human generation is concerned, Spenser seems to have
united the hints taken from Claudius Minos and from Augustine.
The garden is a place of generation and growth, including the
genital organs of both sexes. But it is also a place of conservation,
in which the seminal reasons (like the genes) are preserved throughout the vicissitudes of time. It represents the genital areas of all
men and women in all centuries, beginning with Adam. The
seminal reasons and vegetal souls which go out of the garden in
newly formed bodies return to the garden in the genital areas of
the offspring. Some of the seminal reasons reappear in external
bodies only at long intervals, such as a thousand years; some
which will make the 'uncouth formes' have never appeared at all
but are nevertheless preserved in the 'genital field' or garden of
the body, and at the destined time will make their appearance.

The garden is described by Spenser as

> the first *seminary*
> Of all things that are borne to live and dye
> According to their kynds.   (stanza 30)

In supporting Augustine's theory of the conservation of the
seminal reasons, Abelard quoted Christ's answer to Nathaniel,

---

[1] *De Genesi ad Litteram*, VI. viii, *PL* xxxiv. 344.
[2] Ibid. VI. ix; pp. 344–5.   [3] Ibid. VII. xvi; p. 363. Cf. p. 279 n. 4.

who asked how he knew him: 'When you were under the fig tree, I saw you' (John 1 : 48). This, declares Abelard, was as much as to say: 'You have not at all begun to be known to me for the first time; you whom, through the *seminary* existing from the beginning in the first parents, I have known by prescience.'[1] Vincent de Beauvais writes: 'Just as a seed of any tree has a certain power so that, when buried in the earth, it may be reborn and put forth a sprout . . . so there is in the body what I may call a certain *seminary* whence in the time appointed by God's providence other kinds (*genera*) may be born.'[2] In Genesis 1, the Vulgate uses both *genera* and *species* in describing the creation of plants and animals 'after their kind'. Vincent seems to say that from the 'seminary' within the body will ultimately appear mutations which could be called a different genus; and he therefore implies that these future shapes are transmitted through the seminal reasons now present in bodies. This would account for the 'uncouth formes' growing in the Garden of Adonis.

Mrs. Bennett quotes 'the seminary powers of the members of the body' as being present in the fifth circle of Ficino's descending worlds, the one just above the world of forms in matter.[3] But Ficino uses the word 'seminary' so frequently and so variably that it is hard to limit his use to a particular meaning. He states that Plotinus called corporeal life the seminary world, though the ancients had called it an image of the seminary world;[4] Plotinus' position thus agrees with that of Abelard and Vincent, finding the 'seminary' in the human body. The position of the ancients is that the 'seminary' is incorporeal and that the corporeal world is its reflected image, essentially Mrs. Bennett's position. Even then it is possible to assume that this incorporeal world may be *in* but not *of* matter, just as Venus is infused in matter but is not matter itself (above, p. 237).

We may notice how the details of the garden accord with this interpretation. It has two gates, 'one faire and fresh, the other old and dride', which presumably reflect the states of souls going through them: one the souls about to be born in young babes, the other the souls of old and dried-up persons who have just died and return 'by the hinder gate'. The first gate may be what

---

[1] *Expositio in Hexaemeron, PL* clxxviii. 777ᴮ.
[2] *Speculum Naturale*, xxiv. 44; p. 1744ᴮ.
[3] *PMLA* xlvii. 61.
[4] *Com. in Plotinum*, ii. iii. 18; p. 1641.

Peter Comestor called 'the gate of propagation' (*porta propagationis*) in reference to the sex organs of Adam and Eve.[1] Alanus de Insulis quotes Job's phrase 'ostia ventris' (3 : 10) or 'gates of the womb' as referring to the Garden of Eden; the expulsion of Adam and Eve therefrom was like the expulsion of a child from the womb.[2] Again, Alanus interprets the 'gates' of Job 38 : 8 to mean the vulva.[3] Since the first of Spenser's gates is of iron—or is in an iron wall—there may be some significance in Andrew Marvell's phrase 'the iron gates of life' in allusion to the genital organs;[4] but I have not been able to find Marvell's sources (which may also have been Spenser's). As others have pointed out,[5] the golden wall comes from Claudian's account of Venus' garden, which also has a mount in the middle of the garden and a climate of eternal spring.[6] He also provides an account of the old man Genius—though not by name—and of Nature in the Garden of the Sun.[7]

Several examples of Genius have been noted.[8] To these may be added the account of Gyraldus, who quoted Cebes and gave the usual information about Genius but added that the marriage bed is called *genialis* because in it is the work of generating children.[9] In 'Epithalamion', 399, Spenser uses 'geniall bed' in just this way, invoking Genius as its guardianship. This suggests that *genialis* is used as an alternative form of *genitalis* and perhaps that *genius* is used as an alternative form of *genitus* (born).[10] Ficino uses the terms in this way when he discusses the possibility of rational souls' having existed before joining their bodies: 'Denique varietas geniorum varietatem adducit ingeniorum' ('Thence the variety of things born leads to the variety of things unborn'). Some

---

[1] *Historia Scholastica*, ch. 22, in *PL* cxcviii. 1072–3. Quoted by Vincent de Beauvais in *Speculum Naturale*, xxx. 75, p. 2271E.

[2] *Distinctiones*, *PL* ccx. 994C. [3] Ibid., p. 1012C.

[4] Marvell, 'To His Coy Mistress', l. 44. The phrase recalls to mind the Iron Gates of the River Danube, but these do not seem very relevant.

[5] *Var.* ii. 373, iii. 256, 345.

[6] *Epithalamium de Nuptiis Honori Augusti*, ll. 49–106.

[7] *On Stilicho's Consulship*, ll. 425–45. [8] *Var.* ii. 374–6, iii. 256.

[9] Lilius Gregorius Gyraldus, *Historia Deorum Gentilium*, Syntagma 15, in *Opera Omnia* (edn. of Lyons, 1696), p. 438. Vicenzo Cartari refers briefly to Genius as described by Cebes in *Imagini de gli Dei delli Antichi*: 'Baccho' (edn. of Padua, 1626), p. 369.

[10] In editions of Ovid's *Amores*, ii. xiii. 7, some editions (e.g. the Loeb edn.) read *genialisque arva*, but an edition of Paris, 1580, of the *Heroides* and other works, renders the same passage as *genitalisque arva*. Servius, glossing *genialibus* in the *Aeneid*, vi. 603, states that *geniales* are the female genitals.

persons, continues Ficino, will not admit the pre-existence of rational souls [e.g. Aquinas and Duns Scotus],[1] but Origen and Plotinus argue for it. On entering bodies some souls sink more deeply than others into the Lethean river; i.e. are submerged more deeply in matter.[2] This last remark shows that Ficino is thinking of Virgil's Elysian Fields (*Aeneid*, vi), where souls drink the oblivion of Lethe before proceeding into new bodies and a new earthly existence.

None of the descriptions of Genius is nearly so close to Spenser's account as the picture in Holbein's print, already described (above, p. 35). An aged, bearded man, labelled Genius, stands directly in the gateway to earthly life while the naked babes outside the wall—which would be the inside of Spenser's garden—lift their hands to him appealingly.

Ellrodt speculates as to whether these babes are rational souls or vegetal souls and concludes that they must be the latter.[3] The general belief was that the rational soul did not enter the body at its first conception and definitely was not imparted to the embryo through the parents, as was the vegetal soul. Each rational soul was created directly by God in a body already prepared to receive it, or else was fashioned outside the body and added to the body at an appropriate time. Aquinas and Scotus took the first view as the official doctrine of the Catholic Church. Vincent de Beauvais attributes to the Jews a belief that all souls were created together in the beginning of the world and deposited in one place, and that the Day of Judgement will come after they have all been incarnated into mortal bodies, but not before. But, Vincent adds, Christians say that new souls are created daily to be infused into newly formed bodies.[4] But, whatever the time of its creation, the rational soul did not enter the embryo until some time after

---

[1] Scotus says that rational souls *could* have been made in simultaneous creation but that the official Church doctrine is that each rational soul is made on the day it is infused into a body already 'organized' in the mother's womb (*Summa Theologica*, Q. 118, A. 3, iii. 1036. See also Q. 90, A. 4, iii. 794). He quotes the contrary view of Origen from *De Principiis*, I. vi and II. viii. Aquinas thinks such pre-existence of the rational soul to be impossible (*Summa Theologica*, pt. i, Q. 90, A. 4).

[2] Ficino, *De Immortalitate*, IX. v; p. 216.

[3] Ellrodt, *Neoplatonism in the Poetry of Spenser*, p. 82. Usually, but not always, when the vegetal soul is mentioned by Ficino, the sensible soul is understood to accompany it, since these two are non-rational and hence perishable. Scotus divides them, saying that the vegetal soul is imparted by the parents, but not the sensible soul (*Summa Theologica*, Q. 118, A. 1, iii. 1035).

[4] *Speculum Historiale*, xxv. 127; p. 1047 in *Opera*, vol. iv.

conception. Vincent attributes this opinion to Aristotle and gives his own estimate of seventy days after conception of the embryo as the period before the arrival of the rational soul.[1] Ficino estimates the period as forty-five days or forty-nine days.[2] Most commentators are not so specific, but Dante opined that the rational soul arrived when articulation of the brain cells was complete and the embryo was thus ready to receive its guest.[3] When the rational soul arrives, it takes over the task of 'organizing' the body from the vegetal and sensible souls,[4] which become united with it and under its direction. But the rational soul has nothing at all to do with the generation of the body or its first formation; that is the task of the vegetal soul or, as Ficino says, the non-rational life of the world.[5] Nor is the rational soul subject to repeated generation or absorption into the 'life' of the world; for at death it separates from its companions, the vegetal and sensible souls, and proceeds to the destination adjudged to it by God.[6]

Yet the rational soul is the very principle of form. Spenser writes in 'An Hymne in Honour of Beautie', 132–3 :

> For of the soule the bodie forme doth take :
> For soule is forme, and doth the bodie make.

He is speaking of the rational soul, which is immortal and cannot suffer corruption (line 161). But this soul does not initiate the first beginning of the body. Instead, it takes over the task of 'organizing' form in a body already existing as a foetus. Ficino, like Spenser, declares that the rational soul is form.[7] Stanyhurst says the same in *Harmonia*, p. 6.[8]

In Spenser's garden, the naked babes who appeal to Genius are vegetal souls before conception; they have not yet reached the stage of embryos.[9] The process of clothing them 'with sinfull mire' or flesh will take nine months, after which they will be sent

---

[1] *Speculum Naturale*, xxxi. 49; p. 2329A.

[2] *De Immortalitate*, xviii. vi; p. 406 (45 days); *Com. in Plotinum*, ii. iii. 7; p. 1625 (49 days).   [3] *Purgatorio*, xxv. 67–75.

[4] Vincent, *Speculum Naturale*, xxiv. 31; p. 1733A.

[5] *Com. in Philebum*, Appendix, xxi; p. 1262.

[6] Vincent, *Speculum Historiale*, i. 37; p. 15.

[7] *De Immortalitate*, vi. vii; p. 165, vi. xi; p. 167, x. iii; p. 228.

[8] Cf. p. 239 n. 2.

[9] In this view, I support Ellrodt's opinion against that of C. S. Lewis and Alastair Fowler (see Fowler, *Spenser and the Numbers of Time*, p. 136 n. 1). The babes are human souls-to-be, but not yet rational souls.

out into the world. At some time during the nine months, they will receive rational souls. One might argue that Spenser's failure to mention this point means that it does not take place in the garden, that the 'sinfull mire' refers only to the genital fluids and not to the resultant flesh, that the babes go out of the garden into the world when they enter the womb, not when they leave it. This would bring us nearer to Mrs. Bennett's original position that the garden is a world of forms. Yet, to be sent forth into the world seems a more appropriate description of birth than of conception, though it is true that the babes 'live in mortall state', subject to death, from the moment of their conception. Either point of view can be supported; my own view is that the garden includes the period of foetal life, that Spenser omitted to mention the advent of the rational soul because it is not part of the 'wheel' of generation, and that his reference to forms 'fitt for reasonable sowles t'indew' was sufficient evidence of human presence in the garden.

Genius shares with Fate the responsibility of determining which of the 'babes' shall enter upon life:

> Such as him list, such as eternall Fate
> Ordained hath, he clothes with sinfull mire.   (stanza 32)

Natalis Comes states that all things which are born—whether animals, plants, buildings, or states—have each a proper Genius by which they are perpetually governed; but they are also under the power of the Parcae, or Fate, which decrees that they must ultimately die.[1] Ficino states that Genius, the guardian spirit or daemon which accompanies man throughout life, has particular charge of the embryo during the forty-five days between conception and the arrival of the rational soul. One Genius can care for many human beings, leading them to birth at a time when the stars are favourable. Some attribute more influence to the wisdom of the Genius than to either Fate or Fortune.[2]

These two references associate Genius with Fate. The subjection of new vegetal souls to Fate at the moment of conception probably stems from Virgil's *Aeneid*, vi. 713–14:

> Animae, quibus altera fato
> Corpora debentur.

(Souls to which alternative bodies are assigned by Fate.)

---

[1] *Mythologiae*, III. vi; pp. 106–7.   [2] *De Immortalitate*, XVIII. vi; p. 406.

Ficino enlarges upon this idea: 'Then the soul, by a certain new motion more congenial to itself, turning towards mobile things and thus choosing a mobile life, thence goes forward into Fate, also in a measure before it enters the earthly body and before that body is conceived in the womb.'[1] He also quotes Plato's *Timaeus* to the effect that souls become subject to Fate when first they are joined to their vehicles (bodies).[2]

Since the soul becomes subject to Fate at or before the moment of conception, and since it is not joined by the rational soul for some weeks after conception, it is obvious that the soul described must be a vegetal or vegetal-sensible soul. This description applies to Spenser's 'naked babes' who are not yet clothed with bodies but will be so clothed when so ordained by Genius and Fate.[3] The babes are vegetal or vegetal-sensible souls awaiting transition into corporeal life.

The Wheel of Generation

After the 'babes' have run their course of earthly life, 'they agayn returne backe by the hinder gate' to be replanted and renewed in the garden:

> After that they againe retourned beene,
> They in that gardin planted bee agayne,
> And grow afresh, as they had never seene
> Fleshly corruption nor mortall payne.
> Some thousand yeares so doen they there remayne,
> And then of him are clad with other hew,
> Or sent into the chaungefull world agayne,
> Till thether they retourne, where first they grew:
> So *like a wheele* arownd they ronne from old to newe.
>
> (III. vi. 33)

According to the theory advanced in this chapter, the return of the babes is the survival of the vegetal or vegetal-sensible soul, or of its seminal reasons, in the genital areas of the next generation. The 'hinder gate' which is 'old and dride' suggests an analogy with the dry seed in which a plant preserves its seminal reasons and future potentialities of life. As the seed may re-

---

[1] *Com. in Plotinum*, II. iii. 15; p. 1636.

[2] Ibid. III: 'De Fato', viii; p. 1677.

[3] See Ellrodt's quotation from Boethius on Fate, *Neoplatonism in the Poetry of Spenser*, p. 69.

germinate after a long period of time, so the seminal reasons of a particular soul may be regenerated in new bodies after a thousand years or more.

The usual belief concerning the vegetal and sensible souls is that they perish with the body. Vincent de Beauvais quotes Aristotle's *De Morte et Vita* as authority for the destruction of the vegetal and sensible souls when the body is destroyed.[1] But this does not mean complete extinction. Rather, just as the matter of the body supplies material for other bodily forms, so the souls are reabsorbed into the World-Soul or the vegetal life of the world, and their decaying forms become part of the all-form.[2] They lose their individual identity but remain part of the 'life' of the world. They, like their counterpart matter, are not destroyed but are redistributed.

But Ficino does not wholly agree with this widely accepted theory. He thinks that the vegetal souls may, but do not necessarily, survive as individual entities and may be reclothed with bodily form. It may even happen that the vegetal or vegetal-sensible soul will reunite with the very same particles of matter that made up its body in a past existence, thus becoming physically the same person.[3] The mathematical odds against this occurrence are great, but it could happen. Again, he quotes the opinion of Plotinus: 'He touches upon this opinion: that the souls of all living things being cleansed [from matter] are able to be separated from their present bodies and not to be resolved into the soul of the universe, but to subsist in their own proper being and again to re-migrate to bodies.'[4] These two possible fates of the vegetal-sensible soul—loss of identity through mingling with the World-Soul, or the retention of its identity to return in other bodies—seem to be reflected in Spenser's lines:

> And then of him [Genius] are clad with other hew,
> Or sent into the chaungefull world agayne.

The 'other hew' has caused some debate between Stirling and Mrs. Bennett. She suggested that the phrase referred to the rational soul's promotion to heaven after undergoing the round

---

[1] *Speculum Naturale*, xxiii. 73; p. 1703A.

[2] Ficino, *Com. in Plotinum*, VI. vi. 7; p. 1785, VI. vii. 10; p. 1789.

[3] Ibid. IV. iii. 8; p. 1735.

[4] Ibid. III: 'De Providentia', i. 15; p. 1695. Cf. George Buchanan's *De Sphaera* i. 50–1.

of generation, while he thought that it simply meant the soul's assuming another body.[1] Mrs. Bennett was right in her general idea but wrong in applying it to rational souls, which do not undergo the successive rounds of generation. This exemption of the rational soul from mutability distinguishes the Christian faith from the oriental doctrines of Karma and Nirvana, which are very much like the theories of Ficino as just enunciated.

The cyclical nature of the vegetal-sensible soul's departure and return is expressed in the image of the wheel. Mrs. Bennett and Ellrodt have discussed this wheel in terms of the Fable of Er in Plato's *Republic*, Book x (614–21), where is described the aerial meadow in which souls arrive to assume different bodies.[2] Ficino has something to say about this aerial meadow. He discusses the numerical symbolism of the thousand-year intervals, the number being the cube of ten. The denarius (10) is a 'perfect' number and signifies completion. Hence Virgil uses both the square and the cube of ten. Of the souls whose bodies are not ceremonially buried, he says, 'Centum errant annos' ('They wander a hundred years'; *Aeneid*, vi. 329). Of the souls in the Elysian Fields awaiting rebirth, he says, 'Mille rotam volvere per annos' ('They turn the wheel through a thousand years'; ibid. vi. 748). The aerial meadow, says Ficino, might be considered an obverse of the Christian purgatory, a place of temporal rewards as against a place of temporal punishments; in neither case is the condition eternal. This aerial meadow must be contiguous to those upper plains of Earth which Plato describes in *Phaedo*, 110, in the form of an earthly paradise where the happy inhabitants enjoy perpetual spring. Some place the Elysian Fields in the aerial meadow, but Ficino insists that they are on Earth, since the celestial Elysium is in the eighth heaven [Fixed Stars].[3]

It thus appears that Ficino closely related Plato's Vision of Er to Virgil's description of the Elysian Fields, and that the image of the wheel comes from the latter source. Plato uses the spinning-wheel of the Fates to determine the lots of men's lives, but the birth–death cycle is not described as a wheel, as in Virgil and Spenser. The context of Virgil's line had considerable influence

---

[1] Bennett, *PMLA* xlvii. 57; Stirling, *PMLA* xlix, 521.

[2] Bennett, *PMLA* xlvii. 54; *JEGP* xli. 55; Ellrodt, *Neoplatonism in the Poetry of Spenser*, p. 74.

[3] *Epitome de Republica*, x; p. 1432.

upon medieval ideas concerning purgatory, as I have shown else-where.[1]

Spenser's wheel of generation also has Christian antecedents. In James 3 : 6, already quoted (above, p. 190), the phrase 'ton trochon tēs geneseōs', translated in the Authorized Version as 'the course of nature', is rendered in the Vulgate as 'rotam nativi-tatis nostrae' ('the wheel of our nativity'). This phrase may be reflected in an early print of the Seven Ages of Man, noticed by John Winter Jones, which shows the life of man as a wheel, beginning to revolve from the earth with *Generacio* and returning to the same place with *Corrupcio*.[2] These terms reflect the cycle of life discussed in Aristotle's *De Generatione et Corruptione*, the work on which most subsequent discussions are based. Viewed as a cycle, or wheel, mortal life, death, and returning life seem to imitate the heavens, in which bodies have a circular motion and to some degree control the fluctuating changes in the sublunar world below. It is to this wheel of the sky that we owe the ravages of Time in the garden, a knotty point that has baffled all com-mentators. The most reasonable explanation was given by T. P. Harrison, who thought that the top of the mount containing Venus' bower was immortal, while the rest of the garden was mortal.[3] But the explanation lies elsewhere.

Among the books which Spenser had probably read was Eusebius' *Preparation for the Gospel* (*Preparatio Evangelica*), which E. K. quotes in his gloss on Pan in the May Eclogue of *The Shepheardes Calender*. Eusebius discusses Plato's account of the 'wheel' of the sky in *Politicus*, 269. God guides the wheel in its usual direction but sometimes withdraws his hand. On such occasions, the celestial world of its own will soon begins to revolve in the opposite direction, reversing the course of genera-tion. Eusebius declares that the change involves great destruction of both animal and human life (xi. 32). Bodies long buried in the earth spring again from the earth when the 'wheel of generation' is turned in an opposite direction (xi. 33). After the wheel has counter-revolved by its own will for a time, God takes the helm

---

[1] 'The Pains of the Afterworld: Fire, Wind, and Ice in Shakespeare and Milton', *PMLA* lxxi (1956), 482–95.

[2] See my book *Shakespeare's Derived Imagery* (1953; reprint by Octagon Books, 1967), p. 18.

[3] Harrison, 'Divinity in Spenser's Garden of Adonis', University of Texas *Studies in English* (1939), 48–73.

and turns it into its former circuit, endowing the earth with immortality and perpetual youth (xi. 34).

This notion of recurrent periods when the earth would suffer great destruction from the motion of the heavens had considerable currency. Eusebius illustrates it by quoting Isaiah 34: 4: 'And the heaven shall be rolled together as a scroll', and Isaiah 65: 17: 'And the heaven shall be new and the earth new.' It is this idea of renewal which differentiates such periods of destruction from the Last Judgement. Such destruction and renewal shall come successively in 'the great year of the world', which Natalis Comes thinks will come every 12,000 years, or perhaps 36,000 by modern methods of reckoning.[1] Ficino observes that some persons say 36,000, others 39,000, years as the interval between these times of destruction. The great year of the world comes when all the heavenly bodies have returned to the same position in which they originally stood.[2] Ficino envisions the 'renewal' as a basic change in the seminal reasons themselves. In the great year of the world there will be relatively few mutations of lives; in the following year there will be none at all. Instead, there will be resurrection of the same persons after a period of death.[3] Ficino thus expands upon his idea that already vegetal-sensible souls can 'die' and retain their identity. His notion that such a soul could possibly resume the same material substance and become the same person would be the rule and not the exception after the great year of the world.[4]

Returning to Eusebius, we can see that a reversal of the wheel of generation would cause widespread confusion, if not destruction, among the seminal reasons themselves. All that were lately born in bodies would have to become unborn; the man would return to childhood and then to seminal reasons in the loins of his own parents. If the reversed cycle were allowed to run back through Adam, the human race would cease to exist except as a capability in the matter of Chaos. Yet the earth is renewed to greater happiness and pleasure than before. Thus the ravages of Time in Spenser's garden may mean the apparent destruction of the seminal reasons and their accompanying forms, which had

---

[1] *Mythologiae*, III. xx; p. 147.
[2] *Com. in Plotinum*, v. vii. 3; p. 1767.   [3] Ibid. v. vii. 1; p. 1767.
[4] Not entirely the same person, since the rational soul would be different. It is not subject to cycles of death and rebirth.

seemed immortal but were subject to mortality of a kind in the great year of the world.

Of course, destruction can enter the garden in other ways. From conception to birth, the 'babes' are subject to death in the maternal womb,[1] a matter of daily occurrence. Venus may grieve over the loss of these embryos, though presumably their seminal reasons would remain in the garden under another form. But Venus, the cosmic mother in whose lap Love first awaked in Chaos, would grieve also for the wholesale destruction wrought among the forms in her garden at long intervals of time.

The Paradise of Pleasure

Among the lost works of Spenser, mentioned by the printer of his *Complaints* (1591), are '*Ecclesiastes* and *Canticum Canticorum* translated'.[2] The form used for the title of the Song of Songs suggests that Latin was the language from which the two works were translated. The probable version used was the Vulgate, which had been accepted by the Council of Trent as the authentic translation, out of some forty Latin translations. To study the Church Fathers, as he obviously seems to have done, Spenser would have needed to know the Vulgate. It is quite possible that he had studied other Latin translations as well.

The Vulgate version of the Old Testament did not appear in English until 1609,[3] after Spenser's death. Some highly significant differences between the Latin text and that of other English versions appear in Genesis 2: 4–8. In the main the Authorized Version (1611) follows the earlier English readings of this passage and may be used for purposes of comparison. The Latin text follows:

4. Istae sunt generationes caeli et terrae, quando creata sunt, in die quo fecit Dominus Deus caelum et terram

5. et omne virgultum agri, antequam *oriretur* in terra, omnemque herbam regionis, priusquam germinaret; non enim pluerat Dominus Deus super terram, et homo non erat, qui operaretur terram;

6. sed *fons* ascendebat e terra irrigans universam superficiem terrae.

---

[1] Cf. Ellrodt, *Neoplatonism in the Poetry of Spenser*, p. 81.

[2] Italics not mine.

[3] The Douai Version; the New Testament had been translated in 1582 from the Vulgate, as the Rheims Version.

7. Formavit igitur Dominus Deus hominem de *limo* terrae et inspiravit in faciem eius spiraculum vitae, et factus est homo in animam viventem.

8. *Plantaverat* autem Dominus Deus *paradisum voluptatis a principio*, in quo posuit hominem quem formaverat.

The italicized words are those which mark the principal differences from the English versions. These mention 'every plant of the field before it *was* in the earth', whereas the Latin reads, 'before it *should be born* in the earth'. The difference is significant, allowing for the presence of seminal reasons in the matter of the earth before they appeared in corporeal forms.

Adam was formed by God *de limo terrae*, from slime or mud of the earth, instead of from 'dust', as in the English versions.[1] We have pointed out Spenser's several uses of 'slime' as an equivalent of human flesh (above, p. 137). It is also the 'sinfull mire' which clothes the babes as they leave the garden. In describing Belphoebe's birth, Spenser writes:

> And all her whole creation did her shew
> Pure and unspotted from all loathly crime,
> That is ingenerate in *fleshly slime*. (III. vi. 3)

After Adam's fall because of disobedience, his flesh, which otherwise would have remained pure, was corrupt, and all the works of nature were similarly tainted and made subject to death. Belphoebe's birth from 'the chaste Chrysogone', as Theocritus had called her,[2] was pure in that it involved no coitus before conception and therefore no masculine semen, and no 'sinfull' pleasure, but only the energizing power of the sun, directly applied to matter tempered by moisture. This same explanation was sometimes given for the conception of Christ in the womb of the Virgin Mary.[3] Those who thought the masculine semen necessary

---

[1] The use of 'slime' makes the creation of Adam much more like Prometheus' creation of man from earth mixed with water (Ovid, *Metamorphoses*, i. 80–3).

[2] Spenser's choice of Chrysogone's name probably stems from Gyraldus's account of Theocritus' *Epigrams*, no. 16, in which 'the chaste Chrysogone' gives to her husband Amphicles a statue of Venus Urania, not Venus Pandemos. The couple lived platonically, and Chrysogone remained a virgin (Gyraldus, *Historia Deorum Gentilium*, Syntagma 13, in *Opera Omnia* [edn. of Lyons, 1696], p. 389).

[3] Cf. Sannazarius, *De Partu Virginis*, ii. 372 (*Var.* iii. 250). In Murillo's painting *The Immaculate Conception*, the Virgin is 'clothed with the sun' (cf. Rev. 12 : 1), which is the agent of generation. The first poem in John of Garland's *Stella Maris* (ed. Wilson, 1946) calls Christ 'Sol de sole, nata prolis' ('The Sun from the sun, an

for human generation explained that Mary was impregnated by 'dew' shed from the wings of the Holy Spirit.[1] Spenser glances at this theory also in the first line of Stanza 3:

> Her berth was of the wombe of morning dew.

As earlier stated, the reading 'a paradise of pleasure' inevitably affects the meaning of Genesis 2: 8, stressing the element of sexual enjoyment (above, p. 136). This single variant reading is largely responsible for the gardens of love and paradises where love is exercised without sin that we find throughout medieval folklore.[2] Spenser reflects this reading when he calls his sweetheart's bosom 'the bowre of blisse, the paradise of pleasure' (*Amoretti*, 76). In the June Eclogue of *The Shepheardes Calender*, E. K. glosses 'Paradise' as 'a garden of pleasure, or place of delights', and locates the earthly paradise of Eden somewhere in Mesopotamia. In Hebrew, *Eden* means 'delights' but could also be used as a place-name.

The pleasure of this garden, however, is subordinate to its main purpose: to serve as a garden of generation. At the founding of this garden, there was no animal life or human life in it. Adam was made outside the garden in the Damascene Field,[3] and his first creation involved only his vegetal and sensible souls; the rational soul was added when he was placed in the garden.[4] Animal life in the garden was brought forth *after* Adam was placed there, thus reversing the order stated in Genesis 1. It was this discrepancy that caused Augustine to develop his theory of

offspring born'). In G. M. Dreves's *Analecta Hymnica* (Leipzig, 1904), vol. xlvi, no. 110, a poem on the virgin birth contains these lines:

> Lumine solari nescit vitrum violari,
> Nec vitrum sole nec virgo puerpera prole.

(The glass knows not itself to be violated by the solar ray, neither the glass by the sun nor the bearing Virgin by her offspring.)

Cf. Spenser on Chrysogone: 'Unwares she them conceiv'd, unwares she bore' (above, p. 137).

[1] Cf. Todd's quotation from *Liber Festivalis* (*Var.* iii. 250); Abbot Rupert's commentaries (*PL* clxviii. 201C, 1329A). In Leo Juchae's Latin translation of the Psalms, there appears this marginal note to Ps. 110: 3 (109: 4 in Latin edns.): 'ab utero et ab aurora ros natiuitatis tuae' ('from the womb and from the morning is the dew of your birth'). Editions appeared in 1545, 1584, and 1605.

[2] See the many examples in Meyer and Nutt, *The Voyage of Bran* (London, 1895).

[3] Comestor, *Historia Scholastica*, ch. 13, in *PL* cxcviii. 1067A.

[4] Augustine, *De Civitate Dei*, xiii. xxiii, in *PL* xli. 396; Eucherius, *PL* l. 906C; Angelomus, *PL* cxv. 128A, B. Cf. p. 266 n. 3.

dual creation: first the simultaneous causal creation of form, matter, and the seminal reasons of all future beings; and second, the daily generation of bodies through a union of form and matter.[1]

In the passages quoted above, the English versions make it appear that the order of creation was: incorporeal plants, the fountain or mist, Adam, the garden, corporeal plants, the animals, Eve. Except for the first item, all of these belong to the second creation, the bringing forth of bodies and objects into the corporeal world. But the author of the Vulgate and/or Jerome, who edited it, were not satisfied with this order. Instead of 'eastward' they wrote *a principio* (from the beginning), in order to refer back to *in principio* of Genesis 1: 1. We have already noticed that this was interpreted to mean the first creation of matter, or Chaos, out of nothingness, before any distinct forms had developed. Thus, the Paradise of Pleasure was formed coincidentally with Chaos itself and was figuratively the scene of all future generation except that of Adam, who was specifically exempted by the language of verse 8. To emphasize the earlier creation of the garden, the verb was made pluperfect instead of perfect, *plantaverat* instead of *plantavit*. Jerome defends these readings on the grounds just stated.[2] The change allowed the incorporeal herbs of 2: 5 to be planted in the garden and the fountain to irrigate the garden, which now preceded them in order of time. Thus the garden included both the incorporeal herbs of 2: 5 and the corporeal trees of 2: 9.

Most of the hexameral writers agree that the herbs and plants of 2: 5 refer back to Chapter 1 and the creation of the third day, when the plants were created before the sun, moon, and stars. But this creation was *causaliter* only.[3] From the plan or pattern in the mind of God, the seminal reasons were reflected and placed in the earth as seeds, to emerge as corporeal forms when the ground was irrigated with moisture.

Yet the account in Chapter 1 was stated in terms of plants actually growing in a garden:

11. Et [Deus] ait: Germinet terra herbam virentem et facientem semen

---

[1] *De Genesi ad Litteram*, vi. ii, in *PL* xxxiv. 340.

[2] In *Hebraice Quaestiones in Genesim*, *PL* xxiii. 940–1. Augustine seems not to have used this reading, for he quotes *plantavit* instead of *plantaverat* (*PL* xxxiv. 374).

[3] Augustine, *De Genesi ad Litteram*, v. iv, in *PL* xxxiv. 325.

et lignum pomiferum faciens fructum iuxta *genus* suum, cuius
semen in semetipso sit super terram. Et factum est ita.

12. Et protulerat terra herbam virentem et facientem semen iuxta
genus suum lignumque faciens fructum et habens unumquodque
sementem secundum *speciem* suam.

These verses do not vary significantly from the Authorized
Version except that *genus* and *species* are both interpreted as 'kind',
in Spenser as 'sort' (above, p. 250).

The pre-dating of the garden to the first formation of Chaos in
Genesis 1 : 1 means that this first creation of plants supposedly
took place in the garden. If the seminal reasons were all created
with Chaos (above, p. 266), Genesis 1 : 11–12 marks the first
differentiation and classification among them, the separation into
genera and species. Gregory the Great had modified Augustine's
theory of simultaneous creation by stating that the substance of
all created things was created simultaneously, but not the separate
species of things.[1] In Genesis 2 : 4 we revert to this creation of the
third day which took place just after dry land had appeared and
was called earth. In 2 : 5 the plants are described as living before
they germinated or were born in the earth; they are seminal
reasons and/or incorporeal forms in the garden. With the advent
of moisture in verse 6, they cross over into corporeal existence
and sprout as trees in verse 9. The process is like that of planting
seeds and watering the soil to hasten germination; but as yet there
had been no corporeal plants to produce seeds, so these first plants
existed in the earth as seminal reasons only. In the next generation
of plants, the power of the seminal reasons would be enclosed
in the corporeal seeds. But the Paradise of Pleasure includes both
their corporeal and their incorporeal forms. Spenser's Garden
of Adonis follows the same pattern; its puzzling inconsistencies
simply result from the hexameral tradition.

Spenser describes the plants before their transition to corporeal
form:

> Ne needs there gardiner to sett or sow,
> To plant or prune: for of their own accord
> All things, as they created were, doe grow,
> And yet remember well the mighty word
> Which first was spoken by th'Almighty Lord,

[1] Quoted by Remigius, *Commentarium in Genesim*, PL cxxxi. 59C.

That bad them to increase and multiply:
Ne doe they need with water of the ford
Or of the clouds to moysten their roots dry;
For in themselves eternall moisture they imply.
(stanza 34)

The absence of a gardener—'as yet there was no man to till the ground'—and the absence of moisture are clear reminiscences of Genesis 2 : 5. The injunction to increase and multiply is recalled from Genesis 1 : 22, 28. The 'mighty word' represents the Word or Logos which is the second person of the Trinity. God was God the Father; the spirit borne above the waters (Gen. 1 : 2) was the Holy Spirit. The Word or Logos played its part in creation as the word which expressed the thought in the mind of God; e.g. 'Let there be light!'[1]

In general, the reasoning in the above paragraphs follows that of Augustine. He states that on the third day the nature of plants and trees was created in the earth causally and potentially: 'So indeed the earth, at the word of God, brought them forth before they were born, accepting all numbers of those whom it should extend through the ages according to their kind (*genus*).'[2] To accept 'all numbers' means that the earth received the seminal reasons of all future individual bodies, not merely of their species or type-forms. Explaining further Genesis 2 : 5, Augustine says that certain plants require rain for generation and that others require human tillage: 'But then both were lacking. Therefore God did this by the power of his Word, without rain and without human tillage.'[3] Spenser makes exactly this point about the Garden of Adonis. The incorporeal plants grow without the need of external moisture and human tillage, for they were established as self-subsistent by the Word of God.

Augustine's *rationes seminales* are not the same as the ideas of things existing in the mind of God. They are a stage lower, having been produced at the first creation of matter as reflections of the ideas and as agents for re-creating the ideal forms in material substance. They were accepted by the Scholastics but were denied the power of initiating generation; they were not the efficient cause.[4] They are the forms, or the seeds that blossom into forms,

---

[1] Augustine, *De Genesi ad Litteram*, vi. viii, in *PL* xxxiv. 344. Cf. above, p. 255.
[2] Ibid. v. v; p. 326.   [3] Ibid. v. vi; p. 327.
[4] Cf. Michael J. McKeough, *The Meaning of the 'Rationes Seminales' in Saint Augustine* (Catholic University Press, 1926). Cf. p. 241 n. 1.

in Spenser's garden. He includes the efficient cause in the functions of Adonis (above, p. 252).

The generative character of the Paradise of Pleasure is further stressed in the figurative interpretations of it. Gregory the Great writes:

Paradise is the womb of the human race, whose gates the serpent opened.— Because for every man there is a mother's womb, for this universal human race there existed that highest habitation of Paradise. For from it went out the offspring of the human race as though from a womb and flowed through the gates for the augmentation of progeny just as for the increase of the body. There our conception coalesced, where dwelt the first man, the origin of all men.[1]

A variation of this theme is found in a curious book by the Swiss physician Paracelsus, *Azoth, sive De Ligno et Linea Vitae*. In this book 'concerning the Tree and Line of Life' the author set himself to explore the *arcana* or secrets of things. Man himself is the book in which these secrets can be studied (p. 675).[2] According to Paracelsus, Paradise represents the womb (*matrix*) of the great world or macrocosm, in which all things, including Adam and Eve themselves, were formed. But it also represents the womb of the little world (microcosm) of mankind, the womb which Eve had within herself (p. 681):

For the womb of the macrocosmic and of the microcosmic woman is the same. Whence it also follows that the *Enur* of the womb of a little world is dead if the *Enur* of the womb of the great world lets slip one grain of life. . . . *Enur* is the force and power, and the spiritual seed of power, of the root of any particular tree. For as first the root of a tree perishes, then both branches and fruit and finally the whole tree perish; so likewise the womb, which is nothing other than a branch of Venus in the heaven. For the *Enur* of the womb of the great world is Venus and the moon; and any womb of any woman is a branch of that root and tree of the great world; i.e. of Venus. And just as a pear is the fruit of a tree, so also the womb of any woman is a pear and fruit of its tree; and that tree is Venus and the womb of the great world, yet distributed into four parts according to the four elements. And the small womb of the little world is the fruit and branch of the womb, or of the tree which is the womb. And just as man generates only man,

---

[1] Gregory, *Moralium*, IV. xii, in *PL* lxxv. 649. Alanus quotes these lines in his *Distinctiones*, *PL* ccx. 994B. Italics not mine.

[2] Paracelsus, *Opera* (Latin tr.) (edn. of Geneva, 1658), vol. i, pp. 675 ff. Page references to this edition are given in the text.

so also the womb of the great world generates nothing other than the womb of the little world. And just as from one tree hang many pears, of which one falls more quickly than another since one matures more quickly than another, clearly in the same manner the fourfold tree of the womb of the great world also bears many branches and fruits, which are nothing else than the wombs of the little world.[1]

Paracelsus works out this theme in great detail. In sexual relations, Adam seeks in woman the Paradise which he had lost and in which grew the Tree of Life that gave immortality, while Eve seeks from Adam the eternal substance which caused the generation of life in the original Paradise. (Paracelsus's name for this substance is Limbo [p. 683].) Adam and Eve cannot attain their whole desire, but God allows them to attain an earthly immortality through their offspring, so that mankind may remain in the nature of the world through successive generations (pp. 684–5).

Paracelsus's work clarifies several details for us. It places Venus in the Biblical Paradise of Pleasure and shows in what sense she is the mother of the world. It explains the macrocosmic and microcosmic nature of Paradise as a place of generation, including simultaneously the immaterial seminal reasons and the genital organs of the human race. It suggests that this dual nature of the Garden of Adonis proceeds from current interpretations of the Paradise of Pleasure itself. It represents the Tree of Life as a 'family tree' of the human race, like the tree Yggdrasill of Norse mythology,[2] or like Ficino's World-Tree, with 'the common vegetal power from the World-Soul flourishing whole everywhere in the World-Tree'.[3] In equating Venus (and the moon) with the Tree of Life, it unites classical and Christian symbols of the generation of life.

We have already noted Spenser's account of Love's being woken by Clotho in Venus' lap in Chaos at the time decreed by the Fates (above, p. 258). Clotho's role is explained by Ficino's account of the three Parcae, or Fates, who are daughters of Necessity. Necessity he interprets as the World-Soul, the vegetal part of which is called by three names:

Lachesis, because she is heavy with the seeds of things, and with the lots and forms of lives which she will insert into souls about to descend;

---

[1] Italics not mine.
[2] See Carlyle's *Heroes and Hero-Worship*: 'The Hero as Divinity'.
[3] *Com. in Plotinum*, iv. iii. 8; p. 1736.

afterwards *Clotho*, since by her ordinance she evolves the inserted lots of life into the act of living and spreads them into effect; last, *Atropos*, since by a certain indeclinable progression she conserves and guards lives already evolved into act, even to their inevitable end.[1]

Clotho's part is to promote the seeds and forms from potential to active existence; hence she is pictured as awaking Love from his sleep in Spenser's poem.[2]

Spenser refers again to this appearance of Love in *Colin Clout's Come Home Again*, 799–804:

> For him the greatest of the gods we deeme,
> Borne without syre or couples of one kynd,
> For Venus selfe doth soly couples seeme,
> Both male and female through commixture joynd.
> So pure and spotlesse Cupid forth she brought,
> And in the Gardens of Adonis nurst.

The passage following pictures Love as the agent of creation of the Cosmos from Chaos, the harmonizing force that brought the elements into peaceful concord. The creation is briefly described. After the earth emerges from the waters,

> everie living wight
> Crept forth like wormes out of her slimie nature,
> Soone as on them the suns life giving light
> Had powred kindly heat and formall feature.   (859–62)

The 'slimie nature' of the earth is the *limus terrae* of which God made Adam; Spenser assumes that it was also used for the other animals. His account seems to be an interpretation of Genesis in terms of Lucretius, who wrote that in their first creation animals emerged from 'wombs' in the earth, in the manner of plants.[3]

We have already discussed the masculo-feminine nature of Venus (above, p. 246). The appearance of Cupid, or Love, stems from the first creation in Genesis 1, for the Garden of Adonis, or Paradise of Pleasure, had been created simultaneously with Chaos in the very beginning of all things.

The principal element of Spenser's garden not supplied by the Paradise of Pleasure is the image of the wheel of generation. As

---

[1] *Epitome de Republica X*; p. 1434.

[2] This derivation seems to me more likely than Mrs. Bennett's suggestion of indebtedness to Pico (*Var.*: *Minor Poems*, i. 512).

[3] Lucretius, *De Rerum Natura*, v. 808.

already observed, this detail probably came from the Elysian Fields as described by Virgil. Ficino's own account of the aerial meadow of Plato draws upon Virgil for the image of the wheel of generation (above, p. 274).

Ficino describes the earthly paradise as follows:

> And Plato calls Earth the most ancient goddess of all the gods that are within the sky. He adds that vast regions of the earth, higher in a manner than ours, are inhabited, where stones, metals, plants, and animals are beyond measure more remarkable and more beautiful, where men remain alive for a very long time and in the matter of food are happily nourished with odours, since they are most precious [cf. *Phaedo*, 110]. . . . This is very like those accounts that in the divine gardens, as if in the Elysian Fields, men would have been able to live immortal by only tasting of the Tree of Life.[1]

The accounts of the beauty of the Garden of Adonis, with eternal spring, perennial harvests, and sinless love, are accounts of the Paradise of Pleasure as it would have been if Adam had not disobeyed God. Neither he nor his descendants would have lived there for ever, but after a long life they would have been translated to a higher plane of existence without undergoing the pangs of death.[2]

The various excellent studies of earthly 'paradises' make it unnecessary to pursue the subject further.[3] The elusive quest for a lost perfection, for a lost state of innocence, is the basis of these myths. This aspect of Paradise belongs to the corporeal world, not to the world of forms and seminal reasons. The twofold nature of Spenser's garden reflects the twofold nature of the Paradise of Pleasure and the edifice of interpretation which has been erected upon it.

'TWO CANTOS OF MUTABILITIE'

The Celestial World

We now ascend to 'the star-bearing spheres, and the sublime realm of the shining sky immune to age and immutable with one

---

[1] *De Immortalitate*, XVI. vi; p. 377.

[2] Augustine, *De Genesi ad Litteram*, IX. iii, in *PL* xxxiv. 395.

[3] See Howard R. Patch's *The Other World* (1950) for the most complete treatment; also various articles in James Hastings's *Encyclopedia of Religion and Ethics*; also Mrs. Bennett's articles herein cited.

face', as described by George Buchanan.[1] The whole purpose of
the 'Cantos of Mutabilitie' is to speculate on whether the substance
of these words is in fact true.

The background of the 'Cantos' is the struggle between the
dynasty of Jove and the family of his uncle or uncles, the Titans.
Mutabilitie is called a Titaness. It is the same subject as that used
by Keats in 'Hyperion'. Natalis Comes speaks of the Titans' overthrow as representing 'mutations of the elements'. He also speaks
of the goddess Fortuna as having almost overthrown Jove in
order to seize the rule of heaven for her own hands.[2] Since
we have seen in Chapter I (above, p. 9) the evidence that Mutabilitie is based on Fortuna, Comes's identification assumes added
significance.

Mutabilitie arouses herself some time after the defeat of her
family. She has been allowed to control the world below the moon;
but now she decides to seize control of the moon itself and, when
challenged, boldly asserts her right to rule over all the heavenly
bodies, since all are subject to change. When Jove seeks to contro-
vert her, she appeals to the goddess Nature for a final decision
upon the justice of her claim.

In the argument at Nature's court, Mutabilitie has little difficulty in establishing her claim to dominion over the lower world
and adduces the ravages of Time as evidence of her supremacy
(vii. 47). Jove replies that he and the other gods, as planets, rule
over Time and compel him 'to keepe his course'. As the planets
rule over Time, they also rule over change, or Mutabilitie
(stanza 48). The latter, unimpressed, points out that the planets
themselves constantly change their place and their appearance,
being eclipsed, being dimmed during the day, and varying their
distance from the earth. The basis of her argument appears in
stanza 55:

> Besides, the sundry motions of your spheares,
> So sundry waies and fashions as clerkes faine,
> Some in short space, and some in longer yeares;
> What is the same but *alteration* plaine?

[1]   . . . orbes
Astriferi, et nitidi sublimis regia caeli
Immunis senii, et vultu immutabilis uno.
(*De Sphaera*, i. 39–41)

[2] *Var.* vi–vii. 410.

Onely the starrie skie doth still remaine:
Yet do the starres and signes therein still move,
And even it self is mov'd, as wizards saine.
But all that moveth doth mutation love:
Therefore both you and them to me I subject prove.

The 'starrie skie' refers to the circle of Fixed Stars; 'still' in line 5 means 'at rest'; in line 6, 'still' signifies continuation. The reference is to the slow motion of the stars known today as the precession of the equinoxes; it is this motion which completes a revolution in the great year of the world (above, p. 276).

Spenser's use of the term 'alteration' is highly significant; for Aquinas, interpreting Aristotle, makes a sharp distinction between the process of *alteration* and that of *generation and corruption*: '[Aristotle] therefore first said that Democritus and Leucippus, who made the beginnings of things to be indivisible bodies of infinite figures, from these caused *generation* and *alteration*. For they said that through the congregation and separation of the said figured bodies were caused *generation and corruption*, but through mutation of the order and position of the said bodies was caused *alteration*.'[1]

Here the 'indivisible bodies of infinite figures' are the atoms of Democritus, who expressed the nature of matter in this way. When these atoms conglutinated to form a body, it was said to be *generated*; when they separated, the body was said to be *corrupted*, or to die. But if the body changed its location or appearance while still containing all its conglutinated atoms, it was said to be *altered*.

Again Aquinas writes: 'Therefore to these suppositions he adds that *alteration* occurs when the sensible subject remains the same, namely when there is made a transmutation in its passions or qualities, with no transmutation in its substance.'[2]

Vincent de Beauvais makes a similar distinction based on the same passages from Aristotle. *Alteration* occurs when the body remains the same by number, retaining the same individual particles of its substance, but has mutation in its passions or qualities. Unlike Aquinas, he does not think that change of place should be called *alteration*: that is *ambulation*, while to add or lose part of one's substance is called *augmentation* or *diminution*.[3] Spenser's

---

[1] *Com. in De Gen. et. Cor.*, bk. i, ii. iii. 3.   [2] Ibid., bk. i, iv. x. 2.
[3] *Speculum Naturale*, iii. 42, p. 188c.

Mutabilitie, like Aquinas, includes change of place under her definition of *alteration*.

Aquinas makes another very significant distinction between these terms:

> [Aristotle] therefore first says that from all those philosophers who state that all things were produced from one material beginning it is necessary to say that *generation and corruption* are the same as *alteration*. For they state that that material beginning is a certain 'being' by act, such as fire or air or water, and they state that that is the substance of all things which are generated from it; and, just as matter always remains in those things which are made from matter, so they state that that substance always remains one and the same. This, however, we call *alteration* when, the substance remaining the same from the act of existence, there is made some variation as to form. Whence it follows that there can be no transmutation which is rightly called *generation and corruption*, but only *alteration*. But we say that there is one first substance of all generable and corruptible things, which is not yet 'being' by act but only by potentiality [i.e. first matter]. And therefore whatever from it accepts form, through which is made 'being' by act, is called simply *generation*; but from this whatever, after it has become 'being' by act, undergoes any other form, is said to experience *alteration*.[1]

The effect of this distinction is to identify generation and corruption with birth and death only; changes of appearance are alteration.[2]

Spenser may have had this distinction in mind when he described the 'substaunce' in the Garden of Adonis:

> That substaunce is eterne, and bideth so,
> Ne when the life decayes, and forme does fade,
> Doth it consume and into nothing goe,
> But chaunged is, and often *altred* to and froe.

> The substaunce is not chaungd nor *altered*,
> But th'only forme and outward fashion.　　(III. vi. 37–8)

---

[1] *Com. in De Gen. et Cor.*, bk. i, 1. ii. 2.

[2] The distinction between *generation* as change of substance and *alteration* as change of place is noticed by Richard N. Ringler, 'Spenser's Mutability Cantos', Harvard Dissertation, 1961, p. 41. His references are to Brunetto Latini's *Livres dou Tresor* (ed. Carmody, p. 108) and to Romei's article in *The Frame of Order* (ed. Winney, p. 200). He also discusses the concept of 'equal mixture' as a preservative of the heavenly bodies (p. 43).

The 'But' of the final line means 'except', for substance's innate quality as a substratum of prepared matter is not changed, but its outward form is changed. This constitutes *alteration* of the substance but *generation* of the composite body.

Aquinas also gives some help with the 'wheel' of generation:

And so it does not follow that what is corrupted may secede from the whole nature of things; because, although that which has been corrupted may become non-being, it yet remains as something else which has been generated. Whence matter cannot remain unless it is the substance of some form, and thence it is that by one being corrupted another is generated, and by one being generated another is corrupted; and so there is thought to be a certain *circle* in generation and corruption, by reason of which it has an aptitude to *perpetuity*.[1]

The heavenly bodies, incorruptible themselves, do, however, influence the mutable bodies of the lower world:

But the sun and moon, who are the lower planets according to Aristotle, have most fully the power to cause transmutations in these inferior bodies, whose [condition] is indeed not the best but is something ordained towards the best and leading to it; for inferior bodies, through the transmutation of generation and corruption, follow perpetuity in species, which in the individual they are not able to have.[2]

Thus the heavenly bodies do in a sense 'raigne over Change' in the sublunar world, but are they subject to change themselves? The question which Spenser's Nature is called upon to decide is not whether the stars undergo *alteration*, as the Titaness declares, but whether alteration constitutes mutability. The problem is to set limits to the definition of a word, 'mutability'. Are there several kinds of change, one less 'changing' than another? Can the planets be called 'immutable' when they move from place to place, following an immutable course, but changing position nevertheless? Do they rule over Time, or does Time rule over them? Nature considers the case and pronounces her judgement, admitting that the planets do change but not that they are subject to change:

> I well consider all that ye have sayd
> And find that all things stedfastnes doe hate
> And changed be: yet being rightly wayd,
> They are not changed from their first estate;

---

[1] *Com. in De Gen. et Cor.*, bk. i, III. vii. 6.
[2] *Com. in De Caelo et Mundo*, bk. ii, XII. xviii. 11.

But by their change their being doe *dilate*:
And turning to themselves at length againe,
Doe worke their owne perfection so by fate:
Then over them Change doth not rule and raigne;
But they raigne over Change, and doe their states maintaine.

(VII. vii. 58)

The planets do change, Nature admits, but they do not change from their first estate; i.e. they keep the same material substance *by number*, the identical particles of matter from which they were first made. They also keep the same intelligence or 'soul' assigned to them in the beginning. They seem immortal by comparison with earthly composite bodies and shall endure as long as Time itself, but not perhaps to all eternity.[1] In their circles they seek to perfect themselves by carrying out the will of their Creator and by a *dilation* of their substance.

Ficino uses this term for the action of form within matter when form is *dilated* within the corporeal body,[2] thus suggesting an increasing perfection through form. Rosalie Colie points out the idea in Plotinus' Fifth *Ennead*, where he states that 'forms enlarge [dilate] their being to include matter and to infuse it and its being with their essence',[3] probably the source of the statement by Ficino. Spenser's image of the stars 'dilating' themselves does not imply augmentation of matter, as Miss Colie's word 'include' might suggest. It is rather an expansion of matter, like a crushed sponge that is allowed to expand into its natural shape. Spenser associates such dilation with a greater measure of perfection.

If the stars perform their motions and dilations of their own will, then they can properly claim to rule over change, and Nature credits them with the power to do this. They are voluntarily carrying out the will of their Creator. Aquinas writes: 'For it can be said that the motion of the heaven does not cease, not because of the nature of the place but because of the will of the mover.'[4] He writes of the stars: 'So therefore it happens that bodies of this kind are not moved in their natural motions through an exterior virtue but through an intrinsic virtue which they accepted from

---

[1] *Eternal* things will never have an end. *Sempiternal* things will endure as long as Time itself, but no longer. Cf. p. 249 n. 4.

[2] *De Immortalitate*, I. iii, p. 84; v. x, p. 144; *De Vita Coelitus Comparanda*, ch. i, p. 532.

[3] *Paradoxia Epidemica*, pp. 345–6.

[4] *Com. in De Caelo et Mundo*, bk. i, IX. xxi. 14.

the Creator.'[1] The stars change by their own will and in harmony
with God's will. Plato had envisaged the likelihood of their running backward in their courses if God's hand were removed and
reversing the course of generation among mutable things (above,
p. 275). But Aquinas feels that they voluntarily follow their
courses because of an intrinsic quality received when they were
made. The stars, like men, are pilgrims in space and time, seeking
to prepare themselves for a higher plane of existence: 'For they
do not have the best life, since their life consists of a union of the
soul to the celestial body. Nor also do they have a life the most
sufficient unto itself, since through their motion they pursue the
good.'[2] The assumption is that, if the stars already enjoyed the
best possible life, they would not need to pursue the good which
they already had. The 'best' life is that of the soul freed from any
physical body and resting in God.

George Buchanan expresses his belief that there is one simple
motion of the stars. He does not believe that they ever slow down,
or speed up, or run backward, or get in each other's way, or have
civil war.[3] There is not the confusion that Mutabilitie would
have us believe (*FQ* VII. vii. 49–54). They are moved, says
Buchanan, by the same *vis vegetabilis* which operates in the matter
of the mutable world and which is an aspect of God:

> Nec gens tam barbara terris
> Errat in incultis, ut non cum sidera spectet,
> Fulguraque et vasto tremefactum murmure caelum
> Audiat, esse Deum credat vim scilicet illam,
> Quae regat immensam justo moderamine molem,
> Et moveat nostros per tot miracula sensus.
> Hanc igitur tantam vim, nec rationis egentem,
> Tempore nec lassam, nec fractam viribus aevi
> Credere nos fas est, nec cogi viribus ullis,
> Sed sponte aeternos mundi convertere motus.[4]

(Nor wanders there in savage lands so barbarous a people that, when
they behold the stars and the lightning and hear the skies shaken with
a mighty rumbling, will not believe God to be surely that power
which rules the immense mass with just governance and moves our
senses through so many marvellous things. Accordingly, it is right for

---

[1] *Com. in De Caelo et Mundo*, bk. i, VIII. xviii. 2.
[2] Ibid., bk. i, IX. xxi. 8.   [3] *De Sphaera*, ii. 461–74.
[4] Ibid. ii. 644–53. Cf. the ideas of Justus Lipsius (Sherman Hawkins, 'Mutabilitie
and the Cycle of the Months', in J. R. Elliott, *The Prince of Poets*, p. 299).

us to believe that this great power, neither lacking reason nor wearied by time, nor broken by the force of age, is not driven by any forces but willingly turns the eternal motions of the world.)

This power is the World-Soul of Ficino, operating in its several capacities: as Jove, it operates among the heavenly bodies; as Venus (and, Spenser adds, Adonis), it is the genital power operating among the forms of the changing sublunar world; as Nature, it has a supervisory capacity in both regions.

The Eternal World

After Spenser gave Nature's verdict in favour of Jove and against Mutabilitie, he wrote two stanzas of Canto viii. In accordance with his practice of moralizing upon his subject at the beginning of a canto, he made his comment on what he had just written. He somewhat doubtfully accepts Nature's judgement concerning the heavenly bodies; yet they undeniably do move and undergo mutation of a kind, and the decision of Nature gave scant comfort to a man sick of disasters in a world of change. But Nature had referred to a happier time in the future marked by the 'decay' of mutability:

> But time shall come when all shall changed bee,
> And from thenceforth none no more change shall see.
>
> (vii. 59)

As the poet interprets this prophecy, he derives comfort from it and looks forward to that time of perfect rest:

> When I bethinke me on that speech whyleare
> Of Mutability, and well it way,
> Me seemes, that though she all unworthy were
> Of the heav'ns rule, yet, very sooth to say,
> In all things else she beares the greatest sway:
> Which makes me loath this state of life so tickle,
> And love of things so vaine to cast away;
> Whose flowring pride, so fading and so fickle,
> Short Time shall soon cut down with his consuming sickle.
>
> Then gin I thinke on that which Nature sayd,
> Of that same time when no more change shall be,
> But stedfast rest of all things, firmely stayd
> Upon the pillours of eternity,

That is contrayr to Mutabilitie:
For all that moveth doth in change delight:
But thence-forth all shall rest eternally
With Him that is the God of Sabbaoth hight:
O that great Sabbaoth God graunt me that Sabaoths
    sight!

(viii. 1–2)

Spenser's progression of thought is more succinctly expressed in the words of Henry F. Lyte:

Change and decay in all around I see,
O Thou who changest not, abide with me.[1]

The sense of transiency affects all men. It is in this vein of uncertainty that Spenser writes, and he clings to the one unchanging reality, the promise of eternal rest with God.

The thoughts of Spenser's two final stanzas can be traced in the writings of Ficino and Aquinas; and I add, with some hesitation, Joannis Scotus Erigena, the ninth-century Irish mystic who saw all creation as a vast circuit in time, returning at last to its immaterial origin in God. Since this doctrine of a universal return would destroy the concept of an eternal hell, Erigena's *De Divisione Naturae* had been condemned as heretical and placed on the 'Index Expurgatorius'. However, it seems to have been fairly common in manuscript form and to have exercised great influence over dissident groups within the Church.[2]

First, for Nature's decision as probably being correct, we may note this parallel in Ficino: 'The heaven likewise is not changed in substance while it is revolved in action . . . The heaven also is moved immutably; and while it seems to change certain configurations and extrinsic garments, meanwhile it conserves centre and circumference, and from the same vehicles of times both re-seeks the same things and re-creates like things.'[3]

The heaven's motions are immutable and hence do not constitute mutability. But, like Spenser, Ficino has moments when the

[1] 'Abide With Me', in most church hymnals. For an excellent article relating to mutability as a cause of pessimism see George Williamson, 'Mutability, Decay, and Melancholy', *ELH* ii (1935), 121–50.
[2] Erigena's work is available in *PL* cxxii. Origen, who held almost the same views, is quoted and refuted by Aquinas (*Summa Theologica*, pt. iii, Q. 99, A. 2–3, Supp.). For additional comment on Erigena see the *Catholic Encyclopedia*: 'Erigena'.
[3] *Com. in Plotinum*, ii. i. 3; p. 1596.

whole universe seems subject to change and to ultimate destruction; and he feels the same melancholy regret at this spectacle of change. In his work *On the Immortality of Souls*, he writes:

> But whoever considers the parts of the world below the moon, changing from this being into that being, and conversely; and the parts of the same which are above the moon, crossing everywhere from such being into such being and, because it is everywhere changed, therefore needy and imperfect being; and again the universe itself existing from a certain substance and form, and the substance, which naturally precedes form, able to undergo such form or not to undergo it; and again the world existing not in the manner of parts of a harmonious whole but from parts also fighting among themselves, and the universal body in no wise having being through itself, but entirely through another—i.e. through every cause (the efficient cause certainly), end, form, matter—and therefore vacillating inwardly according to itself; whoever, I say, considers these four [truths] can fully conjecture that the universal mass of the world by its nature will become mutable from being into non-being.[1]

This attitude is almost the same as that in Spenser's first stanza of Canto viii. In his next stanza Spenser comforts himself with the thought of the ultimate disappearance of change in the rest of eternity. A similar progression is shown by Ficino, who in the chapter following the above quotation discussed man's gift of eternal life. Though the angels were created before the beginning of time, and man after that beginning, yet man is allowed to share eternity with them, unlike the beasts, who cannot live always: 'Our souls, born after the beginning of time, yield to the angels; yet they are not temporal. For God, through that point of his *eternity*, which is always the same and oversees the universe and encloses the circle of time, and from which he procreated the angels, so procreates also the souls of men.'[2] On the next page, he adds: 'The terminus of creation to which the soul is directed is within itself, responding only to the *divine eternity*, which is the terminus from which creation proceeded.'[3] The 'Sabbath' of eternal rest appears in a later work of Ficino: 'For they judge that a transformation of this kind [cleansing from sin] can be made up to the end of the world's motion, upon which follows the rest of the eternal Sabbath [*aeterni sabbati quies*], and the eternal blessedness

---

[1] *De Immortalitate*, XVIII. i; p. 399.
[2] Ibid., XVIII. ii; p. 401.   [3] Ibid., XVIII. iii; p. 402.

of the good.'[1] The central lines of the final stanza seem to reflect Aristotle's *Physics*, Book viii, as reported by Aquinas:

> Now, therefore, we must consider what eternity is. To know this, it must be considered that 'eternity' states a certain interminability; for it is called 'eternal' as existing without termini. But, as the Philosopher says in *Physics* viii, in every motion there is a certain generation and a certain corruption in that the movable object ceases to be in the terminus from which it comes and begins to be in the terminus to which it goes. From this it is clear that *all mutability is contrary to eternity*. Therefore, eternity includes not only interminability of being, but also immobility.[2]

This immobility is the equivalent of Spenser's 'stedfast rest', and Spenser explicitly states the opposition between eternity and mutability, as well as stating that *all* motion involves mutation and a certain measure of mutability.

Spenser's view that all things shall be changed and then there shall be no more change repeats the theory eloquently expressed by Erigena, who may similarly have influenced Ficino. Ficino's sentence on the 'terminus' of creation, quoted above, reflects Erigena's opinion that all things return upon themselves to their first beginnings or primordial causes (seminal reasons) to find eternal rest:

> From those [causes] they [substances, essences, reasons] progress materially to procreating this visible world so that when it is dissolved they are dissolved and returned into their substances, so that in those they may rest and set up the *terminus of their mutability*, free from all flux of generation and corruption through increase or decrease in places and times, united to their subject substances so that *eternally* they are made one with them, inseparably and incommutably, by an ineffable unification (*adunatione*).[3]

In Spenser's last two lines, he uses the word 'Sabbaoth' or 'Sabaoth' three times.[4] This could be a verbal echo of Erigena, who, in his climactic vision of all things returning to their point of

---

[1] *Com. in Plotinum*, iii: 'De Providentia', xiii; p. 1694.
[2] Aquinas, *De Tempore*, ch. iv, in *Opuscula Omnia* (edn. of Paris, 1634), vol. v, p. 281.
[3] *De Divisione Naturae*, v. xiv, in *PL* cxxii. 886A.
[4] Cf. D. C. Allen, 'On the Closing Lines of *The Faerie Queene*', *MLN* lxiv (1949), 93–4; L. S. Friedland, 'Spenser's Sabaoth Rest', *MLQ* xvii (1956), 199–203.

origin in God, likewise uses 'Sabbath' three times in one sentence. The context expresses the spirit of Spenser's lines:

I judge that these few paradigms assumed from divine parables are sufficient to show the general and special return of the human race into its beginning, I say into its primordial condition; and into God Himself for those who by their most sincere participation are worthy to enjoy [Him]; and from reversion into its causes of every sensible creature which was fabricated in man or on account of man. Then there will be not only a general Sabbath in all divine works, but also a special Sabbath of Sabbaths in holy angels and holy men; and the house of God will be filled, in which each one is placed in a rank suitable to himself, some lower, some higher, some in the sublimity of nature, some above every natural virtue and around God Himself. And so that great feast will be ordained and celebrated, from which no substance, because it was made by God, is rejected, and into which no vice, because it was not made by God, is introduced. For Nature will be purged, vice will be blown away, the substantial grain will be stored, the flame of God's word will burn up the chaff of wickedness, the secret places of darkness will be lighted, and God will be seen as all in all.[1]

The verbal clues are not sufficient to prove that Erigena was an actual source of Spenser's lines, but Spenser was writing in the tradition which Erigena established: the universal return to God and to the eternal Sabbath at the end of Time, when the entire physical world should be changed and disappear.[2] To both men it seemed 'a consummation devoutly to be wished'.

---

[1] *De Divisione Naturae*, v. 38, in PL cxxii. 1015–16.

[2] I have not discussed at length the *Fowre Hymnes* because I have little to add to existing scholarship. Ellrodt's book is particularly helpful with the study of the *Hymnes*. On the following pages of Ficino's *Opera Omnia*, I have observed references to Sapience: 1215, 1221, 1253, 1369–70, 1558, 1568, 1670, 1768, 1798. Cf. Jon A. Quitslund, 'Spenser's Image of Sapience', *Studies in the Renaissance*, xvi (1969), 181–213.

XII

Conclusion

WHEN Milton declared Spenser 'a better teacher than Scotus or Aquinas', he spoke advisedly.[1] Poetry is superior to philosophy or history, Sidney had said, because it presents their teachings in pleasing language which moves the reader by beauty of expression as well as by substance of thought.[2] Spenser found this opinion illustrated in the Latin verses of Virgil, Ovid, Lucretius, Alanus de Insulis, Palingenius, and Buchanan; in the French of Du Bartas; in the Italian of Dante, Ariosto, and Tasso as interpreted by their commentators. To emulate these in his native English was the task which he set himself. He was not the first to attempt it, for Gower, Langland, Lydgate, Hawes, and Batman had written verse narratives with didactic intent; but Spenser's effort was far more ambitious than any of theirs. His simple announcement in Bryskett's Irish cottage that he was engaged in writing a poem to illustrate the moral virtues (above, p. 2) signalizes his purpose. The allegory, particularly the moral allegory, is the primary essence of *The Faerie Queene*, not an extraneous pattern imposed upon it. In the *Letter to Raleigh*, he explains his choice of allegorical verse rather than direct precepts and admonitions as a method of moral instruction. This moral source of poetic inspiration may prove difficult of acceptance in an age committed to the aesthetic creed of 'art for art's sake'; but the evidence for it is overwhelming. *The Faerie Queene* is a book of religious inspiration and moral instruction, comparable in its purpose with the Revelation of Saint John and the *Divine Comedy* of Dante.

In the wonderful variety of *The Faerie Queene*, certain basic themes repeatedly emerge: (1) the quest for honour and glory, both worldly and unworldly, to be won through the pursuit of

---

[1] *Areopagitica.* Cf. Edwin Greenlaw, 'A Better Teacher than Aquinas', *SP* xiv (1917), 196–217.

[2] *An Apology for Poetry*, in G. Gregory Smith's *Elizabethan Critical Essays*, vol. i, p. 153.

virtue alone; (2) the *psychomachia*, or internal warfare of the soul; (3) the contrast between form and formlessness, both physical and spiritual; (4) the primacy of love as a universal force, both human and cosmic; (5) the need for harmonious personal relationships; (6) man's place in the transiency of the world and in the permanence of God.

In setting forth these themes Spenser has developed to a very high point the technique of allegory. One of his devices is the composite figure or multiple representation, in which a character acts a role as a real person, a role in the external allegory, and a role in the internal allegory, and occasionally several roles in one of these. Throughout this book I have stressed the internal allegory as that feature of the poem which is imperfectly realized by most readers and which seems to have been Spenser's primary concern in writing it. As Wordsworth later aspired to do, Spenser has written a poem on the workings of the human mind, and he has written it successfully. I hope that this book will help the reader to lift the 'covert vele' of allegory and to understand better the substance of *The Faerie Queene*. It is a rich mine that will repay much digging.

APPENDIX

Text of Translated Passages

ABELARD

p. 267: Non modo mihi primum notus esse coepisti, quem a principio in primis parentibus per seminarium existentem per praescientiam novi.

ALCIATUS, with commentaries on the *Emblemata*

p. 191: Quemadmodum lepra tactus contagium spirat, & halitu inficit, ita voluntas praua, aut affectus per aculeum linguae: scorpionis ictus non sic noxius aut viperae: venenum est quidem sub labiis, sed per canalem gutturis ex radice vitae, vbi primum emergit. Index igitur mentis lingua, quae si fraeno regitur, sanam demonstrat; aegram, si effraenis & volubilis. Inuadere alios mordicus rabido cani similem, quae tandem nota est pacati animi? Dissidiorum semina & causas belli spargere, fuliginem candori nominis oblinere, & inducere nubeculam lucenti famae, effutire in vulgus quae secreto commissa, superaddere auctarium crescenti mendacio, dissimulare veritatem & fucare, comminisci, fingere, dilatare quae nusquam & nunquam, vouere diris, execrationibus ferire, allatrare coeli ter sanctum illud & adorandum Numen, periuriis assuescere, contestari falsa, detestari contraria, nonnè cloacam Auerni spirat talis mens, & Acherontaeos puteos, & manifestat se indice lingua? quae mordet, pungit, murmurat, gannit, vlulat, grunnit, stridet, strepit, sibilat, tonat, fulminat, tollit, dejicit, colligit, dissipat, vulnerat, sanat, quando libet, aut quoties interior vis, aut motus dictat. Miraculi loco est, qui parcus in his, nec dictamen audit, aut vim sequitur, cohibito hoc naturae plectro, & vincto ad imperium reginae Prudentiae, cuius iussu se moueat aut coerceat. Lubricitate seducimur interdum & agili flexu membri huius, elabitur enim vt anguilla solet aut muraenula, capta etiam & compressa, è mediis digitis, & nocet priusquam animaduertat ratio: iaculum antevolat celeritate, nec impetus eius nisi ex vulnere iam facto cognoscitur: intercipi nequit dum in cursu est, & ab arcu mentis iam excussa: O stragem spiculi, quam improuisa es atque Euris citatior? . . . Nam silentium autoritatis tantum & ornamenti obtinet, vt homini etiam imperito & indocto prudentiae opinionem conciliet, si garrulitatis vitium nouerit comprimere.

p. 195: Tradunt etiam Gratias in Acidalio fonte, qui est Orchomeni Boeotiae vrbe . . . lauari, quoniam pura esse beneficia oportet, & nihil sordidum, nullam spem retributionis habere . . . Duas affert causas, cur nudae pingantur Gratiae. Prima, quia ad acquirendum amorem & gratiam, necesse est, vt cor ipsum candidum transpareat, purum & absque vllo fictionis velo; in beneficiis itaque vltro citroque collocandis nihil oportet esse duplex aut tectum, sed clara omnia & simplicia.

p. 242: Hic aruum genitale pro virilibus & pudendis posuit, quod sint generationis instrumenta, vt Virgil. 3. Georg.

> *Haec faciunt nimio ne luxu obtusior usus*
> *Sit genitali aruo, et sulcos oblimet inertes.*

Loquendi eandem formulam non est aspernatus August. libr. 18, cap. 23. De ciuitate Dei: Sed voluntati, inquit, membra illa vt caetera cuncta seruirent: ita genitale aruum vas in hoc opus creatum seminaret, vt nunc terram manus, &c. sic aruum genitale *kepos* Graecis, Latinè hortus dicitur.

AQUINAS

p. 288: Dicit ergo primo quod Democritus et Leucippus, qui faciebant principia rerum corpora indivisibilia infinitarum figurarum, ex his causabant generationem et alterationem. Dicebant enim quod per congregationem et segregationem dictorum corporum figuratorum, causabatur generatio et corruptio: per mutationem autem ordinis et positionis dictorum corporum, causabatur alteratio.

p. 288: His ergo suppositis, subiungit quod alteratio est, quando manet idem subiectum sensibile: scilicet quando, nulla transmutatione in eius substantia facta, fit transmutatio in passionibus eius, scilicet in qualitatibus ipsius.

p. 289: Dicit ergo primo quod omnibus illis philosophis qui ex uno principio materiali ponunt omnia esse producta, necesse est dicere quod generatio et corruptio idem sit alterationi. Illud enim principium materiale ponebant esse aliquod ens actu, puta ignem vel aerem aut aquam: et ponebant quod illud esset substantia omnium quae ex eo generantur: et sicut materia semper manet in his quae ex materia fiunt, ita ponebant quod illud subiectum semper manet unum et idem. Hoc autem dicimus alterari, quando, manente substantia actu existentis, fit aliqua variatio circa formam. Unde sequitur quod nulla transmutatio esse possit quae dicitur simplex generatio et corruptio, sed sola alteratio.—Nos autem ponimus omnium generabilium et corruptibilium esse unum subiectum primum, quod tamen non est ens actu, sed in potentia. Et ideo ex eo quod accipit formam, per quam fit ens actu, dicitur simpliciter generatio: ex hoc autem quod, postquam est ens actu factum, suscipit aliam quamcumque formam, dicitur alteratio.

p. 290: Et ita non sequitur quod id quod corrumpitur secedat a tota rerum natura: quia quamvis fiat non ens hoc quod est corruptum, remanet tamen aliquid aliud, quod est generatum. Unde non potest materia remanere quin sit subiecta alicui formae: et inde est quod uno corrupto aliud generatur, et uno generato aliud corrumpitur: et sic consideratur quidam circulus in generatione et corruptione, ratione cuius habet aptitudinem ad perpetuitatem.

p. 290: Sol autem et luna, qui sunt inferiores planetae secundum Aristotelem, habent maxime efficaciam ad causandum transmutationes in istis inferioribus corporibus: quod quidem non est optimum, sed aliquid ordinatum ad optimum et praevium ei; nam corpora inferiora per transmutationem generationis et corruptionis consequuntur perpetuitatem in specie, quam in individuo habere non possunt.

p. 291: Potest enim dici quod motus caeli non cessat, non propter naturam loci, sed propter voluntatem moventis.

pp. 291–2: Sic ergo patet quod huiusmodi corpora suis motibus naturali bus moventur non per virtutem exteriorem, sed per virtutem intrinsecam, quam acceperunt a generante.

p. 292: Non enim habent optimam vitam, cum eorum vita sit ex unione animae ad corpus caeleste: nec etiam habent vitam per se sufficientissimam, cum per motum suum bonum consequantur.

p. 296: Nunc ergo considerandum est, quid est aeternitas. Ad quod sciendum, considerandum est, quod aeternitas dicit interminabilitatem quamdam: dicitur enim aeternum quasi extra terminos existens. Sicut autem dicit Philosophus 8 Physic., in omni motu est aliqua generatio et aliqua corruptio, in quantum mobile desinit esse in termino a quo, et incipit esse in termino ad quem. Ex hoc patet, quod omnis mutabilitas repugnat aeternitati. Includit ergo aeternitas non solum interminabilitatem essendi, sed etiam immobilitatem.

AUGUSTINE

p. 282: Sic enim terra ad Dei verbum ea produxit, antequam exorta essent, accipiens omnes numeros eorum quos per tempora exsereret secundum suum genus.

p. 282: Tunc autem utrumque defuit; ideo fecit Deus haec potentia Verbi sui sine pluvia, sine opere humano.

BOCCACCIO

p. 192: Acidalia è detta, ò dal fonte Acidalio, ch'è consecrato a Venere, & alle gratie in Orcameno Città di Boeotia; doue già gli sciocchi pensauano le gratie sorelle di Venere lauarsi; ouero perche sia cagione di metter molti pensieri, attento che conosciamo di quanti pensieri ella empi gli amanti; & i Greci chiamano i pensieri Acidas.

BRUNO

pp. 102–4: Draco enim magnus et rufus, diabolus est, qui in specie serpentis primum hominem decepit, et nunc quidem propter sanguinem martyrum, quem fundere non cessat, rufus apparet. Hic autem septem capita habere perhibetur; septem videlicet vitia capitalia, quae de matre superbia exorta sunt, ex quibus quasi principiis omnia alia vitia oriuntur. Haec autem sunt vana gloria, invidia, ira, tristitia, avaritia, ingluvies, luxuria, decem vero cornua, omnia alia vitia sunt, quae ab his capitibus derivantur, quae quoniam multa sunt, eum numerum ponere voluit, in quo omnes numeri continentur; non enim progreditur numerus ultra decem. Sed ipse in se revolutus omnes alios numeros complet.

CARTARI

pp. 53–4: La prima, che è detta Clio, significa Gloria, come che per la gloria si induca principalmente l'huomo a dar opera alle scientie.

p. 199: Imagini delle tre Gratie Dee della bellezza, & gratia; Dee ancora della gratitudine, & del beneficio, nominate Eufrosina ò giocondità, Aglaia ò venustà, Thalia ò piaceuolezza; Dee della conuersatione, sociabilità, & amicitia, & di quella allegra vita, che gli huomini desiderano di viuere.

COMES, *Natalis*

p. 193: Primus omnium mortalium Gratiis templum erexit Eteocles quidam Rex Orchomeniorum: nam saepius ad Orchomenios has lotum ire solitas ad fontem Acidalium dixerunt antiqui, vt testis est Strabo libro nono.

pp. 229–30: Oceanus, qui fluuiorum & animantium omnium, & Deorum pater vocatus est ... Ab hoc ipso Oceano videtur putasse Orpheus & antiquorum Deos, & res omnes initium sumpsisse: quippe cum omnia priusquam oriantur, aut intercidant, indigeant humore sine quo nihil neque corrumpi potest, neque gigni, vt sensit Thales ... Hunc eundem Oceanum tradidit Orpheus, & omnes antiquorum theologi principium ortus Diis & rebus extitisse, quia, vt sensit Thales, nihil sine humectatione nascitur aut putrescit, atque omnes elementorum qualitates, quas Deorum nominibus appellarunt, ex humore nascuntur.

p. 231. Materia enim omnis in intellectu forma prior existit, formasque varias semper expetit naturae impulsu, quamobrem in tot formas verti dictus est Proteus.

p. 245 : Nihil est autem aliud Venus, quam occultum coitus desiderium à natura insitum ad procreandum . . . Nata esse dicitur è spuma maris quoniam semen genitale animalium nihil est aliud, quam spuma sanguinis.

p. 245 : . . . quoniam sine vi Solis, nulla esset Venus.

DUNS SCOTUS

p. 251 : Ratio itaque seminalis vel est forma substantialis seminis, vel qualitas consequens necessario formam substantialem eius . . . Nam cum ratio seminalis intendatur ab Auctore naturae, ut sit via ad formas ulteriores et perfectiores, omnibus mixtis possunt rationes hae seminales inesse.

ERASMUS

p. 18 : Metaphora pene semper adest. . . . Allegoria non minus crebra : quanquam & haec quibusdam metaphorae species est. . . . Nonnunquam usque ad aenigma perveni, quod autore Quintiliano, nihil aliud est quam obscurior allegoria : quod genus . . . Dimidium plus toto.

ERIGENA, *Joannis Scotus*

p. 296 : . . . ab eis progrediantur materialiter ad hunc mundum visibilem procreandum, ut eo iterum soluto illa solvantur, et in suas substantias revertantur, ut in eis quiescant, terminumque suae mutabilitatis constituant, omni fluxu generationis et corruptionis per incrementa et decrementa in locis, temporibus, libera, suisque subjectis substantiis unita, ut aeternaliter unum cum ipsis, inseparabile, et incommutabile ineffabili adunatione efficiantur.

p. 297 : Sufficiunt, ut arbitror, haec pauca paradigmata, ex divinis parabolis assumpta, ad generalem specialemque humani generis suadendum reditum in principium suum, primordialem dico conditionem, inque ipsum Deum, in his, qui sincerissima eius participatione digni sunt frui, deque totius sensibilis creaturae, quae in homine et propter hominem fabricata est, in causas suas reversione, quando erit non solum generale sabbatum in omnibus divinis operibus, verum etiam et speciale sabbatum sabbatorum in sanctis angelis, sanctisque hominibus, et implebitur domus Dei, in qua unusquisque ordine sibi congruo constituetur, alii inferius, alii superius, alii in sublimitate naturae, alii super omnem naturalem virtutem circa ipsum Deum. Ac sic coena illa magna ordinabitur et celebrabitur, ex qua nullius substantia, quia ex Deo facta est, respuetur, nullius vitium, quia ex

Deo factum non est, introducetur. Purgabitur enim natura, ventilabitur vitium, recondentur substantialia grana, flamma divinae sententiae delictorum ardebit palea, illuminabuntur abscondita tenebrarum, omnia in omnibus videbitur Deus.

FICINO, *Marsilio*

p. 125: Attende deinceps ad illam animae naturae figuram. In qua sub multiplicis bestiae nomine intellige concupiscendi naturam: sub figura leonis, irascendi uigorem: sub forma hominis rationem. Et uide quam expresse depingat ambitiosi, iniusti, libidinosi hominis uitam, imo miseram seruitutem. Item ibidem accipe formulam, qua possis transitum animarum in bestias ita interpretari, ut in bestiarum affectus et habitus potius quam in corpora migrare dicantur.

p. 244: Merito hic generationis pater est generationis matri propinquus. Primus calor humori primo, illuminator illuminato. . . . Sol per lunarem humorem generationes inchoat, per Venereum generabilium formas absoluit.

p. 245: Virtus quidem Solis uniuersalis hunc hominem, qui est particularis effectus, non produci nisi per hominem alium, tanquam particularem causam, atque propriam.

p. 245: Quanquam si Lunam Veneri similem, humore prorsus aequalem, & uix minus calidam, cum Ioue rite misceas aut Sole, propemodum iam Venerem habes.

p. 245: Cur non igitur ad plantandum (ut cynice loquar) hominem, utamur beneficio Lunae Iouisque & Phoebi? Nam Veneris quidem ad haec officio semper utimur. Sed rectius modo dixissem, semper utuntur. Nam ipsa mihi Venus est Diana.

p. 251: Praecipuas naturalium causas esse uult seminales earum rationes in uegetali animae mundanae natura, quibus semper ordine certo respondeant seminales in speciebus singulis rationes. Sed quo nam pacto ex uniuerso seminario mundi omnia pullulent, multis quaestionibus perscrutatur.

pp. 252-3:... in eiusmodi motu temporeque uarios... habitus anima in seipsa commutat. Qui sane habitus simul omnes esse non possunt: Et cum hic quidem est praesens, iste iam est praeteritus, ille futurus. Hac igitur ratione anima uicissim est atque non est quodammodo, mutatione perpetua. . . . Ipsa uero Identitas ad ens perfectum & stabile pertinens, fluxui huic animali non conuenit. Neque rursus huic competit alteratio tanta, ut ab ipsa natura . . . eadem nec alteratur ab ipsa. Qua uero habitus quosdam uicissim commutando mouetur, eadem alteratur in habitu: Atque ita priores quidem habitus exuens, posteriores autem induens, occidere uidetur, atque renasci, sed rursum proprietatem sibi naturalem, nec nuper accipiens, nec aliquando deserens, neque fit unquam, neque perit . . . quia uidelicet materia in rebus etiam sensibilibus est sempiterna.

p. 253: Notabis in nostro corpore ultra uitale uestigium impressum ab anima mundi, quod nimium est commune, imprimi uestigium quoque uitale propriumque ab anima nostra, atque hanc ab anima mundi diuersam esse, nec ab externis, sed a seipsa potius permutari. Vnde consequens est, nulla eiusmodi mutatione speciem propriam prorsus exuere.

p. 257: Cum tota machina sit animae mundanae subiecta, nihil illi resistere, nihil effluere proprii, nihil alieni contingere: item, totam corporum molem ab ipsa anima per infusam uitam, tum inter se colligari, tum animae deuinciri, prorsusque subesse: animam uero nostram ad corpus accedere, quasi quoddam hactenus mundi membrum, atque iam inde quodammodo uiuens in gremio totius animae, sic illi ferme connexum, sicut foetus in aluo.

p. 258: Non aliter & mundi huius materia, cum principio sine formarum ornamento informe chaos iaceret: illico amore sibi ingenito, in animam se direxit, seque illi obedientem praebuit: atque hoc amore conciliante, ab anima formarum omnium quae in mundo uidentur nacta ornamentum, mundus ex chaos effecta est.

pp. 258, 229 n.: In omnibus denique amor chaos comitatur, praecedit mundum, torpentia suscitat, obscura illuminat, uiuificat mortuos, format informia, perficit imperfecta.

pp. 260–1: In tertio corpus hoc, id est, materiam, sic extensam Deus multis formauit formis, scilicet elementorum atque coelorum, & in coelo confirmauit eam stellarum formis. Sub caelo praeter elementorum formas, formauit eam formis uaporum, lapidum, metallorum, & plantarum & animalium. Materia quidem unica est ubique his omnibus induta formis.

p. 261: Accedit ad haec quod anima mundi totidem saltem rationes rerum seminales diuinitus habet, quot ideae sunt in mente diuina, quibus ipsa rationibus totidem fabricat species in materia. . . . Mox in materiam hanc ita opportune paratam, singulare munus ab idea trahes, per rationem uidelicet animae seminalem. . . . Congruitates igitur eiusmodi formarum, ad rationes animae mundi, Zoroaster diuinas illices appellauit, quas & Synesius magicas esse illecebras confirmauit. Nempe denique credat ad propriam quandam materiae speciem, & tempore certo hauriri omnia prorsus ex anima dona, sed pro opportunitate dona duntaxat seminis quo talis species pullulauit, seminumque conformium. Itaque hic homo humanis tantum adhibitis, non proprias piscium uel auium dotes, inde sibi uendicat, sed humanas atque consimiles.

pp. 261–2 : Natura plura continet in se rerum semina, quam mens ideas. Quum enim naturae seminisque uirtus sit debilior, non potest in uno semine comprehendere, perque unum facere quaecunque idea possidet potestque una. Ergo per plura semina distribuitur, ideae unicae uigor uirtutisque debilitas numero compensatur. Eadem ratione materia in plures perducitur, sub unoquoque semine formas. Accedit ad mundi huius innumerabilem multitudinem dimensio semper diuisioni subiecta, motusque singula uarians, ac rerum inter se commixtio multiplex, congeriesque uirtutum numerumque ex singulis ubique superioribus causis necessitate proueniens. Denique ne rerum mutabilium species aliquando pereant, substantiis numerus singulorum tum successione, tum simul ultra permanentium multitudinem diuinitus augetur.

p. 272 : Tunc animus nouo quodam sui motu propensius ad mobilia uergens, atque ita mobilem uitam eligens in fatum inde prolabitur, quodammodo etiam antequam terrenum corpus ingrediatur, & priusquam id corpus concipiatur in utero.

p. 273 : Tangit inter haec opinionem putantium animas omnium animantium, posse a praesentibus corporibus separari, neque in animam uniuersi resolui, sed in sua proprietate subsistere, iterumque ad corpora remigrare.

p. 284 : . . . communem uim ex mundi anima uegetalem in arbore mundana totam ubique uigentem.

pp. 284–5 : Lachesim quidem, quia rerum seminibus grauida est, & uitarum sortibus atque formis, quas descensuris inserit animabus. Clotho deinde, quoniam insitas uitae, sortes ordine suo euoluit in actum uiuendi, & explicat in effectum. Postremo Atropon, quoniam uitas iam euolutas in actum progressu quodam indeclinabili, ad ineuitabilem usque terminum conseruat atque custodit.

p. 286 : Et Plato terram uocat Deam antiquissimam Deorum omnium qui sint intra coelum. Addit ingentes terrae regiones habitari nostris admodum altiores, ubi lapides, metalla, plantae, animalia sint nostris mirum immodum praestantiora atque pulchriora, ubi homines diutissime uiuant, modicisque alimentis, cum preciosissima sint, odoribusque feliciter nutriantur . . . Haec illis ferme similia, quod in diuinis hortis, quasi campis Elysiis homines sola arboris uitae gustatione immortales uiuere potuissent.

p. 294 : Coelum similiter substantia non mutatur, dum actione reuoluitur . . . Coelum quoque mouetur immutabiliter, ac dum configurationes quasdam, & extrinsecos habitus commutare uidetur,

interea centrum circunferentiamque conseruat, eisdemque curriculis
temporum & repetit eadem & similia recreat.

p. 295: Quisquis autem considerat partes mundi, quae sunt infra
Lunam, de hoc esse in illud mutari, atque econuerso, ac partes eiusdem,
quae supra Lunam sunt, de esse tali in esse tale transire uicissim, &
quia mutatur ubique, ideo indigas imperfectasque esse, rursusque uniuersum ipsum ex subiecto aliquo formaque constare, & subiectum,
qui naturaliter antecedit formam, posse & subire formam talem, &
non subire: item constare mundum non modo ex partibus quantitatis,
sed ex partibus etiam inter se pugnantibus, denique uniuersum corpus
nullo modo per se esse, sed omnino per aliud, quia per omnem causam,
scilicet efficientem, finem, formam, materiam, ideoque secundum se
penitus uacillare, quisquis, inquam, quatuor haec considerat, is plane
coniicere potest uniuersam mundi molem natura sua fore de esse in
non esse mutabilem.

p. 295: Animae nostrae post temporis ortum natae cedunt angelis,
neque tamen sunt temporales. Nam Deus per id ipsum aeternitatis
suae punctum, quod semper est idem, & uniuersum supereminet,
complectiturque temporis ambitum, quo angelos procreauit, animas
quoque hominum procreat.

p. 295: Creationis terminus, ad quem dirigitur anima, in seipsa est,
diuinae solum aeternitati respondens, quae terminus est, a quo creatio
prouenit.

pp. 295–6: Transformationem enim eiusmodi usque ad finem mundani
motus posse fieri arbitrantur, quem sequatur aeterni sabbati quies,
aeternaque beatitudo bonorum.

GIRALDUS CAMBRENSIS

pp. 89–90: In summis autem montium istorum verticibus duo lacus
reperiuntur, sua non indigni admiratione. Alter enim insulam habet
erraticam, vi ventorum impellentium ad oppositas plerumque lacus
partes errabundam. Hic armenta pascentia nonnunquam pastores ad
longinquos subito partes translata mirantur.

Fieri namque potuit ut pars aliqua ripae olim avulsa, radicibus
salicum aliorumque fruticum naturaliter insertorum vinculis astricta
et colligata, paulatim postea per alluvionem incrementa susceperit. Et
quoniam violenta ventorum rapacitate, quae loco tam arduo fere con-
tinua reperitur, ad varias creberrime ripas impellitur, firmas solo tenus
et altas figere radices non permittitur.

GREGORY THE GREAT

p. 283: *Paradisus humani generis uterus, cujus ostia serpens aperuit.*—Quod
unicuique hominum venter est matris, hoc universo humano generi

exstitit habitatio illa summa paradisi. Ex ipsa namque proles humani generis velut ex ventre prodiit, et quasi ad incrementa corporis, sic ad augmenta propaginis foras emanavit. Ibi conceptio nostra coaluit, ubi origo hominum homo primus habitavit.

HAYMO

p. 117: Natura aquilae est ut in senio tantum ei excrescat rostrum et ungues quod non possit se cibo reficere; ascendit autem et tunc adversus solem, donec pennae suae calore exurantur, et deinde decidat in vivam aquam, unde exiens, acuit ad petram rostrum et ungues, et postea cibum capiens, juvenescit. Ita nos occupati multis peccatis, cum tenemur in vetustate Adae, accedimus ad Christum, qui est verus sol, cujus calore et infusione gratiae peccata nostra exuruntur; et inde aquis baptismi lavamur, inde rostrum incurvum, id est malam consuetudinem nostram illidimus et confringimus petrae, id est Christo, cui nos conformantes, vetustatem deponimus et juvenescimus.

p. 118: Atque ita pili sui, et omne innovatur corpus, et plumae illius: sic sancti qui se hic attriverunt mortificando seipsos, innovabuntur per incorruptionem, contemplantes solem justitiae Christum: sicut solem aquila irreverberatis oculis.

LINOCERIUS, *Geofredus*

p. 53: Finxerunt [antiqui] itaque illam Iouis filiam: quia cum *kleio* nihil aliud significet quàm gloriam: si liceat gloriam & nomen bene actorum posteris relinquere, absit vt aliunde repetamus quam à summo Deo, qui è memoria, contemplationeque, bene gestae rei famam nobis parit, nullo aeuo non celebrandam.

PARACELSUS

pp. 283-4: Matrix enim Macrocosmicae & Microcosmicae mulieris eadem est. Unde sequitur etiam, quod *Enur* matricis minoris mundi mortuum sit, si *Enur* matricis maioris mundi granum unum vitae amittit. ... *Enur* est vis & robur, & spirituale semen roboris, unicuiuslibet arboris radicis. Quam primum enim arboris radix periit: tunc & rami, & fructus, adeoque tota arbor periit: Similiter & matrix, quae nihil est aliud, quam ramus Veneris in coelo. *Enur* enim matricis maioris mundi est Venus & Luna: & illius radicis ac arbori ramus est quaelibet matrix cuiuslibet foeminae, id est, Veneris, maioris mundi. Et sicut pyrum est fructus arboris, ita etiam matrix cuiuslibet foeminae pyrum est & fructus suae arboris, & arbor ista est Venus & matrix maioris mundi, in partes tamen 4 distributa secundum 4 Elementa. Et matrix parva minoris mundi fructus est & ramus matricis aut arboris, quae matrix est. Et sicut homo non nisi hominem generat: ita matrix etiam maioris mundi nihil aliud, nisi matricem minoris mundi generat. Et sicut ex una arbore pyra multa dependent, quorum unum altero citius decidit, cum unum altero citius etiam maturescat, eodem plane modo quadruplex etiam arbor matricis maioris mundi multos ramos & fructus fert, qui nihil quam matrices minoris mundi sunt.

PICCOLOMINI, *Alessandro*

p. 3 : Oltra le undici morali uirtù già dette, resta l'ultima, che si domanda Prudentia, la quale, quantunque in un certo modo si possa dir morale; nondimeno intellettual uirtù . . .

p. 12 : Conciosia che non in un medesimo modo fa di mestieri di conuersare con amici, con forestieri, con nobili, con uolgari, con principi, con priuati, con signori, con Gentildonne, e 'l simil dico di tutte l'altre maniere di persone, con chi occorra diuersamente di ritrouarsi : doue sempre innanzi ad ogni cosa si dee considerare la qualità del luogo, del tempo, delle persone, della natura di tai persone, & finalmente d'ogni altra diuersità, accioche ad ogni cosa accommodandosi, non si dica parola, che non sia ben detta.

PICCOLOMINI, *Francesco*

p. 6 : Aufer Iustitiam ex pectore hominum, statim eos inspicies feris infestiores, ac Vrbes syluis syluestriores.

p. 7 : At Liberalitas amplitudine suae Magnificentiae exornata, ei non cedit, verùm potius se illustriorem nititur patefacere : quia si Charitas Theologicarum Virtutum est princeps; Liberalitas, quae ex moralibus ei est simillima, caeteris iure optimo praestare videtur : Et praesertim; quia nulla actione proximius ad Deum accedimus, eique similiores reddimur, quàm dum liberaliter & magnificè aliis opem ferimus. Haec est ea Virtus, qua cunctos nobis Regio quodam nodo deuincimus : quae nutrit egenos, Virtutes alit, fortunae bona in congruentem finem dirigit. Eius actio actionibus Dei & Naturae est simillima : Deus enim sola sua immensa liberalitate Mundum creauit : Natura eius famula, cum pro viribus operetur, suaque munera rebus impartiatur, liberalitatem amplissimè seruat. Haec praeferenda videtur Iustitiae : quia Iustitia aliena bona congruenter distribuit, liberalitas verò distribuit propria, quod longè est difficilius. Et praesertim Magnificentia, quae culmen est liberalitatis, caeteris praeferenda videtur : quia reliquae virtutes omni hominum gradui & conditioni conuenire natae sunt; haec sola praeclarissimum hominum statum & conditionem quaerit, cum solum splendidè natis, & fortunae bonis opulentissimè ditatis conueniat. Demum liberalitas ea est, quae Thesauros e manibus Fortunae aufert, & tutissimè recondet : nam eius munere dicere valemus; Hoc habeo, quodcunque dedi.

pp. 7–8 : Quod Liberalitatis & Magnificentiae est officium; & haec pro-
priè & praesertim digna est nomine Gratiae. . . . Huiusmodi Gratiarum
effusio, Primò & verè soli competit Deo; quia ille solus alio non eget,
ab alio non pendet, pro se ab alio nil sperat: propterea verè Gratiarum
est Viuus fons; a quo primò manat Gratia gratis data.

pp. 8–9 : Erga nos rectè afficimur per Temperantiam, erga alios per
Iustitiam, erga Deum per Pietatem; ita castè, iustè, & piè, viuemus:
Cuius optimae institutionis Castitas siue Temperantia est initium,
Iustitia medium, Pietas finis: ideo in tam salutari fine cum Dei Gloria
iucundissimè requiescamus.

p. 9 : Propterea est altera opinio quorundam, qui censent; Fortunam
esse Deam quandam, Diuinamque potestatem . . . Alii inquiunt esse
intelligentiam quandam, non secus mortali Orbi Praesidentem, ac
Motores coeli praesint orbibus coeli.

p. 10 : Secundò est firma & constans, ratione conseruationis suae
conditionis, suaeque mutabilitatis; est enim immutabiliter mutabilis.

p. 10 : Modus alter proximus est ille Platonis existimantis Diuinam
mentem non indiuiduorum, sed specierum tantum includere ideas;
quibus rationes animae, semina Naturae, participationes & vmbrae
materiei respondeant: qua *aurea catena* ait gradus vniuersi ligari, &
a primo ad vltimum cuncta descendere, ac ab vltimo in primum
reuocari.

p. 11 : . . . quia est semiuirtus, semen virtutis, via ad virtutem: &
oritur ex desiderio honesti, & timore infamiae; quae sunt principia
virtutis, & calcaria ad eam.

p. 12 : Atque harum ipsarum quae ad iucunditatem pertinent; altera in
Iocis, altera in congressionibus ac reliquae vitae communitatibus
vertitur. Nam vir Prudens cum omni hominum conditione, in omnique
actione & sermone, debet seruare decorum; & talem se praebere,
qualem locus, persona, & occasio exposcunt: propterea etiam in
Salibus & iocis tenetur modum seruare, & gratia requietis nonnunquam Iocis debet dare locum; vt se gratiorem reddat aliis, vitam ducat
iucundiorem, animum reficiat, & ad seria se reddat alacriorem.

p. 41 : Sic itaque honor insolubili nodo cum Virtute coniungitur: &
propterea Romani templa Honoris & Virtutis ita iunxerunt; vt nemo
ingredi posset in templum Honoris, nisi transiret per templum Virtutis.

p. 47 : Hac de re proculdubio certi reddi non valemus; rationi tamen
apprime consentaneum censeo, inuentores huius nominis inspexisse
amorem, flagransque desiderium honesti & diuinae conditionis;
vehemens enim ille amor est spiritus hominem eleuans, Heroemque

formans: a quocunque tamen nomen deducatur, parum refert; de hoc consentiunt omnes, Herois nomen denotare gradum & conditionem supra hominem collocatam.

p. 48: Cui opinioni subscribendum non censeo; quoniam Plato aliam Daemonum, aliam Heroum ponit Generationem & conditionem: Heroas oriri affirmat ex amore Deorum erga humanas mulieres, vel virorum erga Deas, vt patet ex Cratylo; Daemonum autem in Timaeo aliam ponit generationem. Propterea censerem ego, ex sententia Platonis Heroas esse; non eos, qui sunt sui natura Daemones, & distribuuntur in aethereos, aereos, & aqueos; sed esse Daemones peregrinos, hoc est animas illustrium Virorum vita functas, solutas a crasso corpore, & ex aureo hominum genere prodeuntes.

p. 48: Hos ego censeo Platonem nuncupasse Heroas, qui etiam dici possunt Daemones aduenae & peregrini; non autem Daemones aqueos, qui sui Natura sint Daemones. Hi a Iamblicho supra humanas animas constituuntur; quatenus sunt animae eorum hominum, qui supra humanam conditionem se extulerunt . . . quia Heroas ab illis, qui sui natura sint Daemones, manifestè distinguit. Colligamus itaque, ex Poetarum commentis Heroem esse Semideum, ex Deo & homine ortum: Ex opinione Platonis esse animam hominis illustri vita functam, solutam a crasso corpore; vel hominem flagranti Virtutis amore supra humanam ~~conditionem~~ eleuatum.
Conditionem

p. 49: Varii apud Poetas referuntur, qui effinguntur a Diis duxisse genus, & Heroes ac Semidei nuncupantur; vt Pan, Hercules, Romulus, Aeneas, & alii: ita quoque Insulae a Plutarcho (ex Demetrii sententia) referuntur, circa Britanniam multae, a Graecis dictae Sporades, quae Geniorum & Heroum esse dicuntur: Sed quoniam haec commenta sunt Poetarum; propterea, quid veri (ex sententia Aristotelis) sub his fabularum inuolucris claudatur, explicandum ac euoluendum occurrit. Heroes sunt illustres homines, qui per eximiam aliquam Virtutem conditionem sunt adepti super humanam refulgentem; per quam vel praeclaram ducunt Vitam, vel vita functi per ora hominum celeberrimè circunferuntur. Hi dicuntur supra hominis conditionem eleuari, quia (vt homini licet) se Diis similes praestiterunt. Dicti sunt ducere genus a Diis: primò, vt denotetur absque diuino afflatu non licere homini ad diuina eleuari: insuper, vt pateat ex sola eximia Diuinorum dilectione, quasi exuperanti charitate, flagrantique desiderio Boni & Honesti, praeclaras ac generosas hominum actiones prodire.

pp. 49–50: Generi heroum opponitur id genus efferatorum hominum, qui ob conspicuam eorum depressionem ac deprauationem ex homine & fera finguntur orti; quales sunt homines illi, qui perperam educati, deteriores euadunt feris; vt inquit Aristoteles in primo de Rep. Ac vt heroici viri parentes proximi nil aliud sunt, nisi Mens ad Diuina conuersa, & vis sentiendi appetendique purgata, & cum mente conformata; Ita parentes viri efferati sunt sensus & appetitio, quasi fera ad sola terrena propensa, quae sibi rationem & Mentem penitus manciparunt: adeò vt accommodatè dicere valeamus, Heroas, efferatosque viros generare seipsos; cum per internas facultates, tanquam per parentes, formentur, ac producantur.

p. 50: Homo enim cum sit Paruus mundus, Magnique mundi Epilogus, Diuinorum & mortalium hymenaeus; Prothei imagine omnem formam recipere, omnemque vitam viuere valet . . . Constat itaque, quid herois, efferatique hominis nomine significetur; & qui sint veri parentes eorum, veraque fabulae Allegoria: Ex quo constat heroem consensione omnium solam denotare praestantiam, & eminentem quandam hominis conditionem.

p. 65: Omne vitium vt vitium, est recessus a lege, ab ordine, a recto, a perfectione, & ab eo quod absolutè & verè est.

p. 65: . . . vt virtus omnis est forma . . . ita vitium omne est defectio, diminutio, & priuatio . . . vitium verò absolutè sit deformitas, deprauatio, & imperfectio . . .

p. 139: . . . de qua Arist. vnà cum Heraclito in secundo Moralium Nicomachiorum cap. 3. dixit difficilius esse voluptati obsistere quàm iracundiae: & Seneca affirmauit; Magnum imperium regit, qui sibi ipsi dominatur; & fortior est qui cupiditatem vincit, quàm qui hostem superat: & Salomon affirmauit fortiorem esse expugnatorem animi expugnatore Vrbium.

pp. 141-2: Amicitia est proborum hominum mutuus, conspicuus, confirmatusque Amor, ex probitatis cognitione consurgens, ad vitae honestae coniunctionem perducens.

p. 142: Amicitia amor est, amoris affectio & comes est desiderium; expetimus autem obiectum assequi, eoque frui: cumulatissimè autem amici probitate fruimur, in vitae coniunctione per actiones ex virtute, tanquam radios ex Sole, prodeuntes.

p. 143: An Amicitia Praeferenda sit Affinitati, et Coniunctioni Sanguinis.

p. 144: Concordia est consensio, & conspiratio plurium ad vnum aliquid; & est latior quàm amicitia; vbi enim amicitia, ibi concordia est; at non econtra: optima tamen concordia ex amicitia consurgit, & est tanquam affectio & fructus eius.

p. 161: Vitii verò imaginem viri eruditi formarunt, manu una ensem, altera coronam gestantem: vt qui vitium superarent, corona honestarentur; qui ei succumberent, ense vsque ad intima cordis transfigerentur.

p. 167: Plato in conuiuio vnà cum Diotima ait, amantem optare ex pulchro aliquid procreare pro sui aeternitate; Cum Aristophane autem inquit, amantem expetere vnitionem cum amato.

p. 168: Copia nonnunquam in solo Amante reperitur: vt Deus, quia bonus, cuncta creat; & quia bonus, amando perficit. . . . Similiter Vir faecundus amans puellam, vt inde materiem recipiat, in qua (pro formanda prole) semen & faecunditatem effundat, dicitur ei praestare . . . vir enim ex interna copia suae faecunditatis diligit, faemina verò ob inopiam; ideo dicitur in i. physic. 81. vt faemina marem, ita materies formam expetit. Vel ea faecunditas est in re dilecta principaliter & verè, vt dum creatura diligit creatorem; & tunc res dilecta praefertur. Vel demum ea faecunditas est in vtrisque; & tunc ambo ratione faecunditatis praestant, ratione indigentiae cedunt: & hoc euenit, dum Amici duo virtute praediti mutuò se diligunt; in vtrisque enim consideratur faecunditas ex propria Virtute prodiens, & indigentia quaedam communionis vitae & aliorum humanam imbecillitatem comitantium. Haec sunt vera de omni Amore, tum honesto tum vtili, tum delectabili. . . . Plato enim considerauit Amantem, vt excitatum ab vmbra pulchri in materie fulgentis, & per furorem Amoris eleuatum ad essentiam Pulchri; cum ex aduerso Aristoteles veras censeat in Materie reperiri formas, & amoris furorem destitutum rationibus & ideis leuiorem iudicet. Demum constat, quomodo bonum & copia gradu eminentiore Amorem parit, quàm id faciat inopia; bonum enim vt bonum faecundum est, suique natura communicabile: ideo expetens propagari, eminentissimum parit Amorem; qualis ille est, quo Deus diligit Mundum.

p. 168: Plato in Conuiuio ex sententia Diotimae inquit, Amorem esse desiderium immortalitatis: & non esse desiderium pulchri, sed generationis partusque in pulchro; quo partu amans seruetur immortalis.

p. 170: Inter Munera Naturae & Bona corporis conspirantia ad constitutionem summi boni hominis hanc vitam viuentis, etiam Pulchritudo enumeratur, quam comitatur Gratia.

p. 184: Primò ratione vniuersae eius latitudinis, Irae enim opponitur gratia & indulgentia, vt Aspasius in secundo Moralium Nicomachiorum cap. 3. manifestauit.

p. 184: Gratia ex sententia Aspasii modo aliquo opponitur Irae; quatenus Ira ex laesione, Gratia & Ingratitudo ad receptum beneficium referuntur: vel saltem Ira vindictam quaerit, Gratia indulget penitus.

p. 23 2 Colligamus itaque, nil in mortalium orbe homine foelicius, nilque eo infoelicius inueniri: propterea Asclepius Atheniensis humanam naturam versipellem imagine Prothei in Mysteriis congruenter significari affirmauit.

PORCACCHI, *Thomaso*

p. 59: Melissa . . . è la gratia preueniente dal diuino amore, che ci fa riconoscere il nostro errore, & leuarci interamente dal uitio.

p. 61: Per il bosco pieno di spiriti, che ei fece tagliare à Praga, ancor che da' Pagani fosse hauuto in religione; si denota che al uero Principe Christiano, amico di Dio, non possono in alcun modo nuocere le illusioni diaboliche.

p. 81: . . . siamo auisati, che niuno christiano può alzarsi da questo centro pieno di uitii, & di peccati à quella cima dell'eterna beatitudine, se prima non si monda l'anima d'ogni concupiscentia terrena con i Sacramenti della Chiesa, confessandosi, communicandosi, & del tutto nettandosi d'ogni macchia, & brutezza, che in questa ualle di miseria ci infetta, & contamina tutti.

RICHARD OF ST. VICTOR

p. 107: Istae sunt duae civitates, una diaboli, altera Dei, ab initio dissidentes, nunquam inter se pacem habentes. Istae sunt duae mulieres, quarum altera superius legitur amicta sole, altera super bestiam coccineam sedere. Collectio namque malorum et universitas bonorum, civitates sunt, et mulieres sunt: civitates, quia numerosa civium suorum multitudine ditantur, mulieres, quia suis viris, Babylon diabolo, Hierusalem Christo copulatae ad multiplicem prolem fecundantur.

SERVIUS

p. 68: Nouimus Pithagoram Samium vitam humanam diuisisse in modum Y literae, s[cilicet] q[uod] prima aetas incerta sit, quippe quae adhuc se nec vitiis, nec virtutibus dedit. Biuium autem Y literae a iuuentute incipere quo tempore homines aut vitia, i.[e.] partem sinistram, aut virtutes, i.[e.] dextram partem sequuntur. . . . Ergo per ramum . . . quem ideo in siluis dicit latere, quia re vera in huius vitae confusione, & maiore parte vitiorum virtus & integritas latent.

p. 68: Sequitur illud Pythagoricum, dicens tenuisse eos viam post errorem syluarum: quae vel ad vitia vel ad virtutes . . . ducit.

VINCENT DE BEAUVAIS

p. 267: Sicut enim semen cuiuslibet arboris habet quandam vim, vt cum obrutum fuerit in terra oriatur & virgultum producat . . . ita est in corpore vt ita dicam quoddam seminarium, vnde suo tempore curante prouidentia Dei aliqua genera oriantur.

Index